Pre-intermediat

Kenna Bourke
Jenna Roden
Nicholas Sheard
Steve Wasserman

Straightforward

Pre-intermediate **Teacher's Book**

MACMILLAN

Macmillan Education
Between Towns Road, Oxford OX4 3PP
A division of Macmillan Publishers Limited
Companies and representatives throughout the world

ISBN 978-0-230-42319-0

Text, design and illustration © Macmillan Publishers Limited 2012
Written by Jim Scrivener
Additional material by Mike Sayer

This edition published 2012
First edition published 2005

Designed by eMC Design Limited
Illustrated by Kathy Baxendale, Mark Draisey, Tim Kahane, Bill Piggins
Cover design by eMC Design Limited
Cover photographs by: Corbis/Roger Tidman (Main); Getty Images/Doug Chinnery; Alamy/Robert Harding Picture Library Ltd; Corbis/Lois Ellen Frank; Corbis/Gerolf Kalt; Alamy/Images & Stories

Full credits for photographs in the facsimile pages can be found in the Student's Book, Workbook, Portfolios, CD-ROM, Teacher's Resource Disc and Digital.

Author's acknowledgements
Mike Sayer
I would like to thank Nicola Gardner, Louise Fonceca and Sally Rigg for their support on this project.

The publishers would like to thank all the teachers from around the world who provided invaluable comments, suggestions and feedback on the first edition.
The publishers would also like to thank the following people for their help and contribution to the second edition:
Tatiana Baytimerova (Russia), Lenka Boehmová (Czech Republic), Dr Manuel Padilla Cruz (Spain), Svetlana Elchaninova (Russia), Jennifer Díaz Green (Dublin), Elena Mokeeva (Romania), Lynn Thomson (freelance editor), Amany Shawkey (Macmillan Egypt), Maria Teresa Rius Villaplana (Spain), Natalia Vorobyeva (Russia).

Printed and bound in Thailand

2016 2015 2014 2013
10 9 8 7 6 5 4 3

Contents

RESOURCE MATERIALS
Straightforward Teacher's Resource Disc

Introduction

STUDENT'S BOOK – STRUCTURE AND APPROACH

For ease of use and practicality *Straightforward* Second Edition is structured to provide one lesson per double-page spread (A/B/C/D), each taking around 90 minutes to complete.

All lessons are interlinked to promote better and more memorable learning, at the same time offering the teacher the flexibility to pick out key sections in order to focus on particular language points.

Additionally, each unit provides extra material in the form of relevant communication activities as well as unit reviews, saving the teacher valuable time.

Each unit contains …
- two to three grammar sections.
- two to four vocabulary sections.
- one functional language section.
- two pronunciation sections.
- four to seven speaking skills sections.
- two reading skills sections.
- two listening skills sections.
- one *Did you know?* section.

Lesson A

STRUCTURE – Clear signposting of each lesson allows both the teacher and the students to feel comfortable and familiar with the progression through the course. Each lesson is linked around different areas of a similar unit topic.

VOCABULARY – Difficult and out-of-context words from the text are given in a glossary so students are not distracted by these lexical hurdles.

GRAMMAR – Clear and uncomplicated explanations present new grammar elements.

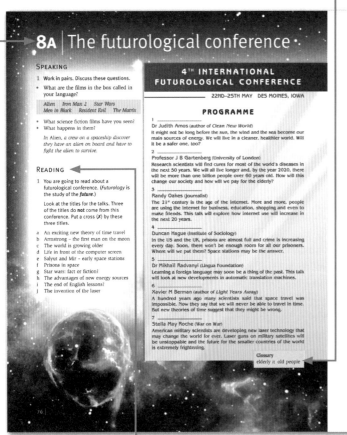

READING – Realistic texts are accessible for the relevant level, and are from a variety of different sources/contexts.

GRAMMAR – Deductive approach to grammar at early levels gives students guidance and scaffolding for learning.

PRONUNCIATION – Listen and repeat exercises address common errors or difficult areas of pronunciation.

Lesson B

STRUCTURE – The second of the unit lessons takes the topic one step further, allowing students to build on what they have learnt in the first lesson and enabling them to really feel comfortable around the wider topic.

GRAMMAR – Students are always supported by the *Language reference* pages at the end of each unit, providing them with a further opportunity to clearly see and understand the language they have just learnt.

SPEAKING – Opportunities to participate in interesting and motivating speaking activities arise naturally as the unit topic develops, giving students the chance to put their language into practice and improve their fluency.

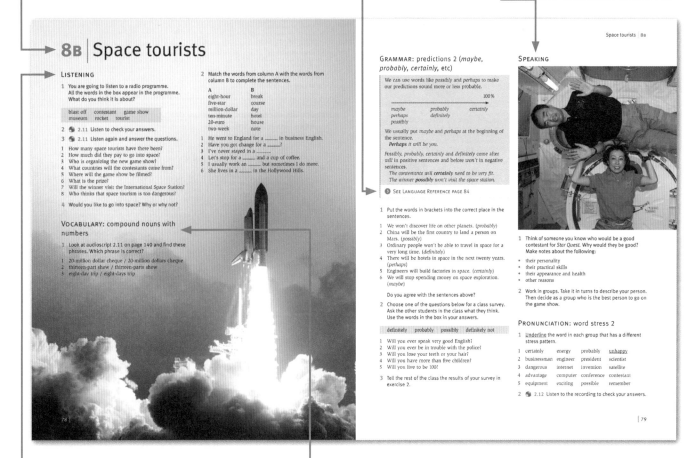

LISTENING – Language is best understood when it is seen or heard in context, and every lesson in *Straightforward* contains either a reading or a listening text.

VOCABULARY – Students are encouraged to look at the context to help them deduce meanings of words – a practical and valuable skill for students to develop.

Lesson C

STRUCTURE – A natural progression in the topic subject introduces new vocabulary and language areas.

GRAMMAR – Associated patterns and language areas are presented through reading and listening, and then developed through clear and straightforward grammar explanations.

8c | Great ideas

Great ideas 8c

LISTENING & SPEAKING

1 2.13 Listen to the recording and match the descriptions 1–5 to the gadgets A–E opposite.

2 Work in pairs. Discuss these questions.

- Which of these gadgets would you like to buy? For who?
- Which of these will sell the most? Put the gadgets in order (1 = best seller → 5 = worst seller).

Strange things for interesting people ...

New gadgets

A Blacklight writer

B Aurora touch clock

C Splats

D Water dispenser

E Key finder

READING

A Great Idea?

Ash Sharma, a second-year business studies student at Thames Valley University, thinks he has found a good way to make money. He needs £5,000 to get his idea off the ground, but his father has refused to help. What do you think? Read both sides of the story and decide for yourself.

My idea is very simple, really. I already have a small website called businessessays.com (1) _____. Business students at university log on to the site and download essays. They have an essay to write for homework, for example, but they need some help with it. On the site, they find the essay they need, download it (2) _____. At the moment, the site is free but if I can improve it, that will change.

I want to make the site much bigger and my idea is to make it really international. I have found some software that can translate the essays into sixteen different languages. It will be easy to use for people from all round the world.

I need about two months to do all the programming (3) _____. When everything is ready, people will pay $2.99 a month to use my service. If it's successful, I will be able to sell advertising, too.

Of course, I can't continue with my university studies and set up the site at the same time. And if I wait, someone else will take my idea (4) _____.

I would like to help my son, but my wife and I agree that it is not a good idea to lend him £5,000 now. There are two main reasons for our decision.

My son has an interesting idea (5) _____. Will his idea work? At the moment, it's impossible to say. Are there any other websites that offer a similar service? How successful are these other sites? How many customers will he need before he starts to make money? If the site is successful, will he need to employ other people? How many? How much will he pay his staff (6) _____?

And finally – is it legal to help students with their homework? When he has a business plan and when he has the answers to these questions, I will think again.

We also think that it is important for our son to finish his university studies before he starts this website. If he leaves now, it will be too risky. What will happen to him if his idea doesn't work? He will find himself with no job and no qualification, (7) _____, he will find it is difficult to get a good job. There are some things in life that we must wait for (8) _____. After he finishes his studies, we will talk about his idea again.

1 Read the magazine article on page 80 and answer the questions.

1 How does Ash think that he can make money?
2 Why does Ash want to leave university?
3 Why doesn't Ash's father want to help him?

2 Read the article again and put the phrases a–h into the gaps 1–8.

a and Ash is still very young
b and I need money to buy the software
c and if he does not have a qualification
d and it is very successful
e and it will be too late
f and use it for their work
g and who will look after the finances
h but he does not have a business plan

3 Work in pairs. Discuss these questions.

- Is the website a good idea?
- Is Ash's father right to refuse to lend him the money?
- Is it wrong to download essays from the internet?

VOCABULARY: adjectives with infinitives

1 Complete these sentences with an infinitive from the box.

to finish   to get   to help   to say   to use

1 It will be easy _____ the new website.
2 It is impossible _____ if Ash's idea will work.
3 Is it legal _____ students with their homework?
4 It's important for my son _____ his studies.
5 It's difficult _____ a good job without a qualification.

Look at the article again to check your answers.

2 How many different sentences can you make from the table?

		easy	to be
It	is will be used to be	possible usual legal dangerous healthy difficult impossible unusual illegal safe unhealthy	to drink to find to have to meet to see to begin to eat to get to make to say to stop	...

GRAMMAR: present tense in future time clauses (first conditional)

When we are talking about future time in clauses with *if, when, after* and *before*, we use the present tense. We can use *will* in the main clause of the sentence.

subsidiary clause	main clause
If it's successful,	I will be able to sell advertising.
When everything is ready,	people will pay $2.99.
After he finishes his studies,	we will talk about his idea again.

The subsidiary clause can also come after the main clause.

I will be able to sell advertising if it's successful.

SEE LANGUAGE REFERENCE PAGE 84

1 Complete the text. Put the verbs in brackets into the correct tense. Use *will* or present simple.

A modelling agency has offered a job in Japan to a sixteen-year-old English school student, Emily. She has decided to take the job. 'If I (1) _____ *(not take)* the job, I (2) _____ *(not get)* the chance again,' she said. Before she (3) _____ *(go)*, she (4) _____ *(have)* a big party for all her friends. 'I'm so excited,' she said. 'When I (5) _____ *(say)* goodbye to my boyfriend at the airport, I (6) _____ *(be)* very sad. But after I (7) _____ *(arrive)* in Japan, everything (8) _____ *(be)* OK.' If she (9) _____ *(be)* successful, the agency (10) _____ *(give)* her more work. 'I've never done this before,' she said, 'but I'm sure I (11) _____ *(be)* good at it when I (12) _____ *(have)* a little experience.'

2 Emily's boyfriend does not want her to go. He thinks she will have problems. Make sentences from the prompts.

1 When she arrives, she won't speak the language.

1 When / arrive / not speak the language
2 If / not speak the language / not make friends
3 If / not make friends / feel very lonely
4 If / feel very lonely / want to come home
5 When / come home / not have any qualifications

3 Can you think of any other possible problems that Emily will have? Make sentences with *if, when, before* or *after*.

4 Complete the sentences so that they are true for you.

1 If I don't go out this weekend, I ...
2 I ... when I have enough money.
3 After I leave the school today, I ...
4 I ... before I am 65.

80

81

LISTENING & SPEAKING – These two skills are often combined for students to use the listening as a model for their own speaking.

READING – Putting language into context and encouraging students to understand the structure will build more confidence in their language.

GRAMMAR – The Inductive or Discovery approach is used as students progress. The teacher provides the framework and the students discover the language themselves, guided by their teacher.

Lesson D

STRUCTURE – The final 90-minute lesson of the unit consolidates everything learnt previously with a focus on the communicative skills and functional language. It aims to bring out the situational element of learning English.

CULTURAL INFORMATION – Students are not expected to learn in a vacuum, and their interests and curiosities are met with *Did you know?* sections. This not only pulls together the language they have been focusing on in a realistic and fresh context, but exposes them to cultural information they may not already know.

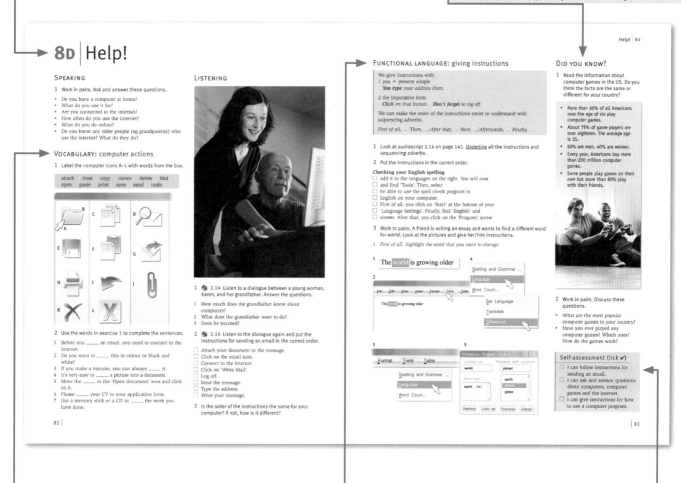

VOCABULARY – Lexis that is practical and immediately applicable to the student's life is drawn out in a natural and engaging way.

FUNCTIONAL LANGUAGE – This section helps students to deal with common, everyday situations in an English-speaking environment – what we might think of as 'survival language'.

CEF/SELF ASSESSMENT – Each unit culminates in a self-assessment box so students can check and monitor their own progress and become more independent learners. The checklist is a selection of clear 'can-do' statements and therefore links to the CEF (Common European Framework) and Portfolio elements of the course.

WORKBOOK

STRUCTURE – Each lesson from the Student's Book has a corresponding single page in the Workbook that builds and consolidates the same vocabulary. It also explicitly highlights what language function the students have been learning.

TRANSLATION – Students are given the opportunity to link the language learnt with their own language and explore similarities and differences.

READING – Extra reading material is provided in the form of a new text at the end of each Workbook unit. This is accompanied by helpful activities that support and promote understanding.

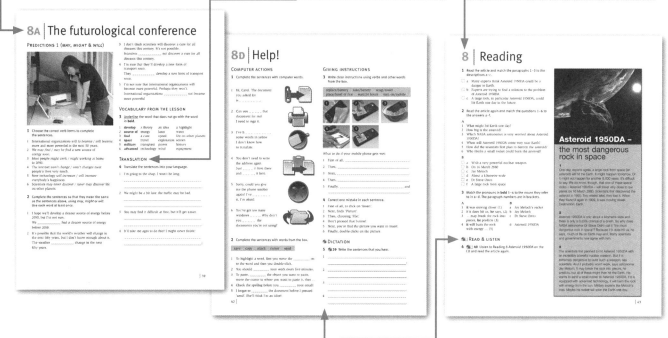

DICTATION – To provide students with integrated listening and writing practice, there is also a series of dictations for them to check their understanding. As students are usually working alone on the Workbook, they are able to work at their own pace and practise key language further.

READING & LISTENING – At lower levels all Workbook and some Student's Book texts are read aloud on the accompanying CD, offering students further listening and pronunciation practice.

WRITING – A special feature at lower levels is that all writing work is contained here, in the back of the Workbook, covering a wide variety of genres pertinent to students' everyday needs.

READING – Each Workbook includes a partial Macmillan Reader for the relevant level at the back of the book, allowing students to naturally expand their language outside of the everyday classes and engage with English fiction.

PORTFOLIO

The Portfolio is like a diary. In it students find …

- a place to keep their own personal record of the work they do during their course.
- a place to write down their thoughts and feelings about the work they do.
- questions to encourage them to think about their English and their studies.
- some puzzles, cartoons, jokes and interesting quotations.

The Portfolio consists of three sections:

1 Before the course:
The introductory pages help students to analyze what they can already do in English and to set targets for the future.

2 During the course:
The diary sections give students the opportunity to record their thoughts as they work through their Student's Book.

There is one diary page for each lesson in the Student's Book.

3 After the course:
At the end of the Portfolio there are some pages to guide students to analyze the progress they have made and to help them assess their English at the end of the course.

THE CEF (COMMON EUROPEAN FRAMEWORK)

The *Straightforward* Portfolios are based on ideas in the Common European Framework (CEF) which bring out the functional element in learning a language. Using the Portfolio will help your students to think more deeply about their learning and to become clearer about the progress they are making in English. Completing the diary sections in the Portfolio can help your students learn the language better. They not only provide the students with writing practice, but also encourage them to reflect on *what* they have learnt and *how* they have learnt it. By reflecting on the language, the students are likely to understand things in more detail and to remember them better.

The Portfolio is designed for students to use on their own as a personal book and diary. However, some teachers may like to include a weekly Portfolio slot in class time.

STRAIGHTFORWARD DIGITAL

NAVIGATION PANE – The navigation pane allows you to select a page from anywhere in the Student's Book.

ENHANCING THE TEACHING EXPERIENCE IN THE CLASSROOM – *Straightforward* Digital is a digital component designed for classroom use. It can be used with an interactive whiteboard or with a computer and projector.

THE DIGITAL BOOK – The *Digital book* allows the teacher to access and display an interactive version of any page from the Student's Book in front of the class. All of the relevant audio, video and reference materials are instantly accessible right on the page.

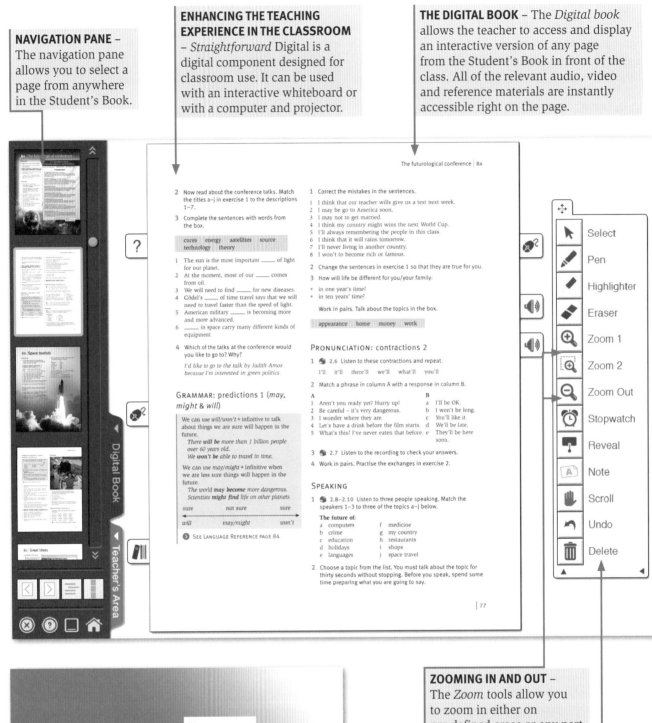

ZOOMING IN AND OUT – The *Zoom* tools allow you to zoom in either on pre-defined areas or any part of the page that you choose.

TOOLBOX – The toolbox provides a number of tools which enable you to interact with the *Digital book* page.

THE TEACHER'S AREA – The *Teacher's area* can be used to create your own material either before or during the class. You can insert and edit text and images, add links to pages from the *Digital book* and insert audio and website links.

NAVIGATION PANE – The navigation pane displays thumbnails of the pages you have created in the *Teacher's area*.

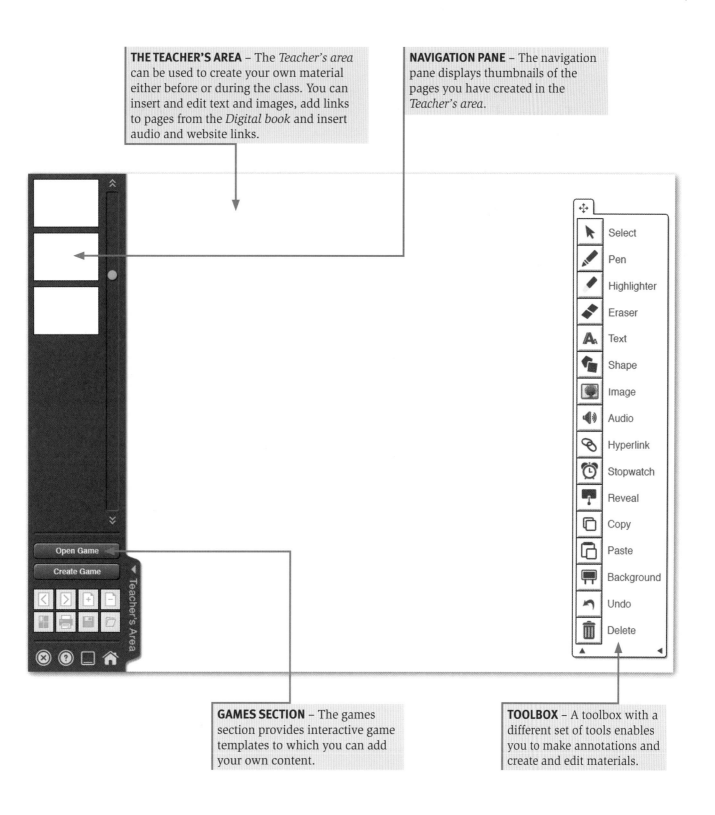

Select
Pen
Highlighter
Eraser
Text
Shape
Image
Audio
Hyperlink
Stopwatch
Reveal
Copy
Paste
Background
Undo
Delete

Open Game
Create Game
Teacher's Area

GAMES SECTION – The games section provides interactive game templates to which you can add your own content.

TOOLBOX – A toolbox with a different set of tools enables you to make annotations and create and edit materials.

STRAIGHTFORWARD DIGITAL

Student's Site

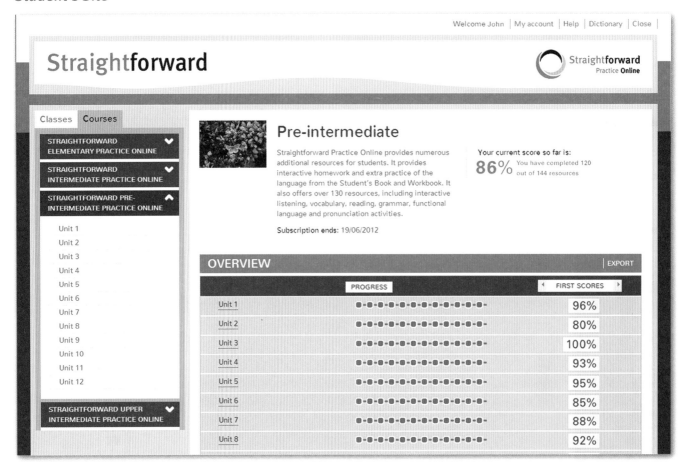

Straightforward Practice Online provides numerous additional resources for students. Accessed through a unique code in the back of the Student's Book, it provides interactive homework and extra practice of the language from the Student's Book and Workbook.

Straightforward Practice Online offers over 130 resources, including …
- bonus interactive listening, vocabulary, reading, grammar, functional language and pronunciation activities to consolidate learning from the print components.
- video.
- interactive word lists with pronunciation and 'email-me-practice' functionality.

Accessing language materials online allows students to take their learning anywhere, any time, in order to better fit their timetable and learning style.

Teacher's Site

Teachers of *Straightforward* Second Edition have the benefit of a dedicated resource website, which supports them with teaching tips, CEF material and extension materials.

Included on the site are:
- *Teaching Tips* from Jim Scrivener.
- CEF checklists and information guides.
- *Teaching Made Simple guides* – PDF manuals from *Straightforward* authors detailing how to use and understand different ELT methodology areas such as learner autonomy and roleplays.
- extra unit-by-unit reading activities from Philip Kerr with a more business-oriented approach.
- author videos.
- photocopiables such as tests, worksheets and companions.

It also acts as a portal to the Interactive Wordlist and *Straightforward Practice Online* where teachers can monitor their students' progress in this online component. This is all accessed using a unique code from the Teacher's Book.

TEACHER'S BOOK

The Teacher's Book offers extensive teaching notes and extra ideas for every lesson.

Short lesson summaries with answers to all exercises (including the Writing activities in the Workbook) and audioscripts.

Suggestions for extra activities for …
• stronger classes.
• weaker classes.
• younger classes.

Supplementary *Language notes* for tricky grammatical and vocabulary information.

1c | Neighbours

WHAT THE LESSON IS ABOUT

Theme	Who makes a good neighbour?
Speaking	Pairwork discussion: talking about your neighbours
	Groupwork: giving and stating reasons; ranking famous people as good/bad neighbours
Reading	*Who would you like as a neighbour?* Newspaper article: results of a British opinion poll
Grammar	*How & what* questions
Pronunciation	The alphabet (and phonemes /eɪ/, /iː/ and /e/)

IF YOU WANT A LEAD-IN …

Introducing the theme: teacher's personal story
• Draw a simple box diagram on the board showing your immediate neighbourhood, eg houses near yours:

```
┌──┬──┬──┬──┐
│  │15│  │  │   (house
├──┼──┼──┼──┤    number)
│  │  │  │  │
└──┴──┴──┴──┘
```

```
┌──┬──┬──┐
│  │  │  │
├──┼──┼──┤
│  │5 │  │   (flat number)
├──┼──┼──┤
│  │  │  │
└──┴──┴──┘
```

• Ask the students to copy the diagram (large enough that they can write notes in the boxes). Write your house/flat number in the relevant box. Talk about your neighbours, where they live, their names, whether you see them often etc. Students make notes about your neighbours, writing each note in the appropriate boxes in their diagram. Afterwards, you can check by eliciting answers for each box and filling in the information in the diagram on the board.
• Ask students to repeat the same activity in pairs, using new diagrams showing the area near their own homes.

SPEAKING

1
• If you did the lead-in above, link directly into this task by asking students to include answers to these questions in their discussion.
• Pairwork. Students discuss the questions about neighbours.

READING

This article examines the results of an opinion poll and explains who British people would like to live next door to. The most popular neighbours are pop star Cheryl Cole and celebrity chef Jamie Oliver.

1
• Students read the article and find out the order the items appear in the text.

> Correct order: 6, 1, 4, 2, 3, 5

2
• Students read the article again. They could then work in pairs to answer the six questions. They need to search for specific pieces of information in the text.

1 310 (31%)
2 a huge mansion
3 many times a year (very often/frequently)
4 Primrose Hill, north London
5 five minutes away
6 some of them are famous

3
• Students must decide which famous person they would prefer as a neighbour. This works best as a whole-class discussion. Ask for reasons. Remind students that they are not discussing which person they like most, but which would be the best neighbour.
• Encourage them to think generally about what it's like to live next to a pop star or a TV celebrity. You could add some of the issues below into the discussion.

Pop star
Positive: you could make friends with her; she might invite you to parties, you could meet other famous people.
Negative: she might be noisy; she might have loud parties; she may attract lots of fans and journalists.

TV chef
Positive: he could give you advice about cooking or invite you to dinner.
Negative: he might have dinner parties without you; there might be journalists and paparazzi outside his house all the time.

Cultural notes: Cheryl Cole & Jamie Oliver

Cheryl Cole
• Cheryl Cole is an English singer and songwriter who was born in 1983. She became famous in 2002 as part of the pop group Girls Aloud. Since the group broke up, she has pursued a solo career and has had number 1 records in the UK. She was married to England international footballer Ashley Cole.

Jamie Oliver
• Jamie Oliver is an English chef and restaurateur who was born in 1975. He became famous for his TV show and cookbook *The Naked Chef* in 1999. Since then, he has made lots of TV programmes and campaigned for healthy food, especially in schools. He owns a number of restaurants in the UK and around the world.

Web research tasks

Cheryl Cole
• Find photos and information about Cheryl Cole and Girls Aloud
Web search key words
• *Image search: Cheryl Cole*
Jamie Oliver
• Find photos and information about Jamie Oliver
Web search key words
• *Image search: Jamie Oliver*
• *Ministry of Food Naked Chef*

GRAMMAR: *how & what* questions

Grammar box
◯ *Language reference, Student's Book page 14*
◯ *Methodology Builder 22: Using Grammar boxes, page 106*

1
• Students write questions to fit the answers.

1 How fast do you drive?
2 What colour is your father's hair?
3 How well do you know your teacher?
4 What time do you (usually) have dinner?
5 How many cousins do you have?
6 What kind of music do you like?

Language notes: how & what questions
• Common words after *how* include: *long* (length of time), *big*, *small*, *rich*, *strong*, *good*, *bad*, *expensive*.
• *What kind of/What type of* - questions asking for a general impression of someone/something. eg A: *What kind of book is it?* B: *It's a biography.* The answer may be a title or a brand name. eg A: *What kind of car does he drive?* B: *It's a Suzuki.*
• *Which* can often be used instead of *what* if you want to emphasize that the answer is a choice between a limited number of possibilities, eg *What/Which book do you want to read?*

2
• Pairwork. Students practise the questions and answers from exercise 1.
• In real life, it's unlikely that full sentence answers would be given to some of these questions. You might want to point out that short answers will often sound more natural, for example, the single word *Grey* is a perfectly good answer to the second question. In fact, it may sound a little odd in a dialogue if the person responding repeats a large number of words from the question.

Weaker/stronger classes
• With a weaker class they can simply read the answers from the exercise.
• A stronger class could be asked to give answers that are true for them.

Drill for How questions
Example:
Teacher: popular / prime minister …
Students: *How popular is the prime minister?*

Teacher cues	Students
rich / the Queen	How rich is the Queen?
clever / Einstein	How clever was Einstein?
late / the teacher	How late was our teacher?
often / you / cinema	How often do you go to the cinema?
often / you / pizza	How often do you eat pizza?
often / she / pizza	How often does she eat pizza?
expensive / Mercedes	How expensive is a Mercedes?
long / football match	How long is a football match?
handsome / Brad Pitt	How handsome is Brad Pitt?

Methodology Builder 4
Cues for sentence-making drills

• In Methodology Builder 2, there were instructions for a question/answer drill. This next kind of drill is a variation. Instead of the teacher saying a question, he/she offers some cue words. The students' job is to use these words to make a sentence or question themselves. So, for example, the drill in this unit works on How and What questions. The teacher offers cues of the key noun(s) and adjective(s)/adverb(s), eg popular/prime minister. The students use these to make a question. Cues can be spoken by the teacher. Alternatively, the teacher could prepare a set of flash cards to hold up with the words written on them.
• A useful extension of the drill would be to get students to ask (and answer) each question with their partner after it has been made.

3
• Students write four questions to find out information about new neighbours. They can use the table to help make questions.

4
• Pairwork. Students compare questions and decide which ones are most interesting.

Alternative procedure
• Rather than just asking students to compare questions, you could turn this into a roleplay if you want to.
• One student asks their questions. The other is the new neighbour who makes up unusual or funny answers.

PRONUNCIATION: the alphabet

1 & 2 🔊 **1.6**
◯ *Methodology Builder 5: Working with phonemic symbols, page 11*
• Ask students to first read the letters in line 1 and see what sound they have in common. Then ask them to agree which one letter from the box could also go in that line. Continue with lines 2 and 3. Don't worry if students don't know phonemic symbols. They will learn them gradually through exercises like this.
• Students often have particular problems confusing the pronunciation of A, I, and E, and also G and J. Check that these are pronounced correctly.
• Students listen to the recording and check their answers.

1J	2G	3X

Extra practice
• If you want students to have more practice in recognizing the three vowel sounds, give students three minutes to find as many rhyming words for each sound as they can, eg *may, play, say,* etc.

Supplementary *Cultural notes* give information and insights into the different cultures of the English-speaking world.

Web research tasks provide opportunities for extension and project work outside class time.

Methodology Builder sections help teachers develop further as professionals by expanding their range of teaching activities and techniques. They give teachers extra ideas and inspiration to try new methods.

CLASS AUDIO CDs

The two CDs contain recordings of all the listening and pronunciation exercises in the Student's Book. The track number for each recording is indicated in the Student's Book rubric. For example, '1.34' means CD1, track 34.

B1   Philip Kerr

Straightforward

Pre-intermediate
Class Audio CDs

Second edition

MACMILLAN

TEACHER'S RESOURCE DISC

METHODOLOGY BUILDER VIDEO MATERIAL – Each Teacher's Book is accompanied by a Teacher's Resource Disc with five short new videos from Jim Scrivener's *Learning Teaching 3rd Edition* that link to the *Straightforward Methodology Builder* sections. They show experienced teachers demonstrating the techniques outlined. Accompanying worksheets promote further discussion about teaching methodology and classroom practice.

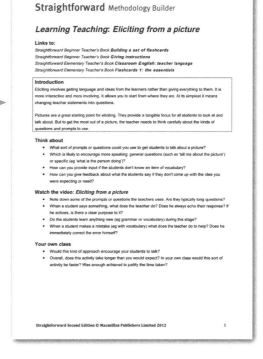

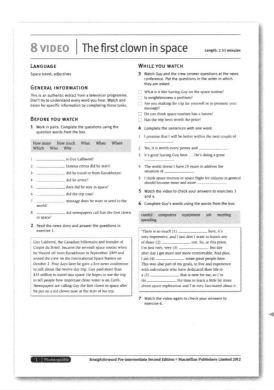

BBC/ITN VIDEO MATERIAL – New class video material from the BBC and ITN (with accompanying worksheets) provides exciting and engaging insights into aspects of contemporary British and world culture and up-to-date trends.

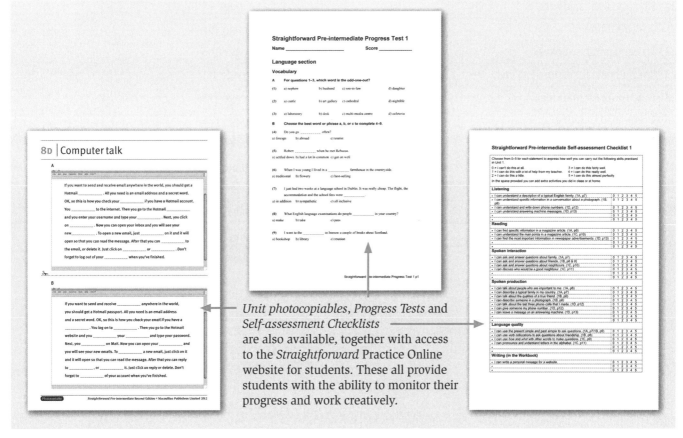

Unit photocopiables, Progress Tests and *Self-assessment Checklists* are also available, together with access to the *Straightforward* Practice Online website for students. These all provide students with the ability to monitor their progress and work creatively.

METHODOLOGY BUILDERS

You will find *Methodology Builders* sections throughout this Teacher's Book. They introduce you to a number of essential teaching techniques and give practical, immediately usable ideas that you can try out in class to extend the range of your teaching. These sections aim to be both informative and inspiring. They can help you find new ways to really exploit material and get the most out of your learners.

DISCUSSION STARTERS – This section suggests a range of possible ideas for using *Discussion starters* in class.

Whole-class mode:

- Ask the questions randomly around the class.
- Make sure you pay more attention to the meaning of what students say rather than focussing too much on accuracy.
- Respond to the ideas and views students state. As far as possible, turn it into a conversation. Get them interested and involved.

Encourage students to listen to each other and respond to each other – rather than having all interaction going via you.

Pairs/groups: Choose one question or statement that you think is particularly interesting. Write it on the board. Put students into pairs or small groups to say what they think about it. After a few minutes a spokesperson from each pair/group reports back to the whole class.

Starting with individuals: Choose a number of the questions and write them on the board (or prepare handouts with them printed on). Ask students to work on their own and write two or three sentences in response to each question/statement. After sufficient thinking and writing time, gather students together in small groups to compare ideas.

TEST BEFORE YOU TEACH – At the start of many units, the Teacher's Book suggests some optional *Test before you teach* tasks. It may feel strange to set tasks that are specifically designed to allow students to use language items that are only taught later in the Student's Book unit. However, these tasks have a number of purposes.

Firstly, they are *diagnostic*, ie they allow you to get an idea of how much the students can already do with the items you plan to teach. This may lead you to change what you do later in some ways. For example, if you realize that students know a lot about one aspect but little about another, you might decide to plan a lesson that spends more time on the latter.

Secondly, they are *motivational*, ie they help students to realize for themselves what they can or can't do. By asking students to do a task which they perhaps can't yet achieve with full success, they may realize that there is some language that they don't yet have full command of. This may help them to see the purpose of the language items when they come to study them.

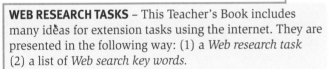

METHODOLOGY GUIDELINES

WEB RESEARCH TASKS – This Teacher's Book includes many ideas for extension tasks using the internet. They are presented in the following way: (1) a *Web research task* (2) a list of *Web search key words*.

All web tasks provide work on relevant reading skills.

Setting up Web research tasks

To allow all students to work simultaneously, you will ideally need to have enough internet-connected computers so that a maximum of three students work per computer.

If this is not possible, you will need to allow some students to work on the task while others do other work, eg allowing a six-minute time slot at the computer for each pair of students.

Running Web research tasks

- The tasks usually give suggestions of useful *web search key words*. We have given these (rather than actual internet addresses) because web addresses tend to change suddenly, whereas these search words are likely to produce good results at any time.
- Alternatively, you might like to set the *Web research tasks* for students to do for homework. Data collected can then be discussed and collated in subsequent class time.

GRAMMAR BOXES – In every lesson of the Student's Book in which new grammar or functional language is introduced, you will find a *Grammar box*. This section suggests a number of typical ideas for using these boxes, as well as a few more unusual options.

- Ask one or two students to read the information aloud to the rest of the class.
- Ask students to work in pairs and read the information aloud to each other.
- Ask students to work in pairs, read and then discuss or ask each other questions about the contents.
- Allow quiet reading time and then ask questions based on the material in the box.
- Use material in the substitution tables (which feature in many of the *Grammar boxes*) to give students simple repetition or substitution drills.
- Ask students in pairs to drill each other.
- Books closed: Before students look at the *Grammar box*, read it aloud to them. At various key points, pause and elicit what the next word or words might be. Clearly confirm right answers. When you have finished, allow students to open books and read the information through quietly.
- Books closed: Write the information from the *Grammar box* on the board, trying to keep the same layout as the book. Leave gaps at key places. Ask students to either copy the diagram and fill it in, or come to the board and fill in the information there. Allow students to discuss the suggested answers before they check with the printed version.

Author's Foreword

A straightforward approach

Dear colleagues

Welcome to the second edition of *Straightforward*. Only six years have elapsed since the first editions were published, but we wanted to keep up to date, to incorporate some of your suggestions, and to make improvements that we thought were necessary. You may have noticed, too, that new editions come out more frequently these days. For many people, the most noticeable and welcome change will be the addition of extra features to make teachers' lives easier, including an interactive whiteboard version and an enhanced website.

Our basic approach, however, has not changed. It remains firmly eclectic, incorporating elements from many different approaches to language teaching. When I meet teachers who are using these books, they sometimes ask me if it is OK to use a slightly different approach (for example, in the teaching of a grammar point) to the one that is suggested in the book. My answer is always an unambiguous 'yes'. Particular students, particular classrooms and particular schools vary too greatly for it to be possible to provide one way of doing things that will be appropriate to everybody.

The core of the course, the Student's Book, is intended to be straightforward: teaching and learning material that is reliable and easy to use straight from the page. The lessons share a number of features:

- All lessons include a balance of language learning and language using (language work and skills work).
- There is a stronger than usual focus on vocabulary development. This involves both the learning of words and phrases and attention to how these items are used (ie the grammar of vocabulary).
- The grammatical syllabus will be familiar, but it is also contemporary, reflecting insights from the analysis of language corpora.
- Every unit (up to and including Upper Intermediate level) contains one lesson that focusses on functional or situational English.
- In every lesson, language is contextualized and presented in either a spoken or written text, and every lesson includes opportunities for either reading or listening. Word lists are provided at the end of every unit in the *Language reference* sections.

- There is a wide variety of types of text, both in terms of content and source (articles, newspaper cuttings, brochures, websites, emails, etc). The topics are varied and the approaches to them are lively.
- Many of the texts focus on aspects of culture in the English-speaking world and encourage intercultural comparison. This work is reinforced by regular *Did you know?* sections that contain further cultural information.
- Every lesson contains opportunities for communicative practice. There are a wide variety of these speaking tasks, so that students have the opportunity to develop a range of communicative skills.

Beyond the core of the course, I cannot recommend strongly enough that you explore the other components. The best place to start is probably with the Teacher's Books, perhaps the best series of teacher's books that I've ever seen. I never usually like to carry around teacher's books (too heavy in my bag!), but I make an exception for these. They form a stimulating teacher-refresher or teacher training course.

If you have a look through the introductory pages here, you'll discover a wealth of ways of adding variety to your teaching. Ringing changes, sometimes just for the sake of it, has helped keep me young-ish, I hope. Researchers confirm that teachers who experiment with change tend to be the happiest ones. I really hope that you'll enjoy the second edition, and I wish you all the best for the rest of this academic year.

Philip Kerr

Philip Kerr   Jim Scrivener

1A | Family life

WHAT THE LESSON IS ABOUT

Theme	Relationships with family and friends
Speaking	Discussion: talking about your family and friends
	Groupwork: describing a typical family in your country
Reading	*Mother Love*. Magazine article: descriptions of families
Listening	Monologue: a description of a typical English family
Vocabulary	Family & friends
Grammar	Questions with *to be*

IF YOU WANT A LEAD-IN ...

Discussion starters

◉ *Methodology Builder 15: Using Discussion starters, page 63*

- *How many people are there in your family? Who is the oldest member of your family? Are there more young people or more old people in your family?*
- *What is the largest family you've ever known?*
- *Do you have relatives you never see?*

Test before you teach: family vocabulary

- Make a list of all the people who came into your home in the last three months (family, friends, etc).

Pre-teach key words: family words

- Draw your own *family tree* on the board. (See example below.) Elicit 'aunt', etc.

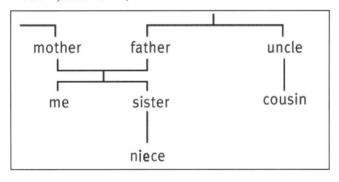

VOCABULARY & SPEAKING: family & friends

◉ *Language reference, Student's Book page 15*

1
- Students match the words in the box with the definitions.

2	colleague	5	cousin	8	son-in-law
3	pet	6	niece	9	aunt
4	son	7	best friend		

2
- Elicit which words have not been defined in exercise 1 (classmate; daughter; grandfather; mother-in-law; nephew; roommate; uncle).

- Ask students to help you construct a new definition for *daughter* on the board. If students find this hard, use the answer for *son* in exercise 1 as a model.
- Pairwork. Students write definitions for the other words. They can use the other definitions from exercise 1 as models.

classmate means 'someone in your class at school'
daughter means 'your female child'
grandfather means 'your mother's (or your father's) father'
mother-in-law means 'your wife's (or your husband's) mother'
nephew means 'your brother's (or your sister's) son'
uncle means 'your mother's (or your father's) brother'
roommate means 'someone you share a room with'

Language notes: family

- *Niece*, *nephew* and *cousin* are often the most confusing words. A *cousin* can be male or female, but *niece* and *nephew* are gender-specific!
- *In-law* as an ending shows that the relationship exists because of a marriage, eg your *mother-in-law* is not your real mother, but is only related to you through your marriage.
  In-laws (usually plural) can be used as a noun in its own right, eg *All my in-laws are at the party.*
- Some interesting and useful collocations are met in the lesson, though not specifically focussed on:
  your closest friend (*Vocabulary & Speaking* 1)
  her future husband (Text – Vera)
  a family pet (*Speaking* 1)

3
- Students think of four family members or friends.
- You could give them three minutes' thinking and preparation time to organize their thoughts and decide what they can say. Ask them to look at the example description beginning *Tara ... .* You could work through another example description before students try the task themselves.
- Pairwork. Students describe the people to their partner. To help students with their listening skills, when one student in each pair is speaking, you could give a task to their partner, such as making notes about the four people described, or thinking of one question to ask about each person.

READING

Students read two texts about the unusual way two women and their families live.

1
- Write the following on the board:
  Vera, South Bank University, Moyo, nurse, electricity
  Judy, 4, 7, juggling, motor home
  Give students a short time to predict what the two texts may be about.
- Students then read the texts and decide which photos are connected with which texts.

Vera Shona: A, D
Judy Boehmer: B, C

2

- Students answer the questions with the information from the texts.

> 1 Clapham, south London
> 2 Zimbabwe
> 3 Moyo
> 4 in a small village in the north of Zimbabwe
> 5 11
> 6 (a 10-metre-long) motor home
> 7 Margaret
> 8 (at a theme park in) Iowa

3

- Students could work in pairs to recall as much as they can about each family. Alternatively, you could collect ideas on the board from the whole class.

4

- Students could work in small groups to discuss the questions. When they have finished, ask groups to summarize their conclusions and tell the whole class.

> *Possible comments:*
> **Text 1:**
> Good: Moyo will have a natural, simple life; he may make more friends; he may learn more about nature.
> Not good: he may miss out on advantages of a richer, western European lifestyle; he may miss out on a European education.
> **Text 2:**
> Good: children have an exciting, enjoyable life; the whole family is working together; children share their parents' life.
> Not good: they may miss out on meeting other children; they may miss school; they may not have a wide choice of future careers; it's dangerous; maybe children need some time away from parents and home life.

Cultural notes: Zimbabwe & circuses

Zimbabwe

- Zimbabwe (pronounced /zɪmˈbɑːbweɪ/) is a country in southern Africa. It borders South Africa and lies between the Limpopo and Zambezi rivers.
- Its official languages are English and two Bantu languages, Shona and Ndebele.
- It was once a British colony, and, before 1980, it was ruled by a white minority government and called Rhodesia. There are a large number of white Zimbabweans in the country.

Circuses

- In Britain, Europe and America many circuses still travel around rather than having one fixed location. They put up their large round tent (the 'Big Top') on open space, eg a field or car park, and perform for a few weeks.
- Families often work together in circuses. Children who grow up in circus families typically join the family act when they are still very young.
- Typical traditional circus acts: jugglers (who throw things and catch them); tightrope walkers (who walk on high ropes); trapeze artists (who go on high swings and 'fly through the air'); animal trainers (who make animals do tricks) and clowns (who are sad-looking funny people with painted faces and big, baggy clothes).

Web research tasks

Zimbabwe

- Find photos of the country, people and lifestyle of villagers in Zimbabwe.
- Find out some information about daily life for a villager in Zimbabwe.

Web search key words

- *Zimbabwe village lifestyle customs*
- *Image search*: Zimbabwe

Circuses

- Find some information about everyday life in a circus. What is it like to work there? How do people get work in a circus?
- Find pictures of five different kinds of circus performance.

Web search key words

- *'circus life' work*
- *Image search:* circus

> **■ ■ Methodology Builder 1**
> **■ ■ Using Web research tasks**
> - *The* web search key words *are ones that are likely to bring up good websites for the Web research tasks, but, as the web changes day by day, there is no guarantee that they will work!*
> - *Web search key words on a single line should be typed in as they are written – ie all the words at once in a single search (rather than word by word as separate searches) with quotation marks (if included).*

GRAMMAR: questions with *to be*

Grammar box

❯ *Language reference, Student's Book page 14*
❯ *Methodology Builder 22: Using Grammar boxes, page 106*

1

- Students match the questions with the short answers.
- To do the task, students will need to notice if the time is present or past and make sure that the personal pronoun matches each noun. NB Students may find question 6 difficult as it uses *there* as a dummy pronoun with no real meaning.

> 1 d   2 b   3 a   4 e   5 f   6 c

Language notes: questions with *to be*

Yes/No questions
(ie ones that lead to *yes* or *no* answers)

- *Is/are/was/were* + noun/noun phrase, eg Was *John late?*
  Is/are/was/were + *there* + noun/noun phrase, eg Is there *a car outside?*
- Other question types appear in the lesson (eg *When does … ?*) but for understanding rather than production.
- This lesson mixes present and past questions (traditionally presented separately). This may seem demanding for students, but the language structures are very similar and students will find that they can quickly gain more communication power simply by switching a past word (eg *was*) for a present word (eg *is*).

- Don't worry too much if students have problems making these questions, as this grammar will be looked at in more detail in future lessons. Don't do a lot of remedial teaching. Maybe, think of this lesson as a sort of informal test to see what students can and can't do. Just make notes of any major problems, for future attention.

Short answers
- All short answers in this lesson follow the patterns:
  Yes + pronoun + am/is/are/was/were
  No + pronoun + 'm not/isn't/aren't/wasn't/weren't
- Alternative short form negative answers are:
  No, + he/she/it's not …
  No, + you/we/they're not …
- Students often have problems finding the correct verb form. It is possible to 'transfer' the *is* verb from *Is he married?* into the answer *Yes, he is* but this doesn't work with *Are you married?*, which requires *I am* or *I'm not* in the reply.
- NB No contraction is possible in *Yes, I am.*
  ✗ *Yes, I'm.*

Wh- questions
- These are made with: *Wh + is/are/was/were*
  (*Wh = where/what/when/why/how*)
- This can be followed with:
  noun or noun phrase, eg Where was *the family's first show*?
  noun/noun phrase + verb (past participle), eg Where was *Vera born*?
  noun/noun phrase + preposition, eg Where is *her husband from*?

How many questions
- *How many* is only used with countable nouns.
- *How many* + noun/noun phrase *is/are/was/were* + there …, eg *How many children are there in Judy's family?*
- In these questions *there* has no particular meaning. It is known as a dummy subject.
- NB The topic of countable/uncountable nouns and *much/many* is looked at in Unit 3.

2
- Students change the answers from exercise 1 in order to make them true for themselves.
- Students could write answers to this exercise individually. However, it might be more interesting to first do it orally in pairs, with one student asking the list of questions to the other student.

Extra task: drill for short answers

Example:
Teacher: *Are you happy?*
Students: *Yes, I am.*

Teacher cues	Students
Are you happy?	Yes, I am.
Is he happy?	Yes, he is.
Is she happy?	Yes, she is.
Are they happy?	No, they aren't.
Was she happy?	No, she wasn't.
Were you happy?	Yes, I was.
Were you at the party?	No, I wasn't.
Was he at the party?	Yes, he was.
Are they here now?	Yes, they are.
Are you married?	No, I'm not.

■ **Methodology Builder 2**
Using simple drills

- *A* drill *is an oral exercise when students say short, restricted pieces of language in order to get more comfortable about forming and pronouncing them. Teachers sometimes feel uncomfortable about using drills, thinking that they are not real communication (or maybe seem too dull). But many students find comfort when they try using a simple piece of language in the safe environment of the classroom. Don't underestimate the value of this kind of practice in manipulating the mechanics of grammar.*
- *This Teacher's Book contains a number of optional drills on tricky language points. The simplest kind of drill is simply 'Listen and repeat'. These are relatively easy for a teacher to invent, so we don't include guidelines for those here. The second type of drill (eg the one in the Grammar section on this page) is a 'question/reply' drill and is set out in frames.*
  1 *Use the first question as an example. Read the question aloud yourself, clearly and naturally – then read the reply. (You could move to a different position to indicate that the reply is spoken by a different person.)*
  2 *Repeat the example but don't say the reply. Indicate that you expect a 'yes' or 'no' answer with a gesture (eg thumbs up) or a cue card (ie a card with 'yes' written on it).*
  3 *Get students to say the answer. If only one or two say it, indicate they should model it for the rest.*
  4 *Repeat the question. Aim to get the whole class giving a fluent reply.*
  5 *Go on to the next question and repeat the procedure. Aim to speed up once students have the idea. Mix up and repeat the questions in various orders to provide challenging practice.*

3
- Focus students' attention on the example. You could do the example as a class on the board. Write up the mixed-up version and elicit possible rearrangements.
- Students work individually to put the words in order to make other questions.

2	What are their names?
3	How old are they?
4	What are their hobbies?
5	Where were your parents born?
6	Who is the youngest person in your family?
7	When was your last family holiday?

4
- Pairwork. Students use the questions from exercise 3 to find out about each other.

SPEAKING

In this listening, a typical English family are being described: their daily and weekend activities, their hobbies, what they like to eat and what they watch on TV.

1 🔘 1.1

- Ask students to look at the list of topic headings (*Children, Family pet,* etc). Students then listen to the recording and decide in which order the topics are heard, writing 1 to 6 in the appropriate boxes.

1	Parents	4	Weekends and holidays
2	Children	5	Food
3	Family pet	6	TV

💿 1.1

The Joneses are a typical English family. <u>Mother</u> Sally is 35 and she is a part-time secretary. <u>Father</u> Mike is 37 and works in an office. Sally is very busy with her job and the housework, so she doesn't have time for any hobbies. Mike likes doing things in the garden and repairing things in the house, but he sometimes goes to the pub with his friends. They have <u>two children</u>: Jason, who is seven and likes football and video games, and his sister, Jane, who is six, and likes playing with her Barbie™ dolls. They have <u>a cat</u> called Snowy.

There is no work or school <u>on Saturdays</u> and the family usually goes somewhere for the day – a walk in the country or a day at the beach. <u>On Sundays</u>, they visit friends and family. <u>In the summer</u>, they go on holiday to Spain for two weeks.

The family has <u>dinner</u> together at half-past six. The children's favourite dinner is chicken and chips, but Sally prefers spaghetti. On Sundays, they always have traditional roast beef or roast lamb. Sally cooks and Mike cuts the meat.

After dinner, they watch <u>TV</u>. They enjoy comedy programmes and soap operas and they always watch the Lottery results. One day they will win and move to a bigger house.

Extra listening task

- Play the recording again. Students answer the questions under each heading about the Jones family. They check their answers in the audioscript.

2

- Pairwork. Students read the questions under each heading and answer the questions about a typical family from their country. They should make notes on their answers.

3

- Groupwork. Pairs meet up with other pairs and compare their ideas. There will be many different views.

Extra discussion

- *Which person in your family do you talk to most?*
- *Who has the most unusual or interesting name in your family?*
- *What hobbies do your family have?*
- *Do you know about the history of your family?*
- *What is similar about people in your family?*
- *How would other people describe your family?*
- *Have your family always lived here?*
- *Who don't you get on with?*

IF YOU WANT SOMETHING EXTRA ...

❯ Straightforward Teacher's Resource Disc *at the back of this book*

1B | Where are they now?

WHAT THE LESSON IS ABOUT

Theme	Old friends
Speaking	Pairwork: discussing friendship
	Communication activity: Facebook™
Listening	Dialogue: a dialogue about an old photo
Vocabulary	Verb collocations (friendship)
Grammar	Questions with auxiliary verbs
Pronunciation	Contractions 1
Did you know?	Discussion: Facebook website

IF YOU WANT A LEAD-IN ...

Discussion starters

❯ *Methodology Builder 15: Using Discussion starters, page 63*

- *Why are friends important? Can you live without friends?*
- *Who are more important to you – friends or family?*
- *Is it better to have a lot of friends or one special one?*

Introducing the theme: friends

- Ask students to write down three questions about *friends.* These can be personal questions, eg *Who is your best friend?* or opinion questions such as *What's the best thing about a friend?*
- Students then stand up and ask their questions to different people.
- Finally, they report back to the whole class about what they found out.

SPEAKING

1
- Students can work in pairs to translate the proverb. Check that they have caught the right meaning. Elicit any similar proverbs in your language. Think about this before class so that you can offer an answer if they can't.

2
- Focus on the proverb *A true friend ...* and the three possible endings. Ask if students agree with these ideas.
- Pairwork. Students find more ways to end the sentence.
- Remind students that most sentences will use the present simple tense as they are about things that are always or usually true.
- Students will also need to remember the third person *-s* ending, eg *listens, makes, knows,* etc.
- NB There are some more quotes about friendship in *Extra discussion* on page 8.

> *Some possible endings (many more are possible):*
> ... helps you when you have a problem.
> ... understands why you are sad.
> ... shares their chocolate with you.

Web research task

❯ *Methodology Builder 1: Using Web research tasks, page 2*

Friends
- Find some more quotations about friendship.
Web search key words
- *quotation friendship*

VOCABULARY: verb collocations (friendship)

❯ *Language reference, Student's Book page 15*

Extra task: presenting friendship collocations

- Here is a story and some collocations you can use with the Repeated anecdote idea in Methodology Builder (3) – see below. Use a photo of two people to introduce the characters. The ↑ symbol shows places to pause.
  Collocations: *oldest friends; got on well; good friends; similar backgrounds; a lot in common; see each other; keep in touch.*
  Story: I want to tell you about Bill. He works for a large computer company. The other person in the photo is Fred. He's one of Bill's ↑ oldest friends. They first became ↑ good friends when Bill bought a used car from Fred. They ↑ got on well immediately because they came from ↑ similar backgrounds, they had ↑ a lot in common, and they both loved working with computers. Nowadays, they never ↑ see each other, but they ↑ keep in touch by email. The car, by the way, is still working!

> ■ **Methodology Builder 3**
> ■ **Repeated anecdotes**
> *This technique is useful for introducing new language items in the context of a story.*
> - *Write the target language items on the board. Just leave them there; don't teach or explain them.*
> - *Introduce the characters of the story using photos or drawings.*
> - *Tell the anecdote.*
> - *When you get to a word just before one of the language items you want to present (indicated in this coursebook by ↑ symbols), pause and wait for students to choose and call out the right item from the list on the board.*
> - *When they get it right, repeat that section of the story yourself with the correct item. Then continue with the rest of the story, pausing before each new item.*
> - *When you get to the end, start the story again and see if students can say the right collocation faster. You may want to tell the story three or four times to give repeated practice. If you keep speeding up, students are unlikely to find this boring and may appreciate the challenge.*

1 & 2 🌐 **1.2**
- Students put the mixed-up text in order. The first sentence is marked [1] as an example.
- Students listen to the recording and check their answers.

> *Correct order: 7, 4, 1, 5, 2, 6, 8, 3*

Alternative procedure

- The text contains collocations that may be new for students and the line breaks are made right in the middle of these. If you think your students may have problems, you could teach the collocations before students do the exercise, using the presentation idea above.

Language notes: collocations

- The collocations are: *oldest friends, get on well, good friends, similar backgrounds, a lot in common, see each other, keep in touch*.
- They appear in the recording as part of longer commonly used phrases (which are also worth learning as bigger chunks of language):
  (She's) *one of my oldest friends*
  (We) *didn't get on well*
  (We) *became good friends*
  (We) *come from similar backgrounds*
  (We) *have a lot in common*
  (We) *don't see each other often*
  (We) *keep in touch*

 1.2

> David is one of my oldest friends. We were at college together. We didn't get on well at first, but later we became good friends. We come from similar backgrounds and we have a lot in common. He lives in Spain now, so we don't see each other very often, but we keep in touch by phone and email.

3

- Students complete the questions with the verbs marked with bold letters in exercise 1.

1 get   2 see   3 have   4 keep

4

- Pairwork. Students ask each other the questions from exercise 3.

Extra practice

- You could offer students further practice of the collocations by using a simple substitution exercise. Write the following sentence on the board:
  She gets on well with her friends.
- Now ask students to change some of the words in the sentence to make a good new sentence.
  For example: Ask students to use *my*. Students will have to say: *She gets on well with my friends.*
  badly (Answer: *She gets on badly with her friends.*)
  He/Our colleagues/The teachers (Answer: *The teachers get on well with their friends*, etc)
- If this is useful, repeat it with more sentences,
  eg *Steve keeps in touch with his family.* – school friends / doesn't / They
  Glyn and Bobby have a lot in common. – My parents / don't

LISTENING

In this listening, a married couple, Adam and Christine, talk about an old photo that was taken in 1973 of Christine, her sister and her friends. Christine wonders what her friends are doing now and Adam suggests checking the internet.

Extra task: pre-listening speaking activity

- In the previous lesson, ask students to bring photos to class. The pictures must be at least three years old and show friends and family. In class, ask small groups of students to look at each other's photos and try to guess who the people are. The person who owns the photo may only answer *yes* or *no* for the first minute of each dialogue. After that they can say more.

1

- Pairwork. Students describe one person in the photo to their partner who guesses which person it is.
- Before you do the exercise, you could remind students of some ways of describing:
  position: *on the left, on the right, at the back*
  clothing: *with dark shoes, in white trousers*
  appearance: *with long hair, with short hair*

2 & 3 🔵 1.3

- Tell students they are going to listen to Christine talking to her husband about the photo. Focus their attention on the eight sentences and ask them to predict if they will be true or false. Ask them to write *T* or *F* next to each sentence. NB Students are only predicting possible answers. They will listen later. Make sure they are clear that the people speaking are not in the photo, but talking about the photo!
- If some finish early, they could compare their answers with others.
- Students listen and compare their predictions with the recording. All the answers are in the first two-thirds of the recording. Students correct the false sentences.

1 T (Susan and Christine)
2 F (Christine was fifteen years old.)
3 T
4 F (Nicholas was a friend of the family.)
5 F (Christine is now married to Adam.)
6 T
7 T

Weaker classes

- If your class is weak at listening, or if you need to replay the recording, you could stop it at the place marked / / in the audioscript.

🔵 1.3

> **C = Christine   A = Adam**
> **A:** Oh look at those red shoes! Very cool …
> **C:** What are you laughing at? Where did you get that photo, Adam?
> **A:** And that lovely flowery dress. You look love-ly.
> **C:** Give me that photo. Where did you find it?
> **A:** It was in this box.
> **C:** Oh God, I look terrible. And look at Susan, next to me on the floor.
> **A:** Susan who?
> **C:** Susan. My sister, Susan.
> **A:** Susan!? Never! How old were you?
> **C:** Well, it was 1973. I remember it well. It was the year that Pink Floyd made *Dark Side of the Moon.* That's what we were singing. God, 1973, that's so long ago, I was only fifteen, and Susan, she was, what, thirteen, I guess. Maybe twelve./ /
> **A:** And who's the boy with the guitar and the pink shirt? A boyfriend?
> **C:** No. That's Nicholas, and he wasn't my boyfriend. He was going out with Helga, my best friend at the time. That's Helga there, with the blonde hair, sitting next to Nicholas. You can see how much she was in love with him.
> **A:** So, who was your boyfriend? The boy in the yellow shirt?
> **C:** Why do you want to know?
> **A:** Well, I am your husband.
> **C:** Hmmm, I'll tell you later. I wonder where they all are now. You know, I mean, what do they do? Are they married? Do they have children, where do they live, that sort of thing.
> **A:** Maybe you'll find them on Facebook.
> **C:** Hey, good idea.

GRAMMAR: questions with auxiliary verbs

Grammar box

⊙ *Language reference, Student's Book page 14*
⊙ *Methodology Builder 22: Using Grammar boxes, page 106*

1
- Students complete the questions with an auxiliary verb from the box.
- In Questions 2 and 3, *does* and *did* are both possible grammatically, but the answer for each is *does* because the *did* is needed for Question 4.

1 is	2 does	3 does	4 did	5 was

Language notes: questions with auxiliary verbs

Popular student errors include:
- Word order (subject *before* auxiliary verb): ✗ *Where you do live?* ✗ *What you are doing?*
- Not using the auxiliary: ✗ *Where you live?* ✗ *Where he go?*
- Forgetting to use the *does* form: ✗ *What do she want?*
- Not using the infinitive: ✗ *Why did he went?* ✗ *When did she arrived?*
- Using the 3rd person singular form instead of the infinitive: ✗ *Where does he lives?*

2
- Pairwork. Students practise asking and answering the questions from exercise 1.

Extra practice: auxiliary verb questions

- Tell students the following short answers one by one, and get them to work out a possible question for each. Do it as an oral exercise or get students to write down their responses. There will be many possible questions for each answer.
  In London, Last Tuesday, Fish and chips, Michael, In December, Writing a letter, At two o'clock, Later, A beautiful picture, Cooking, Her husband, Twelve

3
- Focus students' attention on the text. Ask them to prepare questions which would elicit the information that could fill the gaps. NB Although it looks like a gap-fill, the task isn't to fill the gaps. Students are preparing questions so that the answers would provide information for the gaps.

1	What did she study?
2	Where did she get a job? / Where did she work?
3	Who did she meet?
4	Who did he work for?
5	When did they get married?
6	How many children do they have?
7	Where do Christine and her husband live (now)?
8	Who does she work for?
9	What is he writing?
10	Who does Christine want to get in touch with?

4
⊙ *Communication activities, Student's Book pages 127 & 129*
- Pairwork. Students look at their respective pages and read the texts. Between them the students will know all the information about Christine. They take it in turns to ask each other questions and complete all the information on their page.

1	business management
2	the United Nations in New York
3	Adam
4	the British Embassy
5	two years later
6	seven
7	in West London
8	the International Red Cross
9	his second novel
10	old school friends

PRONUNCIATION: contractions 1

1 **1.4**
- Students listen to the recording. Point out how the pronunciation changes in the contraction. (See *Language notes* below.)

Stronger classes
- You could ask students how they think the items will be pronounced before they listen.

 1.4

1 do not don't   **2** did not didn't   **3** what is what's

Language notes: contractions
- In fluent speech words are frequently contracted, ie sounds and syllables are lost and sounds are changed in order to make the words faster and easier to say, eg *do not* changes from two syllables to one and the vowel sound in /duː/ becomes /dəʊ/.
- The contractions in this lesson are pronounced: /dəʊnt/, /ˈdɪdənt/, /wɒts/, /ˈdəzənt/, /hiːz/, /ðæts/, /ˈwɒzənt/, /wɜːnt/, /huːz/.

2 & 3 **1.5**
- Students work out the contractions.
- If students have a problem with apostrophes, point out that they show where the missing letter is, eg *do not* – *don't*. The apostrophe shows that the letter *o* in *not* has been lost.
- Students listen to check their answers and repeat after the recording.

 1.5

1	doesn't
2	he's
3	that's
4	wasn't
5	weren't
6	who's

SPEAKING

1
- Students read the six questions and correct the errors.

1 Who <u>did you</u> read about?
2 Is she/he ~~be~~ married?
3 How old <u>is she/he</u>?
4 How many children does she/he <u>have</u>?
5 Where <u>is she/he</u> living now?
6 What <u>does</u> she/he do?

Problems are:
– auxiliary verb / subject word order is the wrong way round (1, 3, 5)
– unnecessary auxiliary verb (2)
– wrong form of auxiliary verb (4, 6)

2
> *Communication activities, Student's Book pages 126, 127, 129 & 131*

- Groupwork. This is a 'jigsaw' activity, ie each student in a group of four will see different texts, and they then need to find out information from each other.
- Students turn to their respective pages. Allow enough time for them to read and understand their own text. When ready, they can use questions from exercise 1 to find out information about the other people.
- Students then discuss who they think Christine will get in touch with first.

Extra discussion: a few quotes
- 'A friend is someone who comes in when others go out' (Unknown)
- 'A friend in need is a friend indeed' (ie the most important friend is the one that is there when you need them) (Traditional English)
- 'A friend to everybody is a friend to nobody' (Unknown)

DID YOU KNOW?

1
- Students read the text and then answer the two questions that follow.

Cultural notes: Facebook
- **Facebook** was launched by Mark Zuckerberg and other Harvard students in 2004. It has over 600 million active users worldwide. Facebook users must register, then create a personal profile. They can join common interest groups.

IF YOU WANT SOMETHING EXTRA ...

> Straightforward Teacher's Resource Disc *at the back of this book*

1c | Neighbours

WHAT THE LESSON IS ABOUT

Theme	Who makes a good neighbour?
Speaking	Pairwork discussion: talking about your neighbours
	Groupwork: comparing and stating reasons; ranking famous people as good/bad neighbours
Reading	*Who would you like as a neighbour?* Newspaper article: results of a British opinion poll
Grammar	*How* & *what* questions
Pronunciation	The alphabet (and phonemes /eɪ/, /iː/ and /e/)

IF YOU WANT A LEAD-IN …

Introducing the theme: teacher's personal story

- Draw a simple box diagram on the board showing your immediate neighbourhood, eg houses near yours:

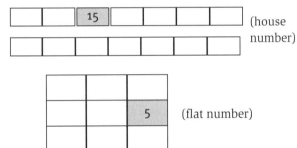

- Ask the students to copy the diagram (large enough that they can write notes in the boxes). Write your house/flat number in the relevant box. Talk about your neighbours, where they live, their names, whether you see them often, etc. Students make notes about your neighbours, writing each note in the appropriate boxes in their diagram. Afterwards, you can check by eliciting answers for each box and filling in the information in the diagram on the board.
- Ask students to repeat the same activity in pairs, using new diagrams showing the area near their own homes.

SPEAKING

1

- If you did the lead-in above, link directly into this task by asking students to include answers to these questions in their discussion.
- Pairwork. Students discuss the questions about neighbours.

READING

This article examines the results of an opinion poll and explains who British people would like to live next door to. The most popular neighbours are pop star Cheryl Cole and celebrity chef Jamie Oliver.

1

- Students read the article and find out the order the items appear in the text.

Correct order: 6, 1, 4, 2, 3, 5

2

- Students read the article again. They could then work in pairs to answer the six questions. They need to search for specific pieces of information in the text.

```
1   310 (31%)
2   a huge mansion
3   many times a year (very often/frequently)
4   Primrose Hill, north London
5   five minutes away
6   some of them are famous
```

3

- Students must decide which famous person they would prefer as a neighbour. This works best as a whole-class discussion. Ask for reasons. Remind students that they are not discussing which person they like most, but which would be the best neighbour.
- Encourage them to think generally about what it's like to live next to a pop star or a TV celebrity. You could add some of the issues below into the discussion.
  Pop star
  Positive: you could make friends with her; she might invite you to parties, you could meet other famous people.
  Negative: she might be noisy; she might have loud parties; she may attract lots of fans and journalists.
  TV chef
  Positive: he could give you advice about cooking or invite you to dinner.
  Negative: he might have dinner parties without you; there might be journalists and paparazzi outside his house all the time.

Cultural notes: Cheryl Cole & Jamie Oliver

Cheryl Cole

- Cheryl Cole is an English singer and songwriter who was born in 1983. She became famous in 2002 as part of the pop group Girls Aloud. Since the group broke up, she has pursued a solo career and has had number 1 records in the UK. She was married to England international footballer Ashley Cole.

Jamie Oliver

- Jamie Oliver is an English chef and restaurateur who was born in 1975. He became famous for his TV show and cookbook *The Naked Chef* in 1999. Since then, he has made lots of TV programmes and campaigned for healthy food, especially in schools. He owns a number of restaurants in the UK and around the world.

Web research tasks

Cheryl Cole

- Find photos and information about Cheryl Cole and Girls Aloud

Web search key words

- *Image search: Cheryl Cole*

Jamie Oliver

- Find photos and information about Jamie Oliver

Web search key words

- *Image search: Jamie Oliver*
- *Ministry of Food Naked Chef*

Grammar: *how* & *what* questions

Grammar box

> *Language reference, Student's Book page 14*
> *Methodology Builder 22: Using Grammar boxes, page 106*

1
• Students write questions to fit the answers.

1	How fast do you drive?
2	What colour is your father's hair?
3	How well do you know your teacher?
4	What time do you (usually) have dinner?
5	How many cousins do you have?
6	What kind of music do you like?

Language notes: *how* & *what* questions

• Common words after *how* include: *long* (length of time), *big, small, rich, strong, good, bad, expensive.*
• *What kind of/What type of* – questions asking for a general impression of someone/something.
eg A: *What kind of book is it?* B: *It's a biography.*
The answer may be a title or a brand name.
eg A: *What type of car does he drive?* B: *It's a Suzuki.*
• *Which* can often be used instead of *what* if you want to emphasize that the answer is a choice between a limited number of possibilities, eg *What/Which book do you want to read?*

2
• Pairwork. Students practise the questions and answers from exercise 1.
• In real life, it's unlikely that full sentence answers would be given to some of these questions. You might want to point out that short answers will often sound more natural, for example, the single word *Grey* is a perfectly good answer to the second question. In fact, it may sound a little odd in a dialogue if the person responding repeats a large number of words from the question.

Weaker/stronger classes

• With a weaker class they can simply read the answers from the exercise.
• A stronger class could be asked to give answers that are true for them.

Drill for *How* questions

Example:
Teacher: popular / prime minister ...
Students: *How popular is the prime minister?*

Teacher cues	Students
rich / the Queen	How rich is the Queen?
clever / Einstein	How clever was Einstein?
late / the teacher	How late was our teacher?
often / you / cinema	How often do you go to the cinema?
often / you / pizza	How often do you eat pizza?
often / she / pizza	How often does she eat pizza?
expensive / Mercedes	How expensive is a Mercedes?
long / football match	How long is a football match?
handsome / Brad Pitt	How handsome is Brad Pitt?

Methodology Builder 4
Cues for sentence-making drills

• In Methodology Builder 2, there were instructions for a question/answer drill. This next kind of drill is a variation. Instead of the teacher saying a question, he/she offers some cue words. The students' job is to use these words to make a sentence or question themselves. So, for example, the drill in this unit works on How and What questions. The teacher offers cues of the key noun(s) and adjective(s)/adverb(s), eg popular/prime minister. The students use these to make a question. Cues can be spoken by the teacher. Alternatively, the teacher could prepare a set of flash cards to hold up with the words written on them.
• A useful extension of the drill would be to get students to ask (and answer) each question with their partner after it has been made.

3
• Students write four questions to find out information about new neighbours. They can use the table to help make questions.

4
• Pairwork. Students compare questions and decide which ones are most interesting.

Alternative procedure

• Rather than just asking students to compare questions, you could turn this into a roleplay if you want to.
• One student asks their questions. The other is the new neighbour who makes up unusual or funny answers.

Pronunciation: the alphabet

1 & 2 ● 1.6
> *Methodology Builder 5: Working with phonemic symbols, page 11*

• Ask students to first read the letters in line 1 and see what sound they have in common. Then ask them to agree which one letter from the box could also go in that line. Continue with lines 2 and 3. Don't worry if students don't know phonemic symbols. They will learn them gradually through exercises like this.
• Students often have particular problems confusing the pronunciation of *A, I,* and *E,* and also *G* and *J.* Check that these are pronounced correctly.
• Students listen to the recording and check their answers.

1 J	2 G	3 X

Extra practice

• If you want students to have more practice in recognizing the three vowel sounds, give students three minutes to find as many rhyming words for each sound as they can, eg *may, play, say,* etc.

Language notes: the alphabet

- This lesson is the students' first meeting in this book with phonemic symbols. NB These represent the sounds of English, not the spelling. So, for example, the phoneme /eɪ/ can be spelt in many ways in different words (eg *game, say, reign, hey*, etc) but still be pronounced the same.
- For many students the phoneme /iː/ is easily confused with /ɪ/ and, depending on their first language, they may have trouble even hearing the distinction. For the moment, it's worth just drawing attention to the fact that /ɪ/ is a short sound and /iː/ is a long sound. The two dots (ː) after the phoneme indicate a long sound.

◼ Methodology Builder 5
◼ Working with phonemic symbols

- *Teachers and students can often be rather nervous about working with phonemic symbols. After all, they look strange, they can be hard to guess, and they are confusable and forgettable!*
- *But, even so, phonemes are extremely useful and a student who knows them can use dictionaries more efficiently, and can find out for themselves how words are pronounced. They can also be quite fun.*
- *Here are a few initial suggestions for working with phonemes and phonemic symbols in class:*
  *1 **Recognition** In the first step, students learn to recognize a sound and distinguish it from other similar ones.*
  *2 **Association** The second step is to associate that sound with a phonemic symbol.*
  *3 **Production** The third (and hardest) step is to produce the sound themselves, alone and in words/ sentences.*
- *Production is often impossible until students have had many chances to notice and hear a sound. For this reason, spend most time on steps one and two.*
- *Don't have unrealistic expectations. There is a lot to learn and if you demand too much, students may switch off.*
- *Play games that help students work with recognizing phonemes and using the symbols. Many familiar vocabulary games, eg* Hangman, *can be easily adapted to work with phonemic symbols rather than alphabetic letters. They make a great filler for the last five minutes of a lesson.*

💿 1.6

1 A H J K	2 B C D E G P T V	3 F L M N S X Z

3 💿 1.7

- Students listen and repeat the letters as they are said in the recording.

💿 1.7

I O Q R U W Y

4 💿 1.8

- Ask students if they know any common British surnames. NB Don't write any on the board.
- Tell them they will hear six very common surnames in the recording. They should listen and write them down. Emphasize that they shouldn't worry about spelling. When they have written their notes, students could compare with each other, but don't check as a whole class. This will be done in the next exercise.

💿 1.8

1	Jones	3	Williams	5	Taylor
2	Smith	4	Brown	6	Davies

5 💿 1.9

- Students listen and check their spelling, correcting it where wrong.
- For answers, see the audioscript below.

💿 1.9

1	Jones J-O-N-E-S	4	Brown B-R-O-W-N
2	Smith S-M-I-T-H	5	Taylor T-A-Y-L-O-R
3	Williams W-I-L-L-I-A-M-S	6	Davies D-A-V-I-E-S

SPEAKING

1

- Students list five famous people, then rank them from 1 to 5 (from best neighbour to worst). Tell them to think about reasons why the people would or wouldn't be good neighbours.

2

- Groupwork. Put students into small groups to compare and discuss their lists, explaining their reasons for their choices. Point out the useful phrases at the bottom of the page.
- You might want to hear feedback from all groups and see who the whole class can agree on as best and worst neighbour.

Stronger classes

- With a stronger group, ask them to come to a consensus, selecting from all their lists, one worst and one best neighbour.

Extra discussion

- *Have you ever had a 'neighbour from hell'?*
- *If your neighbour's pet dog regularly came into your home or garden, what would you do?*
- *What is the worst thing a neighbour can do?*
- *Would you ever go round to your neighbour after midnight and complain?*
- *What are the three most important characteristics of a wonderful neighbour?*
- *Is it better to know your neighbour very well – or not to know them at all?*
- *Would you like to live next door to your country's leader?*

IF YOU WANT SOMETHING EXTRA …

❯ Straightforward Teacher's Resource Disc *at the back of this book*

1D | Making contact

WHAT THE LESSON IS ABOUT

Theme	Making phone calls Understanding spoken & printed messages
Speaking	Discussion: talking about different ways of making contact Pairwork roleplay: phone messages
Reading	Newspaper advertisements: names & details
Listening	Four phone messages: understanding instructions, numbers and pieces of information
Functional language	Phone numbers Phone messages

IF YOU WANT A LEAD-IN …

Test before you teach: phone calls

❯ *Methodology guidelines: Test before you teach, page xxi*

- Do some instant 30-second roleplays (ie short roleplays with no preparation). Put students into pairs: Student A and Student B.
- Tell all As to roleplay a short phone call to B:
  Phone your colleague. You are going to be late for a meeting.
- Stop this after 30 seconds. Set a new task for Bs:
  Phone and ask if your friend wants to go out for a coffee.
- Continue with A and B alternately roleplaying:
  Phone a friend and tell them about a party.
  Phone a Kung Fu teacher. You want to start lessons.
  Phone a cinema. You want to find out film times.
  Phone a shop. You want to get a new job.
  Phone a relative and invite them for lunch.
- Don't worry if students don't know all the language they need. If they get stuck, don't teach any language items, just move on to the next roleplay.

SPEAKING

1
- Pairwork. Students discuss the two questions.
- You could elicit from students possible ways of contacting people. For example:
  face-to-face talk; phone/mobile phone; email; SMS text message; waving and gestures; letters; memos and notes; messages passed via other people; internet chat and discussion boards; advertisements.

2
- Pairwork. Students think back to the last three phone calls they made and answer the questions.
- You could ask students to simply discuss the answers. Alternatively, give them two minutes to prepare a longer monologue using the italicized text as a model.

Extra discussion

- *Do you make a lot of calls? Do you like getting phone calls?*
- *Do you ever call people and have long dialogues, when you will meet them in just a few minutes?*
- *What is the most annoying feature of phones?*
- *Could you live without a mobile phone? If there were no phones in the world, how would it change your life?*

FUNCTIONAL LANGUAGE 1: phone numbers

This listening is a recording of the voicemail answering system of Kate Woods, who works for a recruitment agency. Kate is away today and the system offers some options and alternative phone numbers.

1 & 2 1.10
- Students listen to an answering machine message and answer the multiple-choice questions. The questions call for careful, accurate listening to details.
- Let students listen once, compare together, then play the recording again to check.
- Students look at the audioscript on page 133 and check their answers.

> 1 c   2 a   3 c   4 a

🌐 1.10

> **M = Message   K = Kate**
> **M:** Thank you for calling Sayers Recruitment and Training. To listen to the menu, please press the star button on your telephone now. Thank you. For general enquiries, press 1 followed by hash. For business callers, press 2 followed by hash. To make an appointment with a careers adviser, press 3 followed by hash. Thank you. You have reached the voicemail of:
> **K:** Kate Woods
> Hi, this is Kate Woods. I'm not in the office today, but you can call me at home on 0307 7 double 5 3046 or on my mobile 04 double 7 3201 double 8. That's 0307 7 double 5 3046 at home or 04 double 7 3201 double 8 for the mobile. You can also leave a message after the beep. Thanks.

3

❯ *Communication activities, Student's Book pages 126 & 128*

- Pairwork. Students look at their respective pages. They practise dictating the telephone numbers to each other. Emphasize that accuracy rather than speed is important.

Extra task: teacher dictation

- You can give your students more practice by dictating phone numbers to them. Start slower and get faster as you go on. Get students to practise noticing where the pauses are, indicating the divisions between parts of the number.
  1 *0361 212 4010*   *08 79 0116 262*
  2 *09 391 11 2821*   *00 32 12 99879*
  3 *0777 323 4165*   *9 811 279 1000*
  4 *1 212 39 91 623*   *772 35 35 33*

Language notes: reading phone numbers aloud

- Phone numbers are usually read in blocks of numbers with pauses in between. So, for example, *3267 755 3046* would be read in three separate blocks. Numbers are usually read as individual digits, one by one, eg *3267* would be read *three two six seven*, but sometimes blocks are read as pairs, eg *thirty two, sixty seven*. They are hardly ever read as hundreds or thousands, eg ✗ *Three thousand two hundred and sixty seven,* except in cases where the number is very distinctive and memorable, eg *1001* (which is often the case in TV advertised phone numbers for insurance companies, special offers, etc).

- # is pronounced *hash*
- * is pronounced *star*
- 0 can be pronounced *oh* or *zero*
- Two numbers together (eg *55*) can be said as either *five five* or *double 5*.
- *That's* is often used to introduce a repeat of phone numbers already said.

READING

These advertisements are from the classified ads section of a newspaper.

1
- Students read the eight advertisements. They could work in pairs to sort them into the four categories.
- This is a speed-reading task. Set a fairly tight time limit, eg two minutes, to discourage students from reading every word. Don't explain any vocabulary. Students don't need to understand all details to be able to answer the questions.

> Accommodation: A, E
> English lessons: B, H
> Jobs: F, G
> Making friends: C, D (H is also a possible answer)

Cultural notes: classified ads

- *Classified ads* (advertisements), sometimes known as *Small ads*, are short advertisements in newspapers and magazines. They are often printed in the publication's normal typeface and don't usually have sophisticated photos or wording. They are known as 'Classifieds' because they are typically grouped together with other adverts of a similar type under category classifications, eg *Accommodation, Events, Lonely Hearts,* etc.
- In contrast, *Display ads* are larger, better designed advertisements with big pictures and clever slogans, often placed by product manufacturers.
- *Classified ads* are usually charged by the word, so people placing adverts try to use as few words as possible. Abbreviations are very common, eg *pcm* means 'per calendar month', *WLTM* means 'would like to meet', *GSOH* means 'good sense of humour'.

2
- Students read the advertisements again and answer the eight questions.
- Again, a time limit is a good idea. Encourage students to scan-read, ie speed search for the information rather than reading word-by-word.

> 1 English.
> 2 Sayers Recruitment and Training.
> 3 Notting Hill (London).
> 4 Monday 7.30–8.30.
> 5 To meet new friends.
> 6 £750 per month.
> 7 At the Regent Hotel.
> 8 All languages.

Alternative procedure

- You could do this as a race. Tell students to cover the questions and read them aloud one by one yourself. Tell students not to call out answers but indicate (eg by raising a hand) when they have found an answer. When a number have found the answer, check with one student. NB If you let students call out, the lesson will go at the speed of the fastest students. By asking for students to indicate rather than call out, you allow other students a little more time to find answers and succeed in the task.

3
- Students look back at the advertisements and decide which one would be useful to them if they wanted to go to London to improve their English. They could discuss the question with a partner first before discussing it with the whole class.

LISTENING

In this listening, four people respond to the advertisements in the Reading section. In the first, second and fourth listenings, people leave messages. In the third, the person who answers the phone takes a message.

1 🔘 **1.11–1.14**
- Students listen to the four phone calls and match them to four of the advertisements. They then decide which caller doesn't speak to a recorded message.

> 1 D   2 C   3 G   4 B
>
> Caller 3, Ruby Tuesday, speaks to a receptionist, not a machine.

🔘 **1.11–1.14**

> **1   M = Message   D = Davina**
> **M:** This is 641480. I'm afraid there's no one to take your call right now. Please leave your name and number after the tone and I'll call you back.
> **D:** Ah, yes, hello. Mr Trotter, my name is Davina and I'm, I'm interested in your, erm, advertisement. Could you call me back, please? Any time before 6 o'clock. The number is 0870 double 4 6091. Ask for Davina. Bye.
>
> **2   M = Message   B = Bella**
> **M:** Stuart here. I'm not home at the moment, so please leave a message after the beep.
> **B:** Hello, good morning. This is Bella Moor, that's Moor, M, double O, R. I'm calling about the Kung Fu classes. You can call me back on my mobile, that's 0 double 47 3958 double 2. But I'll try to call you again later.
>
> **3   Re = Receptionist   R = Ruby**
> **Re:** Sayers Recruitment and Training. Can I help you?
> **R:** Hello, yes, erm, I'm, er, I saw your advert and I'm looking for a job, I mean, I'm interested in a new job, and …
> **Re:** Ah, yes, you need to speak to Mrs Sayers, but I'm afraid she's not in the office right now. Could I take your name and number and I'll ask her to call you back?
> **R:** Er, yes, yes. Er, the name's Ruby, Ruby Tuesday and my number is 0308 double 5 71919.
> **Re:** Thank you, Miss Tuesday. I'll pass on your message.
> **R:** Thanks. Bye.
> **Re:** Goodbye.

> 4   M = Message   S = Sara
> **M:** This is 727 23 double 7. I'm afraid there is no one to take your call right now. Please leave your name and number after the beep and I'll call you back.
> **S:** Oh, hello. This is a message for Mary Sharp. I'm interested in having English lessons because I need to prepare for an exam in Spain. Can you call me back? Some time this afternoon before six? My name is Sara and my number is 0308 3 double 4 7031.

2 🔘 1.11–1.14

- Students listen to the recording again and answer the six questions.

> 1   0870 446091
> 2   Anytime before 6 o'clock.
> 3   0447 395822
> 4   Moor
> 5   0308 557 1919
> 6   She needs to prepare for an exam in Spain.

FUNCTIONAL LANGUAGE 2: phone messages

❯ *Language reference, Student's Book page 15*

1 🔘 1.15

- Students listen to the recording and complete the phone messages.
- You could ask students to recall or predict the answers before they listen.

> 1 now   5 interested   9   calling
> 2 name   6 moment   10 mobile
> 3 number   7 message
> 4 name   8 This

🔘 1.15

> 1   M = Message   D = Davina
> **M:** This is 641480. I'm afraid there is no one to take your call right now. Please leave your name and number after the tone and I'll call you back.
> **D:** Ah yes, hello. Mr Trotter, my name is Davina and I'm, I'm interested in your, erm, advertisement. Could you call me back, please? Any time before 6 o'clock. The number is 0870 double 4 6091. Ask for Davina. Bye.
> 2   M = Message   B = Bella
> **M:** Stuart here. I'm not home at the moment, so please leave a message after the beep.
> **B:** Hello, good morning. This is Bella Moor, that's Moor, M, double O, R. I'm calling about the Kung Fu classes. You can call me back on my mobile, that's 0 double 4 7 3958 double 2. But I'll try to call you again later.

2

- Students write their own message using the two texts in exercise 1 as a model.
- Before students do the task, you may want to draw attention to the basic four-step structure of the answering machine messages, and the key chunks of language used in each category (see *Language notes*).

Language notes: answering machine messages

- Recorded messages tend to be structured in four steps:
  1 Stating the location/number/speaker's name: *This is 641480. Stuart here.*
  2 Explaining that no one is available to answer the call: *I'm not home at the moment. There's no one to take your call (right now).*
  3 Requesting information from the caller: *Please leave a /your name and number/message after the beep.*
  4 Saying what the receiver of the call will do: *I'll call you back.*
- When responding, callers often structure their message as follows:
  Greeting / Name (possibly spelt) / Reason for calling / Request to call back or contact / Information on how to contact (phone number/address/good time to call, etc) / Goodbye

3

❯ *Methodology Builder 25: Phone call practice, page 125*

- Pairwork. Students read their roles. Student A is phoning a friend who isn't at home and has to leave a message on the answering machine. Student B takes the role of the answering machine. First, Student B has to give the answering machine message and then they have to make notes about the message Student A leaves.
- So that Student B doesn't waste time while Student A is preparing, ask both students to prepare their own ideas following instructions in the Student A box. Therefore, when the first roleplay is over, they can reverse roles and immediately repeat the task.
- Refer students to the *Useful language box* at the bottom of the page.

Stronger classes

- Because Student B is roleplaying a machine rather than a human, tell them they can't ask Student As to repeat or clarify anything that they don't understand.

4

- Pairwork. Students swap roles and repeat the task.

Stronger classes: funny answering machine messages

- Read out one or two of these more unusual messages. An entertaining writing task for a strong class would be to make their own humorous message:
  1 *Hello. I'm Jim's answering machine. Who are you? Hmm. I've just bought an answering machine. Now how does it work? Eh? Well I pressed the green button. Is anything happening? I don't think so. Beeep.*
  2 *Hello. I am an answering machine, and I just want to tell you that I'm very depressed. I have one million times the memory of my owner, but all I do all day long is answer the phone. And now it's going to do that beep. Here comes the beep. Oh I hate that happy beep. Agggh. Beeep.*
  3 *Hi! Mary's answering machine is broken. This is her fridge. Please speak slowly and carefully because I am a bit slow. I can't record your message … but would you like some food? You do not need to speak. I can see into your mind. When you hear the beep, think about your name and your number. Beeeep. Er er er …*

IF YOU WANT SOMETHING EXTRA …

❯ Straightforward Teacher's Resource Disc *at the back of this book*

Answer key

1 REVIEW
● *Student's Book page 148*

1

1	What
2	When
3	How
4	What
5	What
6	Why
7	How
8	Who

2

1	question 6
2	question 2
3	question 4
4	question 1
5	question 7
6	question 5
7	question 8
8	question 3

3

2	When did her mother die?
3	Where did Athina live?
4	Where do her father and step-mother have a house?
5	Who was Athina's first boyfriend?
6	Where does he come from?
7	What does Athina call him?
8	Where is Athina very popular?

4

1	Do you have a lot in common with him?
2	Are you his best friend?
3	Did he go to school with you?
4	Were you good friends at school?
5	Is he married?
6	Does he live near you?
7	Did you see him yesterday?
8	Can he speak English?

5

a 6 b 7 c 2 d 4 e 8 f 3 g 5 h 1

6

Students' own answers

7

2 Hello, this <u>is</u> 2470362. There's no one at home <u>at</u> the moment. Please leave a message after the beep.

3 Hello, my name is Sayers and I'm calling <u>about</u> your advertisement in the newspaper. My number is 446091. Could <u>you</u> call me back later, please?

4 This <u>is</u> Ruby here. I'm not at home right now. Please leave your message and I'll try <u>to/and</u> call you later. Many thanks.

5 Ruby, are you there? Ruby? It's Stuart. Can you give me a call at work some time <u>this</u> afternoon? Or you can call me <u>on</u> my mobile. It's urgent, OK?

8

1	T
2	T
3	F (Elinor and Diane are sisters-in-law.)
4	F (Elinor is Effie's daughter-in-law.)
5	T
6	F (Mia is Sean's daughter-in-law.)
7	T
8	T

1 WRITING
● *Workbook page 65*

Model answer

Al Campbell (born 1969)
Hi everybody! I hope you're all well. I often think about you all, especially my old friends in the basketball team.
After I left school, I went to live in Los Angeles with my cousins for a year. Then I came back to the UK and studied Film at Sheffield University. I worked in advertising for a few years in London after university, but I didn't like it much. Now I make music videos. I live in Brighton with my wife, Tara, and our two children, Leila and Anastasia.
I'd love to hear from you. Get in touch! I promise to write back!

2A | School days

WHAT THE LESSON IS ABOUT

Theme	Memories of school
Speaking	Pairwork discussion: talking about your school days
	Groupwork: describing a favourite teacher
Listening	Monologues: three people talk about their school days
Vocabulary	Adjective and preposition collocations
Grammar	Past simple
Pronunciation	Regular past simple verb endings

IF YOU WANT A LEAD-IN ...

Pre-teach key words: collecting vocabulary for the lesson

- Write *school* as the headword and the sub-headings: *subjects, verbs, in class* and *people.* Then elicit words for each sub-heading. The most useful set of words to collect for this lesson may be school subjects.

■ **Methodology Builder 6**
■ **Mind map vocabulary collection**

- *A mind map is a visual way of showing how word meanings connect and relate to each other. Many people find words displayed like this easier to remember than the more traditional long word lists many students keep in their notebooks. The diagram may more closely reflect the way we store words in our brains.*
- *Make a mind map by choosing a key word for the centre of the diagram. This word should usually be the word that summarizes the main theme of the words you are collecting. Then decide on other sub-headings and add them to the map as branches from the centre. Collect vocabulary connected to each of these sub-headings. For example:*

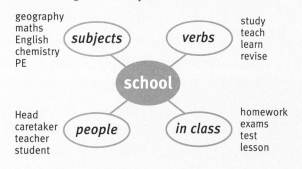

- *You can elicit words from students or present the items yourself. Encourage students to record new vocabulary in this way in their books.*

VOCABULARY & SPEAKING: adjectives with prepositions

> *Language reference, Student's Book page 25*

1
- Ask students to look at the eight sentences and decide which ones are positive and which are negative. Use the first two as an example, pointing out that it's positive if you are good at something, but negative if you are bored.

> positive (+): sentences 4, 5 and 7
> negative (−): sentences 3, 6 and 8

2
- Students think about when they were at school. They can tick the statements in exercise 1 that are true for them and cross those that are not. As these are personal questions, there are no correct answers.
- Students then rewrite the sentences that were not true for them and make them true.

3
- Pairwork. Students read their sentences to each other. Encourage them to discuss each sentence with their partner.

Extra discussion
- *What are/were your favourite subjects at school? Why? What subjects don't/didn't you like? Why?*
- *Should students study things that are directly useful for life or getting a job, eg how to repair a car? how to bath a baby? how to cook?*
  Which school subject do you think is not useful for life?
- *What subject isn't taught at school but should be?*
- *If you could redesign school timetables, what is the biggest change you'd make?*

Language notes: adjective & preposition collocations
- Students will typically make errors in matching the wrong prepositions, eg ✗ *worried on,* ✗ *bored about,* etc (often drawing from their own first language).
- As there is no rule to help learners decide which preposition goes with which adjective, it's important for learners to record and learn the complete collocation rather than just the adjective.
- If you are *fond of* something, you like it and have a loving feeling towards it. For example, *She was very fond of her pet cat* means that she really liked her cat. This is most often used to talk about people and animals.
- If you are *keen on* something, you are very interested in it and excited about it. You can use this to describe hobbies, sports and interests, eg *I'm very keen on horror films.*

LISTENING

In this listening, three people talk about old school memories. Speaker 1 talks about a biology teacher, Speaker 2 talks about a negative school experience and Speaker 3 talks about a positive school experience.

1 💿 **1.16–1.18**

- Students listen to all three speakers and decide which speaker is talking about which topic.

1	b
2	c
3	a (Students could reasonably argue that speaker 2 also talks about his favourite subject, *art*)

Weaker classes

- Play the recordings one at a time and allow students time to compare ideas before moving on.

🌐 **1.16–1.18**

1	Mr Miller taught biology and everybody, well, all the girls anyway, we all loved him. I was afraid of lots of the teachers, but with Mr Miller, I was really fond of him, maybe more than a little fond, actually. You know, he really cared about his students; he was really interested in us, in us as people, I mean. I never missed his lessons. And I always got good grades in his classes. Some of the boys, though, some of the boys weren't very keen on him. Jealous, probably.
2	I didn't like my school at all. I was terrible at most subjects, but I was good at art. The teachers thought I was stupid, and they put me in a class with all the difficult pupils. The teachers weren't interested in us and we didn't worry about them. I never worked in class, I never did my homework, and nobody was surprised when, at sixteen, I failed my exams. I failed all of them except art. I'm a painter now, and people don't care if I have any exams.
3	I didn't really like school very much, but Fridays were OK. Friday was music day and I was really keen on music. Still am. I played the guitar and I sang well, quite well, and the music teachers were always cool. We made a CD with one of them and another organized a gig at the end of term. I had such fun that I didn't want to leave that school.

2 🌐 **1.16–1.18**

- Students listen again. They catch phrases from the recording and make sentences by combining beginnings and endings from column A and B.
  NB The recording will help students to work out possible sentences, but it does not always contain exactly the same wording as the printed exercise.
- You could ask students to try the exercise before they listen again.

1 d	2 a	3 f	4 b	5 c	6 e

3

- Students can work in small groups to compare experiences at school. Ask them if they had any experiences similar to the ones in the recording.

GRAMMAR: past simple

Grammar box

- 〉 *Language reference, Student's Book page 24*
- 〉 *Methodology Builder 22: Using Grammar boxes, page 106*

1

- Students look at the list of infinitives in the table and fill in past simple verb forms. When students have finished, ask them to look at audioscript 1.16–1.18 on page 134 to check their answers.

- You could do one or two examples with the whole class.

1	hated	3	left	5	studied	7	taught
2	listened	4	loved	6	talked	8	tried

2

- Students group the verbs from exercise 1 into four sets according to the grammar headings *a–d*.

a	talked	c	studied; tried
b	hated; loved	d	left; taught

3

- Students complete the dialogue with past simple verb forms.

2	worked	6	didn't have	11	studied
3	lived	7	didn't stay	12	didn't get
4	went	8	left	13	got
5	Did you enjoy	9	Did you do	14	Did you like
		10	didn't go	15	thought

4

- Pairwork. Students use exercise 3 as a model to write a similar dialogue.

Weaker/stronger classes

- Weaker students may produce something with relatively few changes, possibly keeping the verbs as they are.
- Stronger students can be encouraged to use different verbs, as well as changing the information.

Extension task

- When students have finished, they could copy out their text, like exercise 3, with verbs gapped and cues in brackets. In pairs, students swap texts and use them as new exercises for further practice.

Extra practice

- 〉 *Methodology Builder 30: Pelmanism (memory game), page 158*
- Use the Pelmanism game to give students more practice in matching past simple and infinitive verbs.
- You could use these word pairs:

walk, walked	fall, fell
go, went	feel, felt
know, knew	give, gave
get, got	work, worked
fly, flew	try, tried
tell, told	teach, taught
leave, left	have, had

Language notes: infinitive & past simple

- For students the formation of past simple statements is often relatively straightforward. Many students, however, find questions and negatives more problematic. The major difficulty is that these structures use auxiliary verbs and infinitives, rather than the past form.
- Common mistakes arise from forgetting this, eg ✗ *Did he listened?* ✗ *I didn't wanted the coffee.*
  Other common errors are:
  Trying to make a question by inversion, eg ✗ *Failed you the exam?*
  Trying to make negatives by adding the word *not*, eg ✗ *I not wanted the magazine.*

- In questions and negatives, the 'pastness' is indicated by the auxiliary verb *did* rather than by an *-ed* ending or a past form.
- Some teachers find that it helps to present this visually by illustrating how the past ending seems to move and transform into an auxiliary verb. This may also help to show students why there is no past ending on the main verb:

Statement: He listened to the radio.

Question: Did he listen to the radio?

PRONUNCIATION: regular past simple verbs

The main aim of this section is to raise awareness about an aspect of the words students may not have noticed before.

1 1.19
- Ask students to read the explanation and then listen to the pronunciation of the examples.

1.19

open – opened
love – loved
try – tried

want – wanted
decide – decided

Language notes: pronunciation of past simple

- The endings /t/ and /d/ sound very similar and there won't be any major comprehension difficulties if students say them wrongly. The exercises are more important in raising awareness about the number of syllables.
- Students often correctly select between the /t/ or /d/ ending, but often pronounce an extra, unnecessary syllable. Students may assume that all *-ed* endings are pronounced as an extra /ed/syllable, eg
  opened as a three-syllable word ✗ /'əʊpəned/
  (ie *op … en … ed*) rather than as a two-syllable word
  /'əʊpənd/ (ie *op … end*).
  climbed as two syllables ✗/klaɪmed/ (ie *climb … ed*) rather than as one syllable /klaɪmd/.
- Where *-ed* comes after the phoneme /t/ or /d/, you do need an extra syllable. The ending is pronounced /ɪd/, eg *wan … ted*.

2 & 3 1.20
- Ask students to work in pairs and sort the past verbs into the two categories.
- Students listen to the recording to check their answers.

1.20

No extra syllable (NS): helped, worked
Extra syllable (ES): ended, hated, needed, studied, waited

SPEAKING

1
- Ask students to name any films to do with schools or teachers.
- It may be helpful before class to think of some films and TV programmes that students will know, in case they don't remember them themselves.

> Some films with school themes: *Harry Potter series*; *Good Will Hunting*; *Dead Poets Society*; *The Nutty Professor*; *Fame*; *Nicholas Nickelby*; *School of Rock*; *School Daze*.

2
- Ask students to think about a teacher they liked. They read the questions and prepare to talk about him/her. Allow students about two to three minutes' preparation time to read through the list of questions and think about them. The task would also work well if you allow more preparation time so that students can make notes.

3
- Groupwork. Put students into groups to describe their teacher.

Extension task
- You could set a listening task for students who are not speaking. Ask them to decide which of the teachers is the one they would most like to have. At the end, students can come to an agreement.

Cultural notes: American films about education
Freedom Writers
- This is an American film which was made in 2007. It stars Hilary Swank, who plays a teacher from a privileged background who goes to teach in a failing school.
- The film is set in Los Angeles in the 1990s, a time of race riots, and it details the struggles of the students.

Mona Lisa Smile
- This film was made in 2003 and stars Julia Roberts. It is set in the 1950s and is a romantic drama.
- Julia Roberts plays a teacher in a very conservative college who challenges the students and the college to be more liberal.

Web research task
➲ *Methodology Builder 1: Using Web research tasks, page 2*
- Find out about at least one film about schools and/or teachers. Find out about the plot, setting and actors.

Web search key words
- *movies school teachers*

IF YOU WANT SOMETHING EXTRA …
➲ Straightforward Teacher's Resource Disc *at the back of this book*

2B | Irish schools

WHAT THE LESSON IS ABOUT

Themes	Schools in Ireland
Speaking	Pairwork discussion: talking about schools in your town
	Pairwork: comparing schools now & in the past
Reading	*Schools in Europe: The Republic of Ireland*. Magazine article: looking at the Irish education system
Vocabulary	Education
Grammar	*Used to*
Pronunciation	Vowel & diphthong sounds in irregular past simple verbs

IF YOU WANT A LEAD-IN ...

Introducing the theme: schools in the past

- Ask students to think about their parents and imagine what their school days were like. How was the experience different from their own? Allow three minutes for thinking and note-taking.
- Ask students to work in pairs and tell their partner what they think school was like for their parents.

Discussion starters: two different schools

❯ *Methodology Builder 15: Using Discussion starters, page 63*

- Draw two large boxes on the board, one on the left, one on the right.
- Explain that in Edtown there are two schools and the boxes represent these schools. One school – the one on the left – is a very bad school with lots of problems. Elicit from students some of these difficulties. Encourage students to think about the teaching, students, subjects, buildings, behaviour, sports, exams, etc. Write up brief one/two-word notes inside the left-hand building, eg *dirty classrooms*.
- When students have come up with a good range of ideas, turn their attention to the other school. Explain that this school is the opposite of the first one. Ask students to work in small groups and come up with ideas for ways that this school is good. After enough discussion time, get students from different groups to report on their ideas. Make notes in the right-hand box.
- At the end, you can perhaps draw a few conclusions about what is essential in a good school, and ask students to decide how their own memories of school compare with these two.

SPEAKING

1
- Pairwork. Students discuss the questions. Make sure that students answer the *why* question.
- You could ask pairs to make notes of their ideas. After a few minutes, students discuss the ideas with the whole class.

VOCABULARY: education

❯ *Language reference, Student's Book page 25*

1 & 2 💿 1.21
- Students use words from the box to complete the gaps.
- The vocabulary may be new or puzzling for students, but unknown items can probably be worked out from context. Most items are part of common collocations, eg *single sex schools; English education system; compulsory subjects; (school) leaving age; leaving certificate; exam results.*
- Students listen to the recording and check their answers.

1	sex	5	age
2	system	6	certificate
3	compulsory	7	results
4	punishment		

💿 1.21

1. Some schools in England are for boys and girls and some are single sex.
2. In the English education system there are private schools and state schools.
3. Some subjects, like English and maths, are compulsory until the age of sixteen in England.
4. English children must sometimes stay in class at break as a punishment.
5. The minimum leaving age in England is sixteen, but most students continue for another two years.
6. There is no leaving certificate in England, but many students take 'A level' exams when they are eighteen.
7. School students in England get their exam results in the summer holidays after they leave school.

3
- Students change the sentences from the previous exercises to make true statements about their own country.
- This rewriting task needs some thinking as it requires more than just substituting the country name or changing a word or two. Students may need advice on vocabulary or phrases to clearly explain their local situation.

READING

This magazine article looks at the Irish education system, its history of traditional and authoritarian teaching, and the improvements it has made to become one of the best education systems in the world.

1
- Students read the article and decide which heading (a–d) goes best with each paragraph.
- This activity would be most useful with a fairly tight time limit (eg two minutes) to encourage faster reading. Students only need to read as much as is needed to be able to do the task successfully.

2 d   3 a   4 c

2
- Make sure students understand that all the statements are true and the task here is to find evidence from the text to show that they are. Students read the article again and find information that supports each of the statements.

1 *Also possible:* class sizes small; children happy; stay at school after 16.
2 Teaching was very traditional: large classes; teachers used to hit the children; Latin, Greek and religion were the most important subjects.
3 Boys and girls went to different schools; studied different subjects.
4 Girls do better in exams; more girls go to university; most teachers are female.
5 Three compulsory subjects: maths, Irish and English. In addition, two or three extra subjects.

3
- Students note comparisons between education in Ireland and their own country. This could be done by dividing the board into two columns: the left for Ireland, the right for the students' own country. Ask students to turn over their text and recall features of the Irish system item by item. List these down the left side of the board. When the list is complete, ask students to suggest how their own system compares and write this information on the right hand side of the board.

Cultural notes: the Irish education system
- Primary school education in Ireland must start when children are six years old, although many children start when they are four. There are no state primary schools. The English language is used for teaching. Subjects taught include Irish, mathematics, social and environmental studies, arts and crafts, music, physical education and religious instruction. Students do not take a school-leaving exam at the end of primary school. Secondary education lasts from twelve to eighteen. Students first take the junior certificate exams at fifteen and then take leaving certificate exams at eighteen.

GRAMMAR: *used to*

Grammar box
❯ *Language reference, Student's Book page 24*
❯ *Methodology Builder 22: Using Grammar boxes, page 106*

1
- Students transform the sentences using the affirmative and negative of *used to.*
- Students may ask if there is any difference in meaning between the original and rewritten sentences. In fact, past simple and *used to* are very similar, but *used to* suggests these additional ideas: something happened repeatedly, many times, often or regularly; it probably happened some time ago, and doesn't happen any more.
- When they have finished, ask students to look at the three photos. Tell them to work in pairs and discuss who they think the sentences are about.

2 As a child, he used to be called Jonny O'Keeffe.
3 He used to go to a famous school, the North Monastery School.
4 He didn't use to like his school.
5 He used to miss lessons.
6 He didn't use to do well in his exams.
7 He used to spend a lot of time playing pool.

Answer to photo question: Jonathan Rhys Meyers

Extra practice: used to *drills*
❯ *Methodology Builder 4: Cues for sentence-making drills, page 10*
- Use the instruction for *Cues for sentence-making drills.* There will be a number of possible answers for each cue. Accept any that make sense. Students will need thinking time to process the cues. So, don't rush.

Teacher cues	Students (possible answers)
Example: I / toy cars …	I used to play with toy cars.
David Beckham / Manchester United	David Beckham used to play for Manchester United.
Family / very poor	Her family used to be very poor.
I / sports	I used to love sports.
Beatles / a Liverpool club	The Beatles used to play in a Liverpool club.
People / aliens on Mars	People used to think aliens lived on Mars.
Young / hate onions	When I was young, I used to hate onions.
Peter / long walks	Peter used to go for long walks.
Paris / metro	When I lived in Paris, I used to travel by metro every day.

Language notes: used to
Avoidance and overuse
- Students tend to avoid the *used to* structure, often preferring to use past simple.
- A few students overuse *used to*, which quickly sounds unnatural.
- To give realistic practice, keep reminding students about *used to* and integrate practice into future lessons. When doing speaking tasks about the past, remind students that *used to* may also be a possibility.

Confusions
Students often get confused between the meanings, uses and pronunciation of the various structures and words that contain the three letters *use*:
- *Used to* (pronounced /ˈjuːstə/): eg *They used to go to the large disco in the town centre.*
- Main verb *use* (pronounced /juːz/): eg *He always uses Brazilian coffee; Did you use the umbrella? The box was used to carry the bottles home.* (NB Even though the last example has the words *used to*, it still isn't *used to* as studied in this chapter!)
- Noun: *use* (pronounced /juːs/): *This booklet has instructions for use of the new answerphone; What's the use of arriving early?* (ie what is the purpose of …)
- Phrasal verbs with *use*: eg *use up.*
- *To get used to something* and *To be used to something*: Students will probably not have met these items yet; all the same they may cause some confusion. Both refer to a familiarity with something over a period of time.
- There is no present form of *used to.*

Other issues
- The question and negative forms are often trickier for students than statements.
- *Used not to* is a rarer alternative form for the negative, eg *She used not to like long films.*

Pronunciation
- *Used to* and *didn't use to* both have the same sounds: /ˈjuːstə/.
- *To* always has a weak pronunciation, except in some short answers, eg *Do you speak Greek? Well, I used to.*

2

- This is similar to exercise 1, but the challenge here is that *used to* is not possible in all sentences.
- Remind students about when you can't use *used to*, ie events that happened only once – even if that one time extended over a long period of time.

> 2 NP (Not possible)
> 3 NP
> 4 NP
> 5 His family didn't use to have much money.
> 6 His father used to tell funny stories to Frank.
> 7 Frank used to love listening to his father.
> 8 NP

Cultural notes: Frank McCourt & The Pulitzer Prize

Frank McCourt
- Frank McCourt achieved great success with his book *Angela's Ashes*. The book describes the life of an exceptionally poor family in Ireland. The family lived in dreadful conditions and three children died while the father drank the little money he got.
  The book is very sad and moving but also surprisingly funny. A film was made of it. A sequel *'Tis* continues the somewhat happier story of the author's life as a young adult in America.

The Pulitzer Prize
- This refers to a series of US literary awards named after the Hungarian-American newspaper publisher and journalist Joseph Pulitzer (pronounced 'Pull it sir'). There are awards for excellent journalism and for books that deal with important human issues.
- Famous book winners include *The Old Man and the Sea* (Ernest Hemingway), *To Kill a Mockingbird* (Harper Lee) and *The Executioner's Song* (Norman Mailer).

Web research tasks

❯ *Methodology Builder 1: Using Web research tasks, page 2*

Irish writers
- Find a longer biography of Frank McCourt. What were some of the best and worst things in his life?
- Find out the names of some famous books by Irish writers.
Web search key words
- *Frank McCourt biography*
- *famous Irish writers*
Pulitzer Prize
- There is also a Pulitzer Prize for photography. What kind of photographs can win? Find some example photos. Which is your favourite?
Web search key words
- *'Pulitzer prize' photographs*

3
- Students write three *used to* and three *didn't use to* sentences about their time at primary school.
- Check that students are not using *used to* for events that only happened once.

Extension task: writing a childhood/school memoir

- Ask students to write a *memoir* of their own school days as a classroom or homework task. Students may think they remember little of these days, but even so, the experience of writing will often help the memories to come flooding back.
- You could suggest a few of these topics:
  their earliest memories; how they reacted to school

when they were very young; daily life at primary school; people they recall from primary school; their first day at secondary school; people they used to be very close to; things they didn't understand; rules.

PRONUNCIATION: irregular past simple verbs

1 & 2 🔘 1.22
- Students look at the four groups of words. For each group, students decide which word has a different vowel sound from the others.
- Students listen to the recording to check. You could then ask students to listen and repeat from the recording.

> 1 found   2 said   3 lost   4 knew

Extension task
- Extend the activity by asking students to invent interesting sentences that include two or more of the words in them.

Language notes: diphthongs
- Some of the key sounds are diphthongs (ie double vowel sounds, such as the vowel sound in *cow*).
  Bought, caught and *thought* all have the vowel sound /ɔː/, whereas *found* has the diphthong /aʊ/.
  Came, gave and *made* all have the diphthong /eɪ/, whereas *said* has the vowel /e/. Students may get this wrong, as it's commonly mispronounced as /seɪd/ rather than /sed/.
  Broke, drove and *spoke* all have the diphthong /əʊ/, whereas *lost* has the vowel /ɒ/.
  Felt, met and *went* all have the vowel sound /e/, whereas *knew* has the vowel sound /uː/. NB *Knew* is pronounced /njuː/ in British English (not /nuː/, which is US English).

🔘 **1.22**

> 1 bought, caught, found, thought
> 2 came, gave, made, said
> 3 broke, drove, lost, spoke
> 4 felt, knew, met, went

SPEAKING

1
- Students prepare notes comparing schools in their country now and ones in the past. Encourage them to make at least two notes for each of the key word headings.

2
- Pairwork. Pairs meet up and compare ideas. Allow students to refer back to their notes, but the task should be more than simply reading aloud to each other.

Monolingual classes
- Set an additional task to agree five ways that schools are better (or worse) now than in the past.

Multilingual classes
- Make pairs with students from different places. Set an additional task so that students agree on five similarities between their countries and their schools in the past.

IF YOU WANT SOMETHING EXTRA ...
❯ Straightforward Teacher's Resource Disc *at the back of this book*

2c | Red faces

WHAT THE LESSON IS ABOUT

Theme	Embarrassing situations & behaviour
Speaking	Pairwork: discussing embarrassing situations
	Pairwork: discussing ways parents & children can embarrass each other
Reading	*Teacher-talk.* Web page: an internet discussion group
Grammar	Past continuous

IF YOU WANT A LEAD-IN ...

Pre-teach a key word: embarrassing

- Tell a short personal story about an embarrassing incident. For example:
  Last Friday evening, I was making supper when I noticed that I had run out of salt. So I went out to the local shop to buy some. Unfortunately, I left so quickly I forgot to take my key with me. So I tried to climb in through my window. However, I was not a very good burglar and someone walking past saw me. I was still climbing in when the police car came rushing down the street dee-dah dee-dah!
- After the story ask questions to clarify the meaning of *embarrassing*. For example:
  How did I feel? Did I feel stupid? Did my face become red? Did I wish that no one knew about what I did? Did I wish that no one could see me?
  How did I feel the next day when I met my neighbours? Did I feel that I wanted to hide?
  Did I feel proud of my action?

Discussion starters: embarrassing moments

- ❯ *Methodology Builder 15: Using Discussion starters, page 63*
- Ask students: *Have you ever been in an embarrassing situation?* Use some of these memory prompts to see if any students have had embarrassing situations connected with: *school; clothes; meeting people; shopping; sleeping; food; shoes; mobile phones; parties; emails; saying something at the wrong time; keys; money; noises; illness; guests.*

Test before you teach: past continuous

- ❯ *Methodology guidelines: Test before you teach, page xxi*
- Write some times on the board, eg 8am, 1.30pm, 7pm and 11.30pm.
- Ask students to think about what they were doing yesterday at each of these times and make a few notes.
- Ask students to work in pairs and compare what they were doing at these times.

SPEAKING & READING

These messages are from an internet discussion group in which three teachers reveal their most embarrassing moments.

1

- Pairwork. Students read the situations quickly and decide which one they think is the most embarrassing. Tell them to add other embarrassing situations they can think of to the list.

- When they have discussed the situations with their partner, ask a few pairs to say which situations they thought were the most embarrassing.

2

- Students read the three messages and match each one to a situation in exercise 1.

Language notes: vocabulary

- A *costume hire shop* is a place where you can rent unusual clothes for a short time (eg for a party). NB *Costume* means special, unusual, historical or funny clothes. It doesn't mean *suit*.
- *Ring tone:* this is the music that a phone plays when someone calls you.

> Doug – You are wearing the wrong kind of clothes.
> Tamsin – Your telephone rings at the wrong moment.
> Kelly – You fall asleep in a public place.

3

- Students read the texts again and answer the questions.
- You could ask students to write answers individually. Alternatively, allow some individual reading time, then ask students to discuss their answers in pairs.

> 1 To help new teachers get to know each other.
> 2 Doug wanted to get to know his colleagues.
> 3 He thought it was a Hallowe'en party.
> 4 She was the teacher in charge of the exam (ie the invigilator).
> 5 It had a silly ring tone.
> 6 She couldn't find it in her bag.
> 7 It was a beautiful day.
> 8 She heard a noise.

Cultural notes: Hallowe'en party

- **Hallowe'en** (or **All Hallow's Eve**) originated as a celebration in Ireland, but has become famous because of its popularity in the US. It is on the evening of 31 October. The following day is 1 November, the Christian *All Saints' Day*. People believed that on the evening before the day of saints, all the evil and bad spirits of the planet would rush to escape. People used to dress up in costumes to frighten these bad spirits away.
- Nowadays, people celebrate the night with parties or discos. In the US and other English-speaking countries, children dress up as witches, ghosts, skeletons, etc and go from door to door asking *Trick or Treat?*, which means they are asking for a present of sweets or cakes, etc. If they don't get their treat, they will do something bad to you (eg make loud ghostly noises outside the windows). Usually people are prepared for these visitors and have a good stock of sweets and cakes.
- Here is a traditional Hallowe'en rhyme that children can say when *trick or treating:*
  Trick or treat,
  Smell my feet,
  Quickly give me
  Something sweet.

Web research tasks

- Find some typical Hallowe'en decorations.
- Find a recipe for some scary Hallowe'en foods.

Web search key words

- *Image search: Halloween decorations*
- *Halloween food recipe*

4

- Pairwork. Students discuss embarrassing experiences (their own or other people's).
- The prompt ideas in *Discussion starters* on page 22 may be useful here if you didn't use them in the lead-in.

GRAMMAR: past continuous

Grammar box

❯ *Language reference, Student's Book page 24*
❯ *Methodology Builder 22: Using Grammar boxes, page 106*
❯ *Methodology Builder 29: Gap-fill exercises, page 150*

1

- Students do the gap fill task. The timeline diagrams below may help students to see why certain answers are correct:

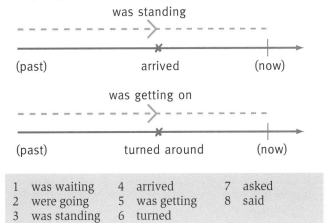

1 was waiting	4 arrived	7 asked
2 were going	5 was getting	8 said
3 was standing	6 turned	

Language notes: past continuous

- Students often think that the past continuous primarily shows a 'continuous' longer lasting activity compared with the past simple. While it is sometimes true that a past continuous activity lasts longer, this is not the defining reason why we use the tense. Past simple activities can also be long lasting, eg *Shakespeare lived for more than 50 years.*
- The tense name is a little unfortunate as there is nothing particularly continuous about it (for this reason some teachers and linguists prefer to call it the *past progressive*).
- When the past continuous tense is used to describe something in progress, when something else happened (in the past simple), this is known as the *interrupted past continuous.*
- Some visual students may find that a timeline diagram can help to clarify this meaning (see *Methodology Builder* on right). The diagram shows that the dog *was running* when *Jeff called*. The *was running* line starts before the other action. The dotted line shows that the *running* may or may not have continued after this.

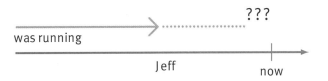

- In written English the past continuous is an important way of setting the background scene before the main events of a story are told, eg *He was walking up and down the hall waiting for the messenger to arrive. Suddenly the door opened ...*

■ Methodology Builder 7
■ Using timelines

- *It can often be difficult to explain in a clear way exactly what 'time' a tense refers to. Sometimes a diagram such as a timeline can make such concepts clearer. It is a simple but powerful way of clarifying and comparing the time references of various tenses.*
- *The basic timeline is a line representing the flow of time, from left to right, from the past towards the future. At some point along the line is the current moment* now. *We can add labels to the line to indicate the period that the line shows (eg a few minutes, hours, a day, months, years, centuries, etc).*

10pm	11pm	12pm	1am	now	2am

- *NB When you first introduce timelines to students, allow enough time to make sure they are clear about these basic ideas, otherwise all the other concepts will not mean much to them.*
- *Once you have established this basic concept of the flow of time, you can place other marks or labels on the line to show how tenses represent our perception of different events in time. This is usually done with the following:*
  Lines or arrows (to show events that have a beginning and end and last a period of time).
  Crosses (to show moments or events that are perceived as happening quickly, in a moment).
  Arrows may also be used to show the relationship between events.
- *In class there are two basic ways to use timelines. You show them: Draw a completed timeline on the board and use it to help explain the meaning of a tense.*
  Elicit from students: Draw the basic timeline (showing only the flow of time) on the board and ask students how they could add to it to show the meaning of an example sentence.

Extra practice: past continuous

- Find some magazine pictures or flash cards with pictures of people doing different actions, eg playing football, eating a meal, etc. Include one (or more) picture(s) showing a bank.
- Give one picture to each student and stress that students must keep them completely secret. Tell students that there was a bank robbery yesterday at three o'clock. If their picture shows a bank, they were a bank robber! If they weren't the bank robber, their picture shows what they were doing at three o'clock yesterday afternoon.
- Divide the class in two and tell one half that they are police officers. The police must ask people what they were doing at three o'clock. Everyone must tell the truth except for the bank robber(s) who must tell a lie about what they were doing.
- After a few minutes, reverse roles and the new police officers ask questions.

- At the end of the task, ask students to recall some of the sentences people said about what they were doing. (You could write them on the board.) Everyone must now try to guess who was/were the bank robbers.
- If students enjoy the game, play it again a few times.

2

❯ *Communication activities, Student's Book pages 127 & 132*

- Pairwork. Students have one minute to study the three cartoons on page 132 and try to remember as many details as possible.
- They then look at the questions on page 127 and see how many they can answer without looking back at the pictures.

> **Picture A**
> 1 The headmaster.
> 2 Kelly.
> 3 A suit.
> 4 They were laughing.
>
> **Picture B**
> 1 In front of the class.
> 2 Her bag.
> 3 In the front row of the class on the left.
> 4 Six.
>
> **Picture C**
> 1 A witch's costume.
> 2 Normal clothes.
> 3 A glass.
> 4 She was dancing.

3

- Pairwork. Students ask and answer the questions about specific times in the past continuous.
- If you want, demand that students give true answers. Alternatively, they can invent answers. Ask them to think of the most unusual and interesting things for the answers. Then feed back with the whole class.

Extension task

- Suggest roles for students to take when giving answers. For example, they answer the *What were you doing …* questions as if they were the US President. Other roles could be: a pop star; head of Microsoft®; an animal in the zoo; a jumbo jet pilot; a bank robber; your teacher; a bird; a policeman.

SPEAKING

1

- Draw attention to the two lists. Elicit an example idea from students for each list to check meaning.
- Groupwork. Students read the sentences and decide which ones go in which list.

> *Probable answers:*
> To embarrass parents: sentences 2 and 3
> To embarrass children: sentences 1 and 4
>
> Students may argue that some answers could fit both categories, eg sentence 2.

2

- Students continue in their groups to discuss the lists and to think of more ideas. They should add at least three more ideas to each list.
- Tell students that they will be asked to present their ideas to the rest of the class. Ask them to think about what they will say and decide who will talk about each idea.

3

- Students make presentations of their ideas to the class.

IF YOU WANT SOMETHING EXTRA …

❯ Straightforward Teacher's Resource Disc *at the back of this book*

2D | Which school?

WHAT THE LESSON IS ABOUT

Theme	Choosing a language school
Speaking	Pairwork decision-making: choosing a language school
	Pairwork roleplay: asking for information
Listening	Dialogue: asking for information in a language school
Vocabulary	School facilities
Functional language	Asking for information
Did you know?	The English language

IF YOU WANT A LEAD-IN ...

Discussion starters: studying abroad

> *Methodology Builder 15: Using Discussion starters, page 63*

For students not studying in an English-speaking country:
- *Would you like to travel to an English-speaking country to study English? Would it help you learn English? What would you enjoy?*
- *Would it be expensive? Is it possible that other people could pay for your study and travel? (Scholarship? Gift? Prize?)*
- *What would improve most in another country – grammar? pronunciation? listening? etc.*

For students away from home who are now in an English-speaking country to study on a language course:
- *Was English study the main reason you came here? Has it helped you study?*
- *What has improved?*
- *Has it been easier to learn English here than at home?*
- *Why did you choose this location?*

For students who live in an English-speaking country:
- *Why is it important for you to study English?*
- *Do the classes help you to live in this country?*
- *Would you like to visit another country to study? Why?*

Test before you teach: asking for information

> *Methodology guidelines: Test before you teach, page xxi*
- Write the following headings on the board: *class size; timetable; lessons; other activities; important information.*
- Put students into pairs for a roleplay: explain that one student is a receptionist at their own school. The other is a person who wants to find out information about the school. Tell students to use the headings on the board to ask and answer questions about the school. Allow two to three minutes for students to ask and answer questions.

SPEAKING

1
- Ask students to look at the information in the leaflet (top half of the page). Ask: *What is it about?* (Answer: *a prize – studying English abroad*); *What is the prize?* (Answer: *a study tour for two people – including flight, accommodation and free course.*)
- Pairwork. Tell students that they have just won the prize! In pairs, students discuss which city they would like to go to.

Stronger classes
- Ask students to state their reasons for or against each location.

Cultural notes: language schools & studying abroad
- Many countries have language schools, ie schools (usually private) that only teach languages. These help local students to get better at languages such as English.
- However, in the UK and other English-speaking countries, language schools mainly provide courses for students who come from other countries to improve their language skills. Students will be living in an environment where they are entirely surrounded by the language they are studying. (Of course, you could also study French, German, Japanese, etc, in English-speaking countries if you wanted to.)

VOCABULARY: school facilities

1
- Students look at the advertisement for the Victoria School of English and match the words in bold to the definitions 1–8.

2	cafeteria	6	flexible
3	fees	7	experienced
4	location	8	qualified
5	tuition		

Stronger classes
- Stronger students could first try the exercise without looking at the advertisement.

2
- Students decide the three most important things to think about when choosing a language school.

Weaker classes
- Help students by first eliciting and writing on the board a list of things to consider. Choose some of these: *location; building; rooms; equipment; decoration; condition; teachers; qualifications; experience; timetables; other students; class size; cafeteria; fees; social programme.*

3
- Pairwork. Students compare their lists with a partner.

LISTENING

In this listening, a man rings up a language school to find out information about French classes.

1 🔘 1.23
- Tell students they will hear a man asking for information at a French language school. Students listen to the recording and underline the correct information from the list.

Stronger classes

- You could simply write the headings (class size, level, etc) on the board and, with books closed, ask students to listen out for the information about each heading.

> Level: Beginner
> Timetable: Tues & Thurs, 8.00–9.30
> Course length: 10
> French club: Friday evenings
> Price: £180

 1.23

> R = Receptionist   P = Patrick
> R: Good afternoon. Bonjour. Can I help you?
> P: Er, yes. Bonjour. Please could I have some information about your school?
> R: Certainly, sir. What would you like to know?
> P: Well, could you tell me about your courses? I mean, for example, how many students are in a class?
> R: There are fifteen students in a class. We have day-time classes and evening classes. And all our teachers are native French teachers. Do you speak any French?
> P: Er, oui. Un petit peu.
> R: Pardon?
> P: Yes, sorry, my accent isn't very good. I think that I'm probably a beginner. Do you have classes for beginners in the evenings?
> R: Yes, we do. On Tuesdays and Thursdays.
> P: And what time are the classes?
> R: Between eight o'clock and half past nine.
> P: Eight to nine-thirty. I see. And how long does the course last?
> R: It's a ten-week course. It starts next Tuesday, actually.
> P: Oh, right. Excellent. And, er, are there any social activities?
> R: Oh yes, we have our French club on Friday evenings.
> P: Sounds fun. Oh, I almost forgot. How much are the course fees?
> R: It's one hundred and eighty pounds for the ten weeks. Would you like a registration form?

2 & 3 1.23

- Students match items from A and B to make typical collocations. Tell them that these items have all been used in the recording.
- Students may argue for other acceptable answers, eg *day-time courses; ten-week class*.
  NB Although *social class* is a common collocation, it has a distinctly different (non-educational) meaning.
- Students listen to the recording again and check their answers to exercise 2.
- You could ask students to indicate (eg by holding up their hand or saying *stop*) when they think that they have heard an item in the recording. Then replay a small section of the recording and get the class to confirm if the item was really there and was correct.

> 1   b – day-time class
> 2   e – native speakers
> 3   d – registration form
> 4   a – social activities
> 5   c – ten-week courses

FUNCTIONAL LANGUAGE: asking for information

> Language reference, Student's Book page 25

1
- Students make questions by rearranging the words in each line. They then look at audioscript 1.23 on pages 134–135 to check their answers.
- Even though all the words are given, students may find this a tricky task. They are likely to make errors with words in the wrong place.

> 2   Could you tell me about your courses?
> 3   How many students are in a class?
> 4   Do you have classes for beginners?
> 5   What time are the classes?
> 6   How long does the course last?
> 7   Are there any social activities?
> 8   How much are the course fees?

Language notes: asking for information

- Some of the questions in this section are straightforward *Wh-* questions:
  What time are the classes?
  How many students are in a class?
  How long does the course last?
  How much are the course fees?
- One question is an inversion:
  Are there any social activities?
- One question uses the 'dummy' auxiliary *do*:
  Do you have classes for beginners?
- One question has a distinctive polite form:
  Could you tell me about your courses?
  (rather than just *Tell me about your courses.*)

SPEAKING

> Methodology Builder 8: Roleplay, page 27

1
- Pairwork. Tell students that they are going to be directors and managers of a new evening school. It could teach anything and be organized in any way they want.
- In pairs, students use the prompt questions to decide how they want their school to be.

Alternative procedure

- You could ask pairs to answer the *What is the school called?* question first. Get pairs to tell their names to the whole class before answering the other prompts. This may give students a chance to settle into the idea of planning a school of their own.

Methodology Builder 8
Roleplay

- *In practice activities, it's important to offer students the chance to speak honestly about themselves and their own lives. However, for most students there is a limit on what varieties of practice they are exposed to in class. They won't get the chance to try out important language in a whole range of situations, eg booking a plane ticket, having a meal at a restaurant, etc. Roleplays are a simple but important way of extending the range of useful practice.*
- *Cues for a roleplay often come in the form of a task description or role card – typically a description of a situation, a job title or a person's character. Some activities allow students to work out their own roles.*
- *When running a roleplay it's worth remembering:*
  1 *Students usually need preparation time: (1) to understand the task and role card; (2) to think of some ideas; (3) to think of appropriate language they can use (maybe finding specific vocabulary items).*
  2 *This preparation time is the time for the teacher to monitor and actively help. Avoid interrupting and interfering too much once students have actually started the roleplay.*
  3 *Remember that a roleplay is a chance to practise using language to communicate. Being fluent and getting one's message across is often more important than getting it 100% correct. Don't forget this when giving any feedback afterwards. Tell students about how well they conveyed (or didn't convey) the message rather than picking on a long list of little grammar points.*
  4 *Don't set up a roleplay and then immediately expect a pair to perform for the rest of the class to watch. Most roleplays work best if all pairs or groups do their speaking simultaneously, so that they don't feel anyone is watching and judging. If some are very good, are funny or interesting, you could ask them to repeat a version for the class to watch at the end. However, beware of forcing unwilling students to embarrass themselves.*
- *If your students really like roleplay, don't limit them to the roleplays in the book. It's very easy to turn many activities into roleplays, eg by simply saying that they should do a speaking activity as if they were in a certain place, or by asking them to adopt a character to do a task. Certainly with stronger students this can often add a significant extra spark to some otherwise routine work.*
  Some cards could have names of situations, eg railway station, bookshop, swimming pool, etc. Others could have jobs, eg policeman, pop singer, etc or personality/mood descriptions, eg you feel very happy, you are very tired, etc. When students start a new speaking task, hand each person a card and ask them to do the task as if they were at the place, or as if they were that person.

2
- Pairs join another pair and compare ideas.

Extension task
- Tell students that the local government will only allow one school to open. Pairs must each make a short presentation for the whole class, describing their school and explaining why theirs is going to be best for the town. Allow students some time after their initial discussions to prepare their presentation.

Web research task
❯ *Methodology Builder 1: Using Web research tasks, page 2*
- Find a good language school for yourself in the UK or Australia.
Web search key words
- *'language school' recognized UK*
- *'language school' recognized Australia*

DID YOU KNOW?

1
- Pairwork. In pairs, students read the facts and discuss the questions.

Alternative procedure
You could turn this into a short quiz instead of a reading activity.
- Write all the numbers from the text on the board (and maybe a few more).
- Books closed: the teacher reads aloud questions based on the facts (eg *How many people in the world speak English as a first language?*).
- Students work in pairs and agree on their answer. They then write it down.

IF YOU WANT SOMETHING EXTRA ...
❯ Straightforward Teacher's Resource Disc *at the back of this book*

Answer key

2 REVIEW

Student's Book page 149

1

1	worked
2	paid
3	went
4	was opening
5	rang
6	was waiting
7	asked
8	was putting
9	replied

2

Possible questions:
1 What could you study there?
2 When did the first students enter the university's business school?
3 When did the first Catholic students arrive?
4 Where did Jonathan Swift and Bram Stoker go to university?
5 When did the first women study at the university?
6 What did Mary Robinson study at Trinity College?

3

Students' own answers

4

1 I used to/didn't use to go to a school near home when I was young.
2 I used to/didn't use to sit at the front of the class.
3 I used to/didn't use to be the teacher's favourite pupil.
4 I used to/didn't use to do extra homework every day.
5 We used to/didn't use to have sport every Wednesday afternoon.
6 I used to/didn't use to enjoy sport.
7 I used to/didn't use to get very good grades in all my subjects.
8 I used to/didn't use to like English lessons.

5

1	Could
2	Are
3	Do
4	How
5	Could
6	How
7	Is
8	What

6

1	question 6
2	question 5
3	question 4
4	question 8
5	question 2
6	question 1
7	question 7
8	question 3

2 WRITING

Workbook page 67

Model answer

Suddenly, we saw a man in the water. He was waving at us and shouting 'Help!'. Mr Miller ran into the sea. I was frightened. It was a long way to swim and the water was very cold. I phoned the police on my mobile.

Mr Miller was holding the man in the water, but the waves were strong and dangerous. We were all watching them now. Suddenly, a police helicopter flew over. It dropped a rope to the two men. Mr Miller caught it and the police pulled the two men up into the helicopter.

After that, the other pupils returned to school. But I went to the hospital. The police asked me and Mr Miller some questions and I spoke to the man. I wrote the things he said in my biology notebook.

Afterwards, I went home and wrote a story about the man in the sea and Mr Miller. I made a lot of spelling mistakes, but I took the story to the local weekly newspaper. A few days later, Mr Miller showed me the newspaper. My story was on the front page: 'Biology Teacher Saves Man's Life', by Alison Hawthorne.

28

3A | Flatmates

WHAT THE LESSON IS ABOUT

Theme	Home life Sharing a flat
Speaking	Groupwork roleplay: solving problems in a shared flat
Listening	A dialogue between two friends about where they live
Vocabulary	Collocations with *house* & *home*
Grammar	Countable & uncountable nouns with *some*, *any* & *no*
Pronunciation	Spelling & sound: *h* and /h/

IF YOU WANT A LEAD-IN ...

Discussion starters: living at home and away

> *Methodology Builder 15: Using Discussion starters, page 63*

For students of school age:
- *When you get older where will you live? Will you want to leave home as soon as possible? Why?*
- *What is your dream home? Would you like to live alone or with friends?*

For adults:
- *How many different places have you lived in your life? Which was the best? Which was the worst?*
- *Is it better to live on your own or to share with other people?*

Introducing the theme: flat-sharing

- Write *flat-share* on the board. Ask students what it means. Confirm by telling a story, either about yourself or about an imaginary character:
  Yourself: If you have ever shared a flat with other people, tell the students why you did it, what was good about it and maybe add a comment or two about any problems or disagreements you had.
  Imaginary character: If you haven't shared, tell a short story about a fictional character *Dana* who came to the capital city, but couldn't afford a flat on her own, and took a room in a flat with three others. She enjoyed the experience but there were constant arguments about who should clean the kitchen! Elicit other potential good and bad things.
- You could also ask if students know of any famous TV shows where characters flat-share, eg *Friends*.

Test before you teach: countable and uncountable nouns

> *Methodology guidelines: Test before you teach, page xxi*
- Write up the following words on the board: *paper*; *rice*; *tea*; *CD*; *cat*; *water*; *juice*; *air*; *chair*; *book*; *lamb*; *food*; *money*; *person*; *map*; *leaf*; *picture*.
- Draw two boxes on the board. Ask students to divide these words into two different groups, one for each box. Tell them not to think about the meaning, but the grammar of the words. They are looking for a reason why these items could be grouped into two separate categories. When they have finished, listen to some of their groupings and reasons. Leave the boxes on the board and say that you will confirm the answers later in the lesson.

VOCABULARY: *house* & *home*

> *Language reference, Student's Book page 35*

1
- Students first think about the questions individually, and then discuss and compare in pairs.

2
- Students choose *house* or *home* to fill each gap.
  NB *House* and *home* are very close in meaning. In this exercise, the reason for choosing one word is because of collocation rather than meaning.
- Ask students how they say *house* and *home* in their own language. Is it two different words or a single word?

2	home	4	house	6	home
3	home	5	home	7	house

Language notes: house & home

- *House* means a building that you live in. *Home* means the place where you live. A house or a flat could both be your *home*.
- *Home* is a more personal and emotional word. We often have a strong personal idea of the place that we are comfortable and happy in.
  NB *A flat* (or *apartment*) is not a house. But a house could be divided into a number of flats!
- *Home* is usually used without an article, eg *come home, go home, get home, leave home*.

3
- Pairwork. Students ask and answer the questions from exercise 2.

PRONUNCIATION: /h/

1 & 2 🔘 1.24
- Students read all the words in the box and decide which do *not* start with /h/.
- Students could work in pairs. They read the words aloud to each other and agree on the pronunciation.
- Students listen to the recording and check.

Honest is pronounced /ˈɒnɪst/.
What is pronounced /wɒt/.
NB In some pronunciations *hotel* is pronounced without an /h/.

🔘 1.24

happy	hospital
holiday	home
honest	house
hotel	what
who	whole

3 & 4 🔘 1.25
- Ask students to work in pairs and practise saying the sentence to each other. Then ask students to try saying it in front of the whole class. This is a tricky tongue twister! Keep the atmosphere fun rather than too critical.
- Students listen to the recording and repeat the sentence.

Language note

- This line comes from a famous musical *My Fair Lady*. In the story, a working-class girl tries to learn how to speak like an upper-class person. She has a problem saying the /h/ sound. (It is sometimes considered lower class to 'drop your aitches', eg saying *'orrible* instead of *horrible*.)

🔘 **1.25**

> In Hertford, Hereford and Hampshire hurricanes hardly ever happen.

Extra practice: more /h/ tongue twisters

- His house is here but hers is on a hill.
- Who's her uncle? How's her aunt?
- Has Helga ever hugged a horse?
- Hairy Harry had a happy hamster.

Language notes: /h/

- Hertford, Hereford and Hampshire are all places in England. In UK pronunciation they are said: /ˈhɑːtfəd/, /ˈherəfəd/, /ˈhæmpʃə/ (or /ˈhæmpʃaɪə/). All have stress on the first syllable.
- A common mistake in this tongue twister is to add an /h/ sound on the front of *ever*. When students do this tell them that most native speakers have a problem with getting this right.

LISTENING

In this listening, Ali, who is having problems at home, tries to convince his friend Charlie to let him move into his flat. Charlie explains the problems there are living in his flat.

1 🔘 **1.26**

- Ask students to read the summary carefully before they listen.
- Play the recording. Students listen and circle the correct answers.

```
1   his family
2   his brothers
3   study
4   four other people
5   do some shopping
```

🔘 **1.26**

> **A = Ali   C = Charlie**
> **A:** Hey, Charlie, do you have any time this week when I can come and look at your flat?
> **C:** Yeah, what about this afternoon? There's nothing to eat in the flat, so I'm going to the shops on the way home to get some food.
> **A:** Pizzas again?
> **C:** No, I want to get some bread and cheese, actually. Anyway, why don't you come with me and look at the flat after that?
> **A:** Yeah, all right. Good idea.
> **C:** So, things are still difficult at home? Still the same problems?
> **A:** Things are worse. We've got twin cousins from London staying with us at the moment. They're sleeping in the room with me and my brothers. Fourteen-year-old twins!
> **C:** Tough, eh?
> **A:** Yeah, and I've got some exams in a week or two. I get no peace and I can't do any work. It's driving me mad.
> **C:** Can't the cousins sleep in another room?

> **A:** No, there's no space in the house. We only have two bedrooms. And my mum's always in the living room watching TV. I can't do my homework in there with the TV on.
> **C:** Well, you know my flat's not very big either, and there are five of us already. No peace there, I'm afraid. We don't go to bed early and, well, I don't want to put you off …
> **A:** No, it's not just that. I can't have any friends in the house. I get no independence. I mean, I love my parents, but I think it's time to move.
> **C:** And you really want to move in with us? I mean, it's only a sofa in the living room. Oh, by the way, the kitchen's a bit dirty. I think it's my turn to do the housework. Haven't you got any better ideas for a place to stay?
> **A:** No. Anyway, let's get that food.
> **C:** Yeah, OK. Oh, have you got any cash on you? Money is a bit of a problem at the moment.

2

- Students read the three phrases and choose the best definition for each. Then students listen again to check if their answer fits in with the recording.
- Ask students to raise their hands or call *stop* when they hear each phrase. Play the short section of the recording again, including the phrase a few times, and ask students to check if the context supports their answer. Ask: *Tell me something in the recording that proves your answer is correct.*

```
1 a   2 a   3 b
```

3

- Pairwork. Students discuss the three questions. During feedback, spend some time discussing the first question. Encourage students to come up with a range of answers.

Stronger classes

- Spend more time on each individual question:
  Question 1: Turn this into a roleplay. Appoint one stronger student to play Ali. Invite Ali to the front of the class and ask him to say what his problems are. Encourage students to give him advice about his situation.
  Question 2: Make two lists – *advantages* and *disadvantages*. Appoint a secretary for each list. Students call out ideas and the secretaries write them up in the appropriate list.
  Question 3: Discuss why – is it personal choice, cultural or financial?

GRAMMAR: countable & uncountable nouns with *some, any* & *no*

Grammar box

- ➲ *Language reference, Student's Book page 34*
- ➲ *Methodology Builder 22: Using Grammar boxes, page 106*

1

- Students divide the list into countable and uncountable nouns.
- If you used the lead-in *Test before you teach: countable and uncountable nouns*, you can now go back to the board and check the answers.

Countable: friends; parents; sofa; space; food
Uncountable nouns: cash; food; independence; money; peace; space

Language notes: countable & uncountable

- When we say something like *two milks* we are missing out a quantity (perhaps to order quickly in a shop or restaurant). *Could I have two milks* is a shortened colloquial form of *Could I have two (glasses/bottles/cartons of) milk*. In a similar way we can say *two breads, three cokes,* etc. The technical name for this missing out words is *ellipsis* (but your students don't need to know that!).

Word	Uncountable meaning	Countable meaning
	(*the general substance or material*)	(*the quantity or container of the substance*)
Milk	The liquid.	A bottle, carton or glass of milk.
Bread	Food made from flour.	A loaf or a slice of bread.
Chocolate	The sweet brown substance.	One single sweet made from chocolate.
Coke	The drink.	A can or bottle or glass of the drink.
Sugar	The sweet substance.	A lump or spoonful of the substance.

- Some nouns can be both countable and uncountable and have different meanings:

Word	Uncountable meaning	Countable meaning
Paper	The material you can write on.	A newspaper.
Wood	The material that comes from trees.	A number of trees growing in one place. A small forest.

In *Grammar* exercise 1:
- These nouns are only countable: *friends; parents; sofa*
- These nouns are typically only uncountable: *cash; independence; peace*
- *Space* is often used as both a countable and uncountable noun:

Word	Uncountable meaning	Countable meaning
Space	(1) The universe.	(3) A gap, an uncrowded place.
	(2) An uncrowded location with no contents.	(4) A period of time with no sound.

- *Foods* is countable and uncountable. In many cases, speakers have a choice of countable and uncountable, eg *She bought baby food; She bought baby foods.*

Word	Uncountable meaning	Countable meaning
Food	(General) Substance to eat.	Particular varieties and types of food, eg health foods, fatty foods.

- *Money* can sometimes be countable when it refers to different currencies, eg *different monies of the world.*

2
- Students choose the correct words to complete the dialogue.

1	problem	5	some	9	some
2	no	6	time	10	an
3	Are	7	any	11	work
4	homework	8	any		

3
> *Communication activities, Student's Book pages 127 & 129*

- Pairwork. Students look at their respective pages. Tell them not to look at each other's picture. Explain that Student A's picture shows Charlie's living room as it usually looks and Student B's picture shows the same room, but after a party. Students find differences between the pictures.
- Ask students to look at the three example questions.
- Remind students of possible language by doing an example with them first. Find a picture of a kitchen. Hold it up and tell students what it is, but don't show them. Tell them to ask you questions, like the example phrases in the Student's Book, to find out what is in the picture.

Charlie's bedroom after the party, from left to right:
1 The table is to one side.
2 There's a glass on the table.
3 There are CDs on the table.
4 There are cups and glasses on the floor.
5 There's a can on the floor.
6 There are some plates and food on the floor.
7 The rug is gone.
8 The sofa cushions are on the floor.
9 The big poster is torn.
10 The plant has fallen over.
11 The picture above the TV is not straight.

SPEAKING

1
> *Communication activities, Student's Book pages 126, 128, 129, 130 & 131*

- Groupwork. Put students into groups. Each student in the group reads a different role card and plans what they want to say to their flatmates.
- When ready, they should have a house meeting to discuss the problems and make a list of four rules that will make the flat happy again. Flatmate C needs to start the meeting.

Cultural notes: flat-shares

- In many UK towns, accommodation is very expensive to buy and even renting costs a lot. So, many students and young people choose to share a flat or house with others.
- Typically, each person has their own bedroom and shares the communal areas (living room, kitchen and bathroom). Bills such as electricity and gas would be split equally between them. However, bills are often a major cause of disagreement as well. Other flashpoints may be: late payment of rent; noise (especially at night); not cleaning up; smoking; eating other people's food.

Web research task
> *Methodology Builder 1: Using Web research tasks, page 2*

- Find a good flat-share in the town you chose to study in in lesson 2D – at a reasonable price. Make notes about the good and bad features of the flat-share you choose.

Web search key words
- *Flat-share* town name

IF YOU WANT SOMETHING EXTRA ...
> Straightforward Teacher's Resource Disc *at the back of this book*

3B | Migrants

WHAT THE LESSON IS ABOUT

Theme	Immigration to and emigration from Scotland
	Living abroad
Speaking	Pairwork discussion: discussing emigration
Reading	*Scotland: the people.* Magazine article: a history of immigration to Scotland
Grammar	*Some*, *many* & *most*
Did you know?	The United Kingdom

IF YOU WANT A LEAD-IN …

Discussion starters: home & away

⊙ *Methodology Builder 15: Using Discussion starters, page 63*

- *Do you like living in your country? List some things that are good about living here/there.*
- *Would you consider going abroad to live and work? For one year? For the rest of your life? Why?*

READING

This encyclopedia entry is about how different waves of immigrants have populated Scotland over the centuries.

1
- Give students a time limit of two minutes to write everything they know about Scotland. (One-word notes not sentences.)
- Pairwork. Students compare their ideas and add anything new to their own lists.
- Compile a full list with the class on the board.

Alternative procedure
- If students have limited world knowledge, don't do the individual/pair task but go straight to the whole-class stage. Elicit ideas but also add some of your own. Clarify the meaning of key items.

Cultural notes: Scotland

Here are some well-known things associated with Scotland and its culture:
- Edinburgh (castle; famous arts festival)
- Glasgow (Scotland's lively second city)
- The Highlands (beautiful countryside with hills)
- Loch (Scottish name for lake)
- Loch Ness Monster (a mythical monster)
- Clans (Scottish families or tribes)
- Many surnames begin with Mc or Mac (eg McDonald)
- Macbeth (fictional prince in Shakespeare play)
- Robert Burns (the most famous Scottish poet)
- William Wallace (Braveheart – famous Scottish leader who challenged the British King Edward I and was executed in 1305)
- Sean Connery (first actor to play James Bond)
- Bagpipes (a musical instrument)
- Kilts (skirts for men)
- Tartan (the criss-cross lined pattern found on kilts)

- Haggis (food made from chopped lungs, liver, heart and oats cooked in a sheep's stomach)
- Porridge (breakfast food made from oats)
- Whisky (Scotland's most famous export – an alcoholic drink. The most important ingredient is Scotland's spring water.)

Scot, Scots, Scottish and Scotch

Four very similar words that are often confused!
- *A Scot* is a person from Scotland (plural *Scots*).
- *Scots* is the language of Scotland, a dialect of English.
- *Scottish* is the most common adjective to describe things from Scotland – like Scottish dancing.
- And … *Scotch* … is whisky and beef.

2
- Ask students to work individually to match the words to the definitions. Let them check their answers in pairs.
- A nice way of checking the difference between *emigration/emigrants* and *immigration/immigrants* is to draw the following on the board:

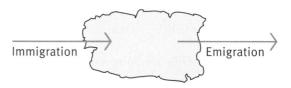

1	colonies	4	invaders
2	tribes	5	settlers
3	immigrants	6	emigrants

3
- Students read the article and decide on the right sentence for each gap.

| 1 e | 2 a | 3 b | 4 d | 5 c |

Weaker classes
- Here are two ways of helping weaker classes complete this exercise successfully:
  1 Ask students to tell you which words are 'key' words in the sentence preceding the first gap in the text. Then ask them to look for similar key words in the list of missing sentences. Ask if this helps them do the exercise. Then tell them to follow this procedure for each gap.
  2 Alternatively, you could tell students which key words to underline in the text in order to give them a lot of support.

Extension task: reading
- Write the following words on the board from the text: *Picts, Celtic, Anglo-Saxon, Pakistan, New Zealand.*
- Ask students, with books closed, to tell their partner what they remember about these words with reference to the text.

SPEAKING

1
- Pairwork. Students discuss the four questions.

Extension task: writing
- You have just arrived in a foreign country where you are going to work for two years. Write a postcard back saying what your first impressions are of the new country and what you already miss about your home country.

Cultural notes: emigration & immigration
- Throughout history people have travelled from one country hoping to make a new life in another. A large part of the population of the US can trace their origins back to immigrants who arrived from Ireland, Eastern Europe, etc.

Web research task

❯ *Methodology Builder 1: Using Web research tasks, page 2*

- Write the name *Ellis Island* on the board and tell students that it is important in the history of immigration to America. Ask for some ideas about why it might be important, then without confirming anything, set the following web research questions:
- Find out some information about Ellis Island.
  1 Where exactly is it?
  2 Why is it important in the history of immigration to the US?
  3 What happened to people who arrived there?
  4 What countries did the people come from?
  5 Can you visit it nowadays?

Web search key words
- 'Ellis Island'

GRAMMAR: *some, many & most*

Grammar box

❯ *Language reference, Student's Book page 34*
❯ *Methodology Builder 22: Using Grammar boxes, page 106*

1
- Students read the sentences and then add the word *of* to some (but not all) of them.

> 1 Many <u>of</u> the passengers …
> 2 Most <u>of</u> the Scots …
> 3 ✓
> 4 ✓
> 5 ✓
> 6 Some <u>of</u> the first immigrants …
> 7 Not many <u>of</u> the new immigrants …
> 8 ✓

Language notes: some, many & most
- If students have a problem with the questions in exercise 1, draw these diagrams on the board and ask students to consider which seems more appropriate for each sentence.

 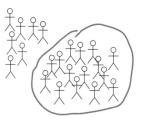

All the passengers   *Many of the passengers*

- If sentences seem to fit *diagram 2*, discuss who is in the big group of *diagram 1* and the two groups of *diagram 2*, eg in question 1, All the passengers *is the big group of* diagram 1 and *Many of the passengers* is the bigger of the two groups in *diagram 2*.
- *Of* is not necessary when we are describing a quantity of something and make no reference to any bigger group of the same thing.
- We use *of* when we want to show a relationship between a smaller part and a bigger quantity.

 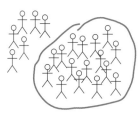

Many students   *Many of the students*
                          (ie not *all* the students)

- You could draw this table under the diagrams and fill the answers in it.

	Diagram 1	Diagram 2
1		Many of the passengers
2		Most of the Scots in America
3	Most Afro-Americans	
4	Some US cities	
5	There aren't many places	
6		Some of the first immigrants
7		Not many of the new immigrants
8	Many Koreans and Japanese	

2
- Show students how to use the substitution table to write new true sentences.
  NB Many sentences are grammatically possible but may make no sense or be untrue.
  You could set a target of five sentences for each student to make.

■ Methodology Builder 9 ■■ Using substitution tables

- *Grammar exercise 2 contains a substitution table. Substitution tables (ST) are arrangements of grammatical items containing a number of example sentences, so that learners can create complete correct sentences by substituting one word/phrase with another. They give a helpful visual insight into the way that the grammatical item is structured.*
- *For some students, information presented in this way may be easier to understand and use than similar data given as explanations or using grammatical terminology.*
- *Here are some ideas for using them:*
  As an aid to introducing a new grammar item
  While you are introducing new items, start to build a partial ST on one part of the board. Add to it as students meet new example sentences and variations.
  As a written record of new grammar
  Write an ST on the board and ask students to copy it.
  As a cue for drilling
  Write an ST on the board and ask students to find and say true sentences from it.
  As a puzzle for students
  Write a partial ST on the board and ask them to copy it and then work out missing words. Or add their own ideas.
  As a cue for writing
  Give students a copy of an ST and ask them to write a paragraph (or story) using at least five (or ten) sentences from the table.

3
- Pairwork. Students compare their sentences.

DID YOU KNOW?

1
- Pairwork. Students quickly do the quiz about the United Kingdom.

1	Edinburgh
2	London
3	Cardiff
4	Belfast

Extension task
- If students want more questions, you could extend the quiz with the following:
  1 *Which countries on the map have their own international football team?* (Answer: *England; Scotland; Wales; Northern Ireland; Ireland*)
  2 *Which country is Manchester in?* (Answer: *England*)
  3 *Can you drive in a car directly from Scotland to England – or do you need to go on a boat?* (Answer: *Yes, you can drive – no problem!*)
  4 *In which country can you look for the Loch Ness Monster?* (Answer: *Scotland*)
  5 *What is 'Ben Nevis' – a mountain, a lake, a famous hotel or a nuclear power station?* (Answer: *It's the highest mountain in Britain. It's in Scotland.*)
  6 *Which country is also known as 'Eire'?* (Answer: *Ireland*)
  7 *Which symbol goes with which country?*
  Shamrock (a small green plant with three leaves) (Answer: *Ireland*)
  Rose (Answer: *England*)
  Dragon (Answer: *Wales*)
  Thistle (a small wild plant with purple leaves and sharp points) (Answer: *Scotland*)

IF YOU WANT SOMETHING EXTRA ...
- ❯ Straightforward Teacher's Resource Disc *at the back of this book*

3c | Home town

WHAT THE LESSON IS ABOUT

Theme	Describing towns
	Living in Montreal
Speaking	Pairwork: describing & comparing towns
Reading	*www.livinginmontreal.com*. Web page: information about town districts
Vocabulary	Describing towns
Grammar	Quantifiers

IF YOU WANT A LEAD-IN …

Introducing the theme: describing locations

- Photocopy a section of a map of your town, showing the centre or the location where your school is. Make enough copies to give one map between three students.
- Put students into groups of three and ask them to think of three things they know of in town that are not marked on the maps (eg a favourite café, a letter box, a swimming pool, etc).
- Put students into new groups. Each student explains the items they thought of. The other students add any new items to their own maps.

Test before you teach: describing a town

❯ *Methodology guidelines: Test before you teach, page xxi*

- Ask students to work in pairs and describe to each other at least 20 things they see in town on their journey from home to school. Tell them not to worry if they don't know the correct words – they can describe the things instead.

■■ **Methodology Builder 10**
■ **Building scenes using cuisenaire rods, toy bricks, real objects, etc**

- *A good alternative to using the board (especially if your class isn't too large) is to create little scenes using cuisenaire rods (small coloured wooden or plastic rods, often used in primary maths teaching), toy building bricks or everyday objects. These can be very powerful teaching aids. You could use them in this lesson to build a town scene and help teach some vocabulary. If you don't have rods or bricks, you'll need to collect some small objects before class. A number of old matchboxes, pens, pencil sharpeners, etc, would be fine.*
- *In class, arrange a table so that all students can see clearly. (They may need to move or stand.)*
- *Start by laying some long objects (eg two pencils) on the table and saying 'This is the Main Street'. Now ask students for some things that they might see on the street. When students suggest things (eg a shoe shop or a letterbox) add an item to the scene. You could ask students which item would be the best one to use.*
- *Don't rush, but make sure that everyone knows what each object represents. Continue to elicit more places and slowly extend the scene until a whole town centre is built.*

- *Occasionally, suggest a new item yourself, perhaps using a word that is new for students. Also go back sometimes and check if students remember what all the objects are.*
- *When you have elicited enough of your town, ask students to copy a picture of the town into their notebooks. When they have drawn the picture, ask students to label each thing in their picture.*

VOCABULARY: towns

❯ *Language reference, Student's Book page 35*

1
- Students first group the words under the four headings, then add to the lists with more words.

---

public transport: bus; Metro; traffic; tram
types of accommodation: flat; house; studio
nightlife, culture: art gallery; bar; cinema; library; nightclub; restaurant; theatre
other: crime; park; pollution; traffic

Stronger classes

- Set a target of finding at least eight additional words.

2
- Students look at the lists and decide on the most important items.
- Discuss with the whole class.

READING

This web page is a mini-guide about living in Montreal written by people who live there. It includes three descriptions on different areas of the city and what each area has to offer.

1
- Ask what students know about Canada. Collect notes on the board. Check the *Cultural notes* on Canada for some possible ideas.
- Tell students they are going to emigrate to Canada. They have chosen Montreal as their home town, but haven't yet decided which district they would like to live in. Focus students on the text and tell them that it describes three separate areas of the town – Verdun, Outremont and Old Montreal. Students read the descriptions of the three areas and decide where they would like to live.
- They then compare with a partner.

2
- Students read the web page again to find which area is referred to in each of the eight sentences.

---

2 V   3 O   4 O   5 OM   6 V   7 OM   8 OM

Cultural notes: Canada

Here are some things that Canada is famous for:
- French and English languages are both used
- The Rockies (mountains)
- Mounties (These are the policemen who ride horses and wear bright red uniforms. *Mountie* is short for *Mounted*, ie on horseback.)
- The world's largest shopping mall (in Edmonton)
- Montreal Jazz Festival
- Niagara Falls (waterfalls on the Canada-US border)
- Calgary Stampede (famous wild west horse-riding event)
- Canada gets a lot of snow. Canadians sometimes drive in their snowmobiles more than their cars!
- The following people are all famous Canadians: Jim Carrey; Celine Dion; Avril Lavigne; Pamela Anderson; Shania Twain; Keanu Reeves; Alanis Morissette; Nelly Furtado; Bryan Adams; Neil Young and Justin Bieber.

Web research task

❯ *Methodology Builder 1: Using Web research tasks, page 2*

- Find ten more interesting facts about Canada.

Web search key words
- *Canada information*

GRAMMAR: quantifiers

Grammar box

❯ *Language reference, Student's Book page 34*
❯ *Methodology Builder 22: Using Grammar boxes, page 106*

1
- Ask students to study the table of information about quantifiers. They complete the gaps in the table with examples from the reading text.

> *quantifiers with plural countable nouns:*
> a lot of good bars and restaurants
> many advantages
> not many Japanese restaurants
> a few good restaurants
> not enough cheap flats
> *quantifiers with uncountable nouns:*
> too much traffic
> a lot of crime
> not much time / not too much crime
> a little crime
> not enough nightlife

2
- Students complete the expressions by choosing the correct options.

1	a lot of	4	not much	7	too many
2	not many	5	a lot of	8	many
3	a few	6	not much		

3
- Students write six sentences about their town using six different quantifiers.
- Put students into small groups to compare their sentences.

Language notes: quantifiers

Quantifiers are words (or phrases) that say how much or how many of something there is (or isn't), ie the quantity. Students have already met a few quantifiers in the coursebook (*some, any,* etc). Quantifiers come before nouns or noun phrases. We have different choices of quantifier depending on:
(1) whether a noun is countable (C) or uncountable (U).
(2) whether the sentence is positive, negative or a question.
(3) how formal the style is (this is not dealt with in this lesson).

The following is a summary guideline for the examples in the Student's Book table:
- *Many* is generally used with (C) in sentences with a negative meaning. *Much* is the (U) equivalent. If there is a positive meaning, we do not usually use *many* or *much*. We use *a lot of* with both (C) and (U). NB *A lot of* can also be used with a negative meaning.
- *Lots of* is an informal alternative to *a lot of*, eg *She has a lot of money; She has lots of money*.
- *Too many* (C) means 'more than is good'. *Too much* is the (U) equivalent.
- *Not many* (C) and *not much* (U) suggest a small quantity.
- *A few* goes with (C). *A little* goes with (U). Although they both refer to a very small quantity, these both have a positive feeling. NB Without the indefinite article the quantifiers have a negative connotation!
- *Not enough* means 'there is less than is needed'. It goes with (C) and (U).

SPEAKING

❯ *Communication activities, Student's Book page 127*

1
- Ask students to turn to page 127 and make brief notes in column A about a town they know (not their home town if other students come from the same town). Point out that they should add comments about *how much* or *how many* restaurants, parks, cinemas, etc, there are, using words such as *not many, a lot,* etc.

2
- Pairwork. Students ask and answer questions to find out about their partner's town. They should note answers in column B.

3
- Students review and discuss their previous dialogue.

IF YOU WANT SOMETHING EXTRA …

❯ Straightforward Teacher's Resource Disc *at the back of this book*

3D | Lost!

What the lesson is about

Theme	Finding your way around Newcastle (UK)
Speaking	Groupwork discussion: comparing Newcastle to towns in your country Pairwork roleplay: directions
Listening	Asking for directions in Newcastle
Functional language	Directions
Vocabulary	Places in a town
Pronunciation	Weak form of *to* (/tə/)

If you want a lead-in ...

Discussion starters: asking for directions

❯ *Methodology Builder 15: Using Discussion starters, page 63*

- *Do you feel embarrassed when you have to ask for directions? When people give you directions (in your own language), do you find them easy to follow?*
- *How would you ask for directions in your own language?*
- *Have you ever got lost somewhere? How did you find your way back? Did you use a map? Did that help you? Did you ask directions?*
- *Are women better at map reading than men?*

Test before you teach: asking for & giving directions

❯ *Methodology guidelines: Test before you teach, page xxi*
- Name a place that everyone knows a few streets away from your school.
- Put students into pairs. One student is a lost visitor and the other is a local. Using their own language (not English), students roleplay asking for directions from the place to the school. When they have completed it successfully, set the same task – but using English. Tell students not to worry if they don't know correct language. Encourage them to do their best in getting the meaning across.

Speaking

1
- Students look at the information box about Newcastle. Ask a few quick questions:
  1 *Do more than half a million people live in the city?* (Answer: *no, 200,000*)
  2 *Is it a good place to go clubbing?* (Answer: *yes – good nightlife*)
  3 *What is the name of the river that Newcastle stands on?* (Answer: *the Tyne*)
  4 *When did the city begin?* (Answer: *Roman times*)
  5 *Does the city have a seaside?* (Answer: *No. The sea is 13 km away.*)
  6 *What sport can you watch in the city?* (Answer: *football*)
  7 *Is the town in the south of England?* (Answer: *No. It's in the north-east.*)
  8 *What kind of art can you see there?* (Answer: *contemporary art*)

2
- Groupwork. Students think of towns or cities in their own country and discuss similarities.

Weaker classes
- Write up this list of check questions on the board and ask students to look at the questions, and to think of a town that has the most *yes* answers to them.
  Is the town ...
    in the north or east of your country?
    on a river?
    near the sea?
    industrial?
    lively?
    near beautiful countryside?
  Does the town have ...
    a similar size population?
    a long history?
    a good nightlife?
    a museum?
    a football team?
- An alternative task would be to compare your own town to Newcastle. Go through the facts one by one and see which are similar.

Extension task: writing activity
- Ask groups to write a paragraph about the town they found that was most similar. Point out the *Bilbao* example to show students how to begin.

Cultural notes: Newcastle
- Newcastle is a city in the north-east of England that was important for industry in the 19th century. It has a famous football team that wear a distinctive black-and-white shirt, and an equally famous brown beer called *Newcastle Brown*. A much-liked modern statue called *The Angel of the North* is at Gateshead across the River Tyne.

Web research task
❯ *Methodology Builder 1: Using Web research tasks, page 2*
- Write these five quiz questions on the board. See how quickly students can find the answers.
  1 Who designed *The Angel of the North?* (Answer: *Anthony Gormley*)
  2 Is there a castle in Newcastle? (Answer: *yes*)
  3 What is the name of the famous bridge over the Tyne? (Answer: *Tyne Bridge!*)
  4 The bridge was opened in 1878 – True or False? (Answer: *false – 1928*)
- Ask students to find a new Newcastle question for the class.

Vocabulary: places in a town

1
- Students look at the map. Ask if they can recognize any of the unlabelled places. They use the words in the box to label the map.

2	art gallery	8	opera house
3	bars and restaurants	9	bus station
4	bridge	10	church
5	castle	11	stadium
6	train station	12	shopping centre
7	cathedral		

2

• Students read the six statements and decide if they are true or false. They then correct the false sentences.

1	T
2	T
3	F (The cathedral is opposite the train station.)
4	F (The opera house isn't next to the castle.)
5	T
6	T

3

• Ask students what locations from exercise 2 they have in their town and where they are.

Extra task

You might want to focus on some aspects of pronunciation of words from the vocabulary exercise:

• Stress focus: Write these words up: *castle; restaurant; gallery; station; shopping; centre; stadium; opera; cathedral.*

• Then write up the following two stress patterns on the board:

☐▫ ☐▫▫

Ask students to decide which of the words, if any, fit the two patterns.

Answer:

☐▫ – *castle; restaurant*; station; shopping; centre; opera*.*

☐▫▫ – *restaurant*; gallery; opera*; stadium.*

* can be pronounced with two or three syllables

• Sounds focus: Ask questions.

1 What is the first sound in *centre*? (/s/)

2 What is the last sound in *bars*? (/z/ – students may think it is /s/)

3 How is 't' pronounced in *castle*? (It's not! It's silent.)

LISTENING & FUNCTIONAL LANGUAGE: directions

In the listening, two female football fans ask local people for directions back to the train station after watching a football match. They can't follow the directions so, eventually, they decide to go for a drink or a pizza instead.

1

• Ask students to look at the map. Ask: *Where is the football stadium? Where is the train station? How do you get from the stadium to the station?*

• Then ask students to look at the photo. Ask: *What can you see? Where are the people?*

• Ask students to look at question 1. Ask them to listen to the recording and to check their answer to question 1.

1	They walk past the church, roundabout, shopping centre, castle and bridge.
2	no

🔊 **1.27–1.29**

K = Kate   **A** = Ali   **M** = Man   **M2** = Man 2

1

K: Come on, Ali. Let's get out of here and find the station.

A: I've no idea of the way. Hang on, I'll ask this guy. 'Scuse me, could you tell us the way to the station, please?

M: Aye. The station you want? Well, turn right when you come out of the stadium, OK? Go straight on. And then, take the first street on the right. Take the first street on the right, OK?

K / A: OK, got that.

M: It's called Strawberry Place, all right. Cross the road, cross onto the other side, and walk a bit, it's not far. Go past the Metro station, on your left. And go to the end of the road. Turn left and you come to a roundabout, all right? And on the other side, you'll see the bus station. It's not hard to find, but you'd better ask for more directions from there.

A: So we go past the Metro, then turn left and look for the bus station? OK, thanks.

M: Aye, that's right. Ta-ra.

2

K: I wonder where the Metro is. He said it was near.

A: Yeah. And he didn't say anything about that church in front of us. And, look, there's a roundabout, but I can't see a bus station.

K: We're lost, aren't we? Come on, let's ask someone. Excuse me, how do I get to the train station, please?

M2: The train station. Just go down this street, keep going, keep going, and it's sort of down there. Not far, you know. You'll see the cathedral, and then the train station is very near after that.

A: Oh, right. Thanks a lot.

3

A: I think we're really lost this time. That man never said anything about a shopping centre.

K: And the shopping centre was ages ago.

A: And he didn't mention that castle we walked past either.

K: No, he talked about a cathedral.

A: Ah well, it's nice here, anyway, isn't it? You see the bridge over there?

K: Yeah, that's the famous bridge, isn't it?

A: Why don't we go into one of these bars? Or we could have a pizza in that restaurant.

K: Good idea. We can always look for the station later.

2

• Ask students to remember or guess what the missing verbs are first. Then play the first part of the recording again and ask students to write in the missing words.

1	Turn
2	Go
3	Take
4	Cross
5	Go
6	Go

Weaker classes

• You could play and pause the recording to give students more time to write. Or you could write the missing verbs (in a mixed-up order) on the board first so that the students listen, then copy the words.

1.27

> **K = Kate   A = Ali   M = Man**
> **K:** Come on, Ali. Let's get out of here and find the station.
> **A:** I've no idea of the way. Hang on, I'll ask this guy. 'Scuse me, could you tell us the way to the station, please?
> **M:** Aye. The station you want? Well, turn right when you come out of the stadium, OK. Go straight on. And then, take the first street on the right. Take the first street on the right, OK?
> **K / A:** OK, got that.
> **M:** It's called Strawberry Place, all right. Cross the road, cross onto the other side, and walk a bit, it's not far. Go past the Metro station, on your left. And go to the end of the road. Turn left and you come to a roundabout, all right? And on the other side, you'll see the bus station. It's not hard to find, but you'd better ask for more directions from there.
> **A:** So we go past the Metro, then turn left and look for the bus station? OK, thanks.
> **M:** Aye, that's right. Ta-ra.

1.26

3
- Students match the phrases in exercise 2 to the correct pictures A–F.

1	B
2	E
3	C
4	D
5	A
6	F

4
- Pairwork. Student A asks Student B for directions using the map of Newcastle. Point out the useful phrases they can use in the blue box. Students can switch roles after doing it the first time.

Language notes: directions
Students may get confused between the verbs *go* and *take*.
- *Go* means 'move in a certain direction'.
- *Take* shows a choice you must make (eg when there are three possible streets to choose between) and usually shows a change of direction or way of moving, for example, when you turn into a new street.

Go	along	
	past	
	straight along	
	straight on	…
	through	
	down	
	to	

Take	the first	street
	the second	turning
	the third	road
	the next	door
	the last	
	the no 73	bus

PRONUNCIATION: *to*

1 1.30
- Ask a student to read the first phrase aloud. Ask how the third word was pronounced, but don't give immediate feedback.
- Play the first sentence in the recording for students to compare. Check if students noticed the weak form pronunciation. You'll probably need to play the sentence again a few times.
- Repeat the procedure again for the other two phrases.

Stronger classes
- You may want to watch out for two other pronunciation points, apart from the weak forms:
  1 *interesting* has three syllables, not four.
  2 *directions* has three syllables, not four.

1.30

> interesting place to visit
> difficult to give directions
> next to the castle

2 & 3 1.31
- Students look through the audioscript and find four more examples of the weak form *to*.
- Students listen to the recording and check.

1.31

> 1 Could you tell us the way <u>to</u> the station, please?
> 2 And go <u>to</u> the end of the road.
> 3 Turn left and you come <u>to</u> a roundabout, all right?
> 4 It's not hard <u>to</u> find.

4
- Students can work in pairs to practise saying the phrases.

Language notes: to
- When small words such as *to, for, of*, etc are pronounced in sentences they typically have a *weak* pronunciation, ie
  (1) they are not stressed.
  (2) the vowel sound changes to a more relaxed, reduced, easier-to-say form.
  (3) the whole word may sound to students as if it has been *swallowed* or *lost*.
- When it is a *weak form*, *to* has the pronunciation /tə/ or just /t/.
- Students who do not know about this feature of English may find it hard to hear the words at all when listening to fluent speech.
- Some languages have relatively even stress on every word and do not lose words in this way. Students may need more practice on this – and even some convincing that it really happens!

> ■ **Methodology Builder 11**
> ■ **Weak forms**
>
> - *Teachers are often puzzled about how to best help students with pronunciation features such as weak forms. One paradoxical problem with weak forms is that as soon as you focus on them in speaking practice, they tend to become stronger rather than weaker! For this reason, it makes more sense to focus in class on the surrounding* stressed *words rather than the weak forms themselves.*
> - *Here is a sequence of ideas to help you practise single sentences, such as in Pronunciation exercise 4.*
>   1 *Ask students to read the sentence you want to practise and mark a dot above every syllable.*
>
>   o o o o o o o o o
>   *It's difficult to give directions.*
>
>   2 *Students now look again at the sentence and try saying it a few times in order to decide where the stressed syllables are. They mark these by turning the dot into a shaded box.*
>
>   o ☐o o o ☐ o☐ o
>   *It's difficult to give directions.*
>
> - *NB There may be different answers. Stress is not fixed. Depending on the context where language is used, and the meaning that speakers want to express, the stress may change!*
> - *Remind students that stress goes with syllables not words.*
> - *Ask students to practise reading the text saying only the stressed syllables, eg ' … diff … give … rec …'. Encourage students to say this a few times, getting faster, and getting a sense of rhythm to the syllables. They will think that this sounds odd, so allow them to enjoy the funniness – but there is a real point to this exercise.*
> - *Now ask students to try to keep to that speed and rhythm, but to put back the missing syllables without slowing down. Of course, to do this they will need to say the other syllables fast and in a weaker pronunciation. Which is exactly what you want them to do.*
> - *Repeat the practice again with the other sentences.*

IF YOU WANT SOMETHING EXTRA …

◗ Straightforward Teacher's Resource Disc *at the back of this book*

Answer key

3 REVIEW

❯ *Student's Book page 150*

1

1 … in the ~~worlds~~ <u>world</u> to live … (line 4)
2 … one hundred ~~city~~ <u>cities</u> around the world. (line 11)
3 … high grades for ~~educations~~ <u>education</u> … (line 13)
4 … ~~entertainments~~ <u>entertainment</u> and culture, … (line 13)
5 … housing, ~~healths~~ <u>health</u> and weather. (line 14)
6 … more and more ~~visitor~~ <u>visitors</u> … (line 16)
7 … there was more ~~crimes~~ <u>crime</u> … (line 19)
8 … the ~~weathers~~ <u>weather</u> and the prices in the shops. (line 23)

2

1 any
2 any
3 No
4 no
5 some
6 some
7 no
8 any
9 any
10 some
11 some

3

1 Did you know that there are many ~~of~~ places in the world called London?
5 There are also some ~~of~~ places called London in Africa.
6 Most ~~of~~ people in London, England, have never heard of these other places.

4

1 a lot of
2 too much
3 not enough
4 a few
5 too much
6 a little
7 many
8 not much

5

1 out
2 take
3 on
4 bridge
5 Go
6 to
7 of
8 to

6

Students' own answers

3 WRITING

❯ *Workbook page 69*

Model answer

Rabat is the capital city of Morocco, and is situated on the Atlantic coast, in the north-west of the country. Together with its 'sister city', Sale, on the other side of the Bou Regreg river, Rabat has a population of about two million.

The most famous site in Rabat is probably the 12th century Hassan Mosque with its enormous, beautiful old minaret. Another popular place to visit is Chellah, the ruins of the old Roman city of Sala Colonia. There are also lovely trees, flowers and thousands of birds.

Rabat's traditional walled market, called the Medina, is a busy, colourful place where you can see all sorts of people and all kinds of products. At the top of the Medina is the fantastic stone gate of the Kasbah des Oudaïas. The view over the Atlantic from the Kasbah walls is unforgettable.

There are many good restaurants in Rabat. Le Dinarjat is a lovely place for a traditional Moroccan meal in the heart of the Medina. During Ramadan, the market stays open all night and there are food stalls and happy crowds in the streets.

Early spring is probably the best time to go to Rabat because the weather is mild and the flowers are at their best. Winter can be cold.

4A | Relationships

WHAT THE LESSON IS ABOUT

Theme	Doing a quiz to find out your relationship 'style'
Speaking	Pairwork: discussing what love is
	Discussing the results of a quiz
Reading	A quiz about relationship styles
Grammar	Present simple
	Frequency adverbs & phrases
Pronunciation	Final -s

IF YOU WANT A LEAD-IN ...

Introducing the theme: relationships

- Ask students to draw a circle in the middle of a piece of paper, and to write their name in it. Then ask them to think of four people they have a close relationship with, and to draw a line from the circle to each person's name. Tell them that the shorter the line, the closer the relationship. Tell them to include husbands or wives, boyfriends or girlfriends, best friends or family members.
- In pairs, students show each other their 'relationship' diagrams and tell each other about the relationship they have with each person.

Test before you teach: present simple

❯ *Methodology guidelines: Test before you teach, page xxi*
- Bring in a photo of a famous person (eg the US President). Explain that as well as going to special events, there are some things the President does every day. Ask students to work in pairs and list the five most interesting things he does every day. Students feed back to other pairs.

SPEAKING & READING

The reading text is a quiz in which students must choose *True* or *False* in response to various statements about their personality. They then find out what 'colour' they are, and, consequently, what sort of relationships they tend to form.

1
- Ask students to discuss the quotes in pairs. Then have a whole-class feedback and find out the views of the class. Elicit any interesting definitions of love from the students.

Weaker classes
- Help students 'define' love by writing *Love is ...* on the board and asking students to finish the sentence in three or four different ways.

Language & cultural notes
- Plato was a Greek philosopher. Tolstoy was a 19th-century Russian novelist, who wrote *War and Peace* and *Anna Karenina*. John Lennon was one of the Beatles, and wrote many famous songs, including *Imagine* and *All You Need Is Love* (the song that the quote comes from).
- The French proverb *Love makes time pass, time makes love pass* means that when you fall in love, you don't notice how quickly time goes by, and that (rather cynically) over time you fall out of love.

- Zsa Zsa Gabor was a Hollywood movie star of Hungarian origin, who was a major star of the 1950s. She was as famous for her romantic affairs with actors such as Frank Sinatra as she was for her acting.
- *Men love with their eyes; women love with their ears* means that men are only interested in physical appearance, whereas women are interested in hearing compliments.

Web research task
❯ *Methodology Builder 1: Using Web research tasks, page 2*
- Students research and find other famous or interesting quotes about love on the internet.
Web search key words
- *love quote*

2
- Ask students to read the statements and to choose *True* or *False*. Students can compare answers in pairs.
- Students then look at their *True* responses only to calculate their score and find out what colour they mostly are. They look at the scoring interpretation at the bottom of the quiz and read about their colour.
- Have a brief class feedback and find out which relationship style is most common in the class.

3
- Ask students to discuss their results in groups of four. You could ask one person from each group to summarize what their group said for the class in feedback.

Extension task
This is an opportunity to introduce or revise some vocabulary for describing people.
- Write the following adjectives on the board: *shy, secretive, emotional, nervous, self-conscious, independent, sociable*.
- Ask students in pairs to look at the sentences in the text and say which ones match the adjectives on the board.

GRAMMAR: present simple

Grammar box
❯ *Language reference, Student's Book page 44*
❯ *Methodology Builder 22: Using Grammar boxes, page 106*

1
- Ask students to rearrange the mixed-up sentences to make questions.

1 What do you do with your friends?
2 Do you like being with other people? (Or: Do other people like being with you?)
3 Do you have friends in other cities?
4 How much time do you spend away from home?
5 What do you do in the daytime?
6 How many texts do you send every day?
7 What do you like doing on your own?
8 What kind of relationship do you have with your parents?

Extra practice: drill practising the -s ending

⊙ *Methodology Builder 12: Substitution drills, page 46*

Example: *I walk to school every day.*
Cue: He   *Answer: He walks to school every day.*

Cue	Answer
She	She walks to school every day.
They	They walk to school every day.
Mary	Mary walks to school every day.
The students	The students walk to school every day.
The dog	The dog walks to school every day.
Peter and John	Peter and John walk to school every day.
The teachers	The teachers walk to school every day.

2
• Pairwork. Students ask each other the questions from exercise 1.

3
• Direct students to look at question 1. Ask students if there are any words from the box above that could be added to the sentence. Quite a number are possible, eg *I always/ often/never get up late in the morning*, etc.
• Students complete all six sentences so that they are true for them.

4
• Do question 1 as an example. Students then make questions for the other sentences in exercise 3.
• Pairwork. Students ask and answer the questions.

> 1   How often do you get up late in the morning?
> 2   How often do you go for a walk in the afternoon?
> 3   How often are you tired in the evening?
> 4   How often do you have dinner in a restaurant?
> 5   How often do you read before you go to bed?
> 6   How often do you visit friends at the weekend?

Extra practice: present simple

• Tell students that you will roleplay a person (or thing). They must try to guess who or what you are – or your job.
  1 I make things. I get up very early every day. They are all ready before six o'clock in the morning. I usually come home at seven o'clock and eat some of the things I made. They smell fresh and delicious. (Answer: *a baker*)
  2 I sleep a lot during the daytime but sometimes I get up and have a little walk around. My owner often gives me food when she sees me. I always go out at night and run around the area and try and catch something to eat. (Answer: *a pet cat*)
  3 I get up at a different time every day. I have an office but I usually go to different places every day. I always take my binoculars (mime using these), *a small tape recorder and a notepad. Sometimes I talk to people but sometimes I follow people and hope that they won't see me.* (Answer: *a private detective*)
  4 I always stand in the street. I usually sleep during the day but I really switch on at night. I feel bright and I light up people's lives. (Answer: *a streetlight*)
• When students have finished, they could make a similar monologue themselves. Students can prepare in pairs and then read their problem to other pairs for them to solve.

Language notes: present simple

This should be a very familiar tense for students by the time they reach this level. It is notorious, though, for also having a number of persistent student errors.
• Linguists have commented on the fact that omission of the third person -*s* ending is a very frequent and long-lasting learner error. Most students know about the -*s*, but for some reason they have difficulty in remembering and using it up to even quite high levels of learning English. For this reason, it's probably helpful to remind students when they get it wrong – but not to get too upset when they never seem to fully learn it.
• Students often place the adverbs of frequency after the verb, eg ✗ *I go never to church.*
• Students often have trouble remembering the situations where it is appropriate to use present simple rather than present continuous, leading to errors such as:
    What are you doing? ✗ *I read my book.*
    ✗ *I am swimming every Tuesday.*

PRONUNCIATION: final -*s*

1 & 2 💿 1.32
• Students listen to the recording. Point out the two different pronunciations with /z/ and /s/.
• Students listen again, but this time they repeat each word.

💿 **1.32**

/z/	goes, lives, days, friends
/s/	likes, wants, books, streets

3 & 4 💿 1.33
• Students could work in pairs to decide which end pronunciation of -*s* is used in each word.
• Ask students to listen to the recording to check.

/z/	knows, learns, spends, parties, problems, questions, things
/s/	maps, talks, writes, facts, states

💿 **1.33**

/z/	knows, learns, spends, parties, problems, questions, things
/s/	maps, talks, writes, facts, states

Extension task: find a friend

• Write the following categories on the board: *likes, dislikes, favourite books and films, habits, type of holidays, plans for the future.*
• Give students one minute to think of how to describe their likes, habits and interests under these headings. They can make notes if they wish.
• When students are ready, ask them to walk around the class and find a student they don't usually get to chat to. Ask students in pairs to tell each other about themselves. After about a minute, ask students to find a new partner.
• After students have spoken to three people, ask them to tell the class which partner they spoke to had the most similar interests.

Language notes: -s pronunciation

- This pronunciation rule applies to both third person verb endings and plural noun endings.
  The *-s* ending is pronounced /s/ when it comes after a word ending in /t/, /k/ or /p/.
  Other word endings are followed by a /z/ or an /ɪz/ pronunciation.
- The word *parties* may puzzle some students. They may think it should have an /s/ pronunciation because it has a /t/ sound. The reason it has /z/ is because the final sound of the singular *party* is /i/ not /t/.
- NB Although it's not featured in this unit, there is also a rarer /ɪz/ ending, eg as in *churches*.

IF YOU WANT SOMETHING EXTRA …

▶ Straightforward Teacher's Resource Disc *at the back of this book*

4B | Wedding bells

WHAT THE LESSON IS ABOUT

Theme	Getting married
Speaking	Describing a wedding
Vocabulary	Weddings
Reading	*If you ask me ...* . Magazine article: discussing the popularity of marriage
Grammar	Present continuous
	Stative verbs
Did you know?	Wedding traditions

IF YOU WANT A LEAD-IN ...

Tell a personal story

- Bring in some photos from your own wedding or a wedding you have attended. Show the photos and talk naturally to students about your memories of the day. You could start by saying: *I'd like to show you some photos of an important day*. Include (but don't spend time on explicitly teaching) some of the lesson's vocabulary, eg *ceremony, groom, bride, ring*, etc.

Test before you teach: present continuous

❯ *Methodology guidelines: Test before you teach, page xxi*
- Think of a busy local place that everyone in class will know – somewhere with lots of people and lots of things happening, eg a shopping mall, a station, a park, etc. Write the name of the place on the board and these sentence starters: *Some people are ...* and *One person is ...*
- Ask students to work in pairs and to imagine what is happening right now in this place. They write six sentences.
- Don't check these immediately but return to them later in the lesson when you have taught the present continuous. Students can then notice if they got the sentences right and can correct errors.

VOCABULARY & SPEAKING: weddings

❯ *Language reference, Student's Book page 45*

1
- Students find the seven items listed in the photos.

Photo A shows the bride, groom and wedding cake.
Photo B shows the ring.
Photo C shows the church.
Photo D shows the bouquet.
Photo E shows the priest.

2 & 3 🌐 1.34
- Students complete the description using words from the box.
- Students listen to the recording and check their answers.

1	ceremony	3	guests	5	speech
2	registry office	4	reception	6	honeymoon

🌐 1.34

The ceremony usually takes place in a church or registry office. After the ceremony, the couple and their guests go to the reception, where they drink champagne and eat the wedding cake. Later on, at the wedding meal, the best friend of the groom makes a speech. The married couple often leave the party early to go on their honeymoon.

4
- Students read the questions and make notes about a wedding they have been to.
- Students describe the wedding to the others.

Alternative procedure

- If you suspect that not many students have been to a wedding, first find out which students have. Make small groups of three or four, making sure each group contains at least one person who has been to a wedding. Students ask questions to each other about the wedding.

Extra task: collecting vocabulary

❯ *Methodology Builder 6: Mind map vocabulary collection, page 16*
- Encourage students to record the vocabulary in their notebooks using a mind map like the one below.

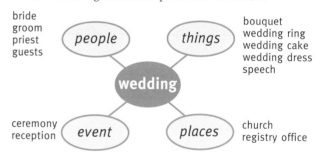

READING

In this magazine article, the writer criticizes her old university professor, who told her students that marriage was a thing of the past. She argues that because marriage is still very popular today, this has proved that the professor's opinion was wrong.

1
- Write the sentence *Marriage is a thing of the past* on the board. Elicit some views from the class, making sure that the meaning of *a thing of the past* is clearly understood by everyone.
- Pairwork. Students continue the discussion, giving reasons.

Language notes: vocabulary

- If something is *a thing of the past* it means that something used to be common and easily available but has become rare or hard to find. NB The thing may still exist. It does not necessarily mean that the thing has disappeared completely. The verb *becoming* is often used with the phrase, eg *It is becoming a thing of the past*.

2

- Students read the article to discover if the author agrees or not that marriage is a thing of the past.
- This could be a tricky task, especially as the key first sentence is missing. Students may get misled by the fact that the article contains views from another person (her university professor) who thinks that marriage is a thing of the past. We can tell that this is not the author's view from the words *she told us* and *she said*. The overall meaning of the later paragraphs should clarify the author's view, which is clearly summarized in the last seven words.

> The writer disagrees.

3

- Students match the sentences to the correct paragraphs.

> 1 b   2 c   3 a   4 d

4

- Pairwork. Students discuss the three sentences. You could extend this to a class discussion if you wish.

GRAMMAR: present continuous

Grammar box

- ❯ *Language reference, Student's Book page 44*
- ❯ *Methodology Builder 22: Using Grammar boxes, page 106*

- As with the present simple, students should be quite familiar with this tense (and may feel that they know everything about it). However, the idea of stative verbs may be new.

1

- Students put the verbs into the present continuous.
- This task is relatively straightforward. Mistakes might include: spelling: ✗ *comeing*, and omitting the auxiliary verb in *is holding*.
- Encourage students to write contracted forms rather than full forms (as they are much more commonly used, though often less familiar to students).
- When students have checked the answers, put them in pairs to decide a possible context for each sentence.

> 1   're coming
> 2   'm trying
> 3   'm telling
> 4   's raining
> 5   are speaking / is holding
>
> *Possible contexts:*
> 1   A daughter/son is calling her/his mum/dad on a mobile phone as she/he comes back after a holiday.
> 2   A student is revising for an exam in the college library. She/He is upset by other loud people.
> 3   A husband is speaking to his wife. He is trying to explain that he didn't go to the pub last night.
> 4   Three children are talking together in their school classroom at break time.
> 5   A radio football commentator is reporting on the World Cup Final.

Weaker students

- If the class still has problems with basic structural points to do with this tense, they may find a drill helpful.
  Example: *I'm walking in the park.*
  Cue: He   *Answer: He's walking in the park.*

Cue	Answer
She	She's walking in the park.
town	She's walking in town.
driving	She's driving in town.
to the airport	She's driving to the airport.
I	I'm driving to the airport.
John	John's driving to the airport.
John and Mary	John and Mary are driving to the airport.
You	You're driving to the airport.
question	Are you driving to the airport?
the pop stars	Are the pop stars driving to the airport?
positive sentence	The pop stars are driving to the airport.
negative	The pop stars aren't driving to the airport.
I	I'm not driving to the airport.
John	John isn't driving to the airport.
question	Is John driving to the airport?

> ### Methodology Builder 12
> ### Substitution drills
>
> - *In this kind of drill, the teacher offers a starter sentence and then a cue word (or words). The students must put the cue word into the original sentence. Sometimes this will be straightforward, just substituting one word for another, eg*
>
> | Cue | Answer |
> | --- | --- |
> | | She likes coffee. |
> | chocolate | She likes chocolate. |
>
> - *If the changed word is always in the same position in the sentence, it is called a simple substitution drill. However, the teacher could also vary the word to be substituted, turn by turn, eg*
>
> | Cue | Answer |
> | --- | --- |
> | | He's going to visit the lawyer. |
> | doctor | He's going to visit the doctor. |
> | Mary | Mary's going to visit the doctor. |
>
> - *This is a progressive substitution drill. On some occasions the cue word will force other changes in the sentence, for example, in verb endings, eg*
>
> | Cue | Answer |
> | --- | --- |
> | | She likes chocolate. |
> | They | They like chocolate. |

- *Sometimes the teacher can give an instruction rather than a cue word, eg*

Cue	Answer
They	*They like chocolate.*
Make a question	*Do they like chocolate?*

- *When students understand this kind of instruction, you can leave out the 'make a' part of the cue and just say 'question'.*
- *This kind of drill provides an interesting challenge for students, as it often demands careful thinking, and prevents students giving automatic responses.*

2

- Students complete the sentences with the correct form of the verb.

1   costs
2   's wearing
3   get
4   isn't wearing
5   keep / are keeping (both possible)
6   Do you ever talk
7   doesn't love
8   doesn't matter

Stronger classes

- Write the following sentences on the board with the words *agree, have, think* in a separate box at the side. Students must use a verb from the box and put it in the continuous or simple form.
- This exercise deliberately offers some more difficult choices between stative and non-stative meanings.

1   *What do you … about the United Nations?*
2   *How many branches does your company …?*
3   *We'll finish the meeting in a minute. We are just … the final cost of the contract.*
4   *Do you … with the results of the questionnaire?*
5   *Where shall we go? Mmm. Wait a minute I'm … about it.*
6   *Hello. Sorry to phone you so early! Are you … breakfast?*

agree
have
think

Answers: 1 *think*   2 *have*   3 *agreeing*   4 *agree*
5 *thinking*   6 *having*

Language notes: stative verbs

- Verbs can refer to events (ie actions, things happening) or states (ie a general condition, without any specific action). For example, in the sentence *I walked into the room* the verb *walked* describes an action, and *walked* is an *event verb*. But in the sentence *I know the answer*, the verb *know* describes a state. *Know* is a *stative verb*.
- This distinction is important because we do not usually use stative verbs in continuous tenses. So, for example, we would not say *I am knowing the answer*, even when the time and meaning seem to require a continuous tense, eg for something happening now.
- However, it's not always easily apparent to students whether a verb is stative or not (eg *wear, love*) and errors arise from this confusion. Many verbs can be used with both a stative and non-stative meaning, eg *She has brown hair* (stative); *She's having lunch* (non-stative).

- Although your students don't need to know yet, teachers should note that the guidelines in the coursebook are guidelines not rules! Some of these verbs may, in certain situations, be used as event verbs, eg *It's costing a lot of money to make this new playroom; Although I'm agreeing to your proposal now, I may vote against it later.* In poetry or advertising, verbs that are usually stative are sometimes made into event verbs in order to make an impact, eg *I'm loving it.*

3

> *Communication activities, Student's Book page 130*

- Students look at the picture on page 130 and write five questions about it. All questions should be about what is happening now and be in the present continuous tense.

4

- Pairwork. Tell students to close books and ask each other the questions they prepared.

Extension task

- You could extend the activity and make it more challenging by repeating it but giving different pictures to each student in a pair. Collect some magazine pictures that show people doing things (make sure the vocabulary isn't too difficult). Distribute the pictures, one to each student, and ask them to prepare questions about their picture.
- When they meet up in pairs, the first student is allowed 45 seconds to study the picture, then close the book. The other student can then ask the questions. Students reverse roles when that's finished.

DID YOU KNOW?

1

- Groupwork. Students read the text about wedding traditions in Britain and America and discuss similarities and differences with their own country.

Extra discussion

- *How much does a wedding cost in your country? Is it important to have an expensive wedding?*
- *How many guests will come to an average wedding? Is it possible to have a small quiet wedding? Is it OK for a boy and girl to travel away from home and secretly marry without telling their family or inviting guests?*
- *What traditions must be followed in wedding celebrations in your country? Are there any traditional foods for weddings? Is music and dancing necessary?*

Web research task

> *Methodology Builder 1: Using Web research tasks, page 2*

- Write up the following places on the board: *Indonesia; Siberia; Sahara; Kenya; Tibet; Japan; Andes.* Ask students to choose one of the places and find three unusual or interesting wedding traditions from the place. If they have access to a printer, you could ask each researching team to find one good illustration of a wedding in that location.

Web search key words

- *wedding tradition* name of country

IF YOU WANT SOMETHING EXTRA …

> Straightforward Teacher's Resource Disc *at the back of this book*

4c | At the movies

WHAT THE LESSON IS ABOUT

Theme	Different kinds of film
Speaking	Pairwork: inventing a film dialogue
	Pairwork – Communication activity: retelling film stories
Listening	A description of a film (*The Holiday*)
Vocabulary	Relationship verbs: phrasal verbs and prepositional collocations
Functional language	Telling stories
Pronunciation	/ɪ/ & /iː/

IF YOU WANT A LEAD-IN ...

Discussion starters: movies

> *Methodology Builder 15: Using Discussion starters, page 63*

- *Do you like going to the cinema? What sort of films do you enjoy most? Do you go because of the film stars or the kind of film?*
- *Should films be censored (ie should someone decide that you can/can't watch certain films?) Which sort of film do you never want to see?*
- *Imagine you are a film director – can you think of a great film that no one has made yet?*
- *What is the worst film ever?*

Introducing the theme: film genres

- Ask students to look at the three photos which come from different kinds of film – what are they? (Answer: *horror; comedy; thriller (or suspense). All are black and white films, so they are probably quite old.*)
- Make three columns on the board with these three headings. Divide the class into three and ask each group to nominate one student as writer to come to the board. Each group then calls out and collects vocabulary, ideas, film stars, etc connected with each type of film, eg horror: monster; frightening; Frankenstein; night-time; mad scientist, etc.

Test before you teach: film stories

> *Methodology guidelines: Test before you teach, page xxi*

- Ask students to think of their favourite film and prepare a few notes in order to tell the story to another student, but they should not name the film, say the name of any people or places or name any key objects, eg they should say 'a young man' instead of 'Luke Skywalker'.
- Put students into pairs to tell their story. Their partner must guess which film is being described.

SPEAKING

1

- Students could work in pairs to explain what they think is happening in each picture.
- You could ask students to use the present continuous to talk about the pictures (though it isn't always the ideal tense!).
- If students are short of ideas, you could help by suggesting the following:

First picture: A mad scientist has just created a monster. The monster is alive! It is speaking!

Second picture: They have just got married. They are going on honeymoon to the Niagara Falls and have just arrived by train. The woman has got lots of luggage and her husband has to carry it all for her.

Third picture: They are in an old house. A stranger has just walked into the room. They are frightened.

2

- Pairwork. Students choose one picture and write a short dialogue that might be spoken by the characters in it.
- If students need help or inspiration, you could suggest a context (see ideas for question 1 above) or a first line.

First picture:
Scientist: *Look! It's alive! It's speaking!*
Second picture:
Wife: *Hooray – at last we've arrived at the Niagara Falls for our honeymoon. Hurry up with the luggage now!*
Third picture:
Man: *Someone's coming into the room! Who is it?*

3

- Ask students to act out their dialogues for the class to watch. The class must guess which picture was used.

Methodology Builder 13
Drama sketches

Drama sketches are one simple task type with a lot of possibilities that can really help to bring practice alive and make it more interesting, more challenging and more memorable. Students and teachers are sometimes a little nervous about any activities with a dramatic element. When students have written a short, performable dialogue, there are a number of guidelines to help make the task more approachable, useful and enjoyable:

- *Don't jump straight from a writing stage to performing in front of the class. This will almost certainly make students nervous, as they will feel unprepared and insufficiently good.*
- *When students have finished writing, get them to first spend some time considering how the text could be spoken, eg ask students to:*
  1 mark all stressed syllables.
  2 decide what feeling the speaker has in each sentence (angry? happy? worried?, etc).
  3 decide what the intonation is in each sentence.
- *Allow students rehearsal time – first reading through the dialogue quite quietly to each other, then standing up and trying it louder and with a few gestures, facial expression and movements.*
- *Maybe, allow students to try out their finished performance with another pair before you gather the whole class together for a class performance.*
- *You may even decide not to have a whole-class stage. It's not compulsory. In some classes, having students perform only to small groups of other students is preferable and less threatening.*
- *You may want to avoid a vote or decision about who was best. Instead, validate every pair by thanking them and picking out good points from each performance.*

LISTENING

In this listening, the film *The Holiday* is being described. It is a sentimental romantic comedy in which an American woman and an English woman swap homes for a holiday. The English woman finds herself in a huge, modern Californian house and falls in love with an American man. The American woman finds herself in a pretty English cottage and falls in love with an Englishman.

1 🔘 1.35
• Direct students to look at the poster. Ask if anyone has seen the film. If anyone has, don't ask them for their opinions until the other students have discussed theirs and guessed what kind of film it is. They may suggest *romantic comedy*.
• Students listen to the monologue and check their answers.

> a romantic comedy

Cultural notes: film genres
• Here are a number of common film genres: action, adventure, animated (cartoon), comedy, crime, fantasy, romantic, historical, horror, musical, science fiction, war, western, non-fiction (documentary).

🔘 **1.35**

> OK, so there are these two women: Amanda, who lives in America, and Iris, who lives in England, and they're both very unhappy. Amanda has split up with her boyfriend, and Iris is unhappy because there's a man she is in love with, Jasper, but he is going to get married to someone else. So, yes, anyway, the two women, they want to change their lives and they decide to swap homes, to go and live in the other woman's house. Amanda arrives in England and she meets Graham, who is the brother of Iris. Amanda and Graham have a lot in common, they talk a lot about their families and so on, and they start going out together. And then, Amanda has to go back to America, but she doesn't go because she realizes that she's in love with Graham, and so she stays in England for a bit.
> At the same time, Iris is in America, and she's still crazy about a guy in England, the one who is getting married to someone else. Iris meets Miles; he's Amanda's best friend, and they get on very well, but Miles is also crazy about someone else, his girlfriend, but he doesn't know that she is cheating on him. So, Iris and Miles become friends, but they both have someone else in their lives. Then, one day, Iris goes home and she finds Jasper at the front door, the one that she was crazy about. But she realizes that she's not in love with him any more, and she sends him away. And Miles splits up with his girlfriend because he finds out that she's cheating on him, and then, yes, then Miles asks Iris out, he asks if she wants to go on a date with him, and she has fallen in love with him, so she says yes. And then they go to England together, and they meet up with Amanda and Graham, and everyone is happy, and, er, that's it, really.

2 🔘 1.35
• Students listen again and write the first letter of the characters' names next to each question.
• Students look at the audioscript on page 136 and check their answers.

Stronger classes
• Find out if the students can answer the questions before listening the second time.

> | | |
> |---|---|
> | 1 | I, G |
> | 2 | A, M |
> | 3 | A |
> | 4 | A, I |
> | 5 | M |
> | 6 | I |
> | 7 | M |

3
• Students discuss the film. If they have seen it, they give their opinion about it. If not, they discuss if they would like to see it. Encourage them to give reasons.

Cultural notes: The Holiday
• *The Holiday* was directed by Nancy Meyers and released in 2006. It starred the American actors Cameron Diaz and Jack Black, and the English actors Kate Winslet and Jude Law.

Web research task
❯ *Methodology Builder 1: Using Web research tasks, page 2*
• Think of a famous film that other students have probably seen. Find ten unusual facts about the film, eg actors who played supporting roles, release date, name of the fictional town in the film, etc. When everyone has their lists, read them out to the class (but don't name the film) and others try to guess the films.

VOCABULARY: relationship verbs
❯ *Language reference, Student's Book page 45*
1
• Students use the six words to complete the gaps in the half-sentences (1–5 and a–e).
• Students may be puzzled that these are not complete sentences. Tell them not to worry about this yet.

> | | | | |
> |---|---|---|---|
> | 1 | out | a | to |
> | 2 | about | b | in |
> | 3 | about | c | up |
> | 4 | in | d | on |
> | 5 | out | e | in |

Language note
• Some common mistakes include ✗ *crazy on someone* ✗ *argument on something* ✗ *married with someone* (not an option in the exercise).

2
• Students now match the beginnings in column A with the endings in column B to make complete sentences that have a sensible meaning.

> | | | | | | |
> |---|---|---|---|---|---|
> | 1 | d (or e) | 3 | c | 5 | a (or c) |
> | 2 | b (or d) | 4 | e (or d) | | |

Extension task: ordering a relationship

- An amusing extension activity would be to work out a natural order for the phrases. Write the following items on the board:

  to ask someone out
  to be crazy about someone
  to have a big argument about something
  to have a lot in common with someone
  to go out together
  to get married to someone
  to be in love with someone
  to split up with someone
  to go on a date
  to fall in love with someone

- Elicit two names (eg Brad and Sally).
- Ask students to work out a complete love story for Brad and Sally – from beginning to end – by using phrases in a sequence. If the idea isn't clear, help them choose the first sentence, eg *Brad and Sally worked in the same office and had a lot in common with each other.*

3

- Pairwork. Students discuss friends, family or people they know, using phrases from exercise 1.

Younger classes

- With teenage classes, there is some danger of embarrassment or attacks of giggles in this discussion, eg when asking *who is going out with who*. You may want to watch and check it doesn't get out of hand.

FUNCTIONAL LANGUAGE: telling stories

1

⊙ *Communication activities, Student's Book pages 126 & 131*

- Groupwork. Ask students to work in groups of four. The first two students are Pair A, the other two are Pair B. Both Pair A and B turn to the pages listed and read the story of a film. They should read it at least twice, making sure they understand it.
- You could ask students to test themselves before moving on to the next phase, ie when they have read the story, they close their books and see if they can recall all the information.

Weaker classes

- Weaker classes may need more time to understand and remember the texts.

2

- Students stay in their original pairs and practise recalling and narrating the story together. Of course, both students in this pair will already know the story, but this is just a preparation for retelling the story later to someone who doesn't know it!
- You can allow students to check back with the original text when there is a doubt or disagreement – or when they want to check something – but discourage telling the story with the book open all the way through.

3

- When students have practised enough to feel confident about telling the story, they join up with a new partner. Each new pair should have one A and one B in it. Students now tell the story of their film to their new partner.

Extension task: telling an example film story

- You could tell a story in this way yourself. Prepare your narration of a film's story before class so that you can tell it in the present simple tense.
- In class, set a gist task or two before you start, eg *Why did Dobbs go to the mountains? Did he get what he wanted?*
- Example: *The Treasure Of The Sierra Madre* (a classic 1948 film starring Humphrey Bogart).

  Dobbs is an American in Mexico. He meets an old man, Walter, who says that he knows where they can find gold. Dobbs and another man agree to go with Walter into wild, deserted mountains. They find gold and work for months to get it out of the ground. But as the amount of gold increases, the three friends start to get more nervous. They dream about what they will do with their wealth but also start to worry that the others want to steal their gold. Dobbs' greed and worry finally makes him go mad. Bandits attack and kill him but they don't realize he is carrying gold. They search the bags for treasure, but think they are just filled with sand. Dobbs' body is left in the desert and the wind slowly blows all his gold dust away.

- When you have told your story check answers to any pre-questions. Focus on your use of the present simple and clarify the reasons why you chose this tense.

Language notes: present simple for past narratives

- Students will be familiar with the use of the present simple to talk about things happening always, usually, generally, etc. This use for telling past narratives is rarer but still often used in colloquial English. It is used when the speaker wants to make a story sound more live and immediate. Thus, it is mainly used for:
  (1) telling personal stories about dramatic or funny events that recently happened to you.
  (2) telling jokes and humorous anecdotes.
  (3) describing the story of a book, film, TV show, play, etc.
- Compare, for example, the joke openings 1 and 2:
  1 *A bear walked into a sports shop and asked the receptionist for a tennis racquet …*
  2 *This bear walks into a sports shop and asks the receptionist for a tennis racquet …*
- The use of the past simple in version 1 has a slight distancing effect – it makes the story seem a bit distant and long ago. In contrast, the second example feels as if it is something closer and more recent. (The word *This* has a similar effect in contrast to *a*.)
- We can use the present simple for personal stories to give a similar effect. The most important thing for students to realize is that this use of the present simple is talking about the past not the present.

Grammar as choice

- An interesting point that arises from this language focus is that not all grammar is simply right or wrong. In many cases we have a choice about how we want to say something. In all the situations where we could use the present simple to tell a past narrative, we could equally well use the past simple. The decision about which to use is a personal choice – not about accuracy, but to do with what kind of impact we want to make with our story. This will depend on where we are and who we are talking to. Some (more formal) contexts will probably be inappropriate for telling present simple past narratives of this kind.

PRONUNCIATION: /ɪ/ & /iː/

1 🌐 1.36

• Students listen to the recording and repeat the words chorally.

🌐 **1.36**

/ɪ/	live, think, still, rich, hit
/iː/	leave, teeth, street, feel, meet

2 & 3 🌐 1.37

• Students read the film titles and mark all /ɪ/ and /iː/ phonemes.
• It may be interesting for students to note how many different spellings a vowel sound can have. In this exercise, /ɪ/ is spelled with *i*, *e* and *y*; /iː/ with *ea*, *ee*, *e* and *ie*.
• Students may argue that the last sound in *Beauty* and *pretty* is /iː/. In fact, the sound is shorter – much closer to /ɪ/ than /iː/ (although it is arguable if it is actually a third phoneme, somewhere in between the two, sometimes written as /i/).
• Students check by listening to the recording. They may need to hear it more than once. Play back the single film titles a few times to help them be sure of what they heard.

> The /ɪ/ sound is in B**i**g, M**i**ssion, **I**mpossible, Pr**e**tty, Rob**i**n, Pr**i**nce (x2), Eg**y**pt
> /iː/ is in B**ea**st, sl**ee**p, **E**T, Th**ie**ves, **E**gypt
> NB The first sound of Egypt is /iː/ not /e/.

🌐 **1.37**

Beauty and the Beast
The Big Sleep
Mission Impossible
Pretty Woman
ET
Robin Hood: Prince of Thieves
The Prince of Egypt

Extra task: dictation

• Tell the students that you will dictate some short sentences which include many /ɪ/ and /iː/ phonemes. (You may want to do only one or two of them.) Students must write down the exact text with as few spelling mistakes as possible. They can compare answers with each other before you write up correct versions. (After students have checked them, you could also use these sentences as tongue twisters for pronunciation practice.)
  1 *He's seen the queen hit that bit of green cheese.*
  2 *This sheep's asleep in the street.*
  3 *Three people with big feet are sneezing in the ship.*
  4 *The bee in the tree will meet the beetle.*
  5 *Jim and me are in the dream team. We'll beat the team from Egypt.*

Language notes: pronunciation /ɪ/ & /iː/

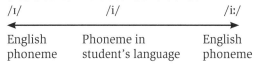

• For students with some mother tongues, the distinction between these two phonemes is very tricky. The initial problem is not making the sound, but being able to hear it when others say it. For many learners, the two sounds will be indistinguishable. This is especially true if their own language has neither sound but a single phoneme that is somewhere between the two:

/ɪ/	/i/	/iː/
←		→
English phoneme	Phoneme in student's language	English phoneme

• When this student hears either /ɪ/ or /iː/, they will tend to hear their own phoneme, ie the sound they expect in their own language. Thus they may say that both /ɪ/ and /iː/ sound the same to them, and will often show amazement that there are two different sounds here.
• So, one way to help students here is by offering ear training, ie giving them the chance to hear examples of the sounds in words and to practise distinguishing between them. To do this with vowel sounds like /ɪ/ and /iː/, teachers often use pairs of words that have the same consonants but differ only in the vowel used, eg *live* and *leave*. The most useful work with these is probably the listening rather than the student production. Don't worry too much if students can't say these perfectly; the first step is to get them to be able to hear the difference. Recognition almost always comes long before good production.

IF YOU WANT SOMETHING EXTRA ...

🔾 Straightforward Teacher's Resource Disc *at the back of this book*

4D | Going out

Theme	Going out with a friend
	Inviting someone out
Speaking	Pairwork: describing an imaginary evening out with a famous person
	Pairwork roleplay: making arrangements to go out with a famous person
	Discussion: describing the social life of people of different ages
Listening	Two phone calls: arranging to go out
Grammar	Prepositions of time
Functional language	Accepting or declining invitations & suggestions

IF YOU WANT A LEAD-IN ...

Discussion starters: asking someone out

❯ *Methodology Builder 15: Using Discussion starters, page 63*

- *When there is a person you would like to go out with, is it difficult to ask them out? Why?*
- *Do you know any great ways to ask?*
- *Is it easier to ask someone you already know as a friend, or a complete stranger?*
- *What happens if they say no? How would it feel to be rejected?*

Test before you teach: prepositions of time

❯ *Methodology guidelines: Test before you teach, page xxi*

- Write *on*, *in* and *at* on the board. Tell students that you will ask them some questions and that they should write answers. The questions will be about when they do things and when things happen. Tell students that they must use one of the words on the board in each answer.
- Read the first question and check it immediately to make sure that students write the prepositions as well as the time expressions.
- Go on to read some or all of the other questions. Don't check the answers immediately, but come back to check them after students have done the exercises in the *Grammar* section.
  1 *When did you have lunch yesterday?*
  2 *When did it last rain?*
  3 *When did the first man walk on the Moon?*
  4 *When does the New Year start?*
  5 *What time did you go to bed last night?*
  6 *When do people like to go on holiday?*
  7 *When is the weather coldest?*
  8 *What time do you usually have lunch?*
  9 *When was the last US Presidential election?*
  10 *When is the biggest public celebration of the year in this country?*

SPEAKING

1
- Ask one or two students to suggest a famous person (film star, pop singer, sportsperson, etc) that would be good to go out with. Ask why their choice would be good, where they would go and what they would do.

- Pairwork. Students discuss their evening out with their partner.

LISTENING

These are two short phone calls. In the first, a woman phones a man to invite him for dinner with her friends. In the second, the man from the first phone call phones a male friend to invite him to lunch with friends.

1 🔘 1.38–1.39
- Write clearly on the board: 1 *How well?* and 2 *Why?* Ask students to listen to two dialogues and answer (1) *How well do the people know each other?* and (2) *Why are they telephoning?*
- In this exercise, students only need to get a general idea of the dialogues. Don't worry if they don't get everything. These will all be clarified in the next exercise.

Dialogue 1
They do not know each other well. The woman is calling to invite the man out. (In this, the first dialogue, Nancy phones Sebastian and asks him for dinner on Saturday. He's busy but they arrange to meet for lunch on Sunday with some of Sebastian's friends.)
Dialogue 2
They know each other well. Sebastian is calling to invite the other man out. (In this, the second dialogue, Sebastian calls his friend Jason to invite him for the lunch on Sunday he has spoken to Nancy about. Jason can't come but might turn up later for coffee.)

Weaker classes
- You could play one recording at a time. After the first recording, pause and allow students time to compare answers to the questions. Replay the first recording a second time if useful.

🔘 1.38–1.39

1 **N = Nancy   S = Sebastian**
S: Yeah, hi.
N: Oh, hi. Erm, Sebastian, hi, it's Nancy. Nancy. We met at Melanie's place last Friday.
S: Oh, right. Yes, hi.
N: I was just ringing to, well, the thing is, some friends are coming to my place for dinner on Saturday, and, erm, well, would you like to come?
S: Oh, that's very kind of you. Saturday, you say?
N: Yep. This Saturday.
S: Sorry, Nancy, I'd love to, but I'm afraid I'm busy on Saturday. It's my parents' wedding anniversary.
N: That's a shame.
S: I tell you what, though. I'm meeting up with some friends for lunch on Sunday. Why don't you come along?
N: All right. Yes, why not?
S: You know the little café on the river? By the bridge? We're meeting there.
N: Yeah, I know. Great.
S: Well, I don't know. Shall we say one o'clock? No, let's say half past one, OK?
N: OK, cool. I'll see you there. Thanks.
S: OK, see you on Sunday, Nancy.

2 **S = Sebastian   J = Jason**
J: Hello.
S: Jason, hi, it's Seb. Sebastian.
J: Hi, Seb. What's up?
S: Hey, listen, a whole group of us are meeting for lunch on Sunday at the river café. Do you fancy joining us?
J: Thanks, Seb, but I'd rather not. You know, I always go running on Sundays.
S: Yeah, I know, but how about doing something different for a change? Just once?
J: I guess I could come along later, maybe. What about joining you for coffee after you've eaten? At about half-past two, something like that?
S: Yeah, OK, great. Good idea. But if you change your mind about the meal …
J: You never know! Let's see what the weather's like, OK?
S: OK. Let's wait and see. But the weather forecast says it's going to rain. See you at the weekend, then. Take care.
J: You take care, too. See you.

2 🔘 1.38–1.39
- Allow students a minute to read the sentences and discuss what the missing information might be with a partner.
- Play the recording again. Students write in the missing information.

1	Friday	4	running
2	wedding	5	coffee
3	one	6	rain

FUNCTIONAL LANGUAGE: invitations & suggestions
❯ *Language reference, Student's Book page 45*

1
- Students choose the correct verb form. All sentences are taken from the recorded dialogues and they can check the correct answers by looking at the audioscript on page 136.
- If students ask why the right answers are correct, there is no easy answer. There isn't any clear rule why some items take an infinitive without *to*, infinitive with *to* or the *-ing* form. These are simply collocation patterns that students must learn.

1	to go	4	going	7	go
2	go	5	going		
3	go	6	going		

2
- Tell students to look at the photo of the two people talking on the phone on page 43. Explain that they are arranging to go out with each other. The dialogue in exercise 2 is a phone call between them. Students choose the correct form for each verb. Tell them not to worry about the three missing lines for now.

1	to go	4	go	7	meet
2	do	5	going		
3	do	6	have		

3
- Students choose which sentence (a–c) goes in which place in the dialogue in exercise 2.

c, a, b

4
❯ *Methodology Builder 16: Practising functional language with situational dialogues, page 68*
- Pairwork. Students choose which character to be and practise reading the dialogue aloud.
- You could ask students to mark stresses, and rehearse, etc.

Stronger classes
- Get students to make a few variations to the dialogue, ie they could choose different people and suggest different places to go to, etc.

5
❯ *Methodology Builder 8: Roleplay, page 27*
- Students imagine that they are a famous person. (They can be a different sex.) Ask them to take a minute to write a short list of things their new character likes and doesn't like doing in the evenings.
- Pairwork. Students meet up (male and female) and try to arrange to go out.

Alternative procedure
- After the preparation time, ask all students to stand up and wander around the room. Students have the chance of meeting up with a number of different people. They should have short dialogues with different people. They should aim to make as many interesting arrangements as possible.

GRAMMAR: prepositions of time
Grammar box
❯ *Language reference, Student's Book page 45*
❯ *Methodology Builder 22: Using Grammar boxes, page 106*

1
- Students complete the sentences with the prepositions.
- In question 7, students may be puzzled that the answer is *in March*. If the sentence said *Our wedding is on March the 14th*, the preposition would be *on* (for a specific date). But the sentence just says that the wedding will be *in* the month (ie the period of time) and pauses, then it mentions the exact date.

1	on	3	in	5	at	7	in
2	on	4	on	6	on		

2
- Students write endings for each sentence so that it is true for themselves.
- If students come from different countries, ask them to write about their home country. If not, they can write answers about their own home town.

Extra task: substitution drill
❯ *Methodology Builder 12: Substitution drills, page 46*
- Students must use the cue word to change the time mentioned in the sentence. The major challenge is that the prepositions will also need to be altered.

Example: *She went there at ten o'clock.*
Cue: nine o' clock *Answer: She went there …*

Cue	Answer
8 o'clock	She went there at eight o'clock.
Tuesday	She went there on Tuesday(s).
Christmas	She went there at Christmas.
summer	She went there in (the) summer.
10th July	She went there on the 10th of July.
lunchtime	She went there at lunchtime.
June	She went there in June.
Friday evening	She went there on Friday evening.
2005	She went there in 2005.
February	She went there in February.
Easter	She went there at Easter.
weekend	She went there at the weekend.

3
• Pairwork. Students compare their sentences.

Language notes: prepositions of time
• All three prepositions studied here have the same meaning, ie they help to answer the question *when* by locating an event at a certain time. We can make a few generalizations about why a time expression should go with *in* rather than *on* or *at*:

At is used for exact times, events and moments, eg *at noon, at 3.30, at lunch* and for some longer special periods eg *at Easter, at the weekend, at New Year.*
In is used with most periods of time longer than a few hours, eg *in the afternoon, in summer, in May, in the last century, in the new year* (ie the period of the whole year rather than just the day of the celebration).
On is used with specific dates or days, eg *on Tuesday, on the 10th of July.*

• Having said that, it's probably more useful for students simply to learn the correct collocation patterns for each time expression, rather than trying to use these guidelines.

SPEAKING

1
• Groupwork. Students describe and compare the social lives of the age groups listed. Point out the phrases in the *Useful language box* that students can use.
• Encourage a range of opinions.

2
• Students discuss whether they have typical views of people from their country.

IF YOU WANT SOMETHING EXTRA …
❯ Straightforward Teacher's Resource Disc *at the back of this book*

Answer key

4 REVIEW

Student's Book page 151

1

Muriel
Why do so many pen pals ~~wants~~ want a romantic relationship?
I am happily married and ~~has~~ have two children.
~~Are~~ Do you want to know more about life in New Zealand?
Steffi
~~Does~~ Do you want to write to me once or twice a week?
My ideal pen pal … ~~don't~~ doesn't find it easy to make friends.
He (or she) …. ~~want~~ wants a friend in a different country.
Jamal
Do you want to ~~improves~~ improve your English?
I ~~likes~~ like talking about sport and music and travel.
I ~~am~~ live in Sweden, but I come from Tunisia.

2

1   We don't often go out on our own.
2   We sometimes have arguments about little things.
3   We usually share all the housework.
4   We speak on the phone six times a day.
5   We talk about our day at work every evening.
6   We always tell each other all our secrets.
7   We never want to have children.
8   We often wear the same colour clothes.

3

1	in	7	on
2	on	8	at
3	at	9	on
4	in	10	on
5	at	11	in
6	at	12	in

4

A: Do you have
B: 'm going
A: Do I know
B: don't think
A: does he work
B: 's making
A: 'm seeing
B: Do you want

5

1   Are your friends also studying English?
2   Does your teacher come from Scotland?
3   Do you often go to restaurants?
4   Are you wearing jeans today?
5   Do your parents like travelling?
6   Is it raining at the moment?

6

a 4   b 5   c 1   d 3   e 6   f 2

7

Students' own answers

8

1   How about tomorrow? Dinner at my place tomorrow?
2   I'd rather not. I'm always tired afterwards.
3   It's kind of you, but I have an evening class this evening.
4   Well, why don't we meet after your class?
5   Would you like to come to dinner this evening?
6   Yes, why not? I'd love to.

9

5, 3, 4, 2, 1, 6

4 WRITING

Workbook page 71

Model answer
Dear Kit,

How are you? How's Jo? Belinda tells me you're both teaching in Budapest these days. What's it like?
My big news is that I left my job at the university last year. One of the Russian professors offered me some work as a translator. I never really liked working in the library, so I agreed. The money isn't great but I can work at home now.
Charlotte's well. She's very excited at the moment because she sold two paintings last week. Now she wants to open a small gallery. It's a nice idea, but we don't have enough money and I don't want to borrow from the bank. I think we need to wait a few years.
I miss our games of chess on Sunday mornings. I still have breakfast at that little chess café we used to go to in Camden. Do you still play?
It would be lovely to see you. We'd love to visit you in Budapest some time!
Write soon!

Greg

5A | Tourist trail

WHAT THE LESSON IS ABOUT

Theme	Tourism in Machu Picchu (Peru) and other places
Speaking	Pairwork discussion: talking about tourism in your country
	Pairwork discussion: Planning improvements in your town for tourists
Reading	*The Ruins of Machu Picchu.* Magazine article: the effects of tourism on Machu Picchu
Vocabulary	Compound nouns
Grammar	Future 1 (future plans)

IF YOU WANT A LEAD-IN ...

Introducing the theme: tourist locations
- Ask students to work individually and write a list of the ten places in the world they would most like to visit – particular locations, not just town names, eg *Eiffel Tower* not just *Paris*.
- Ask students to stand up and mingle with the other students. They should compare lists, asking for reasons why people want to go to certain places. When they have talked to a number of other students, get them to start compiling a list on the board of the top ten most popular places in the class.

Discussion starters: tourism in our country
> *Methodology Builder 15: Using Discussion starters, page 63*

If all students live in the same country:
- *Why do foreign tourists visit your country?*
- *Where do most tourists come from?*
- *Do tourists from your country visit other countries? Which destinations are popular?*

All students:
- *Why do people travel?*
- *Do tourists really see a true picture of the country they visit?*
- *Is tourism good for a country?*

Pre-teach a key word: cable car
- To pre-teach this word, draw a mountain and ask students to think of how people could get to the top. They will probably suggest climbing, a mountain train (and maybe some other ideas); either you or a student can suggest the idea of a cable car. Add the simple illustration to the mountain picture. Tell students the name *cable car*. Ask if they have ever been on one or would like to go on one. NB *Cable car* is the name given to trams (streetcars) in the US (eg San Francisco).

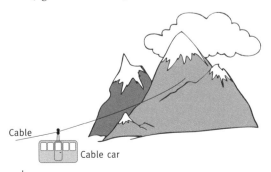

Cable
Cable car

56

Test before you teach: future plans
> *Methodology guidelines: Test before you teach, page xxi*
- Ask students to write down three (genuine) things they are going to do over the next week. When they have written these, they should meet up with another student and tell them what their plans are.

SPEAKING

1
- If you used the *Discussion starters* lead-in, you can move directly from that into this exercise.
- Pairwork. Students discuss the three questions about tourism in their own country.
- After they have finished, you could ask the whole class for their opinions.

READING

This article discusses the effects of modern tourism on Machu Picchu and specifically the arguments for and against the construction of a cable car to the top of the mountain.

1
- Ask students to look at the photo and find out if anyone knows where it is. (Students will probably find the name *Machu Picchu* at the top of the text even if they don't already know it.)
- Tell students that they are going to read a magazine article about that place. Students could work in pairs to guess which of the vocabulary items will be in the text and why.
- This is a prediction exercise. Students can check their answers after they read the text.

Weaker classes
- Give students an example, using the first word *city*, before they work on their own. You could suggest some reasons yourself if they have trouble thinking of any, eg *I think 'city' will be in the text because the place was probably an ancient city hundreds of years ago.*

Optional stage
- Ask students to read the article quickly and find which words from the exercise are in it. (Answer: *All words are in the text.*)

2
- Students read the text and decide which of the seven sentences are true (*T*) and which are false (*F*). They then correct the false sentences.

```
1  F (It was discovered in 1911.)
2  T
3  F (There is a train and a bus that go up to Machu
      Picchu.)
4  T
5  T
6  F (Ana says that she isn't going to stop until the cable
      car idea is dead.)
7  T
```

3
- Students underline any sentences or phrases that make arguments for or against the cable car plan. When they have found these, collect ideas on the board, then ask students to say which they agree with and why.

Extra discussion

- *Is there a tourist place in our country that has similar problems? Tourists bring money to the country, but what problems do they bring? Is it OK for tourism to damage some of our national treasures?*

VOCABULARY: compound nouns

⊙ *Language reference, Student's Book page 55*

1

- Ask students to read the information at the start of this exercise. When they understand the idea, ask them to read the Machu Picchu article again and underline any compound nouns they can find.
- Students may suggest the following as possible answers, though these are probably just describing a particular person or thing rather than being 'fixed' compounds: *American explorer; extraordinary places; Inca bridge; centuries-old path; extra money; large hotel.*

Inca city; city ruins; mountain views; river valley;
tourist destinations; Inca trail; hotel company; cable car;
company spokesman; local people; tour guide;
tea bags; water bottles; tourist centre; souvenir shops;
fast food restaurants; government ministers;
international conference

Stronger classes

- You could set a target number of compound nouns to find, eg fifteen.

Extra practice: compound nouns (1)

- Ask students to work in pairs and look again at the following texts from earlier lessons in the Student's Book: Student A looks at page 10, and Student B looks at page 18. They try and find as many compound nouns as they can from their text. When both partners have their words, they think up a way to use all items in a single short story. They can then compare their stories with another pair.

Extra practice: compound nouns (2) – stronger classes

- Write the following words on the board: *office; park; water; party; bottle; mineral; post; car; company; bank; card; birthday; man.*
- Ask students to work in small groups. They combine the items to find as many compound nouns as they can. Tell them that the words can be reused as often as needed. (Possible answers: *water bottle; bottle bank; mineral water; post office; postman; car park; company car; bank card; birthday card; office party; birthday party*)

Language notes: compound nouns

This is an interesting and often under-studied aspect of English. Here are a few guidelines:

- Compound nouns are different from normal adjective + noun combinations – although it's not always easy to tell which is which. When we use adjective + noun, the adjective helps describe the noun, eg *it's a red car,*

it's a big car, it's a fast car, etc. A compound noun does more than just describing. It is like giving a new name to something. For example, when they invented a phone that you could carry around with you, it was called a *mobile phone*. This was not only describing the kind of phone, but also naming the new thing. *Mobile phone* became a fixed compound widely used by people to name the item, as if it was a noun itself. In contrast, an adjective + noun combination would be used to describe a single example of a thing, eg *That's a tiny phone.*

- In compound nouns, the first word is usually an adjective or a noun. The second word is always a noun.
- It is the second word that carries the main meaning, eg a *streetlight* is a kind of *light* not a kind of *street*.
- The first word acts like an adjective, telling us something more about the noun. It helps us be clearer about exactly what is being talked about. It often tells us what type of thing it is, eg a *video camera* is a camera for taking videos, not a camera for taking still photos.
- When we have specified exactly what we are talking about, it is possible, later in a dialogue, to leave out the first part of the compound because we already know what is being referred to. For example:
  A: *Have you seen the insect spray?*
  B: *Yeah. The spray's over there.*
- It's worth noting that even educated native speakers are often fairly confused themselves about the spelling of compound nouns. Ask someone how to spell some compounds and you'll get a range of answers, eg *street light; streetlight; street-light** or *fairy tale; fairy-tale; fairytale**. As the coursebook says, there are no rules to guide us here, and sometimes even dictionaries differ. *If you're wondering … *streetlight* is usually spelt as one word. The noun *fairy tale* is two words (although when used as an adjective you would make it one word or add a hyphen).
- Although many compounds are fixed items that cannot be altered, it is worth noting that compound nouns are also a creative aspect of language. There are many well-known compounds in English, but there is nothing to stop a speaker expressing a completely new meaning by putting together two words. Imagine, for example, that someone has just invented a chair that has a built-in phone; we could immediately name that phone a *chairphone* (or perhaps call the chair a *phone-chair!*).
- Perhaps we shouldn't worry too much about our students' spelling of compounds, but rather concentrate on raising their awareness of the flexibility of English that allows us to put two nouns together to make a new noun. This creative aspect of language allows students to express a wide range of new meanings, eg *sleeping bag*, without learning any new words, using words they already know.

2

- Ask students to look at the photos at the bottom of page 47. Find out if students can name any of the items, but don't confirm answers yet.

3

- Students use one word from column A and one from column B to name each item in the photos.
- When students have finished, ask them to check their ideas in a dictionary. They should now write a list of the correct spellings, taking care to write the words as one word or two words (there are no hyphenated compounds here), as appropriate.

A	flashlight	G	camping-gas stove
B	first-aid kit	H	video camera
C	backpack	I	sleeping bag
D	guide book	J	sunglasses
E	credit card	K	mobile phone
F	pen knife	L	insect spray

4

- Tell students that they are going on holiday to walk the Inca Trail. Because they are walking, they can only carry a limited number of items with them.
- Pairwork. Students must select the six most useful things to take.

Alternative procedure

- You could organize this as a *Pyramid Discussion*.

> ■ **Methodology Builder 14**
> **Pyramid discussions**
>
> - *Students often find whole-class discussions a little nerve-wracking and teachers often find that two or three students end up dominating, while other students remain quiet because they are shy, don't know what to say, need preparation time, etc. By organizing a discussion as a 'pyramid', some of these problems are answered.*
> - *A pyramid discussion allows students time to think, prepare and try out their thoughts and arguments on small numbers of people before moving on to the whole-class challenge. Pyramid discussions work particularly well with selection and ranking tasks, ie tasks where students are offered a number of options and must select and/or order them (eg choose five qualities of a good teacher; choose the items to take for a Moon landing).*
> - *1 Individually: students think about the problem themselves and write some notes expressing their own opinion (about two minutes).*
> - *2 Pairs: Students meet and compare their notes and discuss them. After about two minutes the teacher adds the instruction that they must reach a compromise about six items they agree on.*
> - *3 When all pairs have reached a compromise, join pairs together into larger groups of four or six. Again students should discuss and finally reach a compromise solution from the whole group.*
> - *4 Bring the whole class back together. By this time students will have explained their views and argued them a number of times, and also had some experience of compromising and reaching agreement. Hopefully, you will find that many more people than usual are ready to take part in a final discussion and compromise solution for the whole class.*
> - *This technique is called pyramid discussion because the interaction and discussion can be imagined diagrammatically as a pyramid, starting small at the top, and widening to take in the whole class:*
>
>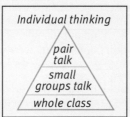
>
> Individual thinking
> pair talk
> small groups talk
> whole class

GRAMMAR: future 1 (future plans)

Grammar box

> ◗ *Language reference, Student's Book page 54*
> ◗ *Methodology Builder 22: Using Grammar boxes, page 106*

1

- Students rearrange the words to make correct questions.

> 1 What are you going to do after the lesson?
> 2 How are you going to get home today?
> 3 Who is cooking your dinner this evening?
> 4 Are you doing anything at the weekend?
> 5 What are you doing for your next birthday?
> 6 When are you going to have your next holiday?

2

- Pairwork. Students ask each other the questions from exercise 1. You can point out the three phrases in the *Useful language box* that they can use.

3

- You could introduce this exercise with a discussion about tourism in your home town, eg *Do tourists come here? Why? What do they like? What don't they like? Do you think our town is welcoming? Could it be more welcoming?*
- Tell students that they are the mayor of their town. They should write a list of ideas for making the town a better place for tourists.
- Pairwork. Each pair should agree on six of their best ideas and then prepare a short presentation for the rest of the class. You could provide more guidance: tell students that for each idea they talk about, they should say something about (a) the current problem, (b) what their idea is, (c) when and how they could start doing something and (d) what good result it will have. Write the following on the board as a reminder: (a) *problem* (b) *idea* (c) *when? how?* (d) *result*.

Language notes: talking about the future

- English has a number of ways of talking about the future. As well as the two forms in this unit, we can also use forms such as *will*, present simple and future continuous.
- In analytical exercises, students can often select the appropriate future form to use. In communicating, however, students tend to avoid using a range of forms, preferring to stick to one or two familiar ways. This reflects the fact that choosing an appropriate future form is quite tricky and there are only general guidelines rather than absolute rules. For this reason, the future is a grammar area that needs to be monitored. Be aware of avoidance (which is often a more serious problem than overt errors) and point out when there is a chance to use a more appropriate form.
- Lesson 5B focusses on deciding whether to use *going to* or *will*.
- In normal spoken English *going to* is often pronounced /ɡənə/. This isn't lazy, or American, or incorrect – it's simply normal fast or fluent speech. Even people who don't believe they say this pronunciation will generally find that they do if they record themselves speaking naturally.

IF YOU WANT SOMETHING EXTRA …

> ◗ Straightforward Teacher's Resource Disc *at the back of this book*

5B | A weekend break

WHAT THE LESSON IS ABOUT

Theme	Staying in a hotel
Speaking	Pairwork: describing the best/worst hotel you have stayed in
Listening	A radio programme about the worst hotel in Britain
Vocabulary	Hotels
Grammar	Future (2) (*will*)
Did you know?	Las Vegas hotels

IF YOU WANT A LEAD-IN …

Introducing the theme: hotels

- Tell students that they are going to stay in a seaside hotel in a nearby country. Ask them to work in pairs and discuss and agree on the ten most important things that the hotel must have.

Discussion starters: hotels

- *Methodology Builder 15: Using Discussion starters, page 63*

- *What are the reasons that people stay in hotels? How long do people usually stay for?*
- *How much would you expect to pay for a hotel in your country?*
- *What differences are there between very cheap hotels and luxury hotels?*
- *If someone offered you the chance to live in a hotel (for a year or more), do you think that would be a good idea?*

VOCABULARY & SPEAKING: hotels

- *Language reference, Student's Book page 55*

1

- Ask students to look at the internet booking form at the top of the page. Explain that after someone fills in this form, the internet search engine will find a number of possible hotels to match the request.
- Students use words and phrases from the box to write the missing items on the form. As an example, ask students to find which item from the vocabulary box is a kind of location. (Answer: *countryside*)

1	countryside
2/3	twin / single
4/5	gym / lift
6/7/8	air conditioning / central heating / minibar

Language notes: hotel vocabulary

- A *single room* is for one person.
- A *double room* and a *twin room* are both for two people. A *double room* has one bed. A *twin room* has two beds.
- A *family room* is a room that accommodates two adults (the parents) plus one or two younger children.
- A *minibar* is a small fridge inside a hotel room, containing a selection of drinks, usually a mixture of alcoholic and soft drinks, and sometimes a few peanuts or other snacks. Hotel guests are allowed to help themselves to this selection, but must pay for any items they use – at prices that are typically higher than shops.

- Not in this exercise – but students may ask: An *ensuite room* is one which also has a private bathroom and toilet, rather than shared facilities along the corridor.
- Guests may also ask for:
  a room with sea/mountain/town views
  tea/coffee-making facilities
  cable/satellite TV
  a trouser press (a sort of ironing machine)
  a business centre (fax, computer, wifi access, etc)

2

- Ask students to look at the first sentence and to think which four hotel facilities from the internet form would be most important for these people. Agree the answer as a whole class, making sure that students state reasons for their choices. NB There is no correct answer.
- Students can work in pairs and do the same for questions 2 and 3.

Possible answers:
1 swimming pool; restaurant; satellite TV; lift
2 internet connection; minibar; gym; restaurant
3 shower; (24-hour) room service; free parking; lift

3

- Students discuss what facilities from the internet form are most important for them. Again, ask them to give reasons.

4

- Pairwork. Make pairs in which at least one student has stayed in a hotel. Direct students to look at the list of questions. Ask students to describe the best and/or worst hotel they have ever stayed in, using these questions as guidelines.
- When ready, rearrange the pairs so that everyone meets a new partner. Students now explain their bad hotel experience to their new partner.

Alternative procedure

- If most of your students have never stayed in a hotel, you could give them five minutes to imagine the worst possible hotel. They could then work in pairs and make notes on ten bad things about this hotel. When they are ready, ask them to imagine they stayed there; they should think of answers to the questions in the book.

Cultural notes: hotel rating systems

- In the UK and other countries, the quality and facilities of hotels are often classified according to a grading system. In fact, there are many different systems, eg stars, rosettes, etc. Some grading schemes are decided by the hotels themselves, some by their hotel owners' associations, some by town or local government, some by independent inspection organizations, etc. This can all lead to some confusion!
- The most common systems used in the UK (and in other countries) are:
  OHRG* ratings: a system of common names for different kinds of hotel, eg *Deluxe, first class, tourist class*, etc.
  Star ratings: from *one star* to *five stars* as an indication of a customer's experience of a hotel. *Five stars* is the top grade and means a place is an excellent and luxurious hotel.

- Of course, different countries can interpret these systems in very different ways. A five-star hotel in one country may actually only count as a three-star in another!
  *Official Hotel & Resort Guide

LISTENING

This listening is a holiday programme on the radio, and is about finding the worst hotel in Britain. Two reporters revisited last year's winner, the Cumberland Hotel in Brighton, and describe how it still has many problems.

1
- Ask students to look at the photo. Elicit any information students can see. Explain that the hotel is in Brighton (a popular seaside holiday resort in the south of England).
- Ask the class to imagine that they are staying there. Do they think it will be a nice hotel? Would they like to stay there? Elicit reasons. Do not confirm any of their ideas yet. Later in the lesson, you can remind students of their first thoughts.

2 🌐 1.40
- Tell students that they are going to listen to part of a radio programme in which two people stay at this hotel. They listen to the recording and tick the problems they hear.

> 1 ✓   2 ✓   6 ✓

Weaker classes
- Write on the board: (a) *programme* (b) *hotel* (c) *people* (d) *jobs* (e) *why?*
- Tell students they will first listen to the opening of the programme. Ask them to find out (a) the name of the programme, (b) the name of the hotel, (c) the names of the two people, (d) the jobs of the two people, (e) why they went to the hotel.
- Play only the presenter's opening speech (up to … *in Brighton for a weekend by the sea.*) and then get students to check their answers in pairs and then with the whole class.
- When students are clear about the basic situation, continue with the rest of the exercise as normal.

🌐 1.40

> **P = Presenter   N = Nicki   M = Manager   G = Gavin**
> **P:** Welcome to *The Holiday Programme*. Today, we continue our search for the worst hotel in Britain. We sent our reporters, Nicki and Gavin Becks, to the Cumberland Hotel in Brighton for a weekend by the sea.
> **N:** When we arrived at the hotel, a sign in the window said 'Vacancies'. We rang the bell, but we had to wait five minutes before the manager finally appeared.
> **M:** Yes?
> **G:** Hello. We'd like a double room for two nights, please.
> **M:** It's ninety pounds a night. No credit cards and you need to pay in advance.
> **G:** That's fine, fine. I'll pay now. Here.
> **M:** Room 51. Fifth floor. On the right. Oh, and the lift's not working. The stairs are over there.
> **G:** Never mind. We'll walk.
> **N:** The room itself was not too bad. There was a good view of the sea from the window, the bathroom was small but clean and the bed looked clean and comfortable.
> **G:** We had a quick (cold) shower, got changed and went back downstairs where we handed in the key.
> **M:** Everything all right?

> **G:** Yes, the room's fine, but the shower's very cold.
> **M:** I know, I know. I'll fix it this evening, OK.
> **G:** That's kind of you. Thanks.
> **M:** What time are you going to come back this evening?
> **N:** I'm not sure. We're going to see a film at the cinema and maybe have a meal afterwards. Why?
> **M:** Well, just remember I close the doors at eleven.
> **N:** Eleven?
> **M:** Eleven.
> **N:** We had a good evening, and when we got back to the hotel, it was two minutes past eleven. The door was locked; we rang and rang, but after fifteen minutes, there was still no answer. We finally decided to give up and look for another hotel. Fortunately, there were vacancies at the Grand Hotel, only a few minutes away.
> **G:** The next morning, after a hot shower, we went back to the Cumberland Hotel to get our bags. When we got there, the manager was standing outside the front door. 'Who do you think you are,' she shouted. 'Waking up all the guests in the middle of the night! Next time you do that, I'll call the police.'
> **N:** 'It won't happen again,' I said. 'We won't be back. We're going to stay at another hotel, thank you very much.' The manager went back into the hotel, came outside with our bags and threw them at us.
> **G:** Britain's worst hotel? This one gets my vote.

3 🌐 1.40
- Students listen to the recording again and put the events in the order that they happened.

> Correct order: 6, 1, 4, 3, 2, 7, 5

4
- Ask students to close their books. Students could work in pairs to retell the story, remembering as many details as they can.

Stronger classes
- Ask students in each pair to take the roles of Nicki and Gavin and retell the story as if it happened to them.

Extension task: roleplay – stronger students
❯ *Methodology Builder 8: Roleplay, page 27*
- This roleplay is probably best done as a spontaneous improvisation rather than with detailed preparation.
- Write the following words on the board: *room; price; key; lift; windows; view; bed; clean; shower; food; door.*
- Put students into groups of four: Students A and B are hotel owners – they can decide if they want to have a wonderful hotel or a terrible one. Students C and D are guests and radio reporters – they can decide to be positive and friendly or negative and suspicious.
- Tell students who they are and that Students C and D have just arrived at the hotel. They should book in, look at the room and ask lots of questions. All students can improvise and invent any details they want. Students can use the words on the board to remind them of possible subjects. At the end of the activity, C and D can give a brief report on the hotel to Students A and B (and maybe to other pairs).

GRAMMAR: future 2 (*will*)

Grammar box

◉ *Language reference, Student's Book page 54*
◉ *Methodology Builder 22: Using Grammar boxes, page 106*

1
- Direct students to look at the four verbs in the box. Show how you can make a sentence by combining *'ll* and a verb, eg *I'll give … .*
- Students do the exercise using *'ll* and one main verb for each question.

1	I'll see	2	I'll think	3	I'll give	4	I'll tell

2
- Ask students to look at the seven problems. These are problems that hotel guests have. Go through the example answer from a friendly and polite hotel manager.
- Students could work in pairs to find a good answer to each problem. NB Not all answers require students to use *'ll*.
- After checking and agreeing on some good answers, you could ask each pair to practise saying the problems and responses to each other. This would be more enjoyable if the guest was quite angry, but the manager was very, very polite! Many responses probably begin with: *I'm sorry, sir/madam* or *I do apologize, sir/madam.*

Possible answers:
2 I'll give you a wake-up call.
3 I'll ask the maid to put some in there immediately.
4 I'll find a different room for you.
5 We have 24-hour room service. I'll get the menu for you.
6 I'll ask the assistant to open the door for you immediately.
7 Oh dear. I'll come up to your room and remove it for you.

3 & 4 🕮 **1.41**
- Remind students that we can say a decision with *'ll* or *going to*. Elicit (or remind them of) the reasons why we choose one rather than the other. Explain that in this exercise they must choose which one to use in each gap.
- Students listen to the recording and check their answers.
- Go through the answers with the class and decide when the speaker makes the decision in each case.
- Pairwork. Students read aloud the completed dialogue.

1	'm going to	5	'm going to
2	'll	6	are you going to
3	'll	7	'll
4	'll	8	'll

🕮 **1.41**

G = Guest   M = Manager
G: Excuse me, I'm going to visit the old part of town this afternoon. Can you tell me the way?
M: Yes, no problem. I'll give you a map.
G: Is it far?
M: No, not far. Do you want to walk or take a bus? It's a nice walk.
G: Oh, well, I'll walk, I think.
M: Or, if you like, I'll take you in my car. I'm going to do some shopping this afternoon.
G: That's kind of you. Thanks. When are you going to leave?
M: About four o'clock.
G: Great. I'll see you here at four o'clock.
M: OK. I'll see you later.

Language notes: will

Some key issues:
- *Will* is quite a problematic word for learners of English because it has so many different uses. Faced with this complexity, students often over-simplify their understanding to a single explanation – that *will* is the future tense. This is partly true, but students need to know that it is only one way of talking about the future and that *will* also has many functional uses (predicting, promising, threats, etc).
- In normal everyday speech, *will* is rarely used. The contraction *'ll* is much more common. Encourage your students to use the contracted form rather than the full form, unless they are speaking in more formal situations.
- *'ll* is pronounced with the dark /l/ sound, ie it sounds more like *ull* in *full* rather than *l* in *light*.
- If students insist on using *will* rather than the contracted *'ll*, it's important that they don't stress it unless they want to show that they have a very strong intention to do something. It can easily sound rude.
- The negative of *'ll* is *won't*. Again, this is much more commonly used than the full form *will not*.
- Questions are made by simple inversion: *Will you …?*

Language notes: decisions made now (will) & *decisions made previously* (going to)

◉ *Methodology Builder 7: Using timelines, page 23*

- In English, there are a number of ways to talk about future events and it is often hard for students to choose correctly between them. This unit introduces one of the few really clear guidelines teachers can offer.
- The key issue is: *When* do I make my decision about what will happen?
  If I make the decision as I speak (ie not planned until that moment), I use *will*.
  If I made the decision before I speak (ie it has already been planned), I use *going to*.

- This context (which you could use with your students) illustrates this difference:
  It's Meg's birthday tomorrow. Peter and Suzie have already decided what to buy her as a present. But Marty forgot it is her birthday!

  Peter: *It's Meg's birthday tomorrow. I'm going to buy her the new Brad Pitt DVD.*

  Suzie: *I'm going to get her a soft toy animal!*

  Marty: *Oh no! Meg's birthday! I completely forgot – what can I get her? I don't know. Ah yes. I know. I'll get her an Italian dictionary. She needs that.*

- In this dialogue, Marty makes his decision while he is speaking. He uses *'ll (will)*. The other two made their decision before they talked. They use *going to*. We can show this on a timeline:

Peter decides	Suzie decides	Marty decides	Meg's birthday
✗	✗	✗	✗

Now

use *going to*   use *will*

NB This is one of those grammar points where, even though the idea may seem quite clear in explanations, it is still quite difficult for students to decide on the spot which is correct, when they are in the middle of a dialogue.

- *Shall* can be used as a (much less common) alternative to *will*, but usually only with *I* or *we*. The meaning of *shall* and *will* is essentially the same, although *shall* can sometimes suggest obligation, duty or definiteness, eg *I shall be there at eight* or *We shall remember them*. The negative of *shall* is *shan't*.

Extra task: drill for will

- In this drill, students are invited to think of creative answers for your problems (as if they are you). They should repeat your problem and then say their answer. Teach them to say *I know. I'll …* each time. There may be many possible interesting and imaginative answers. All the answers are spontaneous decisions and so students will always need to use *'ll* or *will*.

  Problem
  I can't decide what to give my friend for her birthday.
  (Answer: I know. I'll get her a dictionary.)
  Problems
  I can't decide where to go on holiday this year.
  I don't know what to eat for lunch today.
  I don't know where to go tonight.
  I can't decide what film to watch at the cinema.
  I can't decide what mark to give (student's name) for his/her homework.
  I can't make up my mind. What new clothes shall I buy at the weekend?
  What shall I tell the class about next week's lessons?
  I'm tired of teaching. What job can I do instead?

- After your drill, you could ask students to write three or four problems themselves. You could then start a new drill with students asking and responding to each other's problems.

DID YOU KNOW?

1

- Write these words on the board: *Las Vegas*; *Eiffel Tower*; *waterfall*. Brainstorm with students a few things they know about the first two. Ask: *What connection do you think there is between these three things?*
- Elicit some suggestions, but don't confirm their answers. Ask students to read the text and find the answer.

Las Vegas has got huge hotels with amazing features including an Eiffel Tower and waterfalls.

2

- Pairwork. Students discuss the questions in pairs. Then discuss them with the whole class.

Cultural notes: Las Vegas facts and figures

- Las Vegas is in the state of Nevada (in the west of the US, between California and Utah).
- Las Vegas means 'The meadows' in Spanish.
- Las Vegas is the fifth most popular US holiday destination and is the most popular gambling destination in the world. Over 40 million people visit each year.
- In 1910, a law was introduced making gambling illegal in Las Vegas! (It was reversed in 1931.)
- Las Vegas has almost double the number of hotel rooms of New York.
- There are 5005 rooms in the MGM Grand Hotel – which means that if you slept one night in every one, it would take you nearly 14 years!
- The Mirage Hotel has a volcano, a tropical rainforest and over 50 waterfalls. It uses more than four million litres of water every day (in the middle of the Nevada desert!).
- The Luxor Hotel has an Egyptian theme. The strongest light in the world shines from the top of the giant pyramid.
- The town is famous as a place where you can get married quickly. Over 100,000 couples marry each year – that's about 150 a day! It has over 35 wedding chapels.

IF YOU WANT SOMETHING EXTRA …

> Straightforward Teacher's Resource Disc *at the back of this book*

5c | Holiday heaven

WHAT THE LESSON IS ABOUT

Theme	Different kinds of holiday
Speaking	Pairwork discussion: planning a trip for visitors around your country
Reading	*www.heavenholidays.com*. Web page: holiday choices
Vocabulary	Verb patterns
Pronunciation	Silent letters

IF YOU WANT A LEAD-IN ...

Introducing the theme: unusual holidays

- Write the four holiday types from the main text (*Sea holidays*; *Adventure holidays*, etc). Tell students these are all types of holiday.
- Ask students to work in pairs and guess what these names may mean and to think of some example holidays under each heading, eg *rock-climbing* for Adventure holidays, etc.
- Get feedback from the whole class and then ask students to decide which of the holiday types they prefer.

Test before you teach: infinitive/-*ing* form

❍ *Methodology guidelines: Test before you teach, page xxi*

- Write on the board *I hope to …; I'm looking forward to …; I'm very interested in …; I plan to … .* Ask the class to think of the next holiday they would like to take. Each student should copy the four sentence starters and write an ending for each one which is true for them.
- When they have done this, don't check the sentences yet; wait till after students have finished *Vocabulary* exercise 1.

Discussion starters: holidays

❍ *Methodology Builder 15: Using Discussion starters, page 63*

- *What do you think is a perfect holiday?*
- *Would you like to lie on a hot beach for two weeks or would you like to do something more exciting?*
- *Would you like to go on a holiday where you learnt something completely new?*
- *If people visited your country, what are some unusual holiday ideas you could suggest?*

> ### ■ Methodology Builder 15
> ### ■ Using Discussion starters
>
> - *Many units of this Teacher's Book include a number of suggestions for 'Discussion starters'. These usually take the form of questions, provocative comments, etc intended to get students to start thinking and talking, often at the start of a new lesson, when a new topic or theme is being introduced. This Methodology Builder suggests a range of possible ideas for using these in class.*
> *NB There are often a lot of ideas for Discussion starters in the units. Remember that you are definitely not intended to use them all! The idea is to offer you a range of possible ideas so that you can pick ones that you like or which might appeal to your class.*

> *Typical use: working in 'whole-class' mode.*
> - *Ask the questions randomly around the class.*
> - *Make sure you pay more attention to the meaning of what students say rather than focussing too much on accuracy.*
> - *Respond to the ideas and views students state. As far as possible, turn it into a dialogue. Get them interested and involved.*
> - *Encourage students to listen to each other and respond to each other – rather than having all interaction going via you.*
> - *A few don'ts: avoid asking questions routinely person by person round the class (predictable and dull); avoid constant correction (students may say less in an attempt to avoid error); avoid letting one or two strong students dominate to the exclusion of most others.*
> - *Try to give all students a chance to speak. If a loud student talks over a quieter one, try not looking at and not hearing the loud one and wait patiently for the quieter one to have their say.*
> ### *Other ideas*
> - *Pairs/groups: Choose one question or statement you think is particularly interesting. Write it on the board. Put students into pairs or small groups to say what they think about it. After a few minutes, a spokesperson from each pair/group reports back to the class.*
> - *Starting with individuals: Choose a number of the questions and write them on the board (or prepare handouts with them printed on). Ask students to work on their own and write two or three sentences in response to each question/statement. After sufficient thinking and writing time, gather students together in small groups to compare.*
> - *Discussion starters are typically intended to be used in fairly short stages of the lesson. They are mainly for leading into other more substantial later stages. However, occasionally you may find that a topic really takes off, when there is lots of argument and discussion, and a real enthusiasm on the students' part for stating their views. In such cases, you may want to avoid cutting an activity off in its prime, so it's often a good idea to allow an extended time for the stage.*
> - *You can often link smoothly from the discussion starters directly into the activity, text or exercise following.*

READING

This web page advertises four types of holiday: for people interested in the sea; adventure activities; mysterious locations or in history.

1

- Students look at the web page for the different holidays and decide which photo A–H goes with which holiday 1–4.

Sea holidays: B, G	Haunted holidays: A, E
Adventure holidays: D, F	History trails: C, H

2

• Students read the six holiday descriptions and decide which type of holiday they are: *1 Sea holidays*; *2 Adventure holidays*; *3 Haunted holidays* or *4 History trails*.

1	Haunted holidays	4	Adventure holidays
2	Adventure holidays	5	Sea holidays
3	History trails	6	History trails

Cultural notes: reading

• *Scuba* is underwater swimming. The word comes from the initials of the equipment used: *self-contained underwater breathing apparatus*.
• *Swimming with dolphins* has become a popular activity at some resorts. Some people believe that they feel a healing power when they swim next to dolphins.
• *Route 66* was a very long, historic and famous US road, sometimes called *The Main Street of America*. It went from Chicago to Los Angeles. Most of *Route 66* no longer exists, as it has been transformed into motorways.
• *Harley Davidson* is a famous make of motorbike.
• *Mach* is a measurement of speed. *Mach 1* is the speed of sound. *Mach 3* is three times the speed of sound.
• The *MiG-29* is a jet fighter plane which was developed by the Soviet Union in the 1970s and entered active service in 1983.
• Photo E shows a famous image of *Nessie*, the *Loch Ness Monster* in Scotland. It was taken in 1934, but is now widely believed to be a fake.
• *Whisky* is the most important Scottish export. It is made in carefully controlled *distilleries*, and it is illegal for people to make their own.
• *The Feast of Lanterns* is both a Chinese festival early in the New Year and a Japanese Buddhist festival celebrated in July or August. (Here it's a Chinese festival.)
• The *Yeti* is a large human-like creature that is believed to live in the Himalayas. It is also called the *abominable snowman*.
• The *Great Wall of China* is over 6,500 kilometres long. It was built over 2,000 years ago. It is certainly amazing, but many people believe one untrue thing about it! It is often said that it is the only human creation visible from the Moon. However, from the Moon you can only see sea, cloud and desert.
• The *Mayas* were an ancient race that used to live in Central America.
• *Alexander the Great* was a king of *Macedon,* who helped bring together different Greek states. He led Greek armies into many successful battles across Europe and Asia.

Web research task

⊙ *Methodology Builder 1: Using Web research tasks, page 2*

• Offer the class a selection of topics from the listings, eg Nessie; Harley-Davidson; Mayas, etc. Each group should choose a different topic. Students should research and find out some interesting pictures and facts about their chosen topic and report back to the whole class. For example, one group could find more photos of Nessie and report on which ones they think are most convincing.

Alternative web task

• Can you find a live webcam looking out over Loch Ness? A temple? Central American ruins?, etc.

3

• Tell students that the four texts are descriptions of four of the twelve holidays from the web page advertisement. They match each description to the correct holiday (in brackets in the answer key below), and the type of holiday 1–4.

a	2 (Route 66)	c	2 (Mountain Memories)
b	4 (Great Wall)	d	3 (Monster Party

4

• Students could work in pairs to discuss which holiday they are not interested in going on, and their reasons why.

Extension task: reading

• Ask students to write answers to your questions below as you read them. Then ask pairs to compare with each other, and then confirm the correct answers. The questions are in the order that the vocabulary items come in the text. You could mix up the order of questions to increase the challenge.

Teacher questions
• *Look again at the texts on page 50. Find words that mean:*
  1 Know about something by doing it and seeing it yourself. (Answer: *experience*)
  2 Huge, very large, gigantic. (Answer: *titanic*)
  3 An adventurous journey to see animals or other wildlife. (Answer: *safari*)
  4 A car or a ship that is completely damaged and broken. (Answer: *wreck*)
  5 Things that you can remember. (Answer: *memories*)
  6 A public celebration, usually with decorations, singing, dancing, entertainments, etc. (Answer: *festival*)

Extension task: writing

• Write on the board: 5 ✓ 2 ✗ 1 ✗✗✗ or 5 ☺ 2 ☹ 1 ☹☹☹.
• Ask students to imagine that they have just come home after going on one of the holidays from the web page on page 50. They should imagine what it was like and think of five great things that happened, two bad things and one 'near disaster'.
• Students should first make brief notes about these things, then meet up in pairs to tell each other about their holidays. Afterwards, students should write a short report about their holiday, as if they are writing on a web forum.

VOCABULARY: verb patterns

1

• Do the first sentence as an example. Ask students to read it and decide which of the options is correct. They then complete the other sentences on their own.
• Students can check this exercise themselves by looking back at *Reading* exercise 3. All the phrases are in the texts.

1	find	5	spend
2	take	6	visit
3	learning	7	read
4	swimming		

Language notes: verb patterns

• Verbs have different 'going-together' patterns (collocations*)*. Some verbs go with the infinitive with *to.* Some go with the *-ing* form (the present participle, also called a *gerund* when it functions as a noun).

Some verbs (not in this exercise) go with the infinitive without *to* (the bare infinitive).

- Here are some guidelines:
  The following verbs are used only with an infinitive with *to* and never with the *-ing* form: *hope; intend; plan; want; would like.*
  Look forward to is a tricky one. It goes with the *-ing* form even though it has the word *to*. (In this case, *to* is a preposition and is part of the phrase *look forward to* not part of the verb structure that follows.)

2
- Students choose a holiday from the texts on page 50. Give them about three to five minutes to make notes in answer to each of the questions.

3
- Pairwork. Students ask and answer questions from exercise 2.

PRONUNCIATION: silent letters

1 & 2 ● 1.42
- Write the words *comb, night* and *knock* on the board. Ask students how to pronounce them. Help students to say them correctly if they get them wrong. Point out that some of the letters are not pronounced. Cross these letters out: *comb, night* and *knock*. Explain that these are silent letters.
- Students look at the spellings of the words and compare them to the way the words are pronounced. They then circle the silent letters.
- Students then listen to the words in a recording. Pause the recording after each word for students to check their answers.
- Students may need to hear each word more than once.
- The words are pronounced as follows in UK RP pronunciation: /ˈkɑːs(ə)l/; /klaɪm/; /ˈfɒrɪn/; /ˈaʊə/; /naɪf/; /rəˈsiːt/; /gəʊst/; /ˈwenzdeɪ/; /həʊl/ and /rek/.

2	clim**b**	5	**k**nife	8	We**d**n**e**sday
3	forei**g**n	6	receip**t**	9	**w**hole
4	**h**our	7	g**h**ost	10	**w**reck

● 1.42

1	castle	5	knife	9	whole
2	climb	6	receipt	10	wreck
3	foreign	7	ghost		
4	hour	8	Wednesday		

Language notes: silent letters
- Sometimes we can identify a letter that appears to have no obvious connection to any sound pronounced. These are commonly known as *silent letters*.
- Why do we have silent letters? Often the reason is historic; they may show a sound that was pronounced in the past. The spelling has become fixed while our pronunciation has changed.
  In English spelling, there is no one-to-one correlation between letters and sounds, for example, a letter like *a* can be pronounced in many different ways when it is in different words. Often we cannot identify exactly what sound an individual letter makes, but can only say that a group of letters creates a certain sound, eg *ch* is often pronounced /tʃ/.
  The twenty-six letters of the alphabet are not enough to represent all the sounds of English. So we need to use letters in combination as symbols for certain sounds

and, therefore, some may seem to be silent. For example, in the word *ought*, we might say that the *gh* is silent, but maybe we could also interpret the *gh* as part of what helps us to understand that *ou* is pronounced /ɔː/ (not as /ɒ/ or /ʌ/).

3
- Students could work in pairs. Give them two or three minutes to think of some more words with silent letters. Students can check in dictionaries if they have them.
- There are many examples in English. A few words that students might know are: *half; lamb; science; know; autumn; island; taught; business; talk; often.*

Extension task: dictation
- Tell the students that you will dictate some short sentences. (You may want to do only two or three of them.) Students must write down the exact text with as few spelling mistakes as possible. They can compare answers with each other before you write up correct versions. You could also ask them to spot the silent letters (shown in bold).
  1 *I often go to the brigh**t** island in autum**n** and clim**b** up to the castle.*
  2 *I **k**new about science but I taugh**t** business.*
  3 *The **g**host in the **w**reck had half a forei**g**n **k**nife in his **k**nee.*
  4 *I put my thum**b** on the comb.*
  5 *I listened to the bom**b**.*
  6 *I **w**histled as I walked and talked with **Th**omas.*
  7 *I **w**rote t**w**o receipts then signed them.*

SPEAKING

1
- Ask students to read the instructions for the task. Check that they understand that they will need to prepare a one-week programme to introduce the two guests to their own country.
- Students use the list and ideas of their own to make detailed notes on the holiday plans.

2
- Pairwork. Students compare ideas. You could ask pairs to prepare a compromise plan based on the best ideas from the two separate plans.
- Students then describe their plan to the class.

Extra discussion
- *Is it necessary for a holiday to be relaxing? If you came home from a holiday completely exhausted, would that be good?*
- *Is it exciting or foolish to do dangerous things on holiday (eg bungee jumping, paragliding, etc)?*
- *If you go to another country for a holiday, is it necessary to be interested in their culture?*
- *Do you like to read a guide book before you travel? Why? Or is it better to explore and discover things for yourself?*
- *Should you study and read current news about a country before you visit? Is it OK to be ignorant about your holiday country's political situation?*
- *Remember the Machu Picchu text (lesson 5A)? How might tourism be harmful to some of the places in this lesson (eg the wreck of the Titanic)?*

IF YOU WANT SOMETHING EXTRA ...
❯ Straightforward Teacher's Resource Disc *at the back of this book*

5D | Planes

WHAT THE LESSON IS ABOUT

Theme	Air travel
Speaking	Pairwork: describing a journey
	Pairwork roleplay: on a plane
Listening	Air travel: three dialogues at the airport
Vocabulary	Air travel
Pronunciation	Intonation: polite requests
Functional language	Requests

IF YOU WANT A LEAD-IN ...

Discussion starters: travelling by plane

❯ *Methodology Builder 15: Using Discussion starters, page 63*

- *Have you ever travelled by plane? What did you enjoy? What things didn't you like?*
- *On your trip, did you have to wait a long time anywhere? Was the journey comfortable? Did you get any food? Could you eat it? Did your luggage get to your destination?*
- *Is plane travel good value? Is it safe?*

Test before you teach: travelling by plane

❯ *Methodology guidelines: Test before you teach, page xxi*

- Write the following words on the board: *tickets; pack; airport; check-in; security; gate; plane; seat; fly; arrive; luggage; passport; customs.*
- Make pairs or small groups in which at least one person has flown by plane. Tell students that they will be flying to London on business. They must describe the different things that they will do before they arrive there, making at least one sentence for each word on the board, starting with: *We're going to buy the tickets.*
  The words could be used as follows:
  Buy plane tickets; pack bags; go to the airport; check in; go through security; go to the departure gate; get onto the plane; find your seat; fly; arrive; collect your luggage; show your passport; go through customs.

SPEAKING

1

- If you did the *Discussion starters* lead-in, you can go directly from that into this exercise.
- Ask students to take a minute and think of a journey they have had – perhaps one that was very boring or frightening or where something unusual or interesting happened.
- For this exercise, students can describe any journey; they do not need to focus on air travel. However, if you have a class (eg in a company) where you think that most students would have travelled by plane, you could ask them to speak about journeys by plane.
- You could put a few cues on the board: *ticket; cost; problems; other travellers; delays; mistakes; arrival.* These don't have to be discussed, but may suggest some ideas to students who can't think what to talk about.
- Pairwork. Students tell their partner about their journey.

VOCABULARY: air travel

1

- Students look at the three pictures and find the items that match the nouns in the box.

boarding card: picture C – the man is holding it
check-in: the whole place in picture C
overhead locker: picture A – above the passengers' heads
hand luggage: on the conveyor belt in picture B, and the man is carrying it in picture C
seat belt: picture A – the woman sitting at the front has one across her waist
security guard: the large man doing the body check in picture B

2

- Students must number the phrases in a logical sequence, starting with the example: *Book your flight ... .*

Correct order: 11, 1, 9, 3, 5, 8, 7, 2, 10, 6, 4

LISTENING

These are three dialogues about getting on a plane. In the first, a man checks in for his flight. In the second, the same man goes through customs. In the third, the man is on the plane and is being served by a flight attendant.

1

- Students look at the pictures again, one at a time. Elicit accurate descriptions of what is happening in each. Students should use the phrases from exercise 2 in the vocabulary section.
- This task partly involves students changing the grammar of the phrase from the imperative to third person, eg *The passengers are waiting for take-off.*

Stronger classes

- Ask what the man did 20 minutes before each picture (this provides an opportunity to practise many more vocabulary items).

Picture A:
The passengers are sitting in a plane. They've got their seatbelts on and they're waiting for take-off. Some people are reading. An air stewardess is serving drinks and a passenger's drink is falling over.

Picture B:
A man is going through security. A security guard is checking that he isn't carrying anything dangerous on him. His bag is going through the X-ray machine.

Picture C:
A passenger is checking in his luggage. He is holding his boarding card. The check-in assistant is telling him the time to go to the departure gate.

2 🔊 1.43–1.45

- Students listen to the recording and decide which dialogue (1–3) goes with which picture (A–C).

1 C   2 B   3 A

🔘 **1.43–1.45**

---

1   C = Check-in assistant   P = Passenger

C: Good afternoon, sir.

P: Oh, hello. I'm, er, sorry, but I can't find my ticket. It's here somewhere. Ah, here it is. Sorry about that.

C: That's all right. <u>Could I see your passport, please?</u>

P: Yes, sure. Here.

C: Thank you. That's fine. Do you have any bags to check in?

P: No, no, just this. Er, excuse me, but <u>I wonder if I could have a window seat, please?</u>

C: Certainly, yes. 23A. That's a window seat.

P: Great. Thanks.

C: You're welcome. Your plane is boarding in fifteen minutes at twelve-thirty. So, you'd better hurry, I think. It's departure gate 41, boarding at twelve-thirty.

P: OK, right, thanks. Bye.

C: Have a nice flight.

2   S = Security guard   P = Passenger

S: <u>Can you put any metal objects, money, keys and so on, here, please, sir, and walk through the gate?</u>

P: And the phone?

S: Yup, that too.

S: <u>Can you stand over here and put your arms like that, please?</u>

P: Yes, yes, all right, but I'm in a hurry. I've only got five minutes.

S: It's the Dublin flight, is it?

P: Yeah, Dublin. Please. <u>Could you hurry up a bit?</u>

S: Now, <u>could you just empty your pockets, please, sir?</u>

S: Ah, it's a metal comb. I'm afraid you can't take that on the plane, sir. It's a dangerous object.

P: OK, OK. You keep it. Now, can I go?

3   F = Flight attendant   P = Passenger
**   P2 = Second passenger**

F: Would you like anything to drink?

P: Yes, <u>I'd like a coffee, please.</u> Strong. No sugar, no milk.

F: Certainly, sir. And for you, madam?

P2: <u>Just a glass of water for me, please.</u>

F: Certainly, madam. That will be four euros fifty, please, for you sir.

P: It's not free? Oh, right, well, here you are. <u>I'd like to have a receipt, please.</u>

F: I'm afraid we don't do receipts, sir. Here's your water, madam.

P2: Many thanks.

P: I'm sorry, but <u>can I get past?</u> I need to go to the, er, the, you know …

P2: The toilet? Yes, sorry, of course.

P: Sorry.

P2: Mind out! Watch your coffee!

P: Aaagh! That's hot!

---

3 🔘 **1.43–1.45**

- This listening exercise is focussed on accurate listening for small items of detail (eg time, number, place name, etc) rather than general points.
- Students listen to the recording again and answer six multiple-choice questions.

1 b	2 c	3 c	4 a	5 a	6 a	7 c

FUNCTIONAL LANGUAGE: requests
PRONUNCIATION: intonation

❯ *Language reference, Student's Book page 54*

1

- Check that students know what a *request* is (ie asking someone to do something). Ask students to look at audioscripts 1.43–1.45 on page 137 and find a request. If it is correct, ask them to underline it.
- Students can work in pairs to find and agree all other requests in the audioscript. When they have found a number, students should look at the table on the opposite page. There are a number of incomplete possible responses. Students use the audioscript to help them complete the gaps.

> **Requests**
> See audioscripts 1.43–1.45 on this page for requests which are underlined.
> **Responses**
> *Agreeing to the request:* sure; of course; certainly
> *Not agreeing:* I'm afraid that … ; I'm sorry, but …

2

- Students look at the dialogue. Point out the grammar mistake and the correction in the first line: *I like* corrected to *I'd like*. Students read the text, find five more mistakes and correct them.

> 1   I'm afraid ~~but~~ <u>that</u> we're not serving. / I'm ~~afraid~~ <u>sorry</u> but we're not serving.
> 2   I'<u>m</u> afraid that's not possible.
> 3   Could you ~~to~~ fasten your seat belt …
> 4   I wonder if <u>I could</u> go …
> 5   But can you ~~being~~ <u>be</u> quick …

Language notes: requests & orders

- The dividing line between *request* and *order* may be hard to decide. A lot depends on the context and the intonation. If the word *please* is added, an order can often be changed into a request.
- A *request* is usually polite and gives the other person a choice as to whether they do what is asked. They could agree to the request or not. An *order* is when you tell someone what they must do – and you expect them to do it (because of your relative positions, ages, etc).
- In the audioscript, some phrases, eg *Put your arms like that*, seem to be more of an order than a request – but students could argue that they count as requests.
- Another arguable one is *That will be four euros fifty please, sir* (ie I'd like you to pay me 4.50 euros.), which is a formal request for the customer to pay for the goods requested.
- *Just* in *Could I just have …* means *only*, eg I <u>only</u> want a coffee – nothing more.

3 & 4 🔘 1.46

- This exercise focusses on intonation. Ask students to read the introductory information and tell them that each sentence will be said twice. They listen to the two versions of the first sentence and say which version is more polite. Do the same for the second sentence.
- Ask students to work out exactly what it is about the pronunciation that makes a difference. (Answer: *Different intonation. The rude version is flatter or rising. The polite version has a falling intonation.*) Play the sentences again if students are not clear about the differences.

- Play the recording one more time and ask students to repeat the sentences, first chorally, then in pairs to get further practice.

💿 **1.46**

> **Polite:** Excuse me, could I have a coffee, please?
> **Rude:** Excuse me, could I have a coffee, please?
> **Polite:** Can you stand over here, please?
> **Rude:** Can you stand over here, please?

5 💿 **1.47**
- Students listen to seven requests. They mark them with a tick if they are polite, or a cross if they are not polite.

2	✗ rude	4	✓ polite	6	✗ rude
3	✓ polite	5	✗ rude	7	✓ polite

💿 **1.47**

> 1 Excuse me, can I have a window seat, please?
> 2 Could I get past?
> 3 I wonder if I could have another glass of water, please.
> 4 Can you sit down?
> 5 I'd like a black coffee.
> 6 Could you put your bag up there, please?
> 7 Can I see your passport, please?

6
- Pairwork. Students practise reading the dialogue from exercise 2. Remind them to pay attention to getting the intonation right.
- This is an important exercise for the teacher to monitor. While students are practising, go around the groups and give feedback specifically on intonation. If appropriate, model more polite intonation yourself and get students to repeat it.

> ### ■ Methodology Builder 16
> ### Practising functional language with situational dialogues
>
> - *A good way to provide further practice of functional language is to prepare and teach short dialogues that include some of the target items. Here are some ideas using requests from this unit.*
> - *First write a short dialogue. Here is an example:*
>   *John: Excuse me, I'd like these two postcards, please.*
>   *Sally: Certainly. That's £1.30.*
>   *John: And could I have two stamps for Japan?*
>   *Sally: Sorry, I'm afraid that we haven't got any stamps left.*
> - *Also think of some simple illustrations that could go with the story, eg for the first line: picture of John holding two postcards.*

> - *In class, draw the pictures on the board to help you establish the situation (John and Sally in a tourist shop) and then, line by line, elicit ideas from the students about what the characters are saying. Model each correct line yourself (perhaps with slightly exaggerated intonation) and then get students to repeat each line, chorally and in pairs. Slowly build up the dialogue in this way, line by line, with enough repetitions that students get to know it by heart. When they know the whole dialogue, get them to practise it together in pairs.*
> - *NB The idea of this activity is to give students lots of practice rather than just to input the words of the dialogue. Make sure they say the lines many times (not just once or twice). Help students not to get bored with these repetitions by adding new challenges (like working on stress, intonation, saying it faster, etc).*

7
⊙ *Communication activities, pages 129 & 131*
⊙ *Methodology Builder 8: Roleplay, page 27*
- Pairwork. Students read their cue cards and do the roleplays.
- Students should change roles for the two roleplays, so that each student in a pair gets a chance to play both attendant and passenger.

Extra practice: requests & orders
- Hand out five small slips of paper to each student. Ask students to write a request or order on each piece of paper. All requests and orders must be things that people could actually do in the classroom. It's probably a good idea to check an example or two on the board, eg *Please give me Ahmed's coursebook* or *Sit underneath the table.*
- When students are ready, collect in all the slips and mix them up. Redistribute them, five to a student. Tell them not to look at them yet.
- Ask students to walk around the room and mingle with the other students. When they meet someone, they turn over their first slip of paper and say the request or order to the other person, who follows the instruction. When this has been done, the other student takes this slip of paper.
- Students continue to move around and meet others, using the new slips as well as ones they originally had.
- At the end of the activity, you could briefly review the most unusual or interesting requests or orders.

IF YOU WANT SOMETHING EXTRA ...
⊙ Straightforward Teacher's Resource Disc *at the back of this book*

Answer key

5 REVIEW
● *Student's Book page 152*

1

Possible answer:
He is arriving in Krakow on Friday evening and then he is going to look for a hotel. On Saturday morning, he is going to visit the city centre, the cathedral and the castle. At 12.30, he's meeting Grzegorz for lunch at the Wierzynek restaurant. On Saturday afternoon, he is going to catch a minibus to Wieliczka salt mine. On Saturday evening, he is going to a Beethoven concert at the Philharmonica Hall. Then he is going to find a good restaurant in the old town and have dinner. At 9.30 on Sunday, he is visiting the Historical Museum with Marek. Then he is having a picnic with Marek and his friends in the Wolski Forest. At 18.30, he is flying home.

2

1 How is he getting to Krakow?
2 He is catching a plane from Heathrow.
3 Is he going to buy a guide book?
4 No. His friends are going to show him around.
5 Is he going to visit other Polish cities?
6 No. He isn't going to have enough time.
7 Why is he going to stay only two days?
8 He's going back to Poland next year.

3

1 I'll just check.
2 I'll have
3 I'm going to have
4 We'll do
5 is coming

4

1 hearing
2 to spend
3 to climb
4 to do
5 to take
6 to go
7 hearing

5

1 B: ... and I wonder if ~~could I~~ I could change it for a flight in the evening.
2 A: Could I ~~to~~ see your ticket and passport, please?
3 B: I'd like to take the last flight, please.
4 A: I'm afraid ~~but~~ that (*or* ~~afraid~~ sorry, but) the last flight is fully booked ...
5 B: Can I ~~having~~ have a window seat, please?
6 A: ~~I sorry~~ I'm sorry, but I can't do that ...

6

1 facilities
2 location
3 shower
4 twin
5 lift
6 air conditioning
7 room service

5 WRITING
● *Workbook page 73*

Model answer

Dear Kate,

Thanks for your email. I'm really happy that you're coming. You're going to love South Africa!
I am free on Wednesdays, so I can meet you at the airport and take you to your hotel. Could you email me your flight number and the time of your arrival, please?
You asked about a hotel by the sea. I know a very friendly place on the sea that isn't expensive. It's called the Dolphin Inn and it costs about £40 a night with breakfast. It's very central and the manager is a friend of mine. The rooms aren't big but they're very comfortable.
I'd love to go diving while you are here. The sea is very cold in Cape Town but I know some good places we can drive to.
I'd also like to show you around the city. Perhaps on your first weekend we could go up to the top of Table Mountain together?
I'm really looking forward to meeting you.
Best wishes,

Silvia

6A | Junk food

WHAT THE LESSON IS ABOUT

Themes	Elvis Presley
	Junk food
	'Theme' restaurants
Speaking	Pairwork discussion: planning a theme
	restaurant
Reading	*Eating the Elvis Presley Way.* Web book
	review: Elvis Presley's diet
Vocabulary	Food
Grammar	Modifiers

IF YOU WANT A LEAD-IN ...

Introducing the theme: food I like

- Ask students to work in pairs and imagine that they are very rich. Tell them that they can afford to buy and eat any food they want. Ask them what they would choose and to list five typical meals they would have.
- When students have finished, go straight on to *Vocabulary* exercise 1. Ask them if any of the items in the food list are in their list. This can start a good discussion about *luxury* food, *good* food and *junk* food.

Pre-teach a key word: junk food

- Tell a short personal anecdote:
  I came home last night – but I was so tired. I was hungry but there was no food at home. So I went out to (say the name of a well-known local fast food outlet) *and I had* (say a typical junk food meal you could eat there).
- Ask students what they think about your choice of food. Collect some notes on the board to describe it, eg negative: *high in (saturated) fat, sugar and salt; not many fresh vegetables; lots of chemicals and additives; have little real nutrition; bad for your heart; very high in calories and very fattening*
  positive: *tasty; quick; cheap; eating it occasionally won't harm you; good if you are a bad cook; better to have fast food than no food*
- Ask how students can describe such food. Elicit or teach *junk food.*

VOCABULARY: food

❯ *Language reference, Student's Book page 65*

1
- Students tick the items from the list that they can see in the photos.

Items in the photos:		
eggs	hamburger	cookies
pizza	ice cream	potato chips
French fries	donuts	hot dogs

Weaker students

- Ask students to write a name label next to each photo.

2
- Students can work in pairs to discuss which of these foods they eat and how often. (Encourage them to be honest!) Ask them to consider which are really junk foods.

There is no single correct answer here.
Probably *eggs* would be considered the *best* food by most people as they are entirely natural.
Pizza is arguably a reasonably healthy food.
Many doctors would consider *French fries* quite unhealthy and *donuts* the least healthy food, as they are very high in fat and sugar.

Language notes: junk food vocabulary

The shopping list was written in the US (American vocabulary and spelling).
- The term *French fries* is widely understood and used in the UK, although *chips* is more commonly used.
- *Potato chips* are called *crisps* in the UK.
- *Hamburgers* are also called *beefburgers* (though both are made of beef, not ham).
- *Cookies* in the UK is restricted to American-style *biscuits*, such as *chocolate chip cookies*. In the US, *biscuit* refers to a small round soft bread roll.
- *Junk food* is food that doctors or scientists say is high in sugar and salt, cooked in saturated fat and has very poor nutritional value or may be harmful and unhealthy.
- *Snack food* is food that we eat between meals. It is usually a small amount of food. It often refers to packaged savoury snacks such as potato chips, peanuts, etc.
- *Fast food* is food that is made quickly and can be bought quickly and eaten quickly. It needs no cutlery and is often sold in disposable packaging rather than on a plate. It's sold at takeaway restaurants, eg Indian, Chinese.
- *Healthy foods* are foods that doctors or scientists say are good for your health, eg *muesli* and *yoghurt*. This is a little different from ... *health foods,* which are foods that are specifically marketed as being good for you.

Cultural notes: junk food

- In recent years, more people have become aware of the dangers of poor diets. In many countries, there has been a rise in the number of overweight and obese people, and fast food companies have been criticized for encouraging this. Many burger and chicken takeaway restaurants offer 'super-size' menus (extra large quantities of food).
- Fast food, such as hamburgers, fried chicken and chips, are often high in salt and fat and can have many additives (chemicals, flavourings, etc). The fizzy cola drinks that go with burger meals are high in sugar.
- As a result of criticism, many fast food restaurants have started to sell healthier food (eg salads).

Web research task

❯ *Methodology Builder 1: Using Web research tasks, page 2*

- Guess which of these meals has the most calories (the most energy) then research to find out if you were right.
  1 Burger with French fries and a large cola
  2 Your favourite pizza
  3 American fried chicken with chips
  4 A peanut butter sandwich
  5 12 doughnuts
  6 A 300 gram bar of chocolate

Web search key words
- name of food *calories* (eg *burger calories*)

READING

This is a book review of a new biography of Elvis Presley, which specifically looks at Elvis Presley's unusual and unhealthy eating habits.

1
* Students look at the photo of Elvis Presley. Ask them what sort of food they think he ate. If any of the students already know some information about his eating habits, listen to what they say, but don't acknowledge if their ideas are correct or not.

Alternative procedure
* If you think your class is not very familiar with Elvis, introduce this exercise in this way: Write *Elvis* on the board. Ask if students know who he was. If they suggest correct ideas, add notes to the board. If not, tell them some information yourself – see *Cultural notes* on this page.

2
* Students read the text and mark the most surprising information. This is not a fast reading exercise. Students are encouraged to read carefully and really understand the meaning.
* Draw students' attention to the American spellings, *favorite* and *donuts*, in the text.

> *There are no correct answers. Some of the most extraordinary facts in the text are:*
> He had breakfast at five o'clock in the afternoon.
> He ate snack food all day every day.
> He had a fridge in his bedroom.
> He ate lots of chocolate and donuts on his way to see the President.
> His last meal was ice cream and cookies.

3
* Students read the text again and answer the true/false sentences. They then correct the false sentences.

> 1 F (There are over 400 books about Elvis and some of them are about Elvis and his food.)
> 2 T
> 3 F (His eating problems started when he became famous.)
> 4 F (He ate breakfast at 5 o'clock in the afternoon.)
> 5 T
> 6 T
> 7 F (He ate chocolate before meeting the President.)
> 8 F (Elvis loved ice cream.)

4
* Students find a suitable adjective from the text for each gap. Tell students that each sentence contains clues so that they can find the right word. Point out that the words are not in this order in the text.

1	famous	3	favorite	5	sad
2	fascinating	4	hungry	6	serious

5
* If students have not discussed Elvis much so far, ask them to tell you other things they know about him.
* Students say why they think Elvis had eating problems, ie what were the causes? Students may speculate that Elvis's unhappiness was because he was very famous; had too much money; had few friends; had lost contact with reality; was addicted to food, etc.

* You could ask if students see any similarity with problems of more contemporary pop, film or sport stars, eg Michael Jackson.

Extra task: reading
* Ask students to look back at the reading text and collect all references to food – including complete phrases, not just single words, eg *boring school dinners.*

Extra task: writing
* Ask students to work in pairs and compare their own eating habits with Elvis's. Then tell them to write a short comparison of their diet and Elvis's. Put these notes on the board and tell them to include them in their description:
    When you have meals
    What kind of food you typically eat
    What's in your fridge
    What snacks you like
    How often you eat fast food

Cultural notes: Elvis
* Elvis Presley was born in 1935 and died in 1977. He was one of the first and most important rock and roll singers. He made many films and frequently performed in the US, especially in Las Vegas. He had a huge influence over other performers and is still very popular nowadays. His most famous songs include: *Heartbreak Hotel, Blue Suede Shoes, Jailhouse Rock* and *Love Me Tender*. Many of Elvis's fans refuse to believe he is dead and there are often reports of people seeing him shopping in supermarkets, driving a taxi, etc.

Web research task
❯ *Methodology Builder 1: Using Web research tasks, page 2*
* Here is a short list of words and names. Find out what connection they have with Elvis's life.
    1 GI (Answer: *Elvis was a GI soldier in 1958.*)
    2 Blue Suede Shoes (Answer: *This was one of his most successful hits.*)
    3 Las Vegas (Answer: *Towards the end of his life, Elvis regularly appeared at Las Vegas.*)
    4 impersonators (Answer: *After his death thousands of people have made a career as Elvis impersonators, ie people who pretend to be him.*)
    5 Ed Sullivan (Answer: *He appeared on the Ed Sullivan TV show.*)
    6 Sun (Answer: *He made his first record for the Sun label.*)
    7 Tom Parker (Answer: *He was Elvis's manager.*)
    8 Tupelo (Answer: *He was born in Tupelo, Mississippi.*)
    9 Graceland (Answer: *Elvis lived in a house named 'Graceland'.*)

Web search key words
* *Elvis biography*

GRAMMAR: modifiers

Grammar box
❯ *Language reference, Student's Book page 64*
❯ *Methodology Builder 22: Using Grammar boxes, page 106*
* You could ask students to think of different possible adjectives to complete the examples, eg *quite happy; fairly tired; very angry; really sad; extremely hot.* (Students will find more adjectives in exercise 1 below.)

Alternative procedure
* You could introduce these items in a different way. Draw a line on the board and write *weak* at one end

and *strong* at the other. Write up the modifiers in a random order on the board. Ask students to decide where they should go.

1
• Students look back at the text and underline every modifier that they find. They then add the modifiers to the examples in the grammar box.

> quite normal
> fairly sad
> very different
> really serious
> extremely interesting / unhappy

2
• Students put the modifiers in the right position in the sentence. If students are not clear how to do this, remind them that the modifiers come in front of adjectives and to find the adjectives in each sentence first.

> 1 ... very busy   4 ... fairly expensive
> 2 ... a bit slow   5 ... quite nice
> 3 ... really good   6 ... extremely popular

3
• Ask students to think of places in their own town where they can get food. Write the names of some on the board.
• Students work on their own and write six sentences about these places, using modifiers and the adjectives in the box.

Language notes: adverbs of degree

• Modifiers, such as those in this lesson, are classified in grammatical terms as *adverbs of degree.* They can change the strength of the adjective that follows. In many cases they show that there is a different quantity of something.
• Some adjectives are gradable, ie we can use modifiers to vary the strength of the adjective, eg *quite hot, very hot,* etc. Other adjectives (not dealt with in this unit) already represent an extreme and are ungradable, eg *freezing, terrible.* It's usually considered wrong to say ✗ *quite freezing,* ✗ *very terrible,* etc.
• We can arrange modifiers on a diagrammatic line as follows:

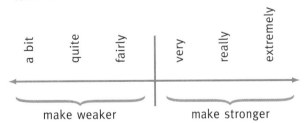

• Your students might ask about other modifiers, not introduced in this lesson. Common ones are: *rather; awfully; so; incredibly.*
NB In US English *real* can be used instead of *really,* eg *It was real cold in there.*

Extra practice: modifiers

• Tell students that you will ask them a number of questions and they should note their answers as you ask each question. Tell them they should not write the questions down but they must include a modifier in each answer.
• Do the first question as an example if you wish, checking people's answers before you move on.

• At the end, students can compare their notes with each other. Ask students if they can remember the question for each answer.
> 1 *If you don't eat for two days, how will you feel?*
> 2 *Look at the photo of Elvis on page 56. How do you think he feels?*
> 3 *What do you think about Elvis in that photo?*
> 4 *How would you feel after eating a burger?*
> 5 *How would you feel after eating six burgers?*

SPEAKING

1
• Write *'theme' restaurant* on the board. Ask if students know what this means. Discuss their special features, whether students have been to one and if they liked it.

Cultural notes: 'theme' restaurants

• A *'theme' restaurant* is one where the decoration, menu, staff uniforms, etc are all connected with a particular topic, eg rock and roll; tropical island; wild west, etc.
• Although they sounded like a great idea in the early 1990s, 'theme' restaurants have not been as successful as expected and many have lost money. The most famous chain, the *Hard Rock Café,* has been more successful than many.

2
• Pairwork. Students work in pairs and plan a 'theme' restaurant. Tell them to work through the questions one by one and write clear answers to each question. This will help them organize their planning.

3
❯ *Methodology Builder 24: Student presentations, page 118*
• Students prepare a presentation for the whole class. At the end, a vote could be taken on the best. You could have a range of winners so that more pairs get acknowledged, eg for the most unusual idea for a theme; the most disgusting food idea; the best restaurant name; the cleverest idea for the uniform; the best presentation, etc.

Debate

• Write one or two debating questions on the board. Divide students into *for* and *against.* Allow some time for students to prepare a short statement of their views. For example:
> 1 *Should junk food advertisements be banned from children's TV?*
> 2 *Some 'theme' restaurants invest too much money on great pictures on the wall and not enough on great food on the plates.*
• Ask two *for* and two *against* speakers to sit at the front. Tell them first to give the class their views (like short speeches) then invite others to join in the discussion. At the end, take a vote to see what opinions people have.

Web research task

❯ *Methodology Builder 1: Using Web research tasks, page 2*
• Find out at least five different 'themes' that have been used in 'theme' restaurants. Which one would you choose if you opened a restaurant?
Web search key words
• *theme restaurants*

IF YOU WANT SOMETHING EXTRA ...

❯ Straightforward Teacher's Resource Disc *at the back of this book*

6B | Slow food

WHAT THE LESSON IS ABOUT

Theme	Traditional food: fast food
Speaking	Pairwork: discussing a food quiz
Reading	*Are you a foodie?* Quiz about eating habits
Listening	Radio programme: an interview about 'slow food'
Vocabulary	Adjectives (opposites)
Grammar	Comparatives
Pronunciation	Word stress 1

IF YOU WANT A LEAD-IN ...

Pre-teach a key word: foodie

- Ask students what they think a *foodie* is. Let students guess various answers. After hearing a few ideas, explain that a foodie is someone who really enjoys food, has a serious interest in food and likes to try different kinds of food.
- Write *Foodies ...* on the board and ask for a suggestion of a way to end the sentence so that it says something a foodie might like or do. Elicit an answer and write it up, eg *Foodies like to eat in exotic restaurants.*
- Ask students to work in pairs and think of five more sentence endings. When they have some good ones, pairs meet up to form groups of four to compare their sentences and discuss.

Test before you teach: comparatives

❯ *Methodology guidelines: Test before you teach, page xxi*

- Draw the following simple pictures on the board:

- Ask students to write three sentences saying some ways in which they think Judy and Sylvia are different. Don't explain any grammar or tell students how to make the sentences.
- When they have finished their sentences, explain that you won't look at them now, but later in the lesson.
- The picture may lead to sentences such as:
    Judy is taller/happier/poorer than Sylvia.
    Sylvia is shorter/unhappier/richer than Judy.
    Sylvia's hat is bigger/more/less attractive than Judy's hat.
    Judy's car is less expensive/older/smaller than Sylvia's car, etc.

SPEAKING

1

- Pairwork. Students work in pairs. They read the quiz questions aloud to each other and compare answers.
- There are no correct answers. When they check their scores, students will find out how much of a foodie they are.

2

❯ *Communication activities, Student's Book page 128*

- Students check their scores.
- Students discuss in pairs if they think the descriptions are true for them.
- Feed back with the whole class. Find out who has the highest foodie score.

Language notes: food vocabulary

- A *microwave dinner* is a *ready-made meal* that usually comes in a single box and can be cooked entirely in a microwave oven. Typical UK microwave dinners are *lasagne, curry, shepherd's pie* (meat with mashed potato). Microwave dinners are also known as *TV dinners*.
- A *recipe book* is a book that tells you how to cook different meals. It lists ingredients and instructions for cooking.

LISTENING

This is a food programme on the radio, in which a reporter goes to Italy to speak to a food expert about how some typical Italian food has changed because of the introduction of bottled sauces, which she says are full of chemicals and artificial preservatives. She promotes the Slow Food movement, which claims that fresh local ingredients taste much better and are much healthier for you.

1 💿 1.48

- Tell students that they are going to listen to an interview on a radio programme about food in Italy. Focus their attention on the list of four programme titles and ask them to guess which title they think will be the best one (with reasons). Then play the recording and allow pairs to discuss which title was the best.

Title 3 is best as it describes Maura's general philosophy.
Titles 1 and 2 are not discussed.
Students might argue for 4 as there is some discussion of the two kinds of pasta.

💿 1.48

J = Jilly   M = Maura
J: Today, we are in the market in Bologna, perhaps the food capital of Italy, but if you come to Bologna hoping to eat spaghetti Bolognese, traditional, authentic spaghetti Bolognese, you will be disappointed. No spaghetti Bolognese in Bologna? I asked Maura Giuliani, an expert on Italian food, to tell me more. Maura, why is there no spaghetti Bolognese in Bologna?
M: Well, we have a dish called 'tagliatelle al ragù', and the sauce is very similar to the sauce you call Bolognese. But we use tagliatelle, not spaghetti. Spaghetti comes from the south of Italy and we do not use it here.

J: How strange!

M: Well, the sauce called 'Bolognese' that you buy in a bottle from a supermarket is even stranger.

J: In what way?

M: Well, it has a very complicated recipe, tomatoes, of course, salt and sugar, but lots of other things and most of them are completely artificial; chemical tomato flavour, artificial colours, and so on. When we make ragù sauce at home, we use local, fresh ingredients. We make a simpler, more traditional recipe. It's healthier for you, and it tastes better. But, and there is a but, it's a lot slower to prepare. Good food is slow food.

J: Yes, absolutely. I understand that you call yourself a 'slow foodie'. What exactly does that mean?

M: Slow Food is a movement that started in Italy back in 1986, but now has members in over one hundred countries. Who are we? Well, it's quite difficult to say because all sorts of people are slow foodies. It's easier to say who we are not …

J: And you are not fast food!

M: Right. We're not pasta sauce in a bottle, we're not a quick hamburger and chips for dinner. We think food is more important and more interesting than that. We're interested in making food more enjoyable, more traditional, slower, better.

J: Maura, thanks. After the market, Maura took us to a demonstration of pasta making.

2 🔊 1.48

- Before students read the passage, point out that *Rome* is underlined because it is not correct. The corrected sentence is written above the passage.
- Tell students to listen to the recording again and find more mistakes.

> … <u>eat</u> spaghetti Bolognese (don't eat)
> … spaghetti <u>is a speciality of Bologna</u> (is not a speciality of Bologna)
> … It is very <u>similar to</u> ragù sauce (different from)
> … Ragù is <u>quicker</u> to prepare (slower)
> … started in <u>France</u> (Italy)
> … in <u>1997</u> (1986)
> … in about <u>twenty</u> countries (fifty)

3

- Students should give reasons for their opinions about slow food.
- Students work on their own to list traditional foods from their countries, and which region they come from.
- Students can then work in pairs to compare and discuss their lists. Explain any unknown items. Discuss if they are slow or fast foods.
- Feed back with the whole class. Collect some of the most interesting foods from different pairs.

Extra discussion

- *Do some countries or cultures have healthier/better food than others? Which national food is the healthiest?*
- *Is a healthy diet boring? Which is the tastiest healthy food?*

Web research task

> ◯ *Methodology Builder 1: Using Web research tasks, page 2*

Choose one of these tasks:
- Find out if people are interested in slow food in your country.
- Find out some more examples of slow food.
- Choose a slow food meal that you would enjoy for your dinner.

Web search key words
- *slow food*

VOCABULARY: adjectives (opposites)

1

- Tell students that all the gapped words in columns A and B are in the audioscript on page 138.
- First let students try the task in pairs.
- When students have completed all the words, they match up the adjectives.

> 2 interesting – e boring
> 3 complicated – b simple
> 4 artificial – a natural
> 5 strange – d normal
> 6 healthy – g unhealthy
> 7 modern – f traditional

Stronger students

- You could replay the audio so that students can spot other possible words.

2

- Explain the example to the students. Tell them that the word *traditional* can be used as an adjective in front of all five nouns and that these are all common collocations.
- Students work on their own and find appropriate adjectives from exercise 1 to go with the other nouns.
- Point out to students that various answers could be possible, though in each question, one or two adjectives go together much more commonly with the nouns. Tell them that many adjectives go together well with a number of the nouns, but not with all, eg *interesting* goes well with *baby; diet; food* and *lifestyle*, but less well with *eating*.

> *Possible alternative answers are shown in brackets:*
> 2 interesting
> 3 fresh
> 4 healthy / unhealthy

3

- Students work on their own. They should write down five nouns that collocate with the adjective they have chosen.
- Pairwork. Students read the nouns (but not the adjective) to their partner, who tries to guess the original adjective.
- It may help to give students an example: *party; film; exercise; time; story* all go with *boring* (as well as *interesting*).

Stronger classes

- Hand out randomly scraps of paper with adjectives already written on. (This will force students to look at all the words and not avoid ones they consider more difficult.)

PRONUNCIATION: word stress 1

1 🔊 1.49

- Students listen to the recording and decide how many syllables are in each of the nine words. For each word, they should write a number (eg *1, 2, 3,* etc). If students are not clear about the idea of syllables, point out the example: *heal / thy* /ˈhelθi/.

Stronger classes

- Ask students to work through the list first and decide how many syllables they think there are before listening to check.

> *The pronunciation given here is the usual pronunciation for British English.*
> 2 difficult /ˈdɪfɪkəlt/ – three
> 3 enjoyable /ɪnˈdʒɔɪəbəl/ – four
> 4 modern /ˈmɒdən/ – two
> 5 important /ɪmˈpɔːtənt/ – three
> 6 complicated /ˈkɒmplɪkeɪtəd/ – four
> 7 simple /ˈsɪmpəl/ – two
> 8 artificial /ɑːtɪˈfɪʃəl/ – four
> 9 traditional /trəˈdɪʃənəl/ – four

2 & 3 🔘 1.49

- Encourage students to say the word out loud, to help them mark the main stress in each word.
- Students listen again to check.
- Students may need to listen more than once to hear where the stress is. Typically this is quite hard for some students to catch.

Weaker classes

- Students may need to listen again while doing the task, rather than waiting to check when they have finished.

🔘 1.49

1 healthy	**4** modern	**7** simple
2 difficult	**5** important	**8** artificial
3 enjoyable	**6** complicated	**9** traditional

Language notes: word stress

- A *syllable* is quite hard to define (though easier to recognize). It usually has a vowel sound – or a vowel sound with consonants on one or both sides.
- All words have a fixed *stress* pattern. This is always heard when the word is pronounced on its own. Word stress is always centred on a *vowel* sound.
- In exercise 2, students are asked to find the main stress in each word. Some longer words have a main and a secondary stress, but at this level it is sufficient to focus on just the main stress. For example, *complicated* actually sounds something like

  □ □□□
  complicated
  (For the purposes of the exercises in this lesson students should find the main stress in each word.)
- When a word is spoken in a sentence, the word stress pattern may be diminished or seem to vanish.
- Do not confuse *word stress* with *prominence* (ie *sentence stress*).

Extra practice: quiz on syllables and stress

- Make teams of three to six students. Draw four columns on the board and ask each team to copy this. Write numbers 0–10 down the left hand column.
- Do an example first. Say *presenter*. Ask students to help you spell the word on the board (write it in line 0, column 2). Ask how many syllables there are in that word. (Write 3 in line 1, column 3.) Ask what the stress pattern is in the word. Put the diagram in line 1, column 4.

	word	syllables	stress
0	presenter	3	□■□
1			
2			

- Teams: Tell students that you will read some more words and they should agree their team answer, and then write the spelling, the number of syllables and the stress pattern for each word. At the end, swap papers between teams and go through the answers on the board, while teams mark each other's papers.
- This is the list of questions and answers. NB When you want to read the questions, read only the words in column 2!

	word	syllables	stress
0	presenter	3	□■□
1	following	3	■□□
2	restaurant /ˈrestrɒnt/	2	■□
3	spaghetti	3	□■□
4	information	4	□□■□
5	chocolate /ˈtʃɒklət/	2	■□
6	recipe	3	■□□
7	sauce	1	■
8	questionnaire	3	□□■
9	interest /ˈɪntrəst/	2	■□
10	comparative	4	□■□□

> ### ■ Methodology Builder 17
> ### ■ Working with word stress
>
> - *Work on raising student awareness before expecting students to be able to produce word stress successfully.*
> - *Useful activities are ones that ask students to listen, count syllables and decide where the stress is.*
> - *It's important that students recognize and can understand how dictionary entries mark stress, but for classroom work, you may find other more memorable ways of showing stress.*
> - *Teachers have different ways of doing this. Here are some popular ways:*
>   *Mark stress on words that you teach by adding squares over the stressed syllables or sticking on cut-out coloured squares.*
>   *If you have access to a box of Cuisenaire rods, children's building bricks or other suitable objects, use these to build stress patterns on a table or shelf.*
>
>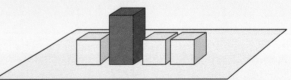
>
> - *Whatever method of showing stress patterns you use, there are a number of tasks you can do with them:*
>   *Say a word. Ask students to make the stress pattern.*
>   *Say a word. Make a pattern yourself. Ask students to say if your pattern is correct or not.*
>   *Ask students to choose and say a word. You make the pattern you hear. Students say what it is.*
>   *Make a stress pattern. Ask students to find five words with that pattern.*

GRAMMAR: comparatives

Grammar box

❯ *Language reference, Student's Book page 64*
❯ *Methodology Builder 22: Using Grammar boxes, page 106*

1
- Ask students why *traditionaler* has been crossed out in 1. Elicit that it is incorrect and that the right answer is *more traditional*.
- Students work on their own and correct the mistakes in questions 2–7.
- Students work in pairs and check their answers.

> 2 ~~healthyer~~ healthier
> 3 more interesting <u>than</u> English
> 4 ~~hoter~~ hotter
> 5 is ~~gooder~~ better
> 6 ~~more later~~ later
> 7 ~~more cheaper~~ cheaper

2
- Students work on their own and choose a possible comparative to fill each space. NB The answer may be more than one word.
- Pairwork. Students compare answers in pairs.

> *Possible answers:*
> 1 tastier
> 2 less healthy
> 3 more popular
> 4 healthier
> 5 more expensive
> 6 more popular

3

❯ *Communication activities, Student's Book page 130*

- Students work on their own. They find as many differences in the pictures as they can.
- Pairwork. Students work in pairs to discuss and compare what they have found. They should explain the differences, using comparatives.

Stronger classes

- You could teach *less* as well as *more*, eg *Fish and chips is less popular now than in the last century.*

Language notes: comparatives

The main problems students have with comparatives tend to be with spelling, and correctly choosing the *-er* form or the *more* form.
- There is no precise rule about which adjectives take *-er* and which take *more*. The best guideline is the one given in the Student's Book, ie longer adjectives, although teachers need to be careful as this is only an approximate guide. In fact many, but not all, two-syllable adjectives take *more*. Almost all three-syllable adjectives take *more*. A few adjectives can take both, eg *more polite/politer*.
- *Than* is often left out when we speak (because it is usually obvious what we are comparing), eg *That table's longer* rather than *That table's longer than the others.*

The commonest mistakes made by students are:
- Using both *more* and *-er* ending, eg ✗ *He was more angrier than the manager.*
- Omitting *than* or using another word, eg *as* instead of *than* – ✗ *The princess was more beautiful as an angel.*
- Using a superlative instead of a comparative, eg ✗ *This flat is biggest than mine.*
- Using *very*, eg ✗ *The sky is very darker than last night.*

IF YOU WANT SOMETHING EXTRA ...

❯ *Straightforward Teacher's Resource Disc at the back of this book*

6c | Coffee break

WHAT THE LESSON IS ABOUT

Theme	Coffee drinking: history and interesting facts
Speaking	Pairwork discussion: talking about your favourite drinks
Reading	*Coffee Break.* Magazine article about coffee drinking habits
Grammar	Superlatives
Did you know?	Starbucks™

IF YOU WANT A LEAD-IN ...

Introducing the theme: coffee & tea

- Write *coffee* and *tea* on the board.
- Ask students to choose which of these two drinks they like best, and then write five true sentences about themselves. Each sentence must have their word (*coffee* or *tea*) in it.
- When ready, get all the *coffee* people to come together in groups of five or six on one side of the room, and all the *tea* people in groups on the other side.
- Bring the class back together. Ask people to read out some of their true sentences. Others must say if the words are true for them as well. The *tea* and *coffee* groups each try to choose five sentences that are true for almost everyone in their group.
- If you use this lead-in, move directly on to *Speaking* exercise 1.

Pre-teach a key word: addict

- Bring in (or draw on the board) a bar of chocolate.
- Draw a sketch of *Chikako*. Explain that she eats chocolate all the time – for breakfast, lunch, supper, between meals. She can't stop. If she doesn't have chocolate, she feels ill! Ask if students know a word to describe her. Write on the board: *She's a chocolate ... .*
- Elicit or teach the word *addict*. Check by asking students for suggestions of other things you can be an addict of. Possible answers: *drugs; TV; video games*, etc.

Stronger classes

- Students may be interested to know that the ending *-holic* has a similar meaning. So, for example, we can talk about an *alcoholic* and a *chocoholic*. People like to invent new *-holic* words, eg *webaholic, filmaholic, danceaholic*.

Test before you teach: superlatives

- Ask students to tell you some foods. Quickly write them all on the board as they call them out, eg *potatoes, burgers, pizza, chips*, etc.
- When you have about ten to fifteen items, write up this table:
  What was/were the ... FOOD you've ever eaten?
- Show students how to make a sentence by adding a word in the space and choosing a food from the list, eg *What was the largest pizza you've ever eaten?* Don't explain the grammar needed for the space.
- Put students into pairs. They think up a sentence using the pattern and ask their partner, who tries to answer truthfully.

- When they have spoken for a while, ask pairs to recall the funniest or most interesting questions and write them down. Tell them you'll check the grammar later in the lesson.

SPEAKING

1

- Pairwork. Students discuss the four questions about drinks.

Language notes: coffee collocations

- The following items commonly collocate with *coffee*:

(verbs)	(adjectives)	
have a (cup of) ~	*black* ~	
pour a ~	*white* ~	
buy a ~	*milky* ~	COFFEE
sip a ~	*strong* ~	
drink (a lot of) ~	*weak* ~	
	Turkish ~	

	(nouns)
	~ *cup*
	~ *bar*
COFFEE	~ *shop*
	~ *house*
	~ *bean*

- In coffee bars people often ask for:
  an espresso (very short strong coffee)
  a cappuccino (espresso coffee with frothy milk)
  a latte (longer coffee with a lot of milk)

READING

This magazine article is about coffee – its origins; the different varieties of coffee there are; famous addicts and how fashionable it has become.

1

- Explain to students that all of the things shown in the photos are in the text.
- Students read the article and decide which photo goes with which paragraph.
- Before students read the article, you could ask them to guess how the photos might be connected to the coffee theme. Ask students to cover up the article, leaving the photos visible. Elicit ideas for each photo, eg *I think it's an explorer who brought coffee from America to Europe.* Don't tell anyone if their ideas are right or wrong (as they will find out by reading).

1 B	2 D	3 E	4 C	5 A

2

- Go through the example with the class.
- Students read the article again and write a sentence about each country.
- Warn students to think carefully about their sentences. It won't always work if they just copy out phrases directly from the article.

2 Finland is the biggest coffee-drinking country in the world.
3 Balzac and Voltaire were French coffee addicts.
4 Indonesian Kopi Luwak is the most expensive coffee in the world.
5 Jamaican Blue Mountain coffee is said to have the best taste.
6 Coffee bars in the United States serve 'coffee art'.
7 The word *coffee* comes from Turkish.

3
• Students find words in the article that fit the definitions.

1 originally   3 bean
2 varieties   4 addicts

Weaker classes
• If you think students might not understand the task, read out these examples and elicit answers:
  A small animal with fur, usually living in a home, or a larger wild animal. (Answer: *cat*)
  Part of the human body. It often means 'love'. (Answer: *heart*)

Web research task
❯ *Methodology Builder 1: Using Web research tasks, page 2*
• Find five reasons why coffee may *not* be good for you.
Web search key words
• *coffee facts*

GRAMMAR: superlatives

Grammar box
❯ *Language reference, Student's Book page 64*
❯ *Methodology Builder 22: Using Grammar boxes, page 106*

1
• Students look back at the article on page 60 and find six examples of superlatives.

the biggest (coffee-drinking country)
the most important (coffee-producing countries)
the best (taste)
the most expensive (coffee)
the most famous (coffee addicts)
the most fashionable (coffee bars)

2
• Students work on their own and write in the correct form of the superlative adjectives. They should not answer the questions yet.

1 The most expensive   5 The longest
2 The best   6 The most popular
3 The largest   7 The heaviest
4 The biggest   8 the oldest

3 & 4 **1.50**
• Pairwork. Students work in pairs to answer the quiz.
• Students listen to the recording to check their answers.

1 c   2 a   3 c   4 b   5 c   6 c   7 a   8 c

 1.50

1 The most expensive meal in the world was in Bangkok in 2007. For their food and drink, the 15 diners paid £150,000.
2 The best caviar in the world comes from the Caspian Sea.
3 The largest restaurant in the world is in Syria. It seats 6,000 people.
4 The biggest donut in the world was made in 2007. It was 6 metres in diameter.
5 The longest hot dog in the world was made in Japan. It measured 600 metres.
6 The most popular fast food in Britain is sandwiches.
7 The heaviest tomato in the world weighed 3.5 kilograms.
8 Scientists think that the oldest soup in the world was made from hippopotamuses.

Web research task
❯ *Methodology Builder 1: Using Web research tasks, page 2*
• Ask students to check on the internet to see if these records have been overtaken since the Student's Book was published.
• Find another amazing food record.
Web search key words
• *longest hotdog record*
• *most expensive meal record*

5
• Pairwork. Students work in pairs and write down a list of about five to ten cafés, bars, hotels, buffets, etc that they know in the locality.
• When pairs have a list, they make some true sentences about these places. The words in the box are ideas, but students do not have to use these.

Language notes: comparatives & superlatives
Many students find it helpful to record (and remember) word lists of adjectives, including the comparative and superlative forms. For example:

happy	*happier*	*the happiest*
bad	*worse*	*the worst*

Here are a few extra points that you might want to know:
• We use *the* in almost all superlative sentences, though there are some cases where it isn't needed. At this level it's probably best to tell students that they should use *the* in every case until they learn about cases where it isn't necessary. If the superlative is followed by *of*, then you must use *the*.
• Typical follow-on phrases after a superlative are *in the world* and *I've ever + past participle*, eg *It's the smallest church in the world* and *That's the worst meal I've ever eaten.*
• We can use superlatives on their own without a noun, eg *This café's the best!* (the best café/the best café in this area/the best café that I know, etc).
• We can use the comparative (as well as the superlative) to compare more than two things or people, eg *Jamaican Blue Mountain has a better taste than Kenyan or Brazilian coffee.*
• Sometimes people use superlatives to compare just two things, eg *This cake's the best.*
Typical student mistakes are:
• using *most* and *-est* in the same sentence, eg ✗ *That was the most loudest concert I've ever seen.*
• omitting *the*, eg ✗ *It was biggest in the world.*

- mixing elements of comparatives and superlatives together, eg ✗ *She was most happier.* ✗ *Which road was the longer?*
- using an incorrect follow-on phrase, eg ✗ *He's the fastest 100 metre runner of the world* and ✗ *That's the tastiest meal I ever eat.*

DID YOU KNOW?

1

- Ask students if they have heard of Starbucks™ and tell them to read the short text.
- They can discuss the three questions in small groups.

Cultural notes: fast food chains

- **Burger King**™ is one of the biggest burger chains in the world. It began in Miami in 1954 and now has about 12,000 restaurants in over 60 countries. Their most famous product is *The Whopper* – a burger sandwich. It was the first burger restaurant to offer *drive-thru* service.
- **McDonalds**© began in California in the 1940s. In 1963 the clown character Ronald McDonald was introduced to publicize the company. Their most famous product, *The Big Mac* (a sandwich with two burgers), was introduced in 1968. *The Happy Meal* was introduced in 1979. It targeted children and offered food and drink with a specially made toy.
  You can find McDonalds© in over 120 countries. Menus are adapted for local culture, conditions and tastes.
- **Domino's Pizza** is a pizza delivery company founded in Michigan in the US in 1960. It is the second largest pizza chain in the US and operates in about 60 countries.
- **Häagen Dazs**® was a New York family-run ice cream business dating back to the 1920s. The company established a reputation for quality and innovative flavours. Their products are now available in over 50 countries.
- **Kentucky Fried Chicken**™, now known as KFC, was founded by Colonel Harland Sanders and has sold chicken since 1939, using a 'secret recipe', which even nowadays is very carefully protected. It sells over a billion chicken dinners per year.
- In recent years some new fast foods have become popular in the US and Britain. Many of these are dishes from various ethnic groups. For example:
  kebabs (Turkish meat and bread)
  bagel (small circular bread roll with various fillings)
  sweet and sour pork (Chinese takeaway restaurants have been popular for many years. This dish is one of the best sellers.)
  blini (Russian pancakes, often served with caviar)
  tortilla (Mexican bread, often filled with meat)
  curry (spicy Indian food, especially popular in Britain)

Extra discussion

- *All the food companies named in the exercise are US in origin. Why do you think the American foods have been so successful? Is it the taste? The convenience? Or just the marketing?*
- *People talk about globalization. Is the influence of US food on the world a positive thing or not?*
- *Which foods from the students' own culture could become popular around the world (like burger and pizza)?*
- *Which of the fast food types mentioned in this unit is the healthiest? The least healthy? The tastiest? The most expensive? The most disgusting?*

IF YOU WANT SOMETHING EXTRA ...

❯ Straightforward Teacher's Resource Disc *at the back of this book*

6D | Class meal

WHAT THE LESSON IS ABOUT

Theme	Restaurants
Speaking	Discussion: talking about restaurants in your town
	Pairwork roleplay: in a restaurant
Listening	A phone call: making a restaurant reservation
	Informal dialogue: a dialogue in a restaurant
Vocabulary	Eating out
Functional language	Making a reservation in a restaurant
Pronunciation	Emphatic stress

IF YOU WANT A LEAD-IN ...

Discussion starters: restaurants

> *Methodology Builder 15: Using Discussion starters, page 63*

- *Do you like going to restaurants? Why? Is the food the most important thing? Or is the atmosphere more important?*
- *If you rarely or never go to restaurants, why? Is it bad value for money? Do you find the food disappointing?*
- *Do you think there should be entertainment while you are eating? If yes, what kind?*
- *What is a perfect waiter like? Should he/she always be polite? What is the worst thing a bad waiter can do?*
- *Is it important to book a restaurant or is it OK just to arrive?*

SPEAKING

1
- Pairwork. Students look at the five types of restaurants and discuss the questions with a partner.
- Ask students as a whole class if they have eaten these types of food and which they enjoy best. Check which ones they can find in their town.
- If there are no restaurants of this type where you live, ask your students why they think this is. Is it a taste that will not appeal locally?

Alternative task

- It's possible that students in your class won't know any (or all) of these and/or may not go to restaurants at all. In these cases, ask students if they know what kind of food is associated with each culture. Use *Italian* as a worked example (Answer: *spaghetti, lasagne, pizza*).
  Possible answers:
  French (long loaves of bread; croissants; cheese; snails; frogs; herbs; sauces; wine)
  Chinese (rice; chicken; beef; noodles; sweet and sour sauces; soy sauce; 1,000-year-old eggs)
  Indian (curry; rice; lentils; tandoori chicken; chapati)
  Mexican (chili; beans; tortilla; tacos)

2
- Elicit students' opinions about local restaurants.

Younger classes

- Students, especially younger ones, may not know much about restaurants. In this case, the task can be done on the basis of what they have heard other people say, or what they can guess, rather than on their own experiences. You could suggest one or two yourself and elicit intelligent guesses about how good they are.

3
- Students discuss which place they would choose for a class meal and why.
- Explain to students that a *class meal* is a meal for the whole class to go to and eat together. It may be a celebration (eg of a birthday) or just for the fun of being together.

VOCABULARY: eating out

> *Language reference, Student's Book page 65*
1
- Ask students some questions about the advertising card for *La Vie en Rose* restaurant, to clarify what kind of place it is.
  1 *Is this a fast food or luxury restaurant?* (Answer: *luxury – it's five stars!*)
  2 *Is it an Italian restaurant?* (Answer: *no – French*)
  3 *Are the cooks from that country?* (Answer: *yes*)
  4 *What kind of atmosphere does it have?* (Answer: *romantic*)
  5 *Where is the restaurant?* (Answer: *near the river on Bridge Street*)
- Students look at the bill and elicit that it's for a meal at the restaurant. Ask them how many people had the meal (answer: *two*).
- Students find the words in the restaurant bill for each of the definitions (1–6). Go through the example with the class and point out that the number of spaces matches the number of letters in the word.

1	*waiter*	5	service charge
2	dessert	6	main course
3	starter		
4	set menu		

2
- Students can work in pairs to compare prices of the items on the bill with typical prices locally.

Language & cultural notes: restaurants

- *Dessert* is not the same as *desert*! Your students are very likely to mix these up!
  Dessert (usually uncountable) has double *s* and has word stress on the second syllable. It is pronounced /dɪˈzɜːt/ or /dəˈzɜːt/.
  A *desert* (countable) like the Sahara or the Gobi, has one *s* and stress on the first syllable. It is pronounced /ˈdezət/.
- *House red* means a low-cost red wine recommended by the restaurant. (There might also be a *house white.*) The word *house* is sometimes used formally to refer to the restaurant, eg 'Mushroom dishes are the speciality of the house'. Restaurant owners sometimes offer their customers 'a drink on the house' (ie a free drink).
- A *tip* (not in this exercise) is the voluntary gift that a customer gives to a waiter or waitress because he/she is pleased with the service.

- A *service charge* is added to your bill by the restaurant. It's usually between 10% and 15%. It is still (in theory) voluntary, and a customer can decide not to pay it if he/she considers the service poor.
- A *set menu* is a small selection of dishes chosen by the restaurant, and is usually a cheaper alternative to choosing from the whole menu.
- *À la carte* (from the French for *from the menu*) is when you choose from the whole menu, when each item has a separate price.
- *La Vie en Rose* is French for *pink-coloured life*. It was the name of a song made famous by French singer Edith Piaf.
- *A party* is a formal term given to a group of people who go to a restaurant or book something else together. This is a special meaning of the word. It doesn't mean there will be music, dancing, balloons, etc!

LISTENING & FUNCTIONAL LANGUAGE 1: making a reservation

In this listening, a student called Betty Mayer rings *La Vie en Rose* restaurant and books a table.

1 **1.51**
- Go through the booking form at the top of the page with the students. Establish that the form would be filled in by a receptionist or waiter when a customer phones to make a booking.
- Students listen to a woman making a telephone booking and fill in the form as if they were a waiter taking the booking.

> Customer name: Betty Mayer
> Number of people: 10
> Day: Friday
> Time: 9.00

 1.51

> **S = Student   W = Waiter**
> **W:** Hello. *La Vie en Rose*. Can I help you?
> **S:** Er, yes, good afternoon. I'd like to book a table for Friday, please.
> **W:** Certainly, madam. For how many people?
> **S:** There'll be ten of us.
> **W:** Yes, that's fine. What time would you like? We open at seven.
> **S:** Oh, no, not seven. Nine. Nine o'clock, if that's possible, please.
> **W:** Yes, certainly, we can do that for you. So, that's a large table for ten at nine o'clock on Friday. Could I take your name, please?
> **S:** Yes, the name's Mayer. M-A-Y-E-R. Betty Mayer.
> **W:** OK, I've got that, Ms Mayer. We look forward to seeing you on Friday evening.
> **S:** Great. So, er, yes, we'll see you on Friday. Bye.

2 **1.51**
- Students listen again and underline the best word for each question. Tell them that they need to find the exact word from the dialogue (not *any* possible word).

1	Can	5	do
2	book	6	take
3	There'll be ten of us.	7	got
4	would you like	8	look

3
❯ *Methodology Builder 8: Roleplay, page 27*
- Pairwork. Students work in pairs: one student is the customer and one is the receptionist. Ask students to use phrases from exercise 1 to roleplay booking a restaurant.
- You could allow some individual preparation time for students to look back over audioscript 1.51 and select a few more sentences they can use.
- You can insist that students change the time, day, number of people in the party, etc.

Extra practice
- To add variety, you could ask students to repeat the roleplay not on the phone, but as if they have just walked into the restaurant. Ask them to stand up, etc.

Stronger classes
- If the class is very strong, ask both the waiters and customers to include a problem. For example:
waiters: no space, restaurant closed for repairs, etc.
customers: vegetarians, must have table by window, etc.

PRONUNCIATION: emphatic stress

1 **1.52**
- As students listen to the phrase, draw their attention to the way that the speaker uses stress to emphasize. He is making a contrast between the two numbers – saying it's *not* one thing but it *is* another.
- Spend some time with this example, allowing lots of students to try it and get it right before moving on to exercise 2.

Extra practice: emphatic stress
- If you would like to offer more examples to your class before they try the exercise, you could read these out and ask them to repeat and say them to each other:
I gave it to Peter the <u>cook</u> not Peter the <u>waiter</u>.
You promised you'd buy me a litre of <u>juice</u> not a litre of <u>water</u>.
The report said she was a good <u>teacher</u> not a good <u>preacher</u>.
I said 'Do it in <u>class</u> not at <u>home</u>!'

 1.52

> Not seven. Nine.

2 & 3 **1.53**
- Ask students to work in pairs and practise saying the four comments. Students should take care to focus on getting the stresses in the right place and also getting them sufficiently stressed (ie loud enough and long enough).
- Students listen to the recording and check their answers.

 1.53

> 1 <u>Friday</u> evening. Not <u>Thursday</u> evening.
> 2 It's <u>Ms</u>. Not <u>Mrs</u>.
> 3 <u>Good</u>? It was <u>excellent</u>!
> 4 No <u>dessert</u>, thanks. Just <u>coffee</u>.

Language notes: emphatic stress

- This kind of stress is *prominence* (*sentence stress*), not *word stress* as looked at in the last unit. Prominence changes the meaning of a sentence.
- *Emphatic* means you use it *to emphasize*. In this unit, we are contrasting one thing that is wrong with another thing that is correct.
- To emphasize, we make a different stress pattern from normal in order to emphasize specific words.
- The stress falls on the syllable that is usually word-stressed in both the contrasting words.
- Students may find it easier to pronounce these if they notice that there is typically a small pause between the two parts of the communication, eg We said *Friday* evening … not *Thursday* evening. Encourage students to make sure they take this pause (and take a breath) as if saying two separate sentences.

LISTENING & FUNCTIONAL LANGUAGE 2: in a restaurant

> *Language reference, Student's Book page 64*

In this listening, Betty Mayer and her group arrive at *La Vie en Rose*. In the first extract, the waiter shows Betty to her table. In the second, the group order their food. In the third, the group talk about the food and ask for the bill.

1 🌐 1.54

- Elicit some descriptions about what is happening in the photo.
- Students listen to the three extracts and answer the questions.

```
1  no
2  two mixed salads; one soup
3  They thought it was very good.
```

🌐 1.54

```
W = Waiter   B = Betty   S1 = Student 1
S2 = Student 2   S3 = Student 3   S4 = Student 4
W:  Good evening, madam. Welcome to La Vie en Rose.
B:  Good evening. The name is Mayer. I have a reservation
    for ten people. Two of them aren't here yet, but they'll
    be here soon.
W:  Certainly, madam. Let me show you to your table. It's
    this way.
B:  Thank you.
W:  Can I take your coats?
S1/S2/S3:  Yes, thanks. / Thanks. / No, that's all right.
W:  Would you like something to drink? Or would you like
    to see the menu first?

W:  Are you ready to order?
B:  Yes, I think so.
S1:  Yes, for starters, I'll have a mixed salad, please.
S2:  And I'll have the soup, I think.
S3:  No starters for me, thanks.
S4:  Mixed salad for me, too, please.
W:  OK, so that's two mixed salads, one soup …
B:  Oh, and could we have a bottle of mineral water,
    please? In fact, make that two. One sparkling, one still.

S1:  Mmm, that was delicious.
B:  Yeah, really good. Marvellous.
S2/S3/S4:  Hmm, yes. / Excellent. / Fantastic soup!
S3:  And the service was good, too. He was ever so
    friendly.
```

```
B:  Well, shall we get the bill?
S1/S2:  Yes, let's. / Yes, let's do that.
B:  Excuse me. Could you bring us the bill, please?
W:  Certainly, madam. I'll get it right away.
```

2 🌐 1.54

- Ask students to listen again and decide the correct order for the sentences.

```
1  I have a reservation for ten people.
2  Let me show you to your table.
3  Can I take your coats?
4  Are you ready to order?
5  No starters for me, thanks.
6  Could we have a bottle of mineral water, please?
7  That was delicious.
8  Shall we get the bill?
```

Stronger classes

- Ask students to predict or recall the order before they listen.

3

> *Methodology Builder 8: Roleplay, page 27*

- Groupwork. Students work in groups to prepare and act out a restaurant sketch. Draw their attention to the useful phrases at the bottom of the page.
- Encourage students to look back at the audioscript for ideas about possible language.
- If you have time, it would be good to do this as a whole story, including the booking.
- Elicit some separate stages and write them on the board. For example:

Booking by phone	*Getting the meal*
Arrival at the restaurant	*Eating the meal*
Greeting	*Talking about the food*
Finding the table	*Asking for the bill*
Ordering drinks	*Paying*
Ordering the meal	*Leaving the restaurant*

Stronger classes

- Elicit some incidents or issues that could make the roleplay more interesting or funny. For example:
  The customers booked a table for ten but only three people have come. The waiter is a little unhappy.
  The customers ordered a vegetarian meal but there is meat in it.
  The bill is incorrect.
  The customers arrive an hour late and their table has been given to another party.
  One customer thinks that the meal is badly cooked and asks to speak to the manager.

Methodology Builder 18
Small bursts of democracy

- *Activities like the restaurant roleplay in this lesson may benefit from a rearrangement of seating (if possible) to make the room look more like a restaurant (or a train carriage, or a plane, or a hotel foyer, etc) though such changes can be noisy and lead to misbehaviour.*

- *Where possible, instructions can be integrated into the discussion in the lesson, eg once students (in normal seating) have prepared their roleplay, ask the whole class (in English) if they think it might be possible to rearrange the room to make it more restaurant-like – and how to do it.*
  Really listen and take note of their ideas. Rather than imposing your own solutions, try to get students to agree what is the best thing to do and how best to do it without undue noise and chaos or time-wasting.

- *In other words, make working with potentially problematic tasks part of the normal process and discussion in your class, rather than simply imposing your own solutions. Humans tend to be more engaged and interested when they have taken an active part in decision-making. Small bursts of democracy in class can help individual activities, as well as general motivation and interest.*

IF YOU WANT SOMETHING EXTRA ...

❯ Straightforward Teacher's Resource Disc *at the back of this book*

Answer key

6 REVIEW

❯ *Student's Book page 153*

1

1 expensive
2 boring
3 unhealthy
4 traditional
5 slow
6 empty

2

1 cheaper
2 more popular
3 better
4 healthier
5 bigger
6 more interesting
7 more important
8 easier

3

1 the best
2 the strongest
3 the worst
4 the busiest
5 the most expensive
6 the hottest
7 the calmest
8 the most famous

4

Students' own answers

5

The strange meals are: 2, 5, 6, 9

6

1 better
2 more authentic
3 slower
4 friendlier
5 the most fashionable
6 the loudest
7 the most uncomfortable
8 higher
9 the most unforgettable

7

1 a, b, d, e, h, i, j
2 c, f, g, k, l

8

1 h, d, a, e, i, b, j
2 c, k, f, l, g

6 WRITING

❯ *Workbook page 75*

Model answer

L'auberge de Richard is a small Swiss-French restaurant in a little village near Lake Geneva.
It's a family restaurant with a very warm, relaxed atmosphere. In winter there's a lovely fire and in summer you can eat outside in a beautiful garden. What I love about *L'auberge de Richard* is that all the food is local and fresh. The menu is very simple, but all the dishes are delicious. I usually start with the tomates farcies – roast tomatoes with herbs. The paté is also a very good starter. There are only really two main courses: roast chicken or roast lamb. I always have the chicken and it is fantastic. Both the lamb and the chicken come with rosti, a traditional Swiss potato dish. The house white wine is surprisingly good. For dessert, I strongly recommend the speciality: tarte a la crème.
The family that run the restaurant seem to love their work. The manager often stops to speak to the guests and waiters are very helpful. *L'auberge de Richard* is not a cheap restaurant but the prices are reasonable. It's a great place for Sunday lunch.

7A | Work experience

WHAT THE LESSON IS ABOUT

Themes	Jobs
	Meeting famous people
Speaking	Pairwork: describing and guessing jobs
Listening	Radio talk show: a radio programme about people who have met celebrities
Vocabulary	Work
Grammar	Present perfect simple
Pronunciation	/æ/ & /ʌ/

IF YOU WANT A LEAD-IN ...

Vocabulary game: jobs

• Write about fifteen letters of the alphabet randomly around the board (some letters can appear two or three times). Divide the class into teams. Ask the first team to think of a job name starting with one of the letters, eg *footballer*. If it's correct, write the job name on the board, give the team a point and cross out the letter. Then it's the next team's turn to think of a new job name (no job name can be repeated). As the game goes on, there will be fewer and fewer letters left. The game ends when all the letters are gone – or no one can think of any more possible jobs.

Discussion starters

❯ *Methodology Builder 15: Using Discussion starters, page 63*

• If students are employed, ask if they like or dislike their job. If your class is school-age or not employed, ask them what they think will be the good and bad features of working. List notes about positive and negative ideas on the board. For example:

Like ...	*Dislike ...*
getting pay	*low wages*
meeting people	*long hours*

• When the students have discussed their opinions with you, ask them to decide which column has the strongest arguments. Then ask students to work in pairs and discuss their own opinions for two minutes.

SPEAKING

1
• Students read the short text and guess the job.
• When students think they know who the person is, they tell the person next to them rather than call it out. Choose one student to say their answer to the class. Other students can confirm or challenge it. Alternatively, read the text aloud yourself and ask students to guess who you are.

> It's the President of the US.

Extra practice: speaking (1)

• You could use more than one example text to give extra practice. Here is one possible further text (to write up on the board or read aloud):

> *A lot of the time I work in a very, very small space, usually with a small number of other people. It's well paid but it's very dangerous too. Often we travel very fast. The view through the windows is amazing – you*

can see the whole planet! We work with very expensive equipment and computers. (Answer: *astronaut*)

Extra task: phrases about work

• Ask students to close their books. Write the words *work* and *deal* on the board. Ask if they can remember the words that came after these words in the text, ie
> work: *work for the government*; *work with lots of different people*; *work in a beautiful office*
> deal: *deal with everything*
If students can't remember, allow them to check back with the text.

• When the phrases are written on the board, ask if students can suggest any other words that could come after the first two words of each example:
> *work for ...* a good boss; my father; a large bank; the local council
> *work with ...* twelve other people; my husband; a team
> *work in ...* a large school; the capital; the head office
> *deal with ...* complaints; difficult people; emergencies

• When a number of examples have been collected, ask students to summarize the ways the prepositions *for*, *with* and *in* are used (see *Language notes* below).

Extra task: recording vocabulary in notebooks

• You could write up notes on *work* + preposition in a simple table such as the one below. This may help encourage students to write their language notes in a more effective way than the traditional long word list.

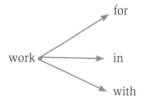

work	for	the government
		a difficult boss
	in	a fizzy drink company
		a large factory
		a small office
	with	nice people
		my father

Language notes: work

You ...
• *work for* ... a person or a company
• *work in* ... a place
• *work with* ... colleagues or other people
NB *Work in* also has another possible use:
• *work in* ... computing; agriculture; education; the construction industry
When you *deal with* something, it means that you take action to do something, especially finding answers for problems, complaints, difficulties, overdue work, etc.
> *The government must deal with unemployment.*
> *I had to spend all morning dealing with my emails.*
> *Will you deal with the visitors?*
• *Deal with it!* (Colloquial English – slightly rude or contemptuous. It means *It's your problem. I'm not going to help you.*)

Cultural notes: the US President & the Oval Office

Students might be interested to know the following facts about the US President and the Oval Office:
• The Oval Office is where the President meets with heads of state, diplomats, his staff, and other important people. When the President speaks on TV or radio, it is often from there.

- The first Oval Office was built in 1909, but it was moved in 1934. Each president has decorated the Oval Office to suit his own tastes.
- The Oval Office is in the west wing of the White House. It has four doors, one of which leads to the Rose Garden. There have been televised broadcasts from the Oval Office by the US President, but only at times of crisis or mourning. President Bush, for example, addressed the nation from the Oval Office after the terrorist attacks of 11 September 2001.

2

- Students use the text they read in exercise 1 as a model for writing their own 'job puzzle'.
- Ask students to first think of a job, and then individually write a new text. They can choose specific famous jobs (like the 'US President' example) or general jobs (like 'charity worker' or 'cleaner').
- Pairwork. Students read their text to their partner, who guesses the job. If there is enough time, let students read their text aloud in groups or to the whole class.

Weaker classes

- Point out that students can make a new description by copying the example text and changing a few key words. You could write this skeleton text on the board if you wish, for example:
  I work for … and I deal with … . I work in … in … . I work with … . It's … well-paid. It's … .
  Weaker students may benefit from working on the writing in pairs (rather than doing it alone).

Stronger classes

- Stronger students may want to write a more adventurous text, straying from the original model.
- When they have written their text, they read it aloud to their partner to guess the job.

VOCABULARY: work

> *Language reference, Student's Book page 75*

1

- Students choose the correct option in the four sentences.

1	jobs; careers	3	job; career
2	work; job	4	career; work

Cultural notes: donuts & dancing chickens

Donut
- *Donut* (see Lesson 6A) is the American spelling; the British is *doughnut*. It's a small fried, sweet cake made of dough. It's often sprinkled with sugar and may be covered in a variety of flavours. Sadly, it is very high in calories.

Dancing chicken
- When companies want to advertise themselves to passers-by on the street, they sometimes pay people to dress up in funny costumes and walk up and down to advertise their products. Brad Pitt's costume was a chicken. And it seems that he was expected to dance too.

2

- Students match the beginnings of the six sentences in column A to the correct endings in column B. They can check their answers in pairs.
- Go through the sentences with the students and clarify that the grammar allows only one possible answer for each question. For example, in question 2: You can be

fired *from* a job and fired *for* something wrong that you do. 2(c) is not a good answer because it is very unlikely that someone would be fired because they cleaned the tables!
- Write the table (from the *Language notes* on this page) onto the board and ask students to copy it.

A	**B**
1 in charge	… of something
2 fired	… from a job/a place
3 work	… as something
4 out	… of work
5 earn	… a living
6 responsible	… for something

1 e	2 d	3 b	4 a 5 f 6 c

Alternative procedure: weaker classes

- The task would probably be easier if you did any teaching input, ie about which beginnings and endings go together, before they tried to do the exercise. Try letting your class see if they can solve the problem first.

Language notes: work

- *Job* and *work* mean the same.
- *Job* is countable (ie we can say *I have three jobs*).
- *Work* is uncountable (ie we can't say ~~I have three works~~).
- Your *career* is the series of jobs you do through your life. It isn't a university course.
- You can get *sacked from your job* (asked to leave). In the US it's more common to say *fired from your job*.
- The following table shows some common collocations with these words:

A	well-paid summer temporary permanent	job	Nice Hard Temporary work Difficult
An	interesting		Interesting
A	long brilliant promising great	career	
An	interesting		

Extra practice: students make an exercise

- When they have finished exercise 2, ask students to make a new exercise themselves following the model. They should write six A and B half-sentences using the language items.
- When ready, they should try their exercise in pairs.

3

- Pairwork. Students look at the six topics. Give students some preparation time to think about how they will answer the questions before they start talking about them. You could remind them to use the vocabulary from the lesson so far.
- Focus students' attention on the example for the first topic, and the expressions *lost her job* and *get another job*.

Extra practice: vocabulary check

- Ask students some personal/general follow-on questions after the exercise. For example:
  Are you in charge of anything?
  Who's in charge of this school?
  Why are people fired from jobs?
  Do you know anyone who has ever been fired? Why?
  What do you work as?

What would you like to work as?
How do you earn your living?
How does Tom Cruise earn his living?
Who's responsible for the class register?
Who's responsible for planning the lesson?

Extra task: famous people quiz

- Many famous people worked in different jobs before they became famous. If your class are interested in this topic, you could set them this quiz.
- First, write all the correct answers (see below) on the board in a random order – plus a few false answers (eg *fireman*; *painter*; *builder*, etc).
- Read out the questions and get everyone to write down what they think is the best answer for each one.
- Alternatively, you could run it as a team competition where the first to answer correctly gets points.
  What did they do before they were famous?
  1 *Sean Connery* (Answer: *Milkman*)
  2 *Sting* (Answer: *Teacher*)
  3 *Bill Clinton* (Answer: *Professor of law*)
  4 *Rod Stewart* (Answer: *Grave digger*)
  5 *Brad Pitt* (Answer: *Delivered refrigerators*)
  6 *Jennifer Aniston* (Answer: *Waitress*)
  7 *Kate Winslet* (Answer: *Worked in a north London food shop*)
  8 *Danny DeVito* (Answer: *Hairdresser*)
  Bonus question: *Which star once went to a holy centre for a year while thinking of becoming a priest?*
  (Answer: *Tom Cruise* – this was mentioned in *Vocabulary* exercise 1, sentence 4.)

LISTENING

In this radio talk show, three people each talk about meeting a famous person while doing their job.

1 💿 2.1

- Students listen to three speakers on a radio talk show. They look at the list of six famous people and decide which speaker met which famous person.

> 1 Valerio met Madonna and Leonardo DiCaprio.
> 2 Michelle met Brad Pitt and Angelina Jolie.
> 3 Tony met Tom Cruise and Tom Hanks.

Optional pre-listening task

- Before you use the listening tasks in the book, you could set an additional pre-task to help students get used to the recording. Ask them to pick out all the famous people's names when they hear them on the recording.

 2.1

> **J = Jerry   V = Valerio   M = Michelle   T = Tony**
> J: Welcome back to *Tell Jerry*. Today we're taking calls from people who've met famous people in their work. Our first caller is Valerio from New Jersey. Valerio, hello. I understand you work as a chauffeur in New York.
> V: Yeah, that's right. It's my own company, man. I'm in charge.
> J: Valerio, have you ever met anyone famous in your work? I mean, have you ever driven any stars in your car?
> V: Yeah, I've had a few. Like, erm, I've had, like, Madonna, recently, Leonardo DiCaprio, yeah, I've had some.
> J: Have you ever spoken to any of them?
> V: No, I've never had, like, a real conversation. Just 'Good day, sir', 'Good day, ma'am', that kind of thing.

> J: OK, thank you, Valerio. And over to our next caller. On the line is Michelle from Santa Monica. Michelle, hi, what do you do for a living?
> M: Hi, Jerry. I'm a customer service assistant in a restaurant. You know, a waitress?
> J: Michelle, who have you met at work?
> M: Brad Pitt and Angelina Jolie. I've served Brad and Angelina.
> J: Hey, what were they like?
> M: I guess, they were, you know, kind of cute.
> J: Michelle, have you ever had any difficult customers? Difficult stars?
> M: I can't tell you that! I'll lose my job, I mean, I'll get fired if I tell you that!
> J: OK, Michelle, thanks. To our next caller. Hi, this is Jerry, who is on the line?
> T: Hello, Jerry. My name's Tony Lewington, calling from Manhattan.
> J: Good afternoon, Tony. Tony, that's not an American accent.
> T: No, I'm from Perth in Australia. I'm working for an ice cream shop in downtown Manhattan. Um, I've met a few stars in the shop. Tom Cruise, for example. And that other Tom, I can't remember his name, the one who was in *The Da Vinci Code*, Tom …
> J: Tom Hanks?
> T: Yeah, that's the one. Nice guy. He paid with a ten-dollar bill and told me to keep the change. Nice guy.
> J: OK. Thank you, Tony, from Perth in Australia.

2 💿 2.1

- Students listen to the recording again and decide which sentence is about which speaker. They write the correct person's initial in each gap.

> 1 T   2 V   3 T   4 M   5 M   6 T   7 M

3

- Students say if they have ever met anyone famous. Do this task fairly briefly with the whole class rather than in pairs, as it's unlikely that many students will have met anyone famous. If someone really has an interesting story to tell you, then you might want to allow a little extra time to hear it and ask questions.

GRAMMAR: present perfect simple

> ❯ *Language reference, Student's Book page 74*
> ❯ *Methodology Builder 22: Using Grammar boxes, page 106*

1

- Students write down the infinitive (base form) of the twelve past participles. When they have finished, they group the verbs into two sets: regular and irregular verbs.

> | | |
> |---|---|
> | done – do | hated – hate |
> | driven – drive | helped – help |
> | drunk – drink | met – meet |
> | earned – earn | served – serve |
> | eaten – eat | spoken – speak |
> | found – find | worked – work |
>
> *regular:* earned; hated; helped; served; worked
> *irregular:* done; drunk; driven; eaten; found; met; spoken

Language notes: present perfect simple

- Regular verbs are easily spotted, as the past participles all end in -ed. In most cases, removing the -ed will leave the infinitive. Although with *hate* and *serve,* we only take away the *d* as the infinitive ends in *e*.
- Irregular past participle forms are trickier and don't follow any consistent formation rules. Students have to learn the infinitive and other forms individually.

2

- Students complete the dialogue, putting the verbs in the past simple or the present perfect simple. Students need to notice the distinction between the beginning of the dialogue, when the talk is about general experiences at some unspecified time in one's life, ie present perfect simple, and the second half of the dialogue in which the talk focusses on a specific showing of the film last night, ie past simple.

> A: <u>Have</u> you ever <u>heard</u> of Thomas Mapother IV?
> B: No, I'<u>ve never heard</u> of him. Who is he?
> A: He's an actor. He'<u>s made</u> loads of famous films.
> B: Well, I'<u>ve never seen</u> a film with him in it.
> A: What about *Mission Impossible*? It was on TV last night. <u>Did</u> you <u>see</u> it?
> B: Yes, but that <u>was</u> with Tom Cruise.
> A: Ah, but Thomas Mapother IV is Tom Cruise's real name. He <u>changed</u> it before he got famous.

3

- Pairwork. Students practise reading the dialogue together.

4 & 5

- Groupwork. Students ask and answer questions using the prompts. They should ask follow-on questions if the reply is *yes*.
- The questions are likely to be present perfect simple *have you ever …?* questions.
- Ask some students to summarize for the class what they found out about the people they spoke to.

Alternative procedure

- You could organize this as a mingle activity. Ask everyone to stand up and walk around, asking questions to different people. Add this instruction: *If you find someone who says 'yes', write their name in front of the appropriate phrase in the book. Try to find two people for each sentence.*

PRONUNCIATION: /æ/ & /ʌ/

1 🔊 2.2

- Students choose and underline any six words from the list. They then listen to the recording and tick each word when they hear it. They should shout *Bingo* when they have heard all six of their words.
  This is a simple Bingo game based around pronunciation. But the game is made harder by the fact that many students find the sounds /æ/ and /ʌ/ very hard to distinguish, and also because some of the words on the recording are repeated.
- When someone shouts 'Bingo', it's important to take time to go through their list and hear what they think each word was.

🔊 **2.2**

> drunk, sang, began, run, drank, swam, ran, begun, sung, swum

2

- Pairwork. Students say one of the words from the table. Their partner must say if it's past simple or past participle. NB If there are any problems, it may be a speaking error, ie the student said the word badly, or it may be a listening error, ie the listener couldn't correctly distinguish the two forms.

Extra task: pronunciation

- If you would like to offer your students some more recognition/production exercises, you could use the following words:
  1 *hat* 2 *hut* 3 *bat* 4 *but* 5 *cat* 6 *cut* 7 *rat* 8 *rut* 9 *mat* 10 *mutt*
- Write the words (with numbers) up on the board and then randomly read a few aloud. Ask students to note which ones you read out.
- Then reverse the roles and get a student to read to you and see if they pronounce them well enough for you to hear the correct one.
- All the words are minimal pairs, ie the only difference between the pronounced words is the vowel sound. Don't worry too much about the meanings of the words – the important thing is the recognition of the different sounds and the association of sounds and spellings.

Language notes: /æ/ & /ʌ/

- Technically speaking, both phonemes /æ/ and /ʌ/ are made in a very similar location within the mouth. Thus they are intrinsically quite confusable. In addition, they may well not correspond precisely to vowels in your students' native language. Even very experienced non-native speakers of English sometimes have trouble pronouncing and distinguishing them.

IF YOU WANT SOMETHING EXTRA …

❯ Straightforward Teacher's Resource Disc *at the back of this book*

7B | Hard work

WHAT THE LESSON IS ABOUT

Themes	Getting and losing a job; being unemployed; salaries
Speaking	Pairwork: talking about your experience of work
	Pairwork: describing an imaginary life
Reading	*Life on the other side.* Magazine article: describing daily life of being unemployed
Vocabulary	Verb collocations (work)
Did you know?	Salaries in the UK

IF YOU WANT A LEAD-IN ...

Discussion starters

❯ *Methodology Builder 15: Using Discussion starters, page 63*

- *How many jobs have you had in your life? Which was the best? The worst?*
- *What makes a job interesting? Is it more important for a job to be interesting or to have a good salary?*
- *What do you think about job interviews?*
- *Is it OK to be unemployed? What problems do unemployed people have?*

Introducing the theme: introductory story

- Tell the story of an imaginary character's job history, including some vocabulary items from *Vocabulary & speaking* exercise 1 along the way, and checking understanding as you go. For example, tell the story of Mike leaving school, looking through job advertisements in the paper, applying, getting an interview, doing badly in the interview, finding another job advertisement, applying, getting the job, having training, etc. You may want a humorous last line to end the story, eg *He finally found his dream job – he became a juggler in the circus!*

Vocabulary revision: cough anecdotes

> ### Methodology Builder 19
> ### Cough anecdotes
>
> - *You could revise some important and confusable words (job; work; career; employed; promoted) by telling a 'cough' anecdote about yourself or an imaginary character.*
> - *Write up the target words randomly on the board. Start your anecdote, but when you get to one of these words cough loudly, eg I had a friend called Bob. He had an amazing < cough > at the bus station. Every time you cough, invite students to tell you which missing word from the board should go in the space.*
> - *Here is a possible anecdote:*
>   *I had a friend called Bob. He had a boring < cough 1 > at a bus station in London, selling tickets. He really wanted to start a < cough 2 > in accounting – but he needed some < cough 3 > so that he could earn some money. It was terrible < cough 4 > but he met lots of interesting people and he was soon < cough 5 > to Office Manager. It was good to be < cough 6 > but*

it was a boring < cough 7 >. One day he was so sick of it that he just got on a bus – and when it left the station, he went with it … all the way to Scotland! He is now < cough 8 > as a circus acrobat in Glasgow!
Answers:
1 job   2 career (or job)   3 work   4 work
5 promoted   6 employed   7 job   8 employed
- *When you go through the answers, point out how a goes with job and career (because they are countable) and some (or no article) goes with work (uncountable).*

VOCABULARY & SPEAKING: verb collocations (work)

1
- Students look at the diagram. Check that they understand what the diagram represents (a possible sequence of events in people's working life).
- Students put the sentences (a–f) in the correct places in the diagram.

> *Possible answers:*
> 2 a   3 e   4 d   5 f   6 c
>
> *You could 'go on a training course' <u>after</u> you get promoted!*

Alternative procedure
- Before students look at the book, write sentences a–f on cards and ask students to arrange them in any logical sequence that tells the story of one person's job history.

2 & 3 💿 2.3
- This short job history provides a brief revision of irregular past forms.
- Students read the short text *Back to Work* and choose the correct past verbs.
- Students then listen to the recording and check their answers. One playing of the recording should be enough.

2	left	6	went	10	got
3	had	7	got	11	lost
4	went	8	was		
5	applied	9	was		

💿 2.3

> When Pat Side's children finished their studies and left home, Pat wanted to find a job. She had no qualifications, so she went on a training course to become an assistant in a home for retired people.
>
> After the course, she applied for many different jobs. She went for a few interviews, but it was six months before she got a job. She was good at her work and, two years later, she was promoted to 'senior assistant'. She also got a small pay rise.
>
> Unfortunately, the home closed a year after that and Pat lost her job.

4
- Students work in pairs and talk about their own work history, using expressions from exercise 1.
- You could ask them to do the speaking activity as:
  a *monologue* (ie one person talks in a 'long turn' while the other listens).
  an *interview* (ie the listener asks questions such as *When did you finish your studies?* and the speaker answers and explains about their work).
  a *discussion* (ie both people speak and listen, comparing their experiences and finding similarities and differences).

READING

The first magazine article describes Pat Side and the difficulties of finding and keeping a job. A journalist met her and discovered they both had exactly the same name. They decide to swap lives and write about their experience. The second article is based on the journalist's experience of being unemployed.

1
- Ask students to read the first paragraph of the magazine article on page 69 and find out what the two women have in common.
- The concept of two women 'swapping lives' may be quite strange to students. Make sure they really understand the idea before you move on to the next tasks. You could check understanding by asking questions about the two people, eg (pointing at a photograph).
  1 *Who is this?* (Answer: *Pat Side*)
  2 *What does she do?* (Answer: *She's unemployed/ a journalist.*)
  3 *What do they have in common?* (Answer: *They are both called Pat Side. They are the same age.*)
  4 *What did they decide to do?* (Answer: *exchange lives*)
  5 *What does that mean?* (Answer: *Pat Side the journalist lived as if she was unemployed for four weeks.*)

> They both have the same name (Pat Side) and are the same age.

2
- Students read the article and answer the questions. They then correct the false sentences. NB The questions are about Pat Side (the journalist) in her temporary new life as an unemployed person.

> 1 T   2 T   3 T   4 F (She didn't enjoy it – she had to walk in the rain and cold, didn't get the jobs she wanted, and began to think it was a waste of time.)

3
- This task contains four extra sections that are missing from the article. Students read them and decide which section (a–d) goes in each of the spaces (1–4). You could let students try this themselves and then compare.

> 1 b   2 d   3 a   4 c

Extra task
- Students may want to discuss the reasons for the answers.
  1 b: because she has an interview and gets six application forms for jobs, and on day 4, she gets an interview for four of the jobs.
  2 c & 3 a: because ... 'half the month' is around 14/15/16 days. She doesn't have enough money on Day 15, so she

couldn't have received her unemployment benefit on Day 14.
4 d: because it's the end of the life-swap experience. 'Four weeks' was the period of time they agreed to exchange lives.

4
- Pairwork. Students discuss the questions in pairs.
- The answer to the first question is given in the *Cultural notes* below. You may want to research the answers to the second and third questions about your own country before the lesson, so that you can add some factual information to the students' speculations.

Alternative procedure
- As you may need to provide some information yourself, you could do these discussion topics as a whole-class activity.

Cultural notes: reading
- *Unemployment benefit* – this is a popular term for a government grant (now officially called the 'Job-seeker's allowance'). It is money the UK government pays (in certain conditions) for those who are out of work.
- *Cheque* – a paper document for transferring money from one organization or person to another. Benefits may be paid by cheque or directly into a bank account.
- *Five miles in the cold and rain* A mile is a lot longer than a kilometre (1 mile = 1.6093 kilometre), so that's quite a long walk! And English rain can be very cold (especially with the cold wind, which makes it feel worse).
- *Chips* are a very cheap food.

SPEAKING

1
- Allow students plenty of preparation time to write notes about a typical day in their new life.

2
- Pairwork. Students discuss their new lives with their partner. They should ask questions to find out more information from each other.

DID YOU KNOW?

1
- Pairwork. Ask students to look at the bar chart and discuss the four questions.
- You could let students have some individual thinking time first before they are asked to give any opinions.

Extra discussion
- *Do you think women and men have similar salaries?*
- *Should there be a minimum wage? Is it right that some unpopular jobs such as cleaners are paid very low salaries?*
- *Is it right that a pop star or a footballer can earn a normal person's yearly salary in a week?*

Cultural notes: UK Minimum Wage
- In October 2011, UK National Minimum Wage rates were £6.08 per hour for those aged 21 and above (the adult rate). It was £4.98 per hour for those aged 18–20.

IF YOU WANT SOMETHING EXTRA ...
- ❯ Straightforward Teacher's Resource Disc *at the back of this book*

7c | Job selection

WHAT THE LESSON IS ABOUT

Theme	Horoscopes about jobs
Speaking	Groupwork discussion: deciding what qualities are needed for different jobs
Reading	Magazine article: an article about horoscopes & work A magazine horoscope
Grammar	Present perfect simple with *already* & *yet*
Vocabulary	Adjectives & nouns (personality)

IF YOU WANT A LEAD-IN …

Pre-teach a key word: astrology (& astronomy)

- Although the word *astronomy* doesn't feature in the lesson, this is a common confusion (even among native speakers) and an interesting language point to put directly to students.
- Write the two words on the board and ask students in pairs to agree on the meanings (and difference in meaning) between the two words. After a minute or so, gather their ideas and confirm a correct answer. *Astronomy* is the study of space, planets, stars, galaxies, etc, in a scientific way, using telescopes and other equipment. *Astrology* is when people believe that the movement of planets and stars can tell you about a person's character, life and future. It is usually considered to be non-scientific.
- Write up a small table like this:
  Noun (thing)   Adjective   Noun (person)
  astronomy
  astrology
- Ask students if they know the *adjective* that goes with each word. Elicit answers and add *astronomical* and *astrological* to the table. Ask *who works* with the two subjects. Add *astronomer* and *astrologer* to the table.
- This little practice also helps prepare students for *Vocabulary* exercise 2, which also works on nouns related to adjectives.

Stronger classes

- With stronger classes, you might want to spend a little time exploring the adjectives, asking for examples of how they could be used, and typical collocations, such as: *an astrological chart*; *What astrological sign are you?*; *She joined an astronomical society in York.*
- Students might be interested to learn that the main use of *astronomical* is not to talk about space, but to talk about something that is very very large, eg *He earned an astronomical salary*.

Introducing the theme: star signs quiz

- This could be a quiz for individuals, pairs or teams.
- Ask students: *Can you remember the twelve star signs in your own language?* Ask them to write them down. Then ask students if there are any that they know in English. They then check with other students and try to get a complete list.

- Read out the following names and ask students to say which ones they think are the names of the English star signs.
  Aquarius, Capricorn, ✗ Vulcan, Scorpio, ✗ Fishy fishy, Taurus, Leo, ✗ BigMacus, Gemini, ✗ Apollo, ✗ Ariel, Cancer, Pisces, Virgo, ✗ Ursa Major, ✗ Saturnia, Sagittarius, Libra, Aries
  NB The ones marked with a cross are not real star signs.

Test before you teach: yet & already

❯ *Methodology guidelines: Test before you teach, page xxi*

- Prepare large sheets of A4 paper, each labelled in large letters with the names of towns: New York; London; Paris; Beijing; Nairobi; Moscow; Singapore. (If you are actually teaching in one of those places, substitute that place for another, eg Lisbon.)
- Place the sheets around the wall of the room, far-apart but visible to all students. Ask everyone to plan a journey around the room, visiting each 'town' in any order they like, eg New York then Nairobi, then Beijing, etc and write a list of town names in order.
- Write these part-sentences on the board:
  Have you been to xxx yet?
  Yes, I've already been to xxx.
  No, I haven't been to xxx yet.
- Don't explain anything about the grammar or say what *yet* and *already* mean if students ask.
- Demonstrate the activity first. Ask a student to start their journey, going to the first location (eg London) and then moving on to their second location (eg Beijing). Explain to the class that when you meet another student, you can only say sentences from the board – nothing else! Ask the student: *Have you been to London yet?* and help the student to respond: *Yes, I've already been to London.* Ask the student: *Have you been to New York yet?* and help the student to answer: *No, I haven't been to New York yet.*
- Ask everyone to stand up and *slowly* make their journey around the world. Remind them to talk to other travellers they meet and only use the items on the board.

READING

This article discusses how seriously horoscopes are taken by some people when making important decisions.

1
- If you used *Pre-teach a key word* or *Introducing the theme: star signs quiz*, you can continue from there straight into this discussion.
- Ask the class the two questions and briefly discuss their views.

Stronger classes

❯ *Methodology Builder 20: Playing devil's advocate, page 92*

- With stronger classes, you could introduce a more provocative edge to the discussion by 'playing devil's advocate', so long as you know your class well and get on with them, eg if your class mainly believes in horoscopes, take a strong anti-horoscope line, and vice versa. If they don't believe them, argue as if you are strongly in favour of them. NB Your aim is to provoke students into discussion, so don't get too carried away with your own performance!

Anti-views

But it's clearly nonsense, isn't it? How can anyone in the modern world believe in such a medieval idea? Will exactly the same things happen today to everyone who has the same star sign?

Pro-views

It's science. A lot of science isn't fully understood yet. Of course the planets can influence humans. Doesn't the Moon make the tides in the oceans? If it's nonsense, why do so many important people believe in it?

■ **Methodology Builder 20**
■ **Playing devil's advocate**

- *In everyday life, when someone plays devil's advocate, they pretend to have strong feelings about something, and disagree or argue with someone with the aim of trying to make the discussion more exciting and interesting. They are not stating their real opinions, but deliberately making an argument more interesting.*
- *This can be a useful strategy for promoting student talk in class. In a discussion, if you expect that everyone will have similar, uncontroversial opinions, play devil's advocate to stimulate strong responses.*
- *It's usually best to play devil's advocate seriously and straight-faced, ie don't wink, smile or give other clues that you are just playing a role; say things as if you really believe them.*
- *At the start of a discussion, make a single strong statement, eg I think smoking is very good for people – and just wait for students to react and argue.*
- *When you collect answers or feedback after an exercise, deliberately offer a wrong answer or two yourself. Don't signal that there is anything strange about this. Just wait for students to work it out and argue their case. This can add some extra challenge to an otherwise routine classroom task.*

2
- Tell students that they are going to read an article that has been torn out of a magazine. Ask if they can see any problems with the text; elicit or point out that some words at the beginning of some of the lines are not easy to read! Tell students not to worry about this just yet.
- Ask students to read the titles and guess which one will be the best summary of the article. When a number of opinions have been voiced, ask students to read the article quickly to decide which title is best.

Title 2 – Why you should read your horoscope

Language notes: reading

- Students may ask about *secret police*. In dictatorships and other countries with limited freedom, the secret police are people who find out about people who are against the government, and try to stop them. This is similar to the *secret service*, which is a government department in many countries used to protect the state and the leaders from terrorism, foreign spies, etc.

3
- Students can work in pairs and agree on what the first word is in each line.

For; minutes; time; studied; future
Like; people; presidents; successful; work; millionaires

Stronger classes
- Students decide whether the words have a capital letter or not.

4
- Students read the article again and complete the sentences with the missing words.

1	waste	4	application
2	believe	5	personality
3	decisions		

Extra task: reading
- Ask students to explain the meaning of *Millionaires don't use astrology. Billionaires do.*
  (Answer: *If you use astrology, it will make you more successful. Very rich people are very rich because they have used astrological information.*)

Extra task: vocabulary
- Ask students to find phrases in the text that mean:
  1 *very busy, overworked* (Answer: *there are a million things to do*)
  2 *prepare for something* (Answer: *get ready*)
  3 *read very carefully* (Answer: *study/studied*)
  4 *stop!* (Answer: *hold it!*)
  5 *here is an extra comment or question* (Answer: *by the way*)
  6 *you may not agree with this* (Answer: *like it or not*)

Cultural notes: horoscopes
- A horoscope can offer general information about personality, lifestyle, typical behaviour and about specific events that are predicted to happen.
- In a daily newspaper, it will usually tell you about predictions for things that will happen in the next 24 hours. In a magazine, the predictions will often be for a longer period, for example a week or a month.
- Most popular newspapers in Britain (such as the *Sun* or the *Mirror*) carry horoscopes, but more serious newspapers (such as *The Times* or *Independent*) do not.
- Horoscope writers get very high salaries – more than many famous reporters.
- It has been reported that Americans spend over $200 million every year on horoscopes.
- Scientific studies of large numbers of babies born at the same time show no obvious similar characteristics.
- Horoscopes seem to work because the writers use sentences that a large percentage of people will think is true about them. Examples are:
  You are someone who is often misunderstood by others.
  You have a warm heart.
  You often regret that you didn't say something important.
  Sometimes you are not sure if you have made the best decision.
  You want other people to like you.

GRAMMAR: present perfect simple with *already* & *yet*

❯ *Language reference, Student's Book page 74*
❯ *Methodology Builder 22: Using Grammar boxes, page 106*

1
• Students complete the dialogue with *already* or *yet*.

A: yet	B: yet
B: yet	A: already
A: already	

Language notes: already & yet

❯ *Methodology Builder 7: Using timelines, page 23*

• These two adverbs are often confusing for students. Both words indicate a time related to now.
Yet means 'not before now'. It shows that something has not happened before now, but you expect it to happen in the future, maybe soon.

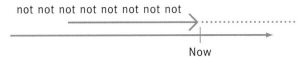

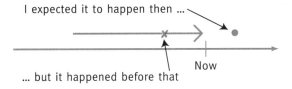

Already means 'before now'. It is used to show that something has happened (although perhaps people didn't expect it to happen).

• The most important guideline is given in the Student's Book: *Already* is almost always only used in positive sentences. *Yet* is mainly used in negatives and questions.
• Word order: *Yet* usually comes at the end of a sentence or phrase. *Already* usually comes after any auxiliary verb and in front of the main verb (except with the verb *be*, when it comes afterwards).

2
• Pairwork. Students read the dialogue and practise saying it more fluently and realistically.
• Before they start, ask students what the relationship between the people might be, what they are talking about and how they think the two people feel. The speakers might be parent and child, discussing school homework. Speaker A is probably impatient and a little angry. Speaker B is probably tired and unhappy. Being clear about feelings will help students to use appropriate intonation when they speak.

3
❯ *Communication activities, Student's Book pages 131 & 132*

• If you used the *Test before you teach* lead-in task, ask students if they can recall the exact three sentences used. If students didn't do the lead-in activity, you might want to do it now as a further practice activity.
• Pairwork. Students turn to their respective pages and ask and answer the questions.

4
• Write *Finish my studies* on the board. Ask students to think of something that is true about themselves using these words. Collect a few answers and check that students are taking the chance to practise using *yet* or *already*. Direct students to look at the example answer.
• Students can work in pairs and do the rest of the exercise orally together.
• Students can then repeat the task, this time writing down their own and their partner's answers.

VOCABULARY: adjectives & nouns (personality)

❯ *Language reference, Student's Book page 75*

1
• Remind students of the twelve star signs (*signs of the Zodiac*). Ask them if they know their own star signs. Let them check the sub-headings in the text at the bottom of the page if they are not sure, but discourage them from reading yet.
• Students think of three people whose birthdays they know. When they have thought of the people, they should read the appropriate parts of the text to see if the horoscope gives correct information or not.
NB Students are *not* asked to read the whole text – only those sections they need to.

Extra task: reading

• In order to give students a reason to read all the texts, you could ask them to check if any of the other star signs give a better character description of themselves than their own star sign text did.

2
• Students should complete the table with words from the horoscope.

1	ambitious	5	intelligence
2	emotional	6	patience
3	imagination	7	skill
4	independent	8	sensitive

Alternative procedure: stronger classes

• Stronger students could try to do the task before they check the text to see if they are correct.

Alternative procedure: weaker classes

• Draw a stick character like this one:

• Explain that the character has no friends and write up these two gapped sentences: (1) *Den is very …* (2) *His biggest problem is …*
• Elicit an answer to the first sentence, by reminding students that he has no friends. (*Den is very lonely.*) Tell students that the second sentence has a similar meaning and the missing word is similar to the word in (1). Elicit or tell students *loneliness*.

- Tell students that *lonely* is an adjective and *loneliness* is a noun. Ask if students can think of any other ways of describing people that have related adjectives and nouns. (Possible answers include: *happy/happiness*; *tired/ tiredness*; *angry/anger*; *hungry/hunger*.)
- Write the words up in a table on the board like this:

Meaning	Adjective	Noun
has no friends	lonely	loneliness
wants food	hungry	hunger

- Then work through the exercise together, filling in the chart for the adjectives and nouns. Students may find it helpful to use a dictionary when doing this task, as most adjectives can be found near their related nouns in alphabetical order.

Extra task: vocabulary

- As well as the items in exercise 2, the text includes many other ways of describing people (adjectives and chunks). Ask students to find some and, as they call out answers, write them on the board. (For consistency write them up in a *he/she* form.)

  She …

    is well-organized
    has very good people skills
    works better on her own
    gets bored quickly
    seems calm
    has natural intelligence
    is honest
    is worried
    is kind
    is strong
    is a good listener

- Students work in pairs. Ask them to describe other members of the class to their partner using these phrases. Remind them that they can use negatives as well, eg *He isn't worried.*

Language notes: adjectives & nouns

- *Ambition, emotion* and *skill* can all be used as C (countable) and U (uncountable) nouns. The (C) and (U) meanings are very similar and lead to few problems if they are mixed up.
  The (U) noun *ambition* refers to a general wish to be successful, whereas the (C) noun is for particular things you want to achieve.
  Emotion (C) and (U) both refer to feelings. Choose singular or plural depending on whether you wish to state that you have a general feeling or a range of different feelings.
  Skill (U) is your general ability to do something. *Skills* (C) are particular abilities in specific areas, possibly as a result of training.
- Depending on their first language, students may confuse *sensitive* and *sensible*.

SPEAKING

1

- Groupwork. Students decide what the most important qualities are for each job in the box. They should agree on the best star sign for each job and give reasons. Remind students that they can use vocabulary from the horoscope.

> *Many answers are possible. These are suggestions:*
> Good *lawyers* are intelligent but not too emotional because they have to work with complex problems, but mustn't become personally involved.
> Good *police officers* must be honest because they are responsible for keeping the law. They must also have very good people skills because they work with members of the public in difficult situations.
> Good *sales people* are patient because they mustn't seem to be in a hurry. They must be imaginative and think of clever ways to interest the customer.
> Good *teachers* must be intelligent because they need to know their subject well. They also need to be good listeners because they need to know what their students are thinking, and what they need.

2

- Students write eight sentences that would describe a perfect boss. They can then work in pairs and describe the perfect boss to their partner.

Younger classes

- School students, who have not experienced employment yet, may find this task trickier. You may want to start with a short discussion about what a boss does and what might be good or bad about him/her.
- You could substitute *school principal/head teacher* or *parent* for *boss* if you feel it would be more productive.

Extra discussion

- *Have you ever read a horoscope that was 100% true for you?*
- *Do you think people who write horoscopes really believe in what they do?*
- *If you could be another star sign, what would you choose?*
- *Would you be happy working for a company that used horoscopes to decide what to do in business?*
- *Do you know of a more accurate way of reading personality or the future?*

IF YOU WANT SOMETHING EXTRA …

> Straightforward Teacher's Resource Disc *at the back of this book*

7D | The recruitment agency

WHAT THE LESSON IS ABOUT

Theme	Finding a job
Speaking	Discussion: talking about finding a job in your town
	Pairwork roleplay: careers advice
Listening	Formal dialogue: an interview in a recruitment agency
Functional language	Asking for and giving advice
Vocabulary	Phrases used in a curriculum vitae
Pronunciation	Email & website addresses

IF YOU WANT A LEAD-IN ...

Pre-teach a key word: advice

- Tell the students a brief situation, eg *I can't decide whether I should buy a new mobile telephone. My old one works OK, but the new ones have such good extra features. But they are expensive!*
- After you have given a brief outline of your problem, elicit some help from the students by asking: *What do you think I should do?*
- Listen to a number of students and then thank them for their good ideas. Write up on the board: *Thanks. You gave me lots of good ... .* Ask pairs to agree what the missing word is (*advice*). If students say *ideas,* acknowledge that this is possible, but ask if they can find another word.
- Elicit a definition of *advice* (your opinion about what someone else should do in a situation – trying to be helpful). Ask what the verb is (*advise*), and point out the different spelling and pronunciation:
Noun: *advice* /ædvaɪs/
Verb: *advise* /ædvaɪz/

Pre-teach a key word: CV

- Ask directly: When you apply for a job, what is the name of the list of all your qualifications and experience? (Answer: *Curriculum vitae* or *CV*. NB In the US, a CV is usually called a *résumé* /rɪsuːmeɪ/.)
- Check by asking: Which of the following would you typically find on a CV?
    Your address (✓)
    Your email address (✓)
    The names of your pets (✗)
    Your height (✗)
    Exams you have passed (✓)
    Your parents' names (✗)
    What you do in your free time (*possibly*)

Pre-teach a key word: recruitment

- Point out the lesson heading *The recruitment agency* and ask students what that means. If they don't know, explain that a recruitment agency is a place that can help companies to find new employees, and for employees to find new jobs.

Test before you teach: giving advice

> *Methodology guidelines: Test before you teach, page xxi*

- Prepare a number of cards (enough for one to each pair of students), each with one of these problems on it:
    1 *You can't decide whether to go abroad for your holiday or stay in this country. Ask for advice.*
    2 *You forgot your friend's birthday last week. What can you do? Ask for advice.*
    3 *You are thinking of inviting friends on a picnic but you don't know what you should do to organize it. Ask for advice.*
    4 *Your friend has stopped going out and spends hours at home just watching TV. What should you do? Ask for advice.*
    5 *You want to redecorate your room – but don't know what to do. Ask for advice.*
- Put students into pairs. Student A (with the card) tells his/her problem to Student B, who should give some advice. Continue the dialogue a little. Every time Student A says something, Student B should try to offer more ideas.
- When students have had a minute or so on their first card, they can hand them on round the room. Student B now has a go with a new card.

SPEAKING

1

- Pairwork. Students discuss the two questions.
- The second question may lead to an interesting discussion about the local situation. Here are some points that may be useful to add to a discussion about the second question:
    1 *Is it easier or harder to find a job if you are well educated or have good qualifications?*
    2 *Which jobs are easy to get locally? (Are they the jobs no one wants?)*
    3 *Is it easier to find a job if you agree to move to a different town?*
    4 *Will your English help you get a job?*
    5 *How important is a good CV?*

Some ways to find a job:
use a recruitment agency; government job centre; family connection; ask your friends if they know of a job; newspaper advertisement; advertisements in shops and offices; internet search; regular emailed job lists; asking directly at places you are interested in; writing to companies; getting higher qualifications; do voluntary work and build a work record that shows you are capable; research carefully and find out exactly who to talk/write to; get careers advice

Younger classes

- Although the topic here, and in the rest of this lesson, may be more difficult for school-age students, who haven't yet experienced looking for work and applying for jobs, they will doubtless still have some opinions and relevant ideas. Students may also be able to relate things that have happened to family or friends.

VOCABULARY: curriculum vitae

1

- Ask students to look at the advertisement for Sayers Recruitment and Training. Quickly check that students know what is being advertised (a recruitment agency).
- Now ask students to look at the six torn-out excerpts. Explain that they are all from one person's CV. Ask students to look carefully at no. 5 and decide which word or phrase from the advertisement the excerpt gives information about (education). Students do the other questions on their own.

1	two referees	4	qualifications
2	professional experience	5	education
3	personal details	6	personal interests

Language & cultural notes: references

- A *referee* is a person who knows you well and is able to write a *reference* about you. When you make a job application, you are often asked to name two or three referees.
- A *reference* is a statement by someone else about you, your work, your personality, your skills, etc. It is typically written by your school teacher, your boss or manager or someone else who has been higher in a workplace than you.
- Some jobs ask you to provide *personal referees* and *professional referees*. A personal referee is usually a friend who could say something about your interests and everyday life. A professional reference would be about your work.

2

- Pairwork. Students use the words and phrases in the advertisement to ask and answer questions with a partner.

LISTENING

In this listening, a woman called Ruby Tuesday goes for an interview at the recruitment agency she phoned in lesson 1D. She currently works in a fast food restaurant but wants to change jobs. The consultant offers her advice.

1 🔊 2.4

- Direct students to look at the form at the bottom of the page. Point out that it isn't a job application form, but is the form that the recruitment agency will fill in about the person who is looking for a job.
- Students listen to the interview and choose the correct information on the form.

Ms
none
computers
fast food restaurant
she doesn't know

🔊 2.4

C = Consultant R = Ruby
C: Come in.
R: Oh, hello. Good morning. I have an appointment.
C: Yes, come in. It's Miss Tuesday, isn't it?
R: Erm, yes, it's Ms, actually. Not Miss.
C: I'm sorry. Come in, have a seat. Why don't you take your coat off?
R: Thanks. And sorry I'm a bit late. I was making a copy of my CV.
C: That's OK. Could I see it? Thanks.
R: I know it's a little short, but I didn't know what else to write. Should I make it a little longer?
C: Well perhaps a little more information would be a good idea. I mean, for example, do you have any qualifications?
R: Not yet, no. But I'm thinking of going to evening classes. It's just, I haven't decided what to study.
C: Well, all in good time. But getting a qualification is definitely something you should think about. And perhaps you could include your personal interests on your CV?
R: Mmm. I could put down computers, perhaps. I'm quite interested in computers and the internet and things like that.
C: What about doing a course in computer skills? Anyway, I see that you're working in a fast food restaurant ...
R: Yes, and I hate it. That's why I'm here. I'm looking for something else. I don't know what. But anything is better than serving hamburgers all day.
C: Well, we'll see what we can do. But first, I think you should think about getting a qualification.
R: You mean you can't do anything for me now?
C: Not really, no, I'm sorry. But I could give you a bit more advice, if you like.
R: Oh, yes, please. Thanks.
C: Well, the first thing is, I mean, if I were you, I'd arrive for interviews on time. It gives a good impression.
R: Yes, I'm sorry about that ...
C: And, erm, what about wearing something smarter next time? I don't think jeans are a terribly good idea for an interview.
R: Oh, right ... Anything else?
C: Well ...

2 🔊 2.4

- Students listen to the interview again and tick the advice given.

✓ 1, 2, 3, 5, 6, 7

3

- Ask students if they agree with the advice about getting a job. Is it helpful? What advice would they give?

FUNCTIONAL LANGUAGE: advice

> *Language reference, Student's Book page 74*

1
- Students rearrange the words to make sentences that ask for or give advice.

> 1 Should I go or should I stay? (Should I stay or should I go?)
> 2 You shouldn't decide too quickly.
> 3 Why don't you think about it?
> 4 I think you should ask your friends.
> 5 If I were you, I'd get a new job. (I'd get a new job if I were you.)
> 6 What about going to a recruitment agency?

Extra task: looking at the sentences
- Students work in pairs to decide a possible situation and speakers for each of the six sentences in exercise 1.
- You could help students to structure their answers by writing up a table on the board with the headings *Where? Who is talking? To who?* and the numbers 1–6 for each of the sentences. Ask students to copy it. Students can then write their answers in the table.

2
- Tell students that questions 1–5 are some problems that a friend has.
- Pairwork. You could put students into pairs with Student A reading problem 1, and Student B giving some advice. They then swap roles, with Student B reading problem 2, and Student A giving advice.
- You could then get feedback from different pairs, and as a whole class agree the best advice for each question.

> *Many answers are possible. Here are some ideas:*
> 2 Why don't you invite someone to have lunch with you? What about asking someone for help with a problem?
> 3 If I were you, I'd tell your boss. I'm sure he'll/she'll understand.
> 4 You should make sure you come on time from now on.
> 5 If I were you, I'd ask for some help. What about taking a holiday?

Alternative procedure
- Students work individually and write their own answers to the problems.

Extension task
- For fun, you could elicit the most unhelpful or funniest advice students can think of for each problem!

Language notes: giving advice
- The sentence heads in this lesson divide into stronger and weaker:

stronger		
↑	1	*You should/shouldn't …*
	2	*I (don't) think you should …*
	3	*If I were you …*
↓	4	*Why don't you …*
weaker	5	*What about … ing*

- The three exponents towards the top of the diagram suggest a strong opinion from the speaker that the listener *should* do what they are told. The speaker is talking with certainty that they know the best thing to do.
- In exponent 2, the verb *think* has some softening effect on *should*.
- In exponent 3, the speaker is imagining what they would do if they found themselves in the same situation.
- Exponents 4 and 5 in the lower part of the diagram are less strong and are closer to suggestions. The speaker is offering possible ideas, but without suggesting that the listener must do them. In fact, the arrows marking stronger and weaker could perhaps also be labelled *advice* and *suggestions*.
- When speaking, advice can be made to sound stronger or weaker by using intonation, volume, eye contact, facial expression, etc. With students, you could practise short dialogues using the same exponents but varying the amount of strength in the advice.
- As with all functional areas, there are many other possible ways that the function can be achieved. In everyday life, much advice is given in quite oblique ways, eg by using statements of information. For example:
  A: *He's an important client but I don't know where to take him to lunch today.*
  B: *There's a good Japanese restaurant on St Andrew's Square.*

3
> *Methodology Builder 8: Roleplay, page 27*
- In this roleplay, students visit a careers advice centre and have an interview. Allow students plenty of time to prepare their ideas for the roleplay. Encourage them to make notes to help clarify what they might want to say.
- You can decide if you want your students to do the activity by answering truthfully about themselves, or as an imaginary character. The first suggestion may be most suitable for adult students who have at least a little work experience, while the second may be more suitable for students in schools.

4
- Pairwork. Students do the roleplay. Student A plays the careers advisor. Student B plays the client (ie the person who is looking for help). When the interview is over, students should swap roles and repeat the task.
- If possible, it will probably help to arrange the seating a little to create an office desk or other appropriate advice-giving arrangement.

Extension task: variation on the roleplay
- Students could repeat the activity for some famous people (eg the Prime Minister, a famous actor, etc) who have suddenly lost their job and now need to get a new career.

PRONUNCIATION: email & website addresses

1 2.5

- Ask students to look at the illustration of a computer screen while they listen to the pronunciation of the addresses.
- After listening, ask students to practise reading the addresses on the screen.
- Many students may be surprised to find out that they are saying these items incorrectly. In some countries, people may have learnt these as English words pronounced in a way that reflects their own language. Listen carefully and give very clear feedback that it's not correct if students say them wrongly.

Younger classes

- As many younger students are very computer literate, you may want to check if they can tell you how to say these before they hear the recording.

🔘 2.5

> davina at sayers dot co dot uk
> www dot sayers hyphen rt dot com
> www dot sayers hyphen rt dot org slash index slash html
> davinasayers (all one word) at srt dot net

Language notes: pronunciation

- The phonemic transcriptions for these items are:
  /æt/; /dɒt/; /ɔːlwʌnˈwɜːd/; /slæʃ/; /haɪfən/.
- *www* is pronounced *double-you-double-you-double-you*.
- In fluent connected speech the /t/ in /æt/ and /dɒt/ is often lost.
- *Slash* is sometimes called *forward slash*.
- *Hyphen* is sometimes called *dash*.
- Another common email pronunciation problem is the character _. This is pronounced *underscore*.
- *.com* is pronounced *dot com* /dɒtkɒm/.
- *.co.uk* is pronounced /dɒtkəʊ dɒtjuːˈkeɪ/.

2

⊙ *Communication activities, Student's Book pages 129 & 131*

- Pairwork. Students turn to their respective pages and take it in turns to dictate the addresses for their partner to copy down.
- Make sure that students don't look at their partner's page until the end. If they check their answers as they go, it may make the task less challenging.

3

- Ask students to work on their own and invent some new email addresses or website addresses.
- Students can then dictate their addresses to a partner.
- There is scope for some humour in this task. You might ask students to first think of two amazing new businesses (with strange products or services). When they have decided that, ask them to decide the web address and email address for each.

Extension task: By the way ...

- In Hungarian the word for @ means *snail*. Do students know of any other symbols that have curious names?

IF YOU WANT SOMETHING EXTRA ...

⊙ Straightforward Teacher's Resource Disc *at the back of this book*

Answer key

7 REVIEW

❯ Student's Book page 154

1

1 's applied
2 's been
3 's already left
4 's done
5 's never needed
6 's thought

2

1 patience
2 skilled
3 imagination
4 ambitious
5 emotional
6 independent

3

a 3 b 4 c 6 d 1 e 2 f 5

4

1 drove
2 haven't given
3 've been
4 've made
5 've never had
6 worked
7 wrote
8 've ever had

5

1 chauffeur
2 nurse
3 model
4 actor
5 waitress
6 engineer
7 journalist
8 teacher

6

Students' own answers

7

1 apply
   a) salary b) company
2 leave
   a) fired b) career
3 living
   a) course b) unemployment
4 charge
   a) responsible b) manager
5 get
   a) horoscope b) experience

8

1 b 2 b 3 a 4 a 5 b

9

1 Do you think I should
2 Why don't you
3 How about
4 What should I
5 You should
6 if I were you

7 WRITING

❯ Workbook page 77

Model answer

> 23 Oakhampton Road
> Eastbourne
> Sussex EA3 3TH
> Tel: 01873 295765
> email:janeh@rmail.com
>
> 23 June 2012
>
> Dear Sir/Madam,
>
> I saw your advertisement for jobs with Bristol Summer Camps Network and I would like to ask for an application form. I am very interested in a temporary job as an art teacher from May to September this year. I would love to work anywhere in France or Italy.
>
> I finished an arts degree at Chelsea Arts College in London last year. Before that, I worked as a French teacher for three years in Bratislava, Slovakia. I have also taught art to children at a special school in Inverness, Scotland. At present, I am studying Art therapy. My CV is enclosed.
>
> I believe I would be good at this job because I love working with young people and I think I can make classes fun and interesting for students.
>
> Please contact me if you need any more information. My address is at the top of this letter.
>
> I look forward to hearing from you.
>
> Yours faithfully,
>
> Jane Hughes

8A The futurological conference

WHAT THE LESSON IS ABOUT

Theme	Studying the future
Speaking	Pairwork discussion: talking about science fiction films
	Monologue: giving a thirty-second talk
Reading	*4th International Futurological Conference*. A conference programme: giving details about a conference on the future
Grammar	Predictions 1 (*may, might* & *will*)
Pronunciation	Contractions 2: *'ll* (dark /l/)

IF YOU WANT A LEAD-IN ...

Teach a key word: futurology

- Write the word *astrology* on the board. Ask students what it means. (They should remember from the last lesson.) Point out that it is made up of *astr* and *ology*. Elicit or explain that *-ology* means 'study of', so *astrology* means 'study of the stars' (*astra* is Greek for *star*). Now write up *futurology* and elicit what it means (study of the future).

Discussion starters

○ *Methodology Builder 15: Using Discussion starters, page 63*

- *Have you ever seen Star Trek™?* (popular US science fiction TV series and films) or, name a TV programme or film that is popular locally. *Will life in the future be like that?*
- *What other things will happen in the future? Will people travel in space? Will people travel in time? Will there be lots of robots? Will the world be better – or worse?*
- *Is it possible to predict the future? Will there be more wars or fewer? Why? Will there be more crime or less?*

SPEAKING

1

- Pairwork. Students discuss the three questions.
- The films in the box are all well-known science fiction films. You may prefer to use the first question with the whole class and clearly establish the term *science fiction* and its pronunciation.
- You could point out to students that they can use the present simple tense to narrate the story of the film (as practised in lesson 4C).

Language & cultural notes: science fiction

- Science fiction is a genre concerned with imagined future lives, events and technology. It often includes journeys in space or time, meetings with alien life, alternative realities and scientific advances.
  NB It's /saɪəns ˈfɪkʃən/ not /fɪktɪɒn/! The term can be shortened to *sci-fi* – pronounced /saɪ faɪ/. (Don't say /sɪ fɪ/!)
- Some other famous science fiction films include: *2001 A Space Odyssey*; *Star Trek™*; *The Fifth Element*; *X-Men*; *Minority Report*; *Blade Runner*; *Close Encounters of the Third Kind*; *AI*; *Solaris*; *Mars Attacks*; *ET*; *Stargate*; *Children of Men*; *WALL-E*; *Inception*

- The following may be useful words for discussing sci-fi films:
  ET (extra terrestrial) – a creature from somewhere that isn't Earth.
  UFO (Unidentified Flying Object) – something in the sky that we cannot identify, ie it may be a flying saucer or it may be a weather balloon or a cloud.
  AI (artificial intelligence) – a thinking machine.
  Robot – an intelligent machine, eg an artificial creature with AI.
  mutant – a creature that has changed in some ways and is different from all others of its species.
  space station – a satellite in space where spaceships can dock.
- The title of this lesson *The futurological conference* is also the title of a science fiction book by Stanislaw Lem, a famous Polish writer.

READING

This programme gives details on the main talks at the 4th International Futurological Conference. They are on renewable energy; increasing lifespan and its effect on society; internet use; prisons in the future; automatic translation; time travel; laser weapons and their impact on the world.

1

- Ask students to look at the text, but not to read it in detail. Elicit what it is (*a conference programme*) and what the subject of the conference is (*futurology*). If you haven't already taught it, ask students to think what *futurology* might mean (Answer: *the study of the future*).
- Point out that items 1–7 are different talks at the conference and that the titles for the talks are missing.
- Students read the titles (a–j) and find the three titles they think would not apply to this conference.

> *The three titles that don't apply:* b, e, j

2

- Students read the conference programme and match the titles to the talks.

> 1 h   2 c   3 d   4 f   5 i   6 a   7 g
> *Answer j is incorrect because the talk is not about the invention of the laser but about its future use on satellites, perhaps in wars.*

3

- Students complete the sentences with the missing words from the box.

> | 1 source | 3 cures | 5 technology |
> | --- | --- | --- |
> | 2 energy | 4 theory | 6 Satellites |

4

- Students study the programme and select two or three talks they would like to go to.
- They can work in pairs and tell their partner about their choice, giving reasons.

GRAMMAR: predictions 1 (*may, might & will*)

Grammar box

> ❷ *Language reference, Student's Book page 84*
> ❷ *Methodology Builder 22: Using Grammar boxes, page 106*

1
- Students find and correct the grammatical mistakes in the sentences.
- They can compare answers in pairs.

> 1   ... our teacher wills give ...
> 2   I may be go ...
> 3   I may not to get married.
> 4   ... might wins ...
> 5   I'll always remembering ...
> 6   I think that it will rains ...
> 7   I'll never living live ...
> 8   I won't to become rich ...

Language notes: predictions 1 (may, might & will)

- *Will, may* and *might* are all modal auxiliary verbs and follow the usual auxiliary rules, including:
  1 No third person -*s*.
  2 They are followed by verb infinitive without *to*.
  3 Questions are made by inversion.
  4 Negatives are made with *not* – and without *do*.
- The distinction mentioned in the notes (about *will* for certainty and *may/might* when we are less sure) is a useful guideline. It is also possible to modify these by adding other phrases. For example:
  I think man will discover time travel is less certain than *Man will discover time travel.* Exercise 1 includes a number of *I think* ... sentences.
- *Might* sounds slightly less certain than *may.*
  I may invite Jane. I might invite Pete.
  In these two sentences Jane is more likely to go to the party than Pete!
- For stronger students, it may be worth mentioning that we can make our sentences sound more uncertain by stressing and lengthening the modal verb. We could help students to learn this by capitalizing the written word, eg *She MAY come to the party* or even by deliberately misspelling it, eg *She maaaaaaay come to the party.*

2
- Students rewrite each of the eight sentences so that they are true for them.

Weaker classes

- You may want to go over possible changes with students before they start. Changes may be:
  Don't use *I think.*
  Change *I think* to *I don't think.*
  Make a positive sentence negative.
  Make a negative sentence positive.
  Change some words, eg country name, competition name, kind of weather, etc.

3
- Pairwork. Students discuss each of the four topics in the box. Make sure that they discuss the immediate future (ie the next year) and the immediate short-term (ten years' time).

PRONUNCIATION: contractions 2

1 🔘 **2.6**
- Students listen to the recording and repeat the words. All the words include the /l/ sound as used in the contraction of the word *will.*

🔘 **2.6**

> I'll
> it'll
> there'll
> we'll
> what'll
> you'll

Language notes: contractions

- In everyday language use (in most varieties of English), very few people fully pronounce every word one by one. To speak fluently, it's normal and natural to use contractions. It's not bad English or 'lazy' English. It's just real English, and so recognizing and using such contractions is important for language learners. Learners can very often sound unnatural if they de-contract words too often.
- As well as *'ll* the other contractions in this part of the lesson are:
  Aren't: this cannot be successfully decontracted in normal spoken questions. ✗ *Are not you ready* simply isn't said in contemporary English and even ✗ *Are you not ready* is very unusual. However, in a negative sentence it is possible to say 'We are not happy'.
  It's: students (as well as many – or most – native speakers) regularly confuse the spelling of *it's* and *its*: the rule of thumb is easy enough, but seems to be tricky to recall and get right in use: *it's* is the contraction of *it is.*
  Its is not a contraction – but is the possessive form of *it*. This is probably particularly confusing as other possessives *do* have an apostrophe – compare *Jane's food, the dog's food, its food.*
- Students sometimes get confused because *it's* can be a contraction of both *it is* and *it has.*
- *Let's.* This is the contraction of the imperative *Let us* and is virtually never said in its decontracted form (unless you are a priest who needs to say *Let us pray* ...).

Language notes: dark /l/

- *Pronunciation* exercise 1 looks at one common contraction and raises a specific pronunciation problem.
- Although there is only a single phoneme shown in dictionary transcripts, the /l/ sound in fact has two distinctly different varieties. In words such as *love, close, live*, etc, the sound is known as *clear /l/*. But there is also another pronunciation known as *dark /l/*.
  The name is quite appropriate as the sound does seem to have a deeper, darker character to it! It can also have syllabic value – in some pronunciations the dark /l/ sound may make a syllable of its own. Students often cannot get the sound correctly because they try too hard to merge it into the preceding syllable, which will tend to lead to a light sound rather than a dark one.
- If your students have problems forming the dark /l/, you might find it helpful to ask them to say it as a separate syllable with a /ʊ/ sound in front of it. For example:
  To pronounce *I'll*, tell students to say *I – ull*, ie /aɪ – ʊl/.
  To pronounce *it'll*, tell students to say /ɪt – ʊl/.

- If students get the wrong /l/ sound, it won't matter too much as the word will still be recognizable.
- It's more important for students to get used to using and hearing contractions than to worry too much about any /l/ problems.

2 & 3 🎵 2.7

- This is a particularly interesting task which works on an area of English – discourse coherence – that coursebooks don't often look at. Most of the expressions in exercise 2 are fixed *chunks*, ie they are regularly used as complete phrases (and should be learnt as such).
- Students match spoken sentences (A) with the likely responses (B).
- Students then listen and check answers to exercise 2.

1 b	2 a	3 e	4 d	5 c

🎵 2.7

> 1 Aren't you ready yet? Hurry up! / I won't be long.
> 2 Be careful – it's very dangerous. / I'll be OK.
> 3 I wonder where they are. / They'll be here soon.
> 4 Let's have a drink before the film starts. / We'll be late.
> 5 What's this? I've never eaten that before. / You'll like it.

Language notes: discourse coherence

- How can students work out which are the correct answers to the questions in *Pronunciation* exercise 2? Although the sentences include possible grammar or vocabulary difficulties for students, the main problem is not essentially a grammatical or a vocabulary one, but one of *discourse* – a term that is typically somewhat unfamiliar to students (and teachers). Discourse refers to the ways that we understand the meaning of language when it is used in communication. Whereas a lot of language study stays focussed at the level of single sentences, a study of discourse features looks beyond the sentence and considers how a whole dialogue or text might hang together.
  For example, consider what helps a learner to connect the sentence *Let's have a drink before the film starts* with the response *We'll be late*. There is a grammatical link between *'s* (us) and *We*, but beyond that, it's hard to find any other grammatical thread or vocabulary similarity. The only way to work out that this is the response is by imagining a possible context for the dialogue, and to think of a detailed possible reason why somebody might give a reply like this, and why it might make sense and seem coherent in this context. We have to work out that *We'll be late* might be given as a response by someone suggesting that there is not sufficient time to have a drink because the film will start before they can finish their drink.
- Thus, students who have problems with exercise 2 won't necessarily be helped by a focus on the language used in the sentences. In fact, this could even be confusing – as, for example, *Aren't you ready yet? Hurry up!* might seem to link linguistically to *We'll be late,* whereas it's only when you think through the possible contexts and dialogues that it is apparent that it doesn't work, and the response *I won't be long* makes a logical reply in the likely context.

4

- Pairwork. Students practise the exchanges from exercise 2.
- Most expressions in this exercise are fixed chunks, ie they are regularly used as complete phrases.

Extra activity: practising chunks with different intonation

- Write one of the responses from *Pronunciation* exercise 2 on the board (eg *I'll be OK.*). Tell students that they must say these exact words, but must show different emotions by changing the intonation. Call out various feelings and get students (chorally or individually) to repeat the sentence according to the instruction. Feelings can include: *You feel very sad; You are angry; You don't really believe what you are saying; You're very happy,* etc. Continue by putting a new chunk on the board and trying again with this one.

SPEAKING

1 🎵 2.8–2.10

- Ask students to look at the list of topics a–j. They listen and decide which of the speakers 1–3 is speaking about which topic.

1 i	2 e	3 f

🎵 2.8–2.10

> 1 Right, er, well, there'll be more and more supermarkets … Um, you see more and more of the same kinds of shops everywhere, you know. Everywhere you go you see the same things, the same chains – so more supermarkets on the outside of the town. Er, the town centres will get quieter and quieter, no – there'll, there'll be less, um, less shops in the town centres and there'll be more bars and cafés and things like that, um, so people will … er, use their cars, I guess, more. Is that thirty seconds yet?
> 2 Everybody says that, er, you know, everybody will need English in the future, but I … I don't think this is true because, um, you know, you need, um, English for computers and the internet and that, but with … with, um … There's more and more Chinese people in the world, so, you know, we'll, maybe, we'll speak Chinese, we'll all need to speak Chinese because, um, 'cos … 'cos we will, and, er, um …
> 3 If you think about medicine now and you think about medicine, say one hundred years ago, the differences, um, are … are incredible because we can … we can do so many things now that we couldn't do then, like, you know, we've got a cure for polio, we've got a cure for lots of diseases, and … and transplants and things, so I guess in the future we'll, you know, carry on and we'll find cures for more and more things and we'll, um … That must be thirty seconds.

2

- Ask students to select one of the topics in exercise 1 and prepare a thirty-second talk on the topic.
- To reduce nerves and stress it might be a good idea to get students to give their talks to small groups (of four to six students) rather than in front of the whole class.

Stronger classes

- With stronger students you might want to try a more demanding game by adapting the long-running and very popular BBC programme *Just A Minute*.

■ Methodology Builder 21
Just a Minute

- *This popular game helps students become more confident at speaking. It is similar to* Speaking *exercise 2. The basic task is the same but:*
  1 Speakers must try to talk for one minute.
  2 Speakers should not hesitate (ie have long pauses, ers or other hesitations).
  3 Speakers must not repeat any words (except for those in the topic title they were given).
  4 Speakers must not deviate too far from the topic set.
- *Organize small groups (of at least four people). Students appoint a speaker and a timer/judge – who will need to be able to time (eg using a digital watch).*
- *The judge sets the topic and asks the speaker to start. The speaker begins talking and the judge starts the 60-second countdown. The other players listen and try to spot one of the problems (hesitation, repetition or deviation). If they hear one, they call out "challenge". The speaker stops talking, the judge stops timing and the challenger says their challenge. If the judge agrees, then the challenger wins one point and takes over speaking about the topic – but only has to talk for the remaining time on the timer, eg 29 seconds. If the challenge is wrong, the original speaker gets one point, takes up the topic again and tries to finish their minute. Speaking and challenging continue until someone finishes the 60 seconds.*
- *The rules given here may be too demanding for many classes. Feel free to vary them as appropriate, eg allowing repetition, allowing preparation time, shortening the time you have to speak, etc.*

IF YOU WANT SOMETHING EXTRA ...

❯ Straightforward Teacher's Resource Disc *at the back of this book*

8B | Space tourists

WHAT THE LESSON IS ABOUT

Theme	Space tourists
Speaking	Groupwork discussion: deciding who is the best candidate for *Star Quest*
Listening	Radio programme monologue: a description of *Star Quest*, a TV game show
Vocabulary	Compound nouns with numbers
Grammar	Predictions 2 (*maybe*, *probably*, *certainly*, etc)
Pronunciation	Word stress 2: three-syllable words

IF YOU WANT A LEAD-IN ...

Teach a key word: game show

- Ask students directly if they know any game shows in their country. If they already understand the idea, students may call out names, which you can collect on the board. If they don't, you could suggest some local examples, eg *Who Wants to be a Millionaire?*
- Establish that a game show is a TV programme. It is a competition usually with prizes – sometimes very big amounts of money, a holiday or a car.

Discussion starters

- *Methodology Builder 15: Using Discussion starters, page 63*
- *Would you like to go on a game show?*
- *Which show would you enjoy being on?*
- *Would you win?*
- *What is the best prize you've ever seen on a game show?*
- *What prize would you like to win?*

LISTENING

This radio programme discusses a new TV game show with contestants from all over Europe, in which the first prize is a seat in a space ship and a visit to the International Space Station. They talk about why NASA might not be happy with this, and give details on how to apply.

1
- Tell students that they are going to listen to a radio programme and that all the words in the box will be in the programme. Ask students to predict from the words what the programme will be about. (See summary above.) Don't confirm or deny any of their ideas yet. However, you might want to note some key ideas from their predictions on the board, which you can refer to and check after they have listened to the recording.

2 🔘 2.11
- Students listen to the radio programme and work out the story. Ask students how close the story is to their predictions. Go back to the six vocabulary items, and to any notes you made on the board, and check how each of them fit in with the recording.
- It may be worth playing the recording two or even three times to ensure that the gist is clear.

Contestants in a new TV game show (which will be filmed in famous science museums) can win the chance to blast off in a rocket and become a space tourist.

🔘 2.11

> Back in 2001, American millionaire Dennis Tito became the world's first space tourist. He wrote a 20-million dollar cheque for the privilege. Since then, there have been another six space tourists, and they have all paid millions for the experience. Others will probably follow soon, but who will they be? One thing is for sure: it certainly won't be you, unless you have a few million dollars. Or perhaps it will be!
>
> A European television consortium, Eurorbit, has announced plans for a new TV game show. The show, which will probably be called *Star Quest*, will have contestants from all the countries in the European Union. It will test the contestants' general knowledge, their skills and their ability to work in a team. Contestants will need to be fit and to speak English, but men and women of all ages are welcome to apply. The programme's organizers hope to film the thirteen-part show at different science museums around Europe – in London, Florence, Paris and at the New Metropolis Science and Technology Center in Amsterdam. And the prize? The winner of the show will take his, or her, seat in a space ship some time next year. After training at the European Space Academy, the winner will blast off for an eight-day trip to the stars and a visit to the International Space Station.
>
> Or perhaps not. Not everyone is happy with the idea. Will scientists in America at NASA refuse permission for the winner to visit the space station? They were unhappy with Dennis Tito's trip and say that this kind of space tourism is too dangerous. 'This idea is so stupid,' said one expert at New York University. However, a spokesman for Eurorbit said that the Americans will probably agree some kind of deal. Whatever happens, he said, the winner of the competition will definitely go into space. But it's possible that they won't be able to visit the space station.
>
> The organizers of the programme are taking applications now. So if you want to be the next space tourist, send your request to contestant@eurorbit.com. That's contestant@eurorbit.com. And good luck!

3 🔘 2.11
- Ask students to listen to the recording again and answer the eight questions.

Stronger classes
- Ask students to predict answers before listening again. Then they listen to the answers and check.

1. seven
2. millions
3. Eurorbit – a Eurovision television consortium
4. The European Union
5. European science museums (in London, Florence, Paris and Amsterdam)
6. an eight-day trip into space
7. Maybe! The prize includes a promised trip to the International Space Station, but NASA is against the idea and may refuse permission
8. NASA

4
• Students could discuss the question in small groups, giving reasons for their opinions.

Extra discussion
• *Would you apply for this competition? Do you think you are the kind of person the TV show is looking for?*
• *If you were the producer of the show, what kind of contestants would be good for getting high audience figures? Do you want bright, funny, attractive people? Fit, sporty people? Serious academics and scientists? Ordinary people – ie the man or woman in the street?*
• *Do you think you will ever go to the Moon in your lifetime? When will it be possible to buy a holiday in space?*

Some more serious questions
• *Why do you think NASA is nervous?*
• *What sort of problems do you think the other astronauts may have if they have a tourist on their space shuttle?*

Cultural notes: space tourism
• It's not easy to become a space tourist. It's very expensive. And it's potentially very dangerous.
• The second space tourist, after Tito, was a South African businessman called Mark Shuttleworth. Since then, only a handful of people have gone into space as fee-paying customers.
• Some writers believe that one million people a year will be travelling into space very soon. That may sound like a lot but remember that over a billion passengers fly on scheduled aeroplane flights every year.
• Japanese scientists aim soon to be able to offer trips into space for as little as $10,000.
• If you are determined to get into space, but don't have the money, you could get a job with one of the many companies that will soon need to work in space: electrical suppliers; chemists; vehicle repairers; hotel staff, etc.

VOCABULARY: compound nouns with numbers

❯ *Language reference, Student's Book page 85*

1
• Ask students to look at the phrases 1–3. Ask if they know which of the options is correct, but don't confirm or deny their guesses. Ask students to look at the audioscript 2.11 on page 140, and to find the items and check which option is correct.
• When students have found the answers, ask if they can work out a rule for the formation of these nouns (ie we do not use the plural *s* in the first part of the compound).

1	20-million dollar cheque
2	thirteen-part show
3	eight-day trip

2
• Elicit from students some possible compounds that they could make from the two columns.
• Students select the best possible compounds to fill the gaps in the six sentences.

1	two-week course	4	ten-minute break
2	20-euro note	5	eight-hour day
3	five-star hotel	6	million-dollar house

Language notes: compound nouns with numbers
• Some other compounds are possible (but do not fit the meaning of the exercise sentences). These are noted below. The tick ✓ indicates a probable compound in everyday English and (✓) indicates a possible but less likely compound.

	break	course	day	hotel	house	note
eight-hour	✓	✓	✓			
five-star	(✓)			✓		
million-dollar	(✓)	(✓)	(✓)	✓	✓	(✓)
ten-minute	✓					
twenty-euro	(✓)	(✓)	(✓)	(✓)		✓
two-week	✓	✓				

GRAMMAR: predictions 2 (*maybe, probably, certainly,* etc)

Grammar box

❯ *Language reference, Student's Book page 84*
❯ *Methodology Builder 22: Using Grammar boxes, page 106*

1
• Students put the word in brackets into the correct place in the sentence.
• When students have completed the sentences, they can check in pairs and then discuss whether they think each sentence is true or not.

1	We <u>probably</u> won't discover …
2	China will <u>possibly</u> be …
3	Ordinary people <u>definitely</u> won't be able to travel …
4	<u>Perhaps</u> there will be hotels in space …
5	Engineers will <u>certainly</u> build factories …
6	<u>Maybe</u> we will stop spending money …

Language notes: predictions 2 (maybe, probably, certainly, etc)
• In addition to the information in the Student's Book, it's worth noting that:
  Perhaps can also go in other places in the sentence including: (1) after the auxiliary verb, eg *He will perhaps arrive before ten.* (2) After main verb *be*, eg *She is perhaps a future President of the US.*
  Perhaps is usually two syllables /pəhæps/, but is also often pronounced as a single syllable /præps/, and *definitely* is usually three syllables, rather than four.
  Probably is in the middle of the coursebook diagram, but this doesn't mean that it represents a 50% chance. If something will *probably* happen, then there is a strong likelihood of it happening, say 70% to 90%. *Maybe* sounds slightly more informal than *perhaps*.

2
• Students choose one of the questions 1–5. Make sure that questions are evenly distributed, so that all students do not select the same one. The simplest way to do this would be by going round the class and giving each student a number from 1 to 5.
• Get students to walk around the class and ask the question to as many people as possible, keeping brief notes about the different answers they hear.
• Remind students about how they can answer when they are asked one of the questions. Point out the words in the box above the questions.

3

- Students report what they discovered with the rest of the class and compare their results.

Alternative procedure

- Ask students to form groups that include members who can report back on different questions.

Extra practice: making predictions

- Remind students about the horoscopes from lesson 7C. Write the following words on the board: *career; house; job; famous; rich; happy; space; travel.*
- Ask students to write a text for their partner with predictions about their future life. Give them a time limit of ten minutes. They must use at least four of the words on the board. Emphasize that the texts should be encouraging, positive predictions (not terrible warnings about sudden death). Encourage students to use language from the lesson. When they have finished, they can read their personal horoscope. Students may also enjoy swapping and sharing other people's texts.

■ **Methodology Builder 22**
Using Grammar boxes

In every lesson of the Student's Book in which new grammar is introduced, you will find a grammar box. These boxes summarize information about the new language being studied. In most cases, no methodological instructions or exercises are offered, so the teacher has many options about how to use them. This Methodology Builder suggests a number of typical ideas for using these, as well as a few more unusual possibilities. In every case, you can mix and match ideas to suit your class.

- *Ask students to quietly read through the information to themselves.*
- *Ask one or two students to read the information aloud to the rest of the class.*
- *Ask students to work in pairs and read the information aloud to each other.*
- *Ask students to work in pairs, read and then discuss or ask each other questions about the contents.*
- *The teacher reads aloud the information to the class.*
- *The teacher allows quiet reading time and then asks questions based on the material in the box.*
- *The teacher uses material in the substitution tables (which feature in many of the grammar boxes) to give students simple repetition or substitution drills.*
- *Ask students in pairs to drill each other.*
- *Books closed: before students look at the grammar box, read it aloud to them. At various key points pause and elicit what the next word or words might be. Clearly confirm right answers. When you have finished, allow students to open books and read the information through quietly.*
- *Books closed: write the information from the grammar box on the board, trying to keep the same layout as the book. Leave gaps at key places. Ask students to either copy the diagram and fill it in or come to the board and fill in the information there. Allow students to discuss the suggested answers before they check with the printed version.*

- *Books closed: use the information in the grammar box to inform your own question-making. Elicit the information, item by item, example by example, from students and note it on the board. When the information is complete, allow students to open their books and find the same content printed there.*

SPEAKING

1

- Remind students of the proposed TV game show *Star Quest*. Ask them if they can think of a possible good candidate – either a friend or colleague or maybe a famous person. Collect and discuss briefly a few suggestions.
- Students write the name of a possible contestant and make notes about why he/she would be good – using the four headings.

2

- Groupwork. Put students into groups. Each student describes their choice and gives reasons. Then the group should select the best candidate.

PRONUNCIATION: word stress 2

1 & 2 🔊 2.12

❯ *Methodology Builder 17: Working with word stress, page 75*

- Students decide where the main stressed syllable is in each word. They underline the word with the different stress pattern.
- Students listen to the recording and check their answers: (underlined in audioscript 2.12 below).

🔊 **2.12**

1	certainly	energy	probably	<u>unhappy</u>
2	businessman	<u>engineer</u>	president	scientist
3	dangerous	internet	<u>invention</u>	satellite
4	advantage	computer	<u>conference</u>	contestant
5	equipment	exciting	<u>possible</u>	remember

- Rather than having the teacher instantly confirm each answer, it is a good idea to let students listen to each word enough times so that they are certain of the answers themselves. They may well have trouble hearing the stress patterns, but it's worth persevering as this is a very awareness-raising thing to do.
- The table below shows you the answers and the stress patterns for all words in the exercise.

The stress patterns are:

1	unhappy □■□	□□□	□□□	□□□	□■□
2	engineer □□■	□□□	□□■	□□□	□■□
3	invention □■□	□□□	□□□	□■□	□□□
4	conference ■□□	□■□	■□□	□□□	□■□
5	possible ■□□	□■□	■□□	□□□	□■□

IF YOU WANT SOMETHING EXTRA ...

❯ Straightforward Teacher's Resource Disc *at the back of this book*

8c | Great ideas

WHAT THE LESSON IS ABOUT

Theme	New products & new businesses
Speaking	Pairwork discussion: discussing & choosing gadgets on a website
Reading	*A great idea?* Magazine article: a new business
Listening	Radio advertisements: descriptions of gadgets
Vocabulary	Adjectives with infinitives
Grammar	Present tense in future time clauses (first conditional)

IF YOU WANT A LEAD-IN ...

Teach a key word: essay

- Read out the following definition and ask students to tell you what it is: *You write this at school or college to show that you understand something and to give your opinions about a particular subject.* (Answer: *essay*)
- It is possible that students will not know the word *essay*, in which case give them the answer and write it on the board. Ask some check questions. For example:
  1 When did you last write an essay? What was it about?
  2 Do people usually write essays in everyday life outside school or college? (Answer: *Not usually, unless they are a professional writer.*)
  3 Is an essay the same as an article? (Answer: *No. An article is intended for publication in a newspaper or magazine. An essay may be published, but is usually just for a teacher to read and mark.*)

Introducing the theme: new ideas

- Write the following on the board: *Films on your mobile phone; Computers under our skin; Flying cars; Free 24-hour doctor on the internet.*
- Explain that these are some recent ideas. Point out that three are products (things you could buy and own) and one is a service (something people do to help you).
- Ask students if they think these are 'great ideas' or not. Ask for reasons. Which ones would students want to have themselves? Ask if students have any great ideas for new products or services. Discuss which ones would be popular.

LISTENING & SPEAKING

In this listening, there are five short radio advertisements giving details about unusual products.

1 🔘 2.13

- Ask students to look at the website page and focus on the five products listed. They can work in pairs and briefly tell each other what they think each item might be.
- Students listen to the five advertisements and note down which one goes with which product.

1 C	2 A	3 E	4 D	5 B

🔘 2.13

1	Looking for a laugh? Get one of these gooey balls and throw it at a window. Just watch your colleagues' faces as it slides down the window making strange shapes.
2	Now you can write secret messages with our invisible ink. With a special ultraviolet light reader, you can read them, too!
3	You can't find your keys? Again! Just whistle and it will flash and beep. You'll find your keys in an instant ... and losing them will be fun!
4	Feeling thirsty? Well, here's your own personal water machine for your desk in the office. It holds eight cups. With this in front of you, you can be sure you'll drink all the water you need.
5	Did you know that colours can change the way you feel? Do you sometimes wake up in the morning feeling (and looking!) grey? With one of these, you can wake up in the morning to a bright, colourful tomorrow.

2

- Pairwork. Students discuss the questions and agree the order on how successful they think the products will be.

READING

This magazine article is about Ash Sharma. He explains why his father should give him a loan for his new business idea and why he should postpone his studies to get his business started. In the second half of the article, his father explains why he won't lend his son the money.

1

- Students read the magazine article and answer the three questions. Tell them not to worry about the eight numbered gaps.

1	By improving his website and selling university essays to students.
2	Because there will be too much work to start the website and study at the same time. He is also worried that someone else may use the same idea before him.
3	He thinks it may not work. There might be other websites offering the same service. He has serious doubts about its success and profitability. He is not sure if it is legal. He thinks Ash should make a business plan and finish his studies before he starts.

2

- Students read the article again and decide where the phrases (a–h) could go in the text.

1 d	2 f	3 b	4 e	5 h	6 g	7 c	8 a

3

- Pairwork. Students discuss the three questions in pairs.

Extra discussion

Business ideas

- *Imagine that you want to start a new business and make a lot of money in a short time. What would you do?*
- *What would be the biggest difficulties in starting a successful business (eg money to start it)?*

• *Do you think that school children and young people can be good business people?*

Essays

(NB These questions raise moral issues and need to be used carefully and sensitively.)

• *Do/Did you ever cheat when writing essays? Do/Did you ever copy sections from a book? Do/Did you ever copy things off the internet?*
• *Imagine that you need to write an essay for a very important qualification. A friend says they will sell you a first class essay for a reasonable price. Would you buy it?*

VOCABULARY: adjectives with infinitives

❯ *Language reference, Student's Book page 85*

1

• Ask students to cover up the article and choose items from the box to fill the five gaps in the sentences.
• When they have finished, ask students to look back at the article on page 80 to find the items and check their answers.

1	to use	3	to help	5	to get
2	to say	4	to finish		

2

• Students could work in pairs and take it in turns to make new sentences from the table. Tell them to try and make sentences that are both grammatically correct and also meaningful. Sentences can be about things that typically happened in the past, what happens in the present or predictions about the future.

Language notes: adjectives with infinitives

• There are many language pairs in this exercise. The patterns are:

It is It will be It used to be	easy/difficult possible/impossible legal/illegal important usual/unusual safe/dangerous healthy/unhealthy	+ infinitive with *to*

GRAMMAR: present tense in future time clauses (first conditional)

Grammar box

❯ *Language reference, Student's Book page 84*
❯ *Methodology Builder 22: Using Grammar boxes, page 106*
❯ *Methodology Builder 27: Grammar auction, page 131*

1

• Students fill the gaps in the text with the correct form of the verbs in brackets. You may want to do the first one together as a class to raise awareness about the kind of problems students will face (no. 1 is both an *if* sentence and a negative).
• Remind students that not all sentences are *if/when/ before/after* ones – so students will need to be very careful when deciding whether they need *will* or not.

1	don't take	7	arrive
2	won't get	8	will be
3	goes	9	is
4	'll have	10	will give
5	say	11	'll be
6	'll be	12	have

Language notes: present tense in future time clauses (first conditional)

• For teaching purposes this rule reduces neatly into one simple guideline and a workable board diagram:

When	...	+	w̶i̶l̶l̶	+	present	+	...
After							
Before							
If							

ie the main guideline is that after these four words we do not use *will*. Instead the present tense is used.
• It's important for students to realize that the meaning remains about the future even though the tense is the present.
• Although the guideline is relatively straightforward, it does seem to be very hard for learners to remember and apply, so don't be too upset if they continue to get it wrong. You're sure to hear your students saying *If I will* ... for months or years to come.
• The structure *If* + present + future is commonly referred to as the *first conditional.*

2

• Check that students have understood the story from exercise 1. Ask them: *Who is Emily? Where is she going? Why? How do you think her boyfriend will feel about this?*
• Students make sentences about what Emily's boyfriend feels about her trip from the prompts. Some extra words and grammatical changes will be needed. Remind students to use the pronoun *she* for each sentence.

2 If she can't/doesn't speak the language, she won't make friends.
3 If she doesn't make friends, she'll feel very lonely.
4 If she feels very lonely, she'll want to come home.
5 When she comes home, she won't have any qualifications.
NB Other variations are possible in some answers, eg using 'going to' in the main clause.

3

• Students can discuss other problems. Remind them to use the grammar they have been studying.

Extension task

• You could extend the discussion by asking students to imagine that they are planning to go to Japan or Mexico for a new job. What do they think will happen to them?

4

• Students write four sentences that are true about themselves using the questions.

IF YOU WANT SOMETHING EXTRA ...

❯ Straightforward Teacher's Resource Disc *at the back of this book*

8D | Help!

What the lesson is about

Theme	Using computers
Speaking	Pairwork discussion: talking about how you use computers
Listening	Informal dialogue: a dialogue about how to send an email
Vocabulary	Computer actions
Functional language	Giving instructions
Did you know?	Computer games in the US

If you want a lead-in ...

Discussion starters: using computers

> *Methodology Builder 15: Using Discussion starters, page 63*

- *Do you regularly use a computer? For work? For communication? For games?*
- *Do you enjoy computers – or are they a necessary evil?*
- *Why is English the international language of computing? Will this change?*
- *What annoys you about computers?*
- *Why do some people find computers so difficult, when others find them very easy?*

Test before you teach: computer words

> *Methodology guidelines: Test before you teach, page xxi*

- Write *undo*, *save* and *paste* on the board. Ask students where they would find all these words (*on a computer*).
- Ask students to work in pairs and think of as many more computer words/phrases as they can (but not names of machines or programs). After two minutes, collect all the words on the board. If you wish, ask students to explain what some of them mean.
- Now tell students to look at all the words and suggest a group of words and the order they would happen in real life. For example:
  switch on > log on > open program > close program > log off > shut down
  select > cut > paste
  open > type > save > close
- There are many possible answers. Students may be able to suggest some you haven't thought of.

Speaking

1
- You could go into this task following straight on from *Discussion starters*.
- Pairwork. Students discuss the six questions.

Extra task: further internet questions
- *Is the internet a good thing? Why?*
- *Is the internet dangerous? How?*
- *Will everyone in the world soon be on the internet?*
- *How do you think the internet will develop over the next ten years?*
- *Will the internet completely replace TV, cinema, letters, etc?*

Vocabulary: computer actions

> *Language reference, Student's Book page 85*

1
- Students label the icons A–L with the words in the box. All these words are verbs describing actions on a computer except for *cursor*, which describes the little pointer that a user moves around the screen.
- With computer-literate students, you could see if they can name the icons without reference to the words in the box.

A	cursor	E	save	I	undo
B	open	F	paste	J	attach
C	copy	G	send	K	delete
D	find	H	print	L	close

Answers K and L could arguably be swapped.

2
> *Methodology Builder 29: Gap-fill exercises, page 150*
- Students use seven of the twelve computer words to fill the gaps in the sentences.

1	send	4	paste	7	save
2	print	5	cursor		
3	delete / undo	6	attach		

Listening

In this listening, a young woman called Karen gives her grandfather instructions on how to attach a photo to an email and send it.

1 🔘 2.14
- Ask students to look at the photo and say what they think is happening. Listen to their suggestions, but don't confirm any yet.
- Students listen to the dialogue and answer the three questions. They can then compare answers in pairs.

1	not very much
2	send an email
3	yes

2.14

> G = Grandfather   K = Karen
> **G:** Karen, could you give me a hand with this?
> **K:** Sure. What are you trying to do?
> **G:** I want to send an email.
> **K**: Yes, OK. Are you online?
> **G:** Erm, not sure.
> **K:** Here, look, <u>first of all</u>, <u>click on that button there</u>. That connects you to the internet.
> **G:** Oh, right. Like this?
> **K:** Yes, that's right. But <u>do it twice</u>, a double click. OK, now you're online. Right, <u>now</u> <u>click on that email icon</u>. There.
> **G:** OK, got it.
> **K:** OK, <u>then</u> <u>click on 'Write Mail'</u>, OK?
> **G:** Yes, OK. There's a lot to remember, isn't there?
> **K:** You'll soon pick it up. Oh, you see the little picture of an address book? <u>You type the address there next to the icon</u>. You're writing to Dad! What are you writing to Dad for?
> **G:** Just to surprise him. And I want to send him one of those pictures you took.
> **K:** Oh, OK.
> **G:** Anyway, what next?
> **K:** Well, <u>next</u> <u>you write your message</u>. In the big space there.
> **G:** It's a short message! S-U-R-P-R-I-S-E. That's it. And the photo?
> **K:** OK, <u>first of all</u>, <u>click there on 'attach'</u>. OK, good, and <u>then</u> we have to find the photo. Here, I'll do it for you. OK, that's it.
> **G:** That's it. So, I just click on 'send'?
> **K:** Yes. And <u>don't forget to log off</u>.
> **G:** OK. Wonderful. Thanks. When will he get it? Does it take long to arrive?

2 **2.14**
- Students listen to the recording again and number the instructions in the correct order for sending an email.

Correct order: 6, 2, 1, 3, 8, 7, 4, 5
You could also type the address after writing your message!

Alternative procedure

- Computer-literate students should easily be able to work out a possible order before listening to the recording. They can then check with the recording if Karen gives the same instructions.

3
- Students compare their way of sending an email with a partner.

One common difference might be that some people will choose to connect to the internet after writing their email. And if the student uses broadband then they are likely to be permanently online and not need to log off.

FUNCTIONAL LANGUAGE: giving instructions

> *Language reference, Student's Book page 84*

1
- Students look at audioscript 2.14 and underline all examples of instructions and sequencing adverbs.

In audioscript 2.14 on this page, the instructions and sequencing adverbs and imperatives have been underlined.

Language notes: giving instructions

- Grammatical imperatives are made using the base form of the verb (the infinitive without *to*).
- Imperatives do not change tense (eg there is no past form), and they do not alter to indicate different persons (eg there is no third person *s*).
- You can add *always* in front of an imperative, eg *Always check that you've typed the address correctly.*
- To make an imperative more polite (ie more of a request or invitation than an instruction) we can add *Do* in front of it, eg *Do come in!* This can also indicate impatience or exhaustion with someone who is not doing what they are told, eg *Do press that button, Bella!*
- You can give a negative instruction (ie a warning) by adding *Don't* or *Never* in front of the imperative sentence. *Don't* usually gives an immediate instruction about the present situation, whereas *Never* gives a general instruction that will apply over a longer time. Examples are: *Don't do that!* or *Don't press that key* or *Never open email attachments from people you don't know.*
- As well as the grammatical form called imperatives, other grammatical structures can have the function of giving an imperative-type instruction.
- Instructions can become a little less direct by using a normal present simple sentence instead of an imperative, eg *You type your address there next to the icon.* The context makes it act as an instruction.
  But be careful, this is different from simply adding the word *You* in front of an imperative which can sound ruder and more forceful – especially if you use more aggressive intonation, and put a pause between the *you* and the imperative, eg *You get over here!* or *You send that email now!* or *You be quiet!*
- You may feel clearer about this difference if you compare these two examples:
  You type your address there.
  You! Type your address there!

2
- Students read the instructions and number them in the correct order.

Correct order: 5, 3, 6, 7, 1, 4, 2

3

- Write on the board: *Dictionary … Thesaurus,* and ask students if they know what the difference is between the two. Almost everyone will be familiar with a dictionary, but fewer may have used a thesaurus. Elicit or give a definition:
A *thesaurus* is a reference book (or computer program) that lets you find words that have a similar meaning to a word you already know. This can be useful when you are writing, if you can't find exactly the right word, or if you want to avoid repeating words too many times.
- Tell students that the pictures show how to use a computer thesaurus program. Tell students to imagine that their friend wants to write *The world is getting older* but feels that the word *world* isn't quite right. How can they find a better word?
- Pairwork. One student looks at the pictures in order and gives instructions to their partner. The partner listens and at the end gives feedback on how clear the instructions were.

Possible answer:
2   Then go to the menu and click on 'Tools'.
3   Select 'Language'.
4   Next select 'Thesaurus'.
5   You will see a list of synonyms for the word. Choose the word you like best and click on 'replace'.
Students could add: Finally you will see your chosen word appear in your text instead of the original word.

Extension task

Other computer instructions

- Computer-literate students may enjoy repeating the instruction-giving task with different computer tasks using their own knowledge rather than pictures. Remind them to use the sequencing adverbs.
How can I put a picture at the top of my text document?
How can I put some of my favourite music tracks onto a CD?
How can I download and use a new screensaver?
How can I get a free internet email account?
How can I protect my computer against viruses?

Non-computer instructions

- For further practice, extend the task to other situations. Ask students to tell someone else:
How to make a cup of tea.
How to make a piece of toast.
How to mend a flat tyre.
- Instructions will be much more interesting when the listener doesn't already know how to do the task being described. For this reason, and for fun, you could try a few imaginary tasks such as the following ones. NB It will be best to allow two or more minutes of preparation time before students give their instructions. Students can tell each other:
How to rob a bank.
How to become President of the US.
How to win the Eurovision Song Contest.
How to be happy.
How to become a millionaire.
How to find the perfect wife/husband.
How to own an airline.

> ### Methodology Builder 23
> ### Total Physical Response (TPR)
> - *Total Physical Response (TPR) is a teaching method often used with beginners. The teacher works with a volunteer student and gives a long list of instructions which the student follows (eg 'Stand up.' 'Walk over to the window.' 'Open the window.' etc). The student is not required to speak at all, but learns a lot by understanding the meanings in context and then doing the actions. If the student misunderstands, the teacher can mime or show the correct action. Later on, (possibly many lessons later) when a student is ready, they may start to give instructions themselves.*
> - *The method is also interesting with students at Pre-intermediate level. Try the following instruction sequence with some of your students. When they have had a go, and understood the idea, ask each student to prepare their own instruction list, which they can then read out to their partner who does the actions.*
> *– First of all stand up.*
> *– Then walk over to the other side of the room.*
> *– After that study the poster on the wall.*
> *– Read aloud one line from the poster.*
> *– Next borrow a book from a nearby student.*
> *– Put the book on your head.*
> *– Then put your hands by your side.*
> *– After that walk across the room without dropping the book.*
> *– Finally give the book to someone you like and say 'Happy Birthday'.*

Did you know?

1

- Students read the text and discuss how similar the US situation is to their own country.

2

- Pairwork. Students discuss the questions about computer games.

Extra discussion: computer games

- *What features make a good game?*
- *What is your favourite game? Describe what happens in it.*
- *If you don't play, why not? Can you imagine any game that might start you playing?*
- *Some computer games make more money than Hollywood films. Why do you think they are so popular?*
- *Are games too violent? Do they have a bad effect on people?*
- *Why do men play more games than women?*

If you want something extra …

❯ Straightforward Teacher's Resource Disc *at the back of this book*

Answer key

8 REVIEW
Student's Book page 155

1

1 The telephone will not be a popular way of communicating. (1876)
2 Heavy machines will never be able to fly. (1895)
3 People won't want to hear actors talking in films. (1927)
4 It might be possible to sell four or five computers. (1943)
5 Computers in the future may weigh no more than 1.5 tons. (1949)
6 We will never use the television for entertainment. (1955)
7 I don't think people will want a computer in their homes. (1977)

2

3 It ~~won't be possibly~~ possibly won't be necessary …
5 Maybe scientists ~~maybe~~ will find …
7 There probably won't be ~~probably~~ another world war.
8 Perhaps we ~~perhaps~~ will make contact …

3

1 plan – Are you going to
2 prediction – will
3 plan – I'm going to
4 prediction – It will
5 prediction – will
6 plan – We're going to
7 plan – is she going to
8 prediction – You'll never

4

1 He won't like it if you do that.
2 If I have time, I'll come and see you.
3 If I need some money, I'll ask the bank.
4 I'll help you if you like.
5 They'll be very sad if you go away.
6 If we don't leave soon, we'll be late.
7 We'll miss the plane if we don't hurry.
8 You'll be ill if you eat that.

5

1 continues
2 will become
3 know
4 will happen
5 grow
6 use
7 will need
8 use
9 will be

6

Correct order: 2, 6, 5, 3, 8, 1, 7, 4

7

1 important
2 unusual
3 easy
4 usual
5 possible
6 difficult
7 legal
8 dangerous

8

Students' own answers

8 WRITING
Workbook page 79

Model answer

Dear Irena,

I hope you arrived safely! This is a quick note to tell you some things about the flat.
Firstly, I took some food out of the freezer before I left and it's on the side. Please help yourself to anything you find. The closest food shop is on Roman Road opposite the train station. While you're here could you please water the plants and feed the cat? Feel free to use the iMac if you want to.
Finally, if you have any problems, call my mother on 0393 774 843. The man next door at No. 12 (Ralph) is very friendly and he will help you with any problems in the flat: water and electricity. When you leave, could you leave one light on and switch the gas off? Have a good time while you're here!

Kristina

WHAT THE LESSON IS ABOUT

Theme	Entertainment: exhibitions, shows and events
Speaking	Pairwork discussion: talking about entertainment in London & your town
Listening	Radio programme: a radio programme about entertainment in London
Vocabulary	*-ing* & *-ed* adjectives
Pronunciation	Diphthongs
Did you know?	Leisure activities in the UK

IF YOU WANT A LEAD-IN ...

Discussion starters: going out

❱ *Methodology Builder 15: Using Discussion starters, page 63*

- *If you have a free day, what do you typically do?*
- *What is your idea of a really good day out?*
- *Do you prefer watching a show or going to an exhibition?*
- *You're going to a concert. What music would you choose?*

SPEAKING & LISTENING

In this radio programme, a reporter gives details about the coming week's music and arts events in London.

1

- Ask students to look quickly at the *What's on* text. Elicit what it is (information about shows, events, etc in London).
- Give students a one-minute time limit to read the text.
- Ask students if they can think of any friend to go with them to the first event (the circus) and why they would choose that person. Listen to a few suggestions from the class. Students then think of a friend or someone else to go with them to each of the other events.
- Pairwork. Students tell their partner who they chose and why, explaining what this person usually likes doing.
- You could make a rule that students can only pick the same person for a maximum of two events – otherwise a student might pick one person to go to all the events.

2 💿 2.15

- Students listen to part of a radio programme and decide in which order the seven events are mentioned.

> *Correct order:* 7, 6, 3, 5, 2, 4, 1

💿 2.15

> **N = Nick   S = Sarah**
> **N:** Now for our weekly look at what's on. Sarah, what have you got for us this week?
> **S:** Well, probably the most exciting concert of the summer is happening on <u>Sunday and Monday</u> this week at half-past seven. Lady Gaga, the incredible Lady Gaga is in town for two nights at the Wembley Arena. If you haven't got tickets, you'll be disappointed, but we've got two tickets to give away in this week's competition. Stay tuned. Also, this week, at the Sound Barrier in Oxford Street, there's a special Brazilian night with top DJs playing the latest sounds from Brazil's coolest clubs. Doors open at ten o'clock and you can dance <u>until four</u> in the morning. The place to be for a really cool night out.

> **N:** Erm, yes, a little past my bedtime, I think. Sorry to be boring and old-fashioned. What else have you got for us?
> **S:** Well, there's a fascinating afternoon of dance at Canary Wharf. It's part of a festival and they've got groups from Switzerland, France and Spain. It all sounds very interesting and it's free. That's Saturday between one and five, and let's hope the weather stays fine.
> **N:** Yes, indeed. Sounds very interesting.
> **S:** And if you're interested in dance, don't forget that you can still see *Mamma Mia*, London's most popular and enjoyable musical, at the <u>Prince of Wales Theatre</u>. Performances are on at half-past seven Monday to Saturday, with an afternoon show on Saturdays <u>at half-past three</u>. No shows on Sunday.
> **N:** Right.
> **S:** The next thing I've got is something for you. This Friday, there's a performance of Verdi's *Requiem* at <u>the Royal Festival Hall</u>. That's half-past seven Friday.
> **N:** Ah, yes, a beautiful piece of music!
> **S:** Isn't it a bit depressing going to listen to a requiem?
> **N:** Pardon?
> **S:** Right, what next? Yes, there's an absolutely fantastic exhibition at the National Gallery. Paintings by <u>the Spanish Impressionist</u>, Camille Pissarro.
> **N:** Pissarro.
> **S:** Yes. You'll be surprised – these paintings are really amazing. Every day <u>from nine in the morning</u> to six o'clock. Ooh, and one last idea. A fun idea for all the family. The Moscow State Circus is in <u>Alexandra Park</u> this week from Tuesday to Sunday. Not to be missed.
> **N:** Thank you, Sarah. Time now to go over to the news room, but stay tuned for details of our competition with two tickets for Lady Gaga ...

3 💿 2.15

- Tell the class that Sarah isn't a very good entertainment reporter. She always makes mistakes. They listen to the recording again, compare it with the events in exercise 1 and underline the text when they find something different.

> Brazilian Club Night: Saturday 10pm–<u>2am</u> (not 4am)
> *Mamma Mia*: <u>Aldwych</u> Theatre (not Prince of Wales Theatre)
> *Mamma Mia*: Saturday <u>3pm</u> (not 3.30pm)
> Verdi's *Requiem*: Royal <u>Albert</u> Hall (not Royal Festival Hall)
> Camille Pissarro: <u>French</u> Impressionist (not Spanish)
> Camille Pissarro: Daily <u>10am</u>–6pm (not 9am)
> The Moscow State Circus: <u>Victoria</u> Park (not Alexandra Park)

4 & 5

- Tell students that Sarah uses some colourful descriptive words to describe the events. Ask if anyone can remember which word in column B was used to describe which event. Collect some ideas, then ask students to listen again and match events with the words.
- Ask students to look at audioscript 2.15 on page 141 to check. Then ask students if they agree with the reporter's choice of adjectives to describe each event.

> 1 g   2 e   3 f   4 b   5 a   6 c   7 d

6

- Pairwork. Students discuss the questions about what they would like to do in London and about entertainment in their own town.

Extra discussion

- *Have you ever seen Verdi's* Requiem *or any of the other events?*
- *Which of these seven events would you least want to go to? Why?*
- *Would you pay a lot of money to see your favourite pop star?*
- *Would you ever buy a ticket from a man outside a concert for three times the price printed on the ticket?*
- *Why do people go to art exhibitions?*

Cultural notes: artists, singers and events

The Moscow State Circus
- The Moscow State Circus is a very popular touring circus with many acrobatic and gymnastic acts. It is particularly well known for *high wire acts* and *trapeze artists*.

Camille Pissarro
- Born in 1830, Pissarro was one of the most important and influential of the French Impressionist painters, although in his lifetime he sold very few of his pictures.

Verdi's *Requiem*
- A Requiem is a funeral mass which is sung traditionally in Roman Catholic churches. Verdi's *Requiem* was composed between 1868 and 1873 in memory of the great Italian composer, Rossini.

Mamma Mia – the Musical
- This musical was originally performed in London's West End in 1999 and is now popular worldwide. It uses the songs of the 1970s Swedish pop band ABBA to tell the story of a girl, on the eve of her wedding, who invites three of her mother's former lovers to the wedding because she wants to know which one is her real father. It was made into a film in 2008.

Lady Gaga
- Lady Gaga is a singer-songwriter from New York who has had a number of international hits and is as famous for her outrageous costumes and stage persona as for her songs.

Web research task

⊙ *Methodology Builder 1: Using Web research tasks, page 2*

- Ask students to find something interesting happening in London over the next month. They should report back to the class. Who chose the most interesting event?

Web search key words
- *London events*

VOCABULARY: *-ing* & *-ed* adjectives

⊙ *Language reference, Student's Book page 95*

1

- Students read the question and discuss the answers. Get feedback on their answers from the whole class and clarify the rules.
- Alternatively, write the sentences on the board, asking the questions and eliciting answers.

> *relaxing* describes the thing that makes him/her feel that way
> *relaxed* describes how the person feels

Language notes: *-ing* & -ed *adjectives*

- This is a language area that learners often find confusing. Even when they understand the point, it can still be hard to recall and use correctly. Unfortunately, errors can be unintentionally humorous or rude, eg when a student went up to a stranger at a party and said: ✗ *Are you boring? You look very boring* when she actually meant to make a polite enquiry to someone who looked *bored*.
  Similarly a student who said: ✗ *I am very disappointing* when he came out of a film when he intended to talk about the film rather than about himself.
- Students will discover the simplest and most useful guideline in exercise 1:
  -ed describes how a person feels.
  -ing describes the person or thing that causes the person to feel like that.
- A board picture can sometimes help to clarify this point:

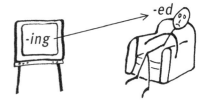

The TV programme is boring … so … Fred feels bored.

- Learner confusion often arises from the fact that the cause of the feeling can be a *human* as well as a thing:

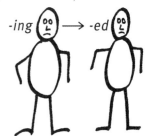

Mike is boring … so … Fred feels bored.

- An interesting way of looking at this grammar problem would be to think of the *-ing* form as an *active* form and the *-ed* form as a *passive* form.
  In other words the *-ing* form is something that a person or a thing *does* (or *is*) – but the *-ed* form is something that is done to someone else.
- Many *-ing* and *-ed* adjectives are related to verbs, ie they are the present participle (*-ing* form) or past participle of verbs.
- The adjectives in this lesson are:

ACTIVE	PASSIVE
annoying	annoyed
depressing	depressed
disappointing	disappointed
exciting	excited
fascinating	fascinated
frightening	frightened
relaxing	relaxed
surprising	surprised
tiring	tired

- Other useful adjectives that students often confuse are:

amazing	amazed
confusing	confused
embarrassing	embarrassed
terrifying	terrified
worrying	worried

2 & 3 🔘 **2.16**
- Students choose the correct adjective for each sentence.
- Pairwork. Students listen to the recording of the four short dialogues and then practise reading the dialogues with their partner.

> 1 excited; boring
> 2 tired; annoying
> 3 relaxing; depressed
> 4 disappointing; surprised

🔘 **2.16**

> **1**
> **A:** I'm so <u>excited</u>. I've got tickets for the Lady Gaga concert.
> **B:** Lady Gaga? I think her music is <u>boring</u>.
> **2**
> **A:** I'm really <u>tired</u>. I didn't get home until three o'clock this morning.
> **B:** I know. And it was extremely <u>annoying</u> that you came home singing.
> **3**
> **A:** I think this music is really <u>relaxing</u>.
> **B:** Really? It makes me feel <u>depressed</u>.
> **4**
> **A:** The concert was a bit <u>disappointing</u>, wasn't it?
> **B:** Yes, I was <u>surprised</u>. Celine Dion is usually so good.

4
- Students finish the sentences so that they are true for them.
- They can then work in pairs and read the sentences to their partner and discuss any interesting comments.

Extra practice
- Ask students to go back through each of the six sentences and make a true sentence using the *-ing* or *-ed* form not used in the original question, eg for question 1, students need to make a true sentence using *frightened*.

PRONUNCIATION: diphthongs

1 & 2 🔘 **2.17**
- Go through the top line of the table item by item and check that students have a good idea how to pronounce them, taking special care over the diphthong sounds. Then ask why *don't* is in the same column as *know*. Make sure students are clear that it is there because it has the same diphthong sound.
- Students can go through the other words with a partner and decide which column each should go in.
- When the pairs have finished, put them into groups of four to discuss and agree on their answers.
- Students listen to the recording and check their answers.

🔘 **2.17**

> **night** /aɪ/ find; kind; quite; time; twice
> **know** /əʊ/ don't; go; home; most; show
> **now** /aʊ/ down; house; out; sound; town
> **name** /eɪ/ fame; place; Spain; state; stay

3
- Students find new items for each column (at least two for each).

> *Many words are possible. These are a few:*
> /aɪ/ light; fine; nine; line; climb; wine
> /əʊ/ toe; low; note; grow; slow; blow
> /aʊ/ how; found; brown; round; cow
> /eɪ/ grey; may; train; way; pain

Extra task: diphthong dominoes
- Prepare a page with about 20 cards, showing pairs of words that contain different diphthongs in them. For example:

> | kind – don't | night – town | go – twice |

- Photocopy and cut these up so that each pair of students has one set. In class, use these as a game like dominoes. Pairs each have half the cards and must take it in turns to play one card next to a previous card so that the diphthong matches. For example:

> | kind – don't | go – twice | night – town |

Language notes: diphthongs
- *Diphthongs* are phonemes that are made up of two vowel sounds said quickly so that the first vowel smoothly glides into the next, as if it is a single sound.
- The diphthongs in RP English are: /ɪə/; /eɪ/; /ʊə/; /ɔɪ/; /əʊ/; /eə/; /aɪ/ and /aʊ/. This lesson only focusses on /aɪ/; /əʊ/; /aʊ/ and /eɪ/.
- Help students to recognize and say diphthongs by getting them to say the first vowel sound a few times; then the second; then the two sounds together one after the other; then lengthening the first sound a little and shortening the second until it is like a smooth single sound. For example:
  e … e …; ɪ … ɪ …; e … ɪ …; e…. ɪ..; eɪ
  NB The first sound of /ɔɪ/ is the same as /ɒ/ (as in *hot, cough,* etc). The first sound of /aɪ/ is similar to /æ/.

DID YOU KNOW?

1
- Ask students to look at the list of seven free-time activities. Tell them that these are things that British people like to do, in order of their popularity.
- Discuss as a whole class how this list compares with people in their own country and with their own tastes.
- Pairwork. Students discuss the three questions.

IF YOU WANT SOMETHING EXTRA …
- ❯ Straightforward Teacher's Resource Disc *at the back of this book*

9B | Reality TV

WHAT THE LESSON IS ABOUT

Theme	Reality TV
Speaking	Groupwork discussion: planning a reality TV show
Reading	*Reality TV – love it or leave it.* Magazine article: the origins of reality TV and its problems
Vocabulary	TV programmes
Grammar	Passive

IF YOU WANT A LEAD-IN ...

Test before you teach: passives

❯ *Methodology guidelines: Test before you teach, page xxi*

• Write these words on the board:
  the   the   the   visitors   conference   manager   drove   to
• Tell students they have to make a good English sentence using all the words. They will probably succeed in finding *The manager drove the visitors to the conference* (or perhaps *The visitors drove the manager to the conference*).
• Now let the class see you erasing the word *drove* in the original set of words and writing up the additional words *by   driven   were* instead. Set the task again – can they find a good English sentence using all the words?
• If the class find the answer *The visitors were driven to the conference by the manager*, ask them if it means the same as the first sentence. (Answer: *The basic meaning is the same.*) Don't analyze it any further.
• If they don't find the answer, tell them that you'll leave the words on the board and you'll check later in the lesson.

Discussion starters

❯ *Methodology Builder 15: Using Discussion starters, page 63*

• *Say the names of some programmes on TV and say which of these are about the lives of real people.*
• *Imagine a programme with no actors or story, but just a camera following the normal life of a normal person every day. Would you watch it? Do you think other people would watch it? Why?*
• *If a TV producer said they wanted to put cameras all round your house and film you for a month, would you agree to it? Why or why not?*

VOCABULARY: TV programmes

❯ *Language reference, Student's Book page 95*

1

• Make sure that students are clear that this is torn out of a TV programme guide, ie listing what programmes are on.
• Ask students if they are familiar with any of the programmes in the TV guide (or with similar ones).
• Students can work in pairs to match the types of programmes with examples of programmes in the listing.

1	game show	5	soap opera
2	chat show	6	documentary
3	sitcom	7	current affairs
4	sports programme		programme

2

• Write up the seven types of programme. Elicit examples of each from the students' country. Check that students are clear about the different types of programme.
• Alternatively, you could do this exercise and the following exercise together as a single pairwork discussion.

3

• Pairwork. Students discuss the three questions.

Extra discussion

• *Which soap operas are most popular in your country?*
• *Some people say 'The advertisements are better than the programmes.' Do you agree?*
• *Which kind of programmes do you think are cheapest for the TV companies to make?*
• *A famous British actor once said 'Television is for appearing on, not for watching.' Would you like to appear on TV? What kind of programme? Would you be good?*

Cultural notes: TV programmes

• TV stations like **game shows** because they are popular and relatively cheap to make. The most common game shows are quizzes, often combining simple questions and an element of luck. Members of the public compete in order to win large cash prizes. *Wheel of Fortune* is a long-running game show in the US and other countries. Players spin a large wheel that shows various large and small money prizes. They then answer questions by guessing letters of the alphabet that come in the answer.
• A **chat show** is a programme in which the host(s) chat to various celebrity guests in an informal way about personal lives and loves, as well as their professional work. In America, *The Tonight Show* is a very famous chat show.
• A **sitcom** (situation comedy) is a comedy that has a new story about the same characters and locations (ie the same situation) every week. Popular sitcoms in the UK are *The Office* (a comedy in the style of a reality documentary, set in an office), and, of course ... the American sitcom *Friends*.
  Friends is one of the most successful TV situation comedy series ever made. It is set in New York and follows the lives of six friends who live there and who spend a lot of time at a café called *Central Perk*.
• A **soap opera** is a story which continues week after week, year after year without end. They are typically set in a particular location and involve the same characters who have various complicated relationships with everybody else. A famous US soap opera is *The Bold and the Beautiful*. In many countries Brazilian soap operas are very popular.
  They are called soap operas because when they started on US radio, they were interrupted by advertisements for cleaning products.
  EastEnders is a long-running UK soap opera. It is set in a fictional east London location called Walford and the stories centre on the many characters who live and work in this area.
  The other very popular TV UK soap operas are *Coronation Street* (the longest running British soap opera, set in a working-class suburb of Manchester), and *Emmerdale* – also set in the north of England.

- A **documentary** is a factual programme, usually focussing on a single topic. In the UK, there are many wildlife documentaries about the lives of animals and birds or about a particular region of the Earth.
- **The news** tells you about important events that have happened in the last 24 hours. **Current affairs** programmes also focus on recent events, but are more reflective and often include discussion, interviews, reports and analysis.

Web research task

⊙ *Methodology Builder 1: Using Web research tasks, page 2*

- Divide the class up so that different students have different countries to research: the UK; the US; Canada; Australia; New Zealand; Ireland.
- Ask students to find a TV programme they would like to watch tonight on TV in the country they are researching.

Web search key words
- *TV tonight country name*

READING

This magazine article discusses the origins of reality TV, how it has expanded worldwide, why TV companies like it and why some viewers don't like it.

1
- Students choose three of the five summary descriptions and match them to the correct paragraphs.

Paragraph 1: b	Paragraph 2: d	Paragraph 3: e

2
- Students read the text again and tick any of the subjects that are mentioned. Remind them that this is not a True/False task. Some sentences may be true – but are they mentioned in this text?

1 ✓	2 ✗	3 ✓	4 ✗	5 ✗	6 ✓	7 ✓	8 ✗

3
- Students can work in small groups to discuss the questions about reality shows.

Extra discussion
- *Why do you think people watch reality shows?*
- *Would you take part in any of these shows? Which one?*
- *Do you think that the people who take part in reality shows are stars?*
- *What in your opinion is the worst programme on TV?*

GRAMMAR: passive

Grammar box
⊙ *Language reference, Student's Book page 94*
⊙ *Methodology Builder 22: Using Grammar boxes, page 106*

1
- Students find three examples of the passive in paragraph 3 of the magazine article and underline them.

1	In France, reality TV <u>is called</u> …
2	… the studios of *Loft Story* (*Big Brother*) <u>were attacked</u> …
3	In Greece, *Big Brother* <u>was described</u> …

Stronger classes
- As there are many examples of passives through the whole text, you could ask students to find as many as they can. (Answers: Paragraph 1: *was called; was shown; was born; was filmed; was watched; are known*. Paragraph 2: *are asked; are made; are published; are sold; are forgotten*).

2 & 3 ⊙ 2.18
⊙ *Methodology Builder 29: Gap-fill exercises, page 150*

- Students select one of the eight words for each gap, changing the grammar so that the word fits.
- As all answers are passives, all verbs will need to be in the past participle form with the correct form of the verb *be*. The verbs are all in the present simple tense, so all auxiliary verbs will be either *is* or *are*. You could allow stronger students to realize this for themselves, whereas it might help if you point it out to weaker students.
- Students listen to the recording and check their answers.

2	are taught	6	is invited
3	are (not) allowed	7	is sent
4	is filmed	8	is given
5	are shown		

⊙ 2.18

Star Academy
Thousands of young people apply to take part in this programme. They send video tapes to the producers and a group of them <u>are chosen</u> to take part. During the series, they live in a castle, where they <u>are taught</u> to sing and dance. They <u>are</u> not <u>allowed</u> to speak to their friends or family and every moment of their life in the castle <u>is filmed</u>. Their lives <u>are shown</u> on TV every evening, and on Saturday there is a special show. A famous TV star <u>is invited</u> on the show and one of the contestants sings a song with him or her. At the end of the programme, there is a vote and one person <u>is sent</u> home. At the end of the series, the winner <u>is given</u> a contract to make an album.

4
- Students choose the correct verb form in each sentence. In this exercise, they need to choose whether it is appropriate to use a passive or not.

1	was shown	5	were taken
2	tried	6	left
3	learnt	7	was told
4	were told		

Language notes: passive
- The grammatical formation of the passive is relatively straightforward – the verb *to be* (in any tense) plus a past participle. For students the bigger problem will be deciding whether a passive is needed or not needed.
- *Grammar* exercise 4 raises a number of interesting problems. The following notes are a commentary on the answers to this exercise, question by question:
Question 1: Compare these two sentences:
  (a) *The TV programme showed the latest news about Haiti.*
  (b) *The TV programme was shown in Haiti.*

Although a TV programme can show *things* (active) such as *news*, in sentence (b) someone (the station or the production company) broadcast the programme. So sentence (b) is passive and has the same meaning as in question 1. The passive is used because we don't know who showed the programme and it is unimportant to the sentence.

Question 2: This is active as the women are clearly the agents who did the trying. The sentence *Fifteen women were tried …* has a different meaning – that they were in court and accused of a crime.

Question 3: *People learn things* (active). *Things* (eg historical facts, new vocabulary, etc) *can be learnt* (passive). Students sometimes use the active verb *learn* when they really need the verb *teach*, eg ✗ *He learnt me three new songs.*

Question 4: Other (unknown) people told the women (passive).

Question 5: We don't know who took the man and women – so it's passive. The important information is about the man and women – and this is placed at the front of the sentence.

Question 6: The woman does the leaving herself (active) – even though she may have been required to do this by the organizers or the rules of the show.

Question 7: Other people (unknown) told the woman about the choice – so it is passive.

5

- Ask if students can think of some reality programmes in their own country. Collect the names on the board.
- Students can work in pairs. Each student chooses one programme and makes true sentences using the table. Their partner should write down the sentences.
- If your students are not familiar with this kind of programme (either because they don't watch them or because they are not shown in their country), go straight on to the following *Speaking* exercise 1, but refer to the table and ask students to use it in their dialogue.

SPEAKING

1

- This activity could be done quickly (five to eight minutes) or, if you want, it could become a useful and enjoyable long activity (30+ minutes).
- Groupwork. Put students into groups of four to six. They plan a reality show of their own using the questions as guidelines.
- Remind students that they will need to make a presentation to the class. Allow them plenty of time to prepare for this.

Weaker classes

- Put students into groups. Tell them they work for a TV company and want to start a new reality show. Ask students to take four minutes to discuss and agree the kind of reality show they want to make. Suggest the general areas: music; relationships and marriage; survival; living together; difficult challenges.
- Ask students to choose a name for the show and to take ten minutes to agree the details of the show. Choose some of these questions and write them on the board:
  1 What exactly happens?

2 How many people are on the show and what sort of people?
3 What do people have to do to win?
4 How long will the show last? (one week? four months?)
5 What is the prize?
6 Are there any unexpected surprises or tricks?
7 Why will it be popular with the audience?

- When students have agreed all the main details, tell them that they will need to make a two-minute presentation to sell their idea to the TV company. Give them five minutes to prepare their presentation.

2

- Groups make a presentation of their plans. The rest of the class acts as a TV production company and asks questions and discusses the ideas. At the end of all the presentations, the class votes for the idea that would make the best show.

■ **Methodology Builder 24**
■ **Student presentations**

- *If handled well, presentations can be an exciting student-focussed activity, but they carry some risk of embarrassing students and teacher. Here are a few key hints to help make presentations work:*

Preparation

- *Make sure students have sufficient preparation time. If students have been working on a different task (eg a decision-making task such as* Speaking *exercise 2), it's easy to forget that they will also need time to prepare the presentation itself. Allow time at the end of the main task for them to do this.*
- *Encourage students to use key-word notes rather than a complete script. Students often think they will be more comfortable reading, but it doesn't work well. Notes make them think and use language live, which generally leads to much better presentations.*

Training students to give presentations

- *Write the ideas in the 'Skills of speaking in front of a crowd' list below on the board and talk about them briefly. If you feel confident, you could give brief demonstrations of doing these things well, contrasted with doing them badly (eg speaking to the audience compared with speaking to the floor).*
- *Ask a few students to come up and let them try ideas out. Repeat in small groups.*

Skills of speaking in front of a crowd

- *Make eye-to-eye contact with the people in the audience (not with their shirts or hair, etc).*
- *Speak to the audience, not to the ceiling, your shoes, the door or your hand.*
- *Practise bouncing your eyes around different people in the room.*
- *Remember – many presentations seem boring to the listeners because the audience can't hear properly. Don't mumble.*
- *Practise projecting your voice. This means making your voice come out clearly and loud enough. It isn't the same as shouting!*
- *Breathe … slowly!*
- *Don't say everything in one rush. Leave pauses in your speech. Give your listeners time to think.*

IF YOU WANT SOMETHING EXTRA …

❯ Straightforward Teacher's Resource Disc *at the back of this book*

9c | Oscars® and raspberries

WHAT THE LESSON IS ABOUT

Theme	The Oscars® ceremony (and the Razzies®)
Speaking	Pairwork discussion: talking about going to the cinema Performance: acting a scene from *Avatar*
Reading	*Oscars® night*. Magazine article: contrasting the Oscar® ceremony and the Golden Raspberry® awards
Vocabulary	Films
Grammar	Passive with agent

IF YOU WANT A LEAD-IN …

Introducing the theme: The Oscars®

- Write up the following on the board:
  De Niro 2
  Penn 2
  Winslet 1
  Pitt 0
- Put students into pairs. Ask them to discuss what the information refers to. If they don't know, add these extra clues:
  The Lord of the Rings – Return of the King 11
  Titanic 11
  Mission Impossible 0
- Confirm the answer. (Answer: *The information is about how many Academy Awards (Oscars®) the people or films won.*)
- When they know the answer, they should then write three things they know about the Oscars®.
- When ready, collect the students' extra information on the board and leave it there until the reading text has been looked at, at which point the facts can be checked as an extra reading task.

SPEAKING

1
- Pairwork. Students discuss the questions about cinema-going.

Extra discussion
- *Do you choose to see a film because of the story or the actors?*
- *Have you ever seen a film that everyone liked – except for you? (Or you liked and everyone hated?)*
- *Is it better to watch a film at the cinema or on DVD, video, TV? Why?*
- *If a film has won some prizes, eg 'Best Film', does that encourage you to see it?*
- *How important is the music in a film? How important are special effects to a film?*

VOCABULARY: films

> *Language reference, Student's Book page 95*

1
- Ask students if they have seen the film *Avatar*. If not, ask them to look at the poster advertising the film. Elicit information or guesses about the content of the film.
- Students then find words/phrases in the text about the film that match the five definitions.

1	soundtrack
2	is set
3	stars
4	director
5	special effects

Extra task
- Ask students in pairs to tell their partner what they know about the director and stars of *Avatar*, and, if they have seen the film, what they can remember about the soundtrack or special effects.

Cultural notes: Avatar
- The plot: Jake, a paraplegic war veteran, is taken to another planet, Pandora, where a race of tall, blue human-like people called the Na'vi live. A military unit there wants him to infiltrate the Na'vi tribe with the use of an 'avatar' – while sleeping, Jake's mind controls a tall, blue version of himself that makes him look like one of the Na'vi. They want Jake to find secrets of the tribe to help the military take over the Na'vis and so that they can mine for a precious mineral there. Jake falls in love with the beautiful Na'vi alien Neytiri and helps the tribe resist the military and the destruction of their planet.
- *Avatar* was released in 2009. It cost at least $200 million to make because of its amazing special effects, and it was a huge box office success. Despite all its nominations, it only won three Oscars®.

2
- Pairwork. Students discuss the two questions about films in town at the moment.

Web research task
> *Methodology Builder 1: Using Web research tasks, page 2*
- What films are currently showing in your area (or have been on TV recently)? Choose one film and find out some information about its story, actors, etc. Go on the web and find out if anyone has seen the film and written a review.
- Prepare a report on the film for the rest of your class.
Web search key words
- 'film title' *review*

READING

This magazine article contrasts two very different film awards, both taking part at the same time in Hollywood: the Oscar® ceremony (for the best in film) and the Golden Raspberry® awards (for the worst in film).

1

• Students read the article and find how the Oscars® and the Raspberries are connected. This is quite a demanding first task, and requires some detailed reading and understanding of the whole text.

> The Oscars® and Golden Raspberries® (Razzies®) are both award ceremonies for the cinema. They both happen on the same night in the same town (Hollywood). Both ceremonies are shown on TV. The Oscars® are very expensive to run, but the Razzies® are very cheap. In the Oscars®, awards are given for good films, acting, etc; Razzies® are given for bad performances, films, etc.

Alternative procedure

• If you want a gentler introduction to the text, you could use the lead-in *Introducing the theme*, and use the notes collected on the board, to make an introductory first task. Check if the facts are mentioned in the text and if they are true.

2

• Students read again and decide if each sentence is about the Oscars® or the Golden Raspberries®. Students could mark sentences with *O* or *R*.

> 1 O   2 R   3 R   4 R   5 O   6 O   7 R   8 O

3

• Students could discuss the question about their favourite and least favourite films with a partner.

Extra reading task: memory

• Tell students that you will set a memory test. Give them a few minutes to remember facts from the text, then ask them to close their books.
• Write the following on the board: 23.30 / 1929 / 250 / $10 / $5,000 / $20 million / 25.
• Ask students to copy the numbers and then give them three minutes to write down what each number refers to. Then let students check their answers by looking at the text again.
  (Answers:
  23.30 = *the stars arrive at the Oscars®*
  1929 = *the first Oscars® ceremony*
  250 = *the number of people who attended the first ceremony*
  $10 = *the cost of a dinner ticket at the first ceremony*
  $5,000 = *the cost of producing the Razzies®*
  $20 million = *the money TV companies pay for rights (permission to broadcast) to the Oscar® show*
  25 = *the number of years the Razzies® have been organized*)

GRAMMAR: passive with agent

Grammar box

❯ *Language reference, Student's Book page 94*
❯ *Methodology Builder 22: Using Grammar boxes, page 106*

1

• Students choose the correct form for the verbs. All verbs are to be put into the past simple passive.

1	was invented	5	was played
2	was seen	6	were written
3	was made	7	was won
4	was opened	8	was employed

Language notes: passives with agent

We can use *by* + agent:
• When we want to put an emphasis on who/what did something.
• When we want to place information about who/what did something at the end of a sentence for a dramatic effect, saving the new information until last, eg *The most violent riot in the country's history was started by a policeman.*
• When we want to make a fluent, direct link to the following sentence, eg *The picture that sold for $10,000 was painted by Monica. She is a three-year-old chimpanzee.*

2

• Students first rewrite the sentences in the passive using the sentence stems given.

> 1 A ship is hit by an iceberg.
> 2 Most of Andy's toys are thrown away by his mother.
> 3 The role of the cabaret singer is played by Nicole Kidman.
> 4 An alien is helped to return home by a boy and his friends.
> 5 The most advanced technology was used by the director.
> 6 This film was divided into two parts by the producers.
> 7 This story of ancient Rome was directed by Ridley Scott.

Extra practice: passive endings

• This practice exercise will help your students work on making good passive sentences. Tell them that you will read the endings of some sentences. They must write a true beginning for each. Do an example first:
  … by Shakespeare.
  Possible answers include: *Hamlet was written by Shakespeare.*
  Explain that there will be many possible answers. For weaker classes, point out that all answers will be in the form *X was Y by Z*, where *X* is a book, film, etc, *Y* is a past participle, and *Z* is a person or people.
  1 … by Steven Spielberg.
  2 … by Kylie Minogue.
  3 … by our teacher.
  4 … by Leonardo da Vinci.
  5 … by this class.

3

- Tell the students that the sentences in exercise 2 are about famous films. As an example, ask them which film sentence 1 is about. Students must now match the other sentences to the film names in the box.

1	*Titanic*	5	*Avatar*
2	*Toy Story 3*	6	*Harry Potter and the*
3	*Moulin Rouge*		*Deathly Hallows*
4	*ET*	7	*Gladiator*

4

- Pairwork. Students use the table to write their own sentences about films, books or TV programmes. It's important that they write these sentences, because they will need to work more with them in the next exercise.
- You could allow students to have ten minutes internet research time to collect information to help them make their sentences. But make sure that they choose films that will be known by the other students.

5

- Pairwork. Students rewrite the sentences from exercise 4 to make questions.
- You may want to take some time to clarify the formation of questions in the passive.

6

- Pairwork. Pairs meet up with another pair. Each pair asks the other pair their questions.

Language notes: passive questions

- Passive questions are formed by using:

wh- question word	+ verb *be* in correct tense	+ past participle	+ …

SPEAKING

1

- Pairwork. Students practise reading the dialogue aloud.

2

- Students perform their dialogues.
- Organize the feedback as an Oscar® awards ceremony. Appoint small groups to be responsible for each award, eg three pairs will be responsible for the *Best Male Actor* award. They should make a list of nominations and then write the winner on a folded piece of paper, which they read out. You could write these typical lines on the board: *The nominations for Best … are … , … , … and … . And the winner is … .*
- Possible awards are:
  Best film; best male actor; best female actor; best special effects.
  For fun, and if students spend longer preparing, you might want to add: best music; best costume, etc.

Extra task: pitching a film

- Explain to students that before getting the funding to make a film, producers sometimes have to 'pitch' an outline of the film to top Hollywood executives. Tell the class that they are going to pitch an idea for a new film.
- Divide the class into groups of three or four and give them the following questions (you could put them on a handout, the board or an overhead projector, or you could dictate them):
  What is the title of your film?
  What genre is it?
  Where and when is it set?
  What is the plot?
  How will it end?
  Which director are you going to hire?
  Who are the central characters?
  Why are these characters interesting?
  Which Hollywood stars will play these roles?
  Who will the film appeal to?
  How much money do you need?
- Give students five to ten minutes to prepare their ideas. When they are ready, ask groups to come to the front of the class and pitch their films. The rest of the class are the 'executives'; they must decide whether to give the producers the money, and whether the film is an Oscar® or a Razzie.

Extra task: interviewing a star

- Divide the class into pairs. Half the pairs are Hollywood reporters. The other pairs are Hollywood stars. Tell the stars to talk together and to 'invent' their career – tell them to think about films they have made recently and films they are about to make. Tell the reporters to think of questions to ask the stars about their careers.
- After three or four minutes, mix the pairs so that there is a star with a reporter. The reporters ask their questions and the stars improvise answers.
- In feedback, ask reporters to report what their star said to the class.

IF YOU WANT SOMETHING EXTRA …

❯ Straightforward Teacher's Resource Disc *at the back of this book*

9D | Box office

WHAT THE LESSON IS ABOUT

Theme	Concerts
Speaking	Pairwork roleplay: at the box office
	Pairwork discussion: describing a concert
Listening	Telephone calls: four people buy tickets on the phone
Functional language	At the box office
Pronunciation	Saying dates

IF YOU WANT A LEAD-IN ...

Introducing the theme & vocabulary: concert halls

- Ask students to tell you locations in your town where people can see concerts. Write the names on the board, making sure that they include small places (ie bars or clubs) as well as large concert halls or theatres. If you live in a small town, you may need to think about the nearest big city for this task.
- Put students into groups. They should tell each other about any performances they have seen at any of these locations, and whether they prefer seeing a concert in small or large places.
- Continue the discussion with the whole class and see if people agree.
- Students may conclude that big places are good because you can see bigger shows and more famous artists. Small places are good because you can get closer to the performers and there is often a better atmosphere.

SPEAKING

1

- Pairwork. Students discuss which artists they know about and which they would like to see.

Cultural notes: the events

- **The Metropolitan Hall** in this lesson is fictional, though many towns have a concert hall with this name.
- **Los Van Van** is Cuba's most popular band.
- **Salsa** is a lively, jazzy dance from Cuba and South America with Spanish and African influences. It has a distinctive five note rhythm, which has a strong effect on the listeners so that they feel that they have to get up and dance.
- **Justin Timberlake**
  A popular singer who first became famous as a member of NSYNC. His first solo album *Justified* was a big hit.
- **Coldplay**
  An English rock band, formed in 1996, which has had a lot of critical and chart success. Its lead singer, Chris Martin, is married to Gwyneth Paltrow, the film star.
- **Red Hot Chili Peppers**
  Schoolmates who formed a band in Los Angeles and then became famous for their outrageous behaviour. As they matured, the music became more popular.

- **Cecilia Bartoli**
  A classical singer from Italy. She has worked with many famous conductors and performers and has made many successful recordings.
- **Swan Lake**
  Tchaikovsky's work is probably the most famous classical ballet. The story is based on a fairy tale: Princess Odette has been changed into a white swan by an evil magician. Prince Siegfried falls in love with her but fails to save her and she dies.
- **Shakira**
  Colombian singer with a Lebanese father, she achieved great success in Latin America before breaking onto the world scene with her first English language album *Laundry Service* and a huge hit single *Whenever, Wherever*.
- **Messiah**
  One of the great choral works, Handel wrote this in 24 days in 1741. It is sometimes performed by gigantic choruses of over 3,000!
- **Mr Bean**
  A fairly naive and often idiotic comedy character performed by Rowan Atkinson in a series of short TV films that are mostly silent.
- **Wynton Marsalis**
  Wynton Marsalis is a trumpet player, a jazz and classical performer as well as a composer. A septet is a group of musicians with seven members.
- **Justin Bieber**
  A Canadian singer/songwriter who was discovered after he placed videos of himself performing on YouTube.
- **Tribute bands**
  In recent years, *tribute bands* and *tribute acts* have become increasingly popular. They are *impersonators* (people who look like and sound like the real performers). Probably Elvis Presley is the most imitated singer. Some tribute bands have very clever, funny names, often including a pun such as The Beat Alls, The Rolling Clones, Ironically Maiden, Led Zepagain, NU2 (U2 tribute), Think Floyd, REMAKE (REM tribute), Bjorn Again (ABBA tribute, named after one of the original artists).
- **Beauty and the Beast**
  A classic fairy tale by Italian author Giovanni Straparalo in 1550. The story was made into a Disney® cartoon and a spectacular musical.
- **Johann Strauss**
  Johann Strauss was the 'Waltz king' of 19th century Vienna. (Waltzes are dances for two people with a strong DUM-da-da DUM-da-da rhythm.) His 170 waltzes include *The Blue Danube*, *Tales From the Vienna Woods* and *Roses From The South*. The New Year's Day concert is traditional in Vienna and many other places.

PRONUNCIATION: dates

1 🔊 2.19

- Pairwork. Students test each other saying the numbers. They discuss and agree together which pronunciations are correct or not.
- Students then listen to the recording and check.
- It may be helpful to play the recording with lots of pauses, so that students can really compare what they say. A possible strategy would be:

T: *Say the first number again to each other.*
Pairs: (speak)
T: *Listen to this number on the recording.*
T: (plays one number from the recording)
T: *Was that the same as yours? Try again.*
T.   *OK. Now say the next number.*
Pairs: (speak)
T: *Now listen ...*
T: (plays next number)
etc

1	12–13 August	5	5 November
2	22 August	6	16 November
3	21 September	7	2 December
4	3 November	8	31 December

🔘 **2.19**

> first, second, third, fourth, fifth, sixth, eleventh, twelfth, thirteenth, fifteenth, sixteenth, twentieth, twenty-first, twenty-second, twenty-third, twenty-fourth, thirty-first

🔘 **2.21**

> On the seventh of August, we have the Cuban salsa band, Los Van Van. Then, for two nights, on the twelfth and thirteenth of August, we have Justin Timberlake. Coldplay are coming on the twenty-second of August, and we have the Red Hot Chili Peppers on September the third and fourth. For lovers of classical music, there is an evening with Cecilia Bartoli on September the twenty-first. Also, beginning on October the thirty-first, you can see Tchaikovsky's *Swan Lake*. Shakira is coming on the third of November, and on the fifth of November we have Handel's *Messiah*. The sixteenth of November is *A Night with Mr Bean* and on November the twenty-second, the Wynton Marsalis Septet are in town. Justin Bieber is coming on the second of December, and on the fourth of December there is a special tribute to the Beatles. From December the seventeenth to the twenty-fourth, we have our children's show, *Beauty and the Beast*, and finally on the thirty-first of December, there is the Johann Strauss New Year concert.

2 🔘 **2.20**

- Ask students to look at the six ways of writing dates. Tell them that they will hear two different ways of saying this date. Before students hear the recording, briefly ask pairs to guess what the missing words might be.
- Play the recording for students to complete the missing words.

> 1   September <u>the</u> twentieth
> 2   <u>The</u> twentieth <u>of</u> September

🔘 **2.20**

> 1   September the twentieth.
> 2   The twentieth of September.

Language notes: writing dates

- Months always start with capital letters.
- You can abbreviate month names when writing them. These are all three letters long and are usually written with a full stop. The abbreviations are:
  Jan. Feb. Mar. Apr. (May) Jun. Jul. Aug. Sep. Oct. Nov. Dec.
- When abbreviating dates as just numbers, the order that the numbers are written in is different in different cultures. This can sometimes lead to confusion – or even serious errors. It is worth raising students' awareness about this before it leads to a problem.
- If you are visiting a web page and see the date 03/06/07, what date might this be?
  In the UK and some countries of Europe, the order is Day/Month/Year – so 03/06/07 is the third of June in the year 2007.
  The same written date – 03/06/07 – in the US would be the sixth of March because they use the order Month/Day/Year.
  Japan uses Year/Month/Day, so 03/06/07 would be the 7th of June 2003.
  The international standard (which is becoming more widely adopted on internet sites) is Year/Month/Day. To avoid confusion the year is always written as four figures, eg 2007/06/03.

4

- Each student should think of four dates that are important to them. These can be day and month – or could include a specific year.
- Pairwork. Tell students not to look at their partner's paper. Partners ask each other what their dates are.
- When they hear the dates, they should write them down as a dictation and then ask why they are important, making a brief note about that.
- Tell students that they must only check their partner's original paper after they have heard all the dates, and are certain that they have written them correctly.

Language notes: pronunciation of ordinal numbers

Numbers used to show dates (or the position something has in a sequence) are known as *ordinal numbers*. A few of these may cause problems for students:
- In most cases the ordinal number is formed by simply adding *-th* to the number. However, *1ˢᵗ*, *2ⁿᵈ* and *3ʳᵈ* have special words which need to be learnt: *first, second, third*.
- Ordinal numbers above 20 that include *1ˢᵗ*, *2ⁿᵈ* or *3ʳᵈ* (eg *21ˢᵗ, 22ⁿᵈ, 23ʳᵈ, 31ˢᵗ, 42ⁿᵈ*, etc) also work in this way: *twenty-third, thirty-first*, etc.
- *20ᵗʰ* has three syllables: /ˈtwentɪəθ/, although it can also be pronounced quickly as /ˈtwentjəθ/.
- The dictionary pronunciation of *5ᵗʰ* is /fɪfθ/, although in fluent speech it is often pronounced /fɪθ/. This may be easier for students to say.
- Similarly *6ᵗʰ* is in the dictionary as /sɪksθ/, but is often said as /sɪkθ/.
- In the same way: /twelfθ/ is often pronounced /twelθ/.
- *15ᵗʰ* is pronounced /fɪfˈtiːnθ/ – not /faɪvtiːnθ/.

Language notes: pronunciation of dates

- When saying whole dates, there are three common ways used in the UK. The two in the coursebook are:
  Month + *the* + ordinal number
  The + ordinal number + *of* + Month

3 🔘 **2.21**

- Direct students to look again at the concert programme. Point out that there are eight missing dates.
- Explain that students will hear a recording that includes this information. Ask students to listen and fill in the dates they hear in the correct places on the programme.

- The third way was considered a little American until recently but is now very common:
  Month + ordinal number (eg *I'll see you October seventh*).
- To say what today's date is we usually use *It's ...*, eg *It's January the fifth.*
- Dictionaries show *-teenth* numbers having the stress on the *-teenth* syllable. However, when saying a date, the stress is sometimes not on the last syllable, especially when the speaker wants to make sure the date is understood, eg *It's the <u>thir</u>teenth of <u>May</u>; On the <u>seven</u>teenth of <u>Decem</u>ber.*
  NB The word *of* is pronounced as a weak form pronunciation, ie /əv/ rather than the full form/ɒv/.

LISTENING

In this listening, four different people phone Trevor at the Metropolitan Box Office to book tickets for different performances.

1

- All the vocabulary in this task is to do with choosing and buying a concert ticket. Students select the correct vocabulary item to fill each gap in the six sentences.

1	box office	4	sold out
2	booking fee	5	matinee
3	credit card	6	circle

2

- Pairwork. Students ask and answer the questions from exercise 1.

3 & 4 🔘 **2.22–2.25**

- Make sure students are clear about how the table is organized. Check by asking a quick question or two, eg *How much does speaker 2 pay for tickets? Who will speaker 4 see?*
- Tell students they will listen to four phone dialogues. They fill in the missing information in the ten numbered spaces.
- Students listen to the recording again to check their answers.

1	three
2	£240
3	Wynton Marsalis Septet
4	22 November
5	two
6	Red Hot Chili Peppers
7	one
8	£46
9	circle
10	£170

🔘 **2.22–2.25**

1
BO = Box office   M = Mary
BO: Metropolitan Box Office. This is Trevor speaking. Can I help you?
M: Yes, hello. I'd like to book three tickets for *Beauty and the Beast*, please.
BO: Certainly, madam. How many tickets do you want?
M: Three, please.
BO: Yes. And what date would you like?
M: The Tuesday before Christmas. December the twenty-third.
BO: And would you like the matinee or the evening performance?
M: Oh, the matinee, the matinee. It's for a young child, you see.
BO: OK. Well, we've got all tickets available for that performance. What sort of seats would you like?
M: The front of the stalls if you have them.
BO: We do indeed. Those seats cost eighty pounds each, so that'll be three times eighty, that's two hundred and forty.
M: Two hundred and forty.
BO: Right. Can I have your name, please?

2
BO = Box office   B = Becky
BO: Metropolitan Box Office. This is Trevor speaking. Can I help you?
B: Hello, good afternoon. I'd like two tickets for Wynton Marsalis, please.
BO: Yes, the Wynton Marsalis Septet. Saturday the twenty-second of November. Half-past seven.
B: Have you got anything in the circle?
BO: Front or rear?
B: How much are the seats at the front?
BO: I've got two right in the middle at the front for thirty-eight pounds.
B: Oh, great. Fine.
BO: So, that's seventy-six pounds altogether. Could I take your details, please?
B: Yes, the name's ...

3
BO = Box office   S = Stephen
BO: Metropolitan Box Office. This is Trevor speaking. Can I help you?
S: Yeah, I want a ticket for the Red Hot Chilis on the fourth of September.
BO: The Red Hot Chili Peppers? I'll just check for you. September the fourth ... No, I'm sorry, sir, we're sold out.
S: What about the other day? The third of September.
BO: Yes, we've got a few tickets left in the rear stalls.
S: Oh, great. How much are they?
BO: Er, they're forty-six pounds, including a booking fee of two pounds.
S: How much?
BO: Forty-six pounds altogether.
S: Forty-six pounds!? Forget it.

4
BO = Box office   P = Pablo
BO: Metropolitan Box Office. This is Trevor speaking. Can I help you?
P: Good afternoon. I'd like two tickets for the evening with Cecilia Bartoli, please.
BO: Certainly, sir.
P: The best seats you've got, please.
BO: I'll see what seats we've got available. We've got a couple of seats at the front of the circle at eighty pounds each.
P: Oh, fantastic.
BO: And there's a booking fee of five pounds, so that'll be one hundred and seventy pounds altogether.
P: Fine.
BO: Could I take your details, please ...

Language notes: buying tickets

- Most concert halls and theatres have their own *box office* (the place in the building where you can buy tickets).
- If you buy tickets somewhere else, you may be charged an extra *booking fee* to do this, often between 10% and 20% of the face value printed on the ticket. This may sometimes be called a *service fee* or a *handling fee*. This is how a ticket agency makes its profit (as they themselves probably bought the ticket at face value). For some big concerts, you cannot avoid a booking fee wherever you get your ticket.
- When a concert is *sold out* at the box office, it may still be possible to buy a ticket at a higher price from an agency or to get one for twice, or up to ten or 20 times, the face value from a *ticket tout* (someone selling tickets illegally, often right outside the concert venue). Many theatres and halls have shows in the afternoons some days a week. These are called *matinees.*

FUNCTIONAL LANGUAGE: at the box office

❯ *Language reference, Student's Book page 94*

1
- Students complete column A with an ending from column B to make a complete sentence.
- Students look at audioscripts 2.22–2.25 to check their answers.

1 j	2 e	3 b	4 g	5 i
6 d	7 h	8 c	9 f	10 a

2
- Pairwork. Students roleplay phoning the box office and booking tickets for a show. Remind students to use language from exercise 1.

◼ Methodology Builder 25 Phone call practice

One of the real-life difficulties of a phone call is that the speakers can't see each other. Everything has to be understood from what is said; there is no eye contact, there are no compensatory facial expressions or gestures, documents being discussed cannot be seen by both people, etc. Another difficulty is that the sound quality is often poor and words can be hard to catch. Here are a few ideas to give students realistic practice in the classroom:

- *Even if the seating in your class is fixed or hard to move, you may be able to ask students in each pair to sit back-to-back or side-to-side (so they can't easily make eye contact).*
- *If students are sitting face-to-face, ask them to hold their coursebook, or a piece of paper, between them when phoning, or ask them to close their eyes.*
- *Get students to sit a greater distance apart than normal. They may need to speak a little louder.*
- *Different pairs' dialogues may criss-cross and interfere with each other (which may provide an interesting extra distraction).*
- *Of course, if your students mainly need confidence building and language practice rather than immediate needs to make real phone calls, then often the best way to practise is simply as a normal face-to-face exercise.*
- *If you don't move the students at all, you can still ask them to hold up a mimed phone to their ears. Tell them to speak to the phone rather than to the person opposite.*

SPEAKING

1
- Allow students a few minutes to choose a concert they've been to. Tell them to read the questions and think about them, and to make short notes about their own answers.
- If you have students who have never seen a concert, tell them to imagine going to a concert of someone they would really like to see.

2
- Pairwork. Students tell each other about their concert.

IF YOU WANT SOMETHING EXTRA ...

❯ Straightforward Teacher's Resource Disc *at the back of this book*

Answer key

1

1 tired
2 annoyed
3 bored
4 exciting
5 frightened
6 disappointing
7 interesting

2

Students' own answers

3

1 is owned
2 are paid
3 are made
4 is watched
5 are known
6 are shown
7 are looked
8 is seen

4

1 was; built
2 was; called
3 were received
4 was; hit
5 were saved
6 was; directed
7 were; played
8 were won

5

1 The Titanic was built in 1911 in Belfast.
2 The captain of the ship was called Edward Smith.
3 Six, or possibly seven warnings about icebergs were received by the ship.
4 The ship was finally hit by an iceberg at 11.40pm on April 14ᵗʰ 1912.
5 About 700 people were saved from the ship.
6 The film was directed by James Cameron.
7 The main roles in the film were played by Kate Winslet and Leonardo DiCaprio.
8 Eleven Oscars® were won by the movie.

6

1 is watched
2 pay
3 writes
4 see
5 is introduced
6 are based
7 is called
8 are played
9 is thought
10 earn
11 star

7

Correct order: 2, 4, 7, 1, 6, 5, 3, 8

9 WRITING
❯ *Workbook page 81*

Model answer

Peter Ibbetson was made in 1935 and has recently come out on DVD. It is not a very famous film, though it stars Gary Cooper, one of the greatest Hollywood actors of all time. It was directed by Henry Hathaway. The screenplay was written by Constance Collier and is based on a novel by George du Maurier.
Peter Ibbetson is a simple, but incredibly romantic story about the power of love. It begins with two close childhood friends, Gogo and Mimsy. When Gogo's mother dies, he has to move away from Mimsy. Many years later, Peter (Gogo) is employed by the Duke and Duchess of Towers to design some buildings. The duchess is Mimsy and she and Peter fall in love. The duke tries to kill Peter, but shoots himself. Peter is sent to prison and the duchess becomes very ill. Every night, however, they walk with each other in their dreams in a strange and beautiful landscape.
This film is especially interesting because of the special effects of the dream scenes. A lot of people fall in love with this film because there is something very innocent, brave and hopeful about it.

10A | Animal lovers

WHAT THE LESSON IS ABOUT

Theme	People and their pets
Speaking	Pairwork discussion: talking about pets & animals
	Pairwork – Communication activity: guessing animals
Reading	*The United States of animals*. Magazine article: Americans' attitude towards their pets
Grammar	Present perfect simple with *for* & *since*

IF YOU WANT A LEAD-IN ...

Discussion starters

❱ *Methodology Builder 15: Using Discussion starters, page 63*

- *Do you have a pet? What is it called? When did you get it? How old is it? Is it well-behaved? Does it cause you any problems?*
- *Why do people keep pets?*
- *Do some people like animals more than humans?*

Animal vocabulary game

- Divide the class into teams. Set a time limit. Teams must find an animal for every letter of the alphabet. Allow students to use dictionaries. Start the teams off with a few examples together: A *alligator;* B *bear;* C *cat.* At the end of the time, award one point for each correct animal found.

Test before you teach: present perfect with *for* & *since*

❱ *Methodology guidelines: Test before you teach, page xxi*
- Ask students to look in their bags or pockets and find three things they own. (You could ask students the day before to bring in some special possessions.)
- Write on the board:
  I've had this since + time/date
  I've had this for ... years/months/days
- Students can work in groups of three. Ask them to show their possessions to each other and say something about them. Point out the sentences on the board (but don't go into explaining the grammar). Say that students could use them in the dialogue if they want to, but don't demand that they do so.

SPEAKING

1
- Pairwork. Students work in pairs, first to discuss the first question about pets, then to agree on the best pet from the box for each of the four people in the photos. Finally, students talk about their own favourite animal.

READING

This magazine article describes how crazy Americans are about animals and how much money some famous stars spend on their pets.

1
- Students can work in pairs to make a list of any famous Americans who have pets. If they know little about celebrities, do this stage quickly as a whole-class task, writing up any celebrity names suggested by the students.
- When students have made their list, they should read the article and underline all celebrity names in it.

Famous people listed in the article:
Oprah Winfrey; Leonardo DiCaprio; Naomi Campbell; Joan Rivers; Uma Thurman; Wayne Gretzky; Cher

2
- Direct students to read the seven sentences that explain how Americans are crazy about pets. Tell them that four of these explanations are in the article. Ask them to read again and choose the correct ones.

✓ 1, 3, 5, 7

3
- Students compare views in their own country with the views they have read about in the article.

Extra discussion

- *A friend has offered you a monkey as a pet. Would you say 'yes' to this present? Why or why not?*
- *Do people look like their pets?*
- *Do pets behave like their owners?*
- *What is the biggest pet you have ever seen?*
- *What is the strangest pet you have ever heard about?*

Web research task

❱ *Methodology Builder 1: Using Web research tasks, page 2*
- Ask students to find the most unusual animal to get as a class pet. Write up these questions on the board and ask students to make sure they find answers to them.
  1 *Name of animal.*
  2 *What it looks like (colour, size, number of legs, etc).*
  3 *What it eats.*
  4 *Why it is a good pet.*
  5 *How much does one cost?*
- At the end, the class can discuss which is the best suggestion and choose it as a class pet.
Web search key words
- *unusual pets*

GRAMMAR: present perfect simple with *for* & *since*

Grammar box

❱ *Language reference, Student's Book page 104*
❱ *Methodology Builder 22: Using Grammar boxes, page 106*
❱ *Methodology Builder 7: Using timelines, page 23*

1 & 2 💿 2.26
- This is a challenging discrimination exercise. Students choose either the present perfect or past simple of the verbs in brackets to fill the eleven gaps. Point out that students will need to put more than one word in some gaps.
- If students are having problems, remind them that the writer is writing now. If events started in the past and continue up to now, then we need the present perfect. If the events are entirely in the past, we cannot use the

present perfect. You could put the following reminder diagrams on the board – all answers fit one of these three diagrams.

(A) From the past up to now = present perfect

Now

(B) A moment in the past = past simple

Now

(C) A period in the past that *doesn't* come up to now = past simple

Now

• Students listen to the recording and check their answers.

> *The letters A, B or C indicate which diagram (above) the verb form fits.*
>
> | | | | |
> |---|---|---|---|
> | 1 | A has lived | 7 | A have been |
> | 2 | A has loved | 8 | C were |
> | 3 | B found | 9 | A has never worried |
> | 4 | A has found | 10 | A has been |
> | 5 | C had | 11 | A hasn't left |
> | 6 | B had | | |

🔘 **2.26**

> Oscar Werbeniuk, who is 61, <u>has lived</u> all his life in the same New Jersey house. He <u>has loved</u> animals, especially cats, since he was a child. He <u>found</u> his first cat, Tabatha, in the street in 1981, and he <u>has found</u> another 43 cats since then. But Tabatha – who died in 1990 – <u>had</u> babies and Oscar soon <u>had</u> more than a hundred cats. For the last fifteen years, there <u>have been</u> more than two hundred cats in his house. Oscar is lucky because his parents <u>were</u> very rich, so he <u>has never worried</u> about money. In fact, since 1999, Oscar <u>has been</u> so busy that he <u>hasn't left</u> his house.

3

• Students complete the phrases with *for* or *since*.

> | | | | | | |
> |---|---|---|---|---|---|
> | 1 | since | 5 | since | 9 | since |
> | 2 | for | 6 | for | 10 | for |
> | 3 | since | 7 | for | 11 | since |
> | 4 | since | 8 | for | 12 | since |

Alternative procedure

• This would also work well as an oral exercise, ie a drill. Call out a random time and the students must say the phrase including *for* or *since*. For example:

Teacher:	*yesterday*
Students:	*since yesterday*
Teacher:	*an hour*
Students:	*for an hour*

• It may be useful to ask students to record these in their notebooks, classifying answers under two columns: *for* and *since*. For example:

for	since
a day or two	*2002*
three years	*Monday*

Language notes: present perfect simple with *for* & *since*

> ❯ *Methodology Builder 7: Using timelines, page 23*

• This is a grammatical area that consistently causes problems for students. First, the present perfect is a tense whose meanings do not have exact equivalents in most languages. Second, the words *for* and *since* (along with *ago, from, until* and *during*) seem to be rather confusable concepts relating to different ways we can view time.

• Timelines are often a helpful way of clarifying the periods of time referred to.

• *For* indicates a period of time with a beginning and end. After the word *for* we say the length of time, eg *for six months; for six years; for six minutes*.

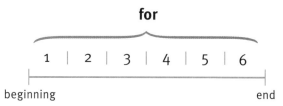

In the present perfect tense, the period lasts up to the moment now.

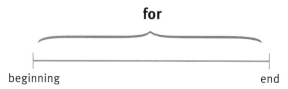

• NB *For* is a weak form /fə/ in sentences made using this structure – it is almost never stressed. If students have a problem, encourage them to read the word as if it is only an *f*, eg *She's worked there ften years*.

• *Since* tells us when something started and is almost always used with a perfect tense. We say the starting moment or time, eg *since two o'clock, since January, since the first time we met*. The action or event is still continuing now and may (or may not) continue into the future.

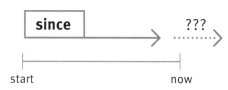

• Students tend to make errors by confusing various items and using them wrongly together:
> ✗ *I've been here for two weeks ago.*
> ✗ *I've been here since two weeks.*
> ✗ *I am here since Tuesday.*
> ✗ *I am staying here since Tuesday.*
> ✗ *I've been here for Tuesday.*

• *Since* is usually not correct with the past simple (we use *from* instead). The sentences *I've been here since eight* and *I waited from eight till ten* are both good, but the next sentence sounds wrong:
> ✗ *I was here since eight.*

- Sometimes a sentence is grammatically correct but is said with the wrong meaning. For example, when talking about past time students may say:
  I am here for two weeks.
  This is a correct sentence, but with a present and future meaning (*I will be here for a total period of two weeks*) rather than a past one.

4

- Students can work in pairs to find different possible endings for the sentence heads. Make sure that both partners write down all the questions.
  NB Sentence 1 could have a present perfect continuous ending, but as this has not yet featured in the coursebook, it is more likely that students will not use this.

> *Some possible endings for 1:*
> … a student; in this town; at this school; interested in films; a fan of Justin Timberlake; unhappy
> *Some possible endings for 2:*
> … that wallet; those shoes; that idea; your hair like that; my pen in your bag; your cold
> *Some possible endings for 3:*
> … Michael; about us; my password; each other; the family; the truth

More practice: for & since

- Before class, think of a number of true sentences about your own life. Each sentence should include the target grammar (present perfect with *for* or *since*), eg *I've lived in my flat since 2011* or *I've taught this class for six weeks.*
- Write the time phrases on the board, eg *2011, six weeks* and in a separate column write the key nouns/noun phrases, eg *my flat, this class.* Tell the class that all the words are about true things in your own life. They must ask you questions to find out about your life by using the present perfect and by selecting times and nouns. Tell them that you will only answer questions that use perfect English grammar!
- For each attempt, first give feedback on the grammar by saying *The grammar is good* or *The grammar is not good.* If the grammar is good, you can then say either *The sentence is true* or *The sentence is not true.* For example, the feedback to *Have you lived in your flat since seven weeks?* is *The grammar is not good.*
  The feedback to *Have you lived in your flat for seven weeks?* is *The grammar is good* and *The sentence is not true.*
  The feedback to *Have you lived in your flat since 2001?* is *The grammar is good* and *The sentence is true.*
- NB This is an exercise to take slowly.

Stronger classes

- Encourage everyone to make a decision about whether a sentence's grammar is good or bad by pausing dramatically after you say *The grammar is …*, and silently gesturing for students to say what they think before you conclude the sentence yourself with either *good* or *not good.*

> ### ■ Methodology Builder 26
> ### ■ Slowing down
> - *The temptation in teaching is to go quickly and race through coursebook exercises one after the other. But it's important to remember that just because students have done an exercise, it doesn't necessarily mean that anyone has learnt anything.*

> - *Learning is not an automatic result of turning pages – though many students (and teachers) seem to assume that it will happen. In fact, learning requires that students are engaged, ie listening, processing ideas, being involved and thinking. It's important to make sure that your teaching allows time and space for this to happen. For this reason, one of the most important teaching skills is finding the right pace in a lesson. Here are some ideas:*
> 1 *A lesson that is too slow feels boring and uninvolving to students. But be careful not to go to the other extreme. A lesson that is too fast is also uninvolving for many students because they can't keep up with it and can only respond by mentally switching off. Make sure that you are teaching at the speed of the class rather than flying at the speed of your fastest and strongest students.*
> 2 *Find the right pace by slowing down the speed at which you go through material, but asking lots more questions to more students. Ask questions to a range of students rather than just accepting answers from the ones who call out first. (If they do call out, try being deaf to them and waiting until the students you asked can answer.)*
> 3 *Experiment with longer waiting times after you ask a student a question. Don't jump in immediately if they don't answer in the first two seconds – count a few more seconds in your head. Allow some real thinking time. Longer waiting means that you will need to become more comfortable with silence in the classroom. Train yourself not to feel uncomfortable with thinking silences. It is not necessary to have voices filling every second of class. (Getting comfortable with silence is typically a very difficult thing for teachers to get used to.) Consciously experiment with stretching the waiting silences in your lessons. Can you find the maximum that you are comfortable with?*
> 4 *Your school or director may require that you finish a certain amount of work in a period of time. Don't let this requirement make you feel that you are forced to do the book at a fast speed instead of really making sure that students are learning.*

5

- Pairwork. Make new pairs so that students are not working with their previous partner. Ask and answer questions from exercise 4.

SPEAKING

1

❯ *Communication activities, Student's Book page 132*
- Pairwork. Students look at the illustration. One student chooses an animal without telling their partner which animal it is. Their partner must ask questions (only ones with *yes* or *no* answers) and guess what the animal is. The example questions may be helpful, but students will need to think of other questions as well.

IF YOU WANT SOMETHING EXTRA …

❯ Straightforward Teacher's Resource Disc *at the back of this book*

10B | Stress

WHAT THE LESSON IS ABOUT

Theme	Causes and cures for feeling stressed
Speaking	Pairwork: discussing stressful jobs
	Groupwork: ranking stressful experiences
Reading	Magazine article: an article about stress
Vocabulary	Collocations with *get*
Grammar	Present perfect simple for unfinished time

IF YOU WANT A LEAD-IN …

Teach a key word: stress

- Tell a personal anecdote, something like the example below. If you want to, you could dramatize it by adding some 'stressed' actions, eg moving around a lot; breathing faster; wiping your brow; looking around jerkily, etc.
  Oh goodness, I have so many things to do. I don't know where to start. I have to mark all this homework, and I have to prepare seven lessons, and my child has a cold, and I have to fill in these application forms. Oh gosh – it's just too much. I think I'll explode … or maybe I'll cry.
- At the end of your story write up this sentence-head on the board:
  Our teacher feels really, really …
- Ask students to work in pairs and agree the best word to finish the sentence.
- Collect feedback and clarify why *stressed* is the best answer.
- Ask students what things make them feel stressed. Ask how they know that they (or other people) are stressed, ie what are the symptoms?

SPEAKING & READING

This article is about stress. It discusses how serious a problem it can be to your health, some of the main causes of stress and how it can affect businesses.

1

- Use the first word in the box, *accountant*, as an example. Ask students if they think the job is stressful or not. Elicit reasons why it may be stressful, eg *Accountants work for long hours. If they make a mistake, it can have very serious results.*
- Pairwork. Students look at the other jobs and decide what is stressful in each job. When they've finished, students must decide which jobs are most stressful.

2

- Students read the article and decide which of the three titles is best.
- Students may ask what *adrenaline* and *cortisol* are. Don't tell them but say that they will find out in the article.

> *The best title is:* Are you suffering from stress?
> Adrenaline and cortisol are mentioned but are not the subject of the article.
> The article mentions stress at work but doesn't list which jobs are stressful.

> The article is addressed to the reader *you* and asks if the reader feels stressed.

3

- Students answer the seven comprehension questions.

> 1 *Any three from this list:* headaches; stomach aches; difficulty in breathing; skin problems; feeling sad or nervous for no good reason; wanting to cry; getting angry
> 2 Over half of the adult population.
> 3 Adrenaline and cortisol.
> 4 Heart problems, coughs and colds.
> 5 Kenny Dalglish and Winona Ryder.
> 6 40 million.
> 7 They are offering relaxation and stress management classes.

Cultural notes: Kenny Dalglish & Winona Ryder

- Kenny Dalglish is a former Scottish international footballer, who has managed a number of football teams, including Liverpool and Celtic.
- Winona Ryder is a slim, dark-haired actress who has starred in *Heathers*, *The Age of Innocence*, *Little Women* and *Black Swan*.

4

- Students can work in pairs to discuss and compare the stressfulness of their own lives.

GRAMMAR: present perfect simple for unfinished time

Grammar box

- ❯ *Language reference, Student's Book page 104*
- ❯ *Methodology Builder 22: Using Grammar boxes, page 106*

1

- Students decide if each phrase is (U) unfinished time or (F) finished time.
  NB The answer to some questions will vary depending on the actual time when students are answering it. The concept of *finished/unfinished* is also partly to do with the speaker's opinion rather than fact, ie *this morning* is unfinished time if it is still morning when students answer the question, but is finished time if it is later in the day, and the morning is already in the past.

> yesterday – F
> in 1998 – F
> in my life – U
> in the last month – U
> last month – F
> last week – F
> one year ago – F
> since last year – U
> this month – U*
> this week – U*
> today – U*
> this morning – U (if it is still the morning) F (if it is the afternoon of the same day)
> (* *unless the speaker is talking at a time they consider is at the end of the day/month/week, such as bedtime, end of the working day, midnight, etc*)

2

* Students choose the correct verb form for each sentence. Use the diagrams in the *Language notes* below if they find the decisions difficult.
* In some questions, an alternative answer is possible, but is much less likely.

> *Less likely answers are in brackets.*
> 1 went
> 2 've done (did)
> 3 've made (made)
> 4 was
> 5 've been
> 6 haven't had (didn't have)
> 7 had

Language notes: present perfect simple for unfinished time

❯ *Methodology Builder 7: Using timelines, page 23*

* If you want to use these ideas for a presentation to students, draw these three diagrams on the board and explain or elicit the information from students.

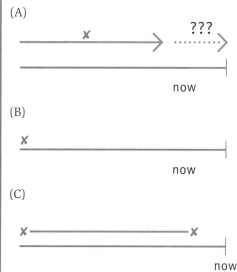

(A)

???

now

(B)

now

(C)

now

* Clarify that (A) shows an event happening in a period of time that comes up to the present and possibly continues after the present.
* It's important that students are clear that the event in (A) is in the past, but the exact time is not stated or imprecise and that the period of time in which the event happened is seen as continuing up to the present.
  For example: *I've talked to her this week.*
  The talking happened in the past, but we don't know exactly when, only that it happened at some point in the week that started seven days ago and continues up to the present.
* In contrast, (B) and (C) show events that are entirely in the past. The events have finished before the present moment, and the period of time in which they happened has also finished.
* Ask students which diagrams go with which tense. (Answer: *(A) present perfect; (B) and (C) past simple.*)
* An interesting problem arises with sentences that include *today, this week, this month*. Choice of tense will depend on (a) the actual time when the speaking is happening, and (b) the speaker's own opinion about whether the current time period is finished or unfinished.
  If the words are said during or in the middle of the time period, the present perfect will be used.

If the speaker considers the time period is still unfinished (ie still in progress), they will use the present perfect, eg *I've done a lot of work this week.*
If the speaker considers the time period finished or almost finished (perhaps because it is the end of the week, or they have completed all the work they had to do) they will use the past simple, eg *I did a lot of work this week.*
* This is an example of grammar being about speaker choice as well as about fact.
* Students may find the similarity of *last month* and *in the last month* confusing. *Last month* is a finished period in the past. *In the last month* is a period of time up to the present moment. The former would naturally go with past simple, the latter with present perfect, eg *I went there last month; I've been there twice in the last month.*

> ### ■ Methodology Builder 27
> ### ■ Grammar auction
> * *The grammar point in this lesson lends itself well to a grammar auction, but the technique can be used for many grammar items, or even a range of mixed grammatical forms.*
> * *Before the lesson prepare about 5–10 good sentences using your target language. Then add another 5–10 sentences using the target language, but each with one common error. Cut the sentences up and mix up the separate pieces of paper. So, for example, you might have the following:*
>   1 *I saw a good film two weeks ago.*
>   2 *He's lived in London for last year.*
>   3 *They've been to Prague last month.*
>   4 *I've had a lot of work to do this week.*
>   5 *She's left school in 1998.*
>   6 *How often have you been to a concert last year?*
>   7 *How often did you go shopping in the last two weeks?*
>   8 *I never saw a lion in my life.*
>   9 *They played tennis in the park last week.*
>   10 *How many cups of coffee have you had today?*
>   *(Sentences 2,3,5,7 and 8 are incorrect)*
> * *In class, divide students into teams of about four or five people. Write the team names on the board and add the number 200 next to each.*
> * *Explain the rules:*
>   *Each team has 200 pounds in their bank.*
>   *You will read out some sentences (and write them on the board if you want). Students must try to buy correct sentences and not buy any incorrect ones. Teams should aim to buy as many good sentences as they can.*
> * *Read out the first sentence. Teams discuss secretly and decide if they think it is good. Then teams start to bid the money they would like to spend (as if it was an auction). For example, Team A might bid £2 and Team C might bid £10. Team A might then bid £12 and win the sentence. You should minus the amount from their bank, and give the winning team the sentence.*
> * *Continue till all the sentences have been sold.*
> * *Remind teams not to spend all their money on one sentence!*
> * *At the end, go through the sentences one by one and let students decide which ones are correct.*

- *The wining team is the one with the most correct sentences.*
- *If you want to, you could write or copy all the sentences and let students study them before the auction.*

3
- Students rewrite the sentences so that they are true for them. They could then work in pairs and say their new sentences aloud to each other.

Weaker classes
- You could suggest ways that students can change the sentences:
  Simply repeat the original sentence.
  Change the sentence into a negative.
  Change the quantity of something, eg *a lot* into *a little*.
  Change a period of time, eg *the last two weeks* into *the last month*.
  Change a noun phrase for another, eg *a big party* into *a meal with friends*.

4
- Students put the verbs in brackets into the correct form.

1	did you drink	5	did you eat
2	have you seen	6	have you been
3	have you taken	7	were you
4	have you spent	8	have you visited

Extra practice: stronger classes
- Ask students to make more questions similar to those in exercise 4.

5
- Pairwork. Students read the questions to each other and answer them.

VOCABULARY & SPEAKING: collocations with *get*

⟳ *Language reference, Student's Book page 105*

1
- Students complete column A with a phrase in column B.

1 b	2 g	3 e	4 a	5 d	6 c	7 f

2
- Ask students to arrange the events in exercise 1 in order from most to least stressful. Don't compare answers as a class.

Language notes: collocations with get
- There are three separate grammatical uses of *get* in this lesson's exercises. For simplicity, it makes sense to present these all as phrases or *chunks of language* to learn in their own right, rather than to analyze them in detail. But as the teacher, you should probably know how they work!

get/got + adjective
- *get/got* + adjective means '*become/became*' *She got very ill* means 'She became very ill'.

get into/got into
- This is a phrasal verb meaning to 'become involved in something bad'.
  They got into trouble means 'They became involved in trouble'.
  They got into financial difficulties means 'They became involved in financial difficulties'.

get/got + past participle
- This has a passive meaning (substituting the verb *get* for *be*).
  She got promoted means 'Someone promoted her'.
  He got fired means 'Someone fired him'.
- This passive structure can also be used to talk about things people do together or do to themselves.
  They got divorced means 'They divorced each other'. (Someone did something so that they would both be divorced.)
  They got married means 'They married each other'. (Someone did something so that they would both be married.)

3
- Groupwork. Students compare their opinions and try to reach a consensus on the four most stressful events.

4
- Ask students to read the short text *Dealing with Stress*. They can then discuss in small groups if these are helpful ideas. Which ones work? Which ones don't work? What else can you do?

Cultural notes: stressful events
- Scientific research suggests the order of stressfulness in *Vocabulary* exercise 2 may be: 4–6–7–5–1–2–3.
- Other very stressful events include: pregnancy; new baby; your child has serious health or discipline problems; arguments; relationship problems; being a victim of crime; prison sentence; limited income; overspending (eg with a credit card); taking out a big loan; retirement; death of a close family member or friend.

Web research task

⟳ *Methodology Builder 1: Using Web research tasks, page 2*
- Set some stress-related tasks, one to each pair of students:
  1 Find a good relaxation exercise that we could do in class.
  2 Find out what *endorphins* are.
  3 Find some questions to test how stressed you are.
  4 Find at least five more suggestions to help you deal with stress.

Web research key words
- *stress*

IF YOU WANT SOMETHING EXTRA …
⟳ Straightforward Teacher's Resource Disc *at the back of this book*

10c | Marathon men

WHAT THE LESSON IS ABOUT

Theme	Marathons
	Sports
Speaking	Pairwork: talking about how fit you are
Listening	Radio programme: a news report about the marathon runners, Ranulph Fiennes & Mike Stroud
Vocabulary	Sport
Grammar	Present perfect simple with *been* & *gone*
Pronunciation	/ɔː/
Did you know?	Sports in Australia

IF YOU WANT A LEAD-IN ...

Teach a key word: marathon

- Tell the class that you have a quiz question for them. Explain that you are thinking of a word (*marathon*) and they must guess what it is. You will give them five clues. They must try to find the word with the smallest number of clues.
- Write the first clue on the board: *42,195*. Ask if anyone knows what word you are thinking of. If someone guesses correctly, congratulate them (and ask some check questions to see if the whole class knows what the word means). If no one gets it right, go on to the next clues, one by one, until they get it, or you win because no one gets it after five clues!

Clues

1 *42,195* (Answer: *the length in metres of a marathon*)
2 *NYC* (Answer: *New York City – location of a famous marathon*)
3 *Athens* (Answer: *the town the first runner ran to*)
4 Add the word *metres* after the number *42,195*
5 *Olympics®* (Answer: *the most famous and important race*)

Test before you teach: been & gone

> *Methodology guidelines: Test before you teach, page xxi*

This game introduces the idea of *been* and *gone*.
NB Make sure you are really clear about these instructions before you start!

- Prepare two large (eg A4 size) pieces of paper, one with the word *been* in large letters, the other with the word *gone*.
- On another two or three pieces of paper, write in large letters names of places, one to each sheet, eg *New York; the supermarket; the Moon; the sports centre; the café*. Pin these place names up in various places around the walls of the room.
- Invite three students to the front of class. Give the *been* card to one and *gone* to the second. Tell them to hold the cards down so the words are not visible.
- Ask the third student to walk to the Moon. When he/she gets there, say *He's/She's gone to the Moon*, and gesture to ask the student with *gone* to hold up their card. Don't explain the grammar at all, or do anything else to draw attention to it. After a few seconds, when everyone has seen the word, gesture to the student to hide the card again.
- Now ask the travelling student to walk back to the front where you are. Say *He's/She's been to the Moon* and

gesture to ask the student with *been* to hold up their card. After a few seconds, gesture to the student to hide the card again.
- Now ask the travelling student to walk to the café. Say *He's/She's ...* and gesture to the class to tell you which of the two card-holding students should show their cards. Whatever they say, after a few seconds indicate that the student with *gone* should hold up their card. Say *He's/She's gone to the café*. After a few seconds, gesture to the student to hide the card again.
- Now continue by asking the student to walk to various places, saying the start of sentences and eliciting which verb should be shown.
- Make sure you include some journeys in which the student goes from one location to another (rather than coming back to the front). This would require two *gone* verbs in a row.

SPEAKING & VOCABULARY: sport

> *Language reference, Student's Book page 105*

1
- Students read sentences and decide which ones are true for them.

2
- Pairwork. Students discuss answers to the questions in exercise 1 with a partner. Encourage them to say more than just the basic information.

3
- Students match the pictures with the words. They can then work in pairs to agree answers.

A	golf	F	aerobics
B	squash	G	running
C	weight training	H	yoga
D	tennis	I	swimming
E	cycling		

4
- Students write the words in the correct column. When answers have been checked, ask students if they can see any reasons the sports go with each verb.

do	**go**	**play**
aerobics	cycling	golf
weight training	running	squash
yoga	swimming	tennis

Language notes: do, go, play + sports

- There are no precise rules about when we can use *play, do, go* with sports, and students will need to learn these collocations item by item. However, the following guidelines may be helpful:
  We *play* games – usually competitively with one or more other people, eg *play football*; *hockey*; *water polo*; *volleyball*. Things we *play* often have (1) a ball; (2) points or scoring; (3) a winner at the end.
  Sports that have the verb *go* are frequently outdoor activities and usually involve movement from one place to another, eg *go walking*; *climbing*; *canoeing*; *car racing*; *surfing*.

Sports that go with *do* are often ones that we do by ourselves, mainly for our own improvement, rather than in competition with others, eg *do exercises*; *callanetics*; *circuit training*.

- However, these are only guidelines and are not consistently true. For example, consider: *play chess*; *go bowling*.
- In colloquial English, when we add a word/phrase that specifies a quantity, such as *some* or *a lot of*, we can frequently use the verb *do* with items that don't normally go with the word:
  I'm going to go running.
  I'm going to do some running.

5

- Students can first discuss the two questions in small groups. Then collect answers from the whole class and see if everyone agrees.

Extension task: survey

- Pairwork. Students think of one more question about sports they would like to ask other people in their class.
- Collect all the questions on the board (and add the two from the book). Ask everyone to choose two questions.
- Tell students to stand up, move around and ask their two questions to as many people as possible. They should keep a note of answers they hear.
- Put students into groups to report back on what they learnt from their survey.

LISTENING

In this radio sports programme, there is a report on the New York Marathon in which two British runners who took part, the explorer Ranulph Fiennes and his doctor Mike Stroud, succeeded in completing seven marathons in seven days in seven countries.

1 & 2 ● 2.27

- Tell students that they are going to listen to a radio sports programme and that all the photos are part of the programme.
- You could put students into pairs to discuss what the story is about and how it could include all the photos.
- You can ask to hear students' ideas about possible stories, but don't confirm or deny any predictions yet. This will come in the next stage.
- You could write students' ideas on the board, then use this as a checklist for students when they are listening. Then after the listening, as feedback, check each prediction one by one to see whether it was correct.

> At this year's New York Marathon, Fiennes and Stroud finished their seventh marathon in seven days in seven different places (including the Antarctic and Cairo). Fiennes has recently had a heart operation. Together they earn millions of pounds for charity by going on expeditions and doing unusual things.

● 2.27

> **P = Presenter S = Sunil**
> **P:** ... and now it's over to Sunil Gupta in New York to bring us up to date with news of this weekend's big event, the New York Marathon.
> **S:** Yes, it's all over here. This year's winner of the men's race was the Kenyan, Martin Lel, in an official time of 2 hours 10 minutes and 30 seconds. In an exciting finish, Lel pushed last year's winner, Rodgers Rop, into second place. Another Kenyan, Margaret Okayo, took the women's race in a time of 2 hours 22 minutes and 31 seconds. But the big event of the afternoon for many of the spectators in Central Park was the arrival of two Britons, Ranulph Fiennes and Mike Stroud. Despite their slow time of almost five and a half hours, they will surely be in *The Guinness Book of Records*.
> For Fiennes and Stroud, this was an incredible seventh marathon in seven days in seven different continents. Their marathon began last week in Patagonia in the deep south of South America. In the last week, they have been to the Antarctic, Sydney, Singapore, London and Cairo, completing a marathon at each stopover. Incredibly, Ranulph Fiennes suffered a heart attack earlier this year and had a heart operation just three months ago. Fiennes and Stroud have raised millions of pounds for the British Heart Foundation by completing the marathon in New York today. On previous expeditions, they have raised more than four million pounds for a multiple sclerosis research centre and two million pounds for a breast cancer clinic. They have been to the North and South Poles, and they have walked across the Andes. The two runners, however, did not celebrate at the party in Central Park after the race. A spokesman for the British Heart Foundation said, 'Both runners have gone home. They caught a plane to London earlier this evening. Dr Fiennes has gone to join his wife before going into hospital for a check-up on his heart next week. Dr Stroud has gone to London for a day of rest before returning to work on Tuesday morning.' This is Sunil Gupta reporting from New York's Central Park.

3 ● 2.27

- Students listen again and choose the best option for each of the six questions.

> 1   Martin Lel
> 2   2 hours 22 minutes and 31 seconds
> 3   Patagonia
> 4   Sydney, Singapore and Cairo
> 5   four
> 6   into hospital

4

- Students suggest great sporting heroes from their own country and describe their achievements to the whole class.

Cultural notes: marathons

- Marathons were until recently something that only experienced professional athletes took part in, but they have become very popular since the 1970s, and nowadays many ordinary people join in.
- A marathon is 42,195 metres long (which is 26 miles 385 yards).
- The first marathon was run by a Greek soldier between the town of Marathon and Athens, so that he could tell people that the enemy Persians had been defeated. Unfortunately he died soon after this amazing effort (which was probably a lot shorter than modern marathons).
- The length of marathons has changed a lot over the years (but of course everyone in one race ran the same length). The fixed length was only set after 1921.
- The New York City Marathon began in 1970 in Central Park and had only 55 runners. It cost just over $1,000. Nowadays, the NYC marathon is raced through many famous districts and streets of New York including the Bronx, the 59th Street Bridge and First Avenue, ending in Central Park. It attracts over 30,000 people and virtually stops the city.
- Many other places now hold marathons including Berlin, Las Vegas, London, Loch Ness, Madrid, Paris, Prague, The Sahara, Antarctica and Venice ... and Walt Disney® World!
- If a marathon sounds like too much for you, many places organize *half marathons*.
- The Olympic Games® traditionally finish with the marathon.

Web research task: marathons

⊘ *Methodology Builder 1: Using Web research tasks, page 2*

- Find out:
  1 where the closest marathon or half-marathon to your home town is.
  2 who won the last New York marathon (male and female).
  3 what the record for the fastest marathon ever is (male and female).

web search key words
- *marathons* name of country
- *New York marathon winner*
- *marathon record*

GRAMMAR: present perfect simple with *been* & *gone*

⊘ *Language reference, Student's Book page 104*

1
- Students match each sentence with a diagram.

1	*gone* – He is still there.
2	*been* – He has come back.

Language notes: present perfect simple with been & gone

- In dictionaries you will find *been* listed as the past participle of the verb *be*, but one interesting way of looking at this grammar point is to consider *been* as also a past participle of the verb *go*, ie the verb *go* has two alternative past participles rather than one:

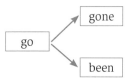

Gone suggests that the journey has not yet finished. *Been* always means that the journey has completely finished, as in the lesson's diagram showing going and coming back. This is a different meaning of the word *been* compared with the past participle of the verb *be*.

- *Been* is usually pronounced as an unstressed weak form /bɪn/ in normal fluent speech. Be careful not to train your students to over-pronounce the word as ✗ /biːn/.

2 & 3 💿 2.28

- Students choose *been* or *gone* to complete the dialogue. Remind them that they can choose the correct answer by deciding whether the subject has (A) been and come back or (B) gone and is still there.
- Students listen to the recording to check their answers.
- Point out that sentence 5 is a question. When we ask if someone has travelled to a particular place, the normal form is *Have you been there?* (not *Have you gone there?*). This is natural because the person you are asking must have come back if you are speaking to them!
- Pairwork. Students then practise reading the dialogue together.

1	gone	4	gone	7	been
2	gone	5	been		
3	been	6	been		

💿 2.28

Jane:	Hello.
Mark:	Hi, it's Mark here. Is Rick there, please?
Jane:	Hi, Mark. No, I'm sorry. He's <u>gone</u> away for the week.
Mark:	Oh? Work? Holiday?
Jane:	Both. He's <u>gone</u> to Patagonia – for a walk.
Mark:	Oh, I've <u>been</u> there. Twice. It's really nice. Why didn't you go with him?
Jane:	Because my boss has <u>gone</u> to Nepal on business so I'm in charge of the office.
Mark:	Nepal? Nice!
Jane:	Have you <u>been</u> there, too?
Mark:	Yes, I've <u>been</u> a few times, actually.
Jane:	Really? I've only <u>been</u> there once. I liked it.
Mark:	Yes, it's an excellent place for walking.
Jane:	Yes. Well, I'll tell him you called.
Mark:	OK. Thanks. Bye, Jane.
Jane:	Bye, Mark.

PRONUNCIATION: /ɔː/

1

- You may want to clarify what sound the words are missing before they start to add the letters to the words. With stronger classes, let them work it out for themselves as they do the exercise.

1	before	5	report	9	thought
2	four	6	called	10	walking
3	New York	7	sport		
4	north	8	sort		

2 & 3 **2.29**

- Students must work out which words contain /ɔː/.
- Students then listen to check their answers. Remember that listening is the first problem in pronunciation. It may be that some students cannot hear the sound in some words. Help them by giving a number of chances to re-hear the recording.

All the words contain /ɔː/ apart from (7) *squash* and (10) *would*.

2.29

(*The phonemic transcriptions for these words are in brackets.*)
1 awful /ˈɔːfəl/
2 caught /kɔːt/
3 cause /kɔːz/ (NB not /kɔːs/)
4 daughter /ˈdɔːtə/
5 important /ɪmˈpɔːtənt/
6 morning /ˈmɔːnɪŋ/
7 squash /skwɒʃ/
8 thought /θɔːt/
9 walk /wɔːk/
10 would /wʊd/

Language notes: /ɔː/

- This sound is often quite a puzzle for students! Some students' mother tongue may not have any sound like this and learners frequently say a sound like /əʊ/ instead.
- /ɔː/ is a long vowel sound. The two dots indicate length. It is possible to keep making the sound as long as you have enough breath.
- In southern UK pronunciation, it is the sound of the word *or*. (NB Without any /r/ sound at the end!)
- In American English, many speakers do not distinguish between /ɔː/ and /ɒ/. To make the sound /ɔː/ the space inside the speaker's mouth should be quite large, like a cave. The jaws shouldn't be too far apart. The lips will be quite rounded and the tongue quite low with its back part raised a little – though not raised very much.
- Students may not believe that some of the listed words in exercise 1 (or 2) are really pronounced with /ɔː/. This is often because they have become so familiar with something they have learnt wrongly, or they have frequently heard it mispronounced.
- Students may find words like *sport* and *New York* more difficult if the same or similar words are used in their own language, but with a pronunciation different from the English one.
- Students are sometimes misled by the spelling into an incorrect pronunciation. When the /ɔː/ is spelt with -or (eg *for; report; north; important; order; sort*), they seem to get it correct more often, but when it is spelt in other ways (eg *awful; caught; called; thought; walking*), the spelling may cause some confusion and a range of different mispronunciations.

DID YOU KNOW?

1

- Elicit from students their guesses about which sports are popular in Australia.
- Students read the short text and check which guesses are correct.
- Pairwork. Students discuss the questions about sports in their own country.

IF YOU WANT SOMETHING EXTRA ...

❯ Straightforward Teacher's Resource Disc *at the back of this book*

10D | Doctor, doctor

WHAT THE LESSON IS ABOUT

Theme	Doctors, illness and health
Speaking	Pairwork roleplay: at the doctor's
Listening	Dialogue: two doctors' appointments
Functional language	At the doctor's
Vocabulary	Body & health
Pronunciation	Sentence stress

IF YOU WANT A LEAD-IN ...

Teach a key word: patient

- Draw a simple sketch of two matchstick people sitting facing each other with a table or desk between them. Explain that the person on the right is a doctor. Ask the class who the other person is. Elicit or say *She's a patient.*
- Ask some check questions. Point to the patient and ask:
  Is this person a doctor? (Answer: *No.*)
  Is this person ill? (Answer: *Probably.*)
  Why is she talking to the doctor? (Answer: *She wants help for her illness.*)
  How can the doctor check her? (Answer: Many answers, eg *take her temperature, listen to her chest,* etc)
  What can the doctor give her? (Answer: *medicine – or a prescription for medicine*)

Test before you teach: illnesses

> *Methodology guidelines: Test before you teach, page xxi*

- This activity requires a little acting from the teacher, so only do it if it suits your personality or teaching style, and you feel happy about this element of performance.
- Come into class looking very miserable. Sit down and make it clear that you are not feeling well. You could, for example, cough; rub your stomach and groan; feel your forehead and wipe it; blow your nose (or sneeze); rub the top of your head (or your back).
- When students show some interest, chat with them about how you feel and ask for suggestions about what you could do. You don't need to bring in deliberately specific illnesses or cures, just let the dialogue flow naturally for a few minutes. Make sure students get chances to speak as well as you, asking questions and giving advice.
- After a short time, tell the class that you went to see your doctor this morning and he gave you a pill. Ask the class if you should take it. Put your hand in your pocket and take out an imaginary tablet (or a real sweet), put it in your mouth and have an instant, magic cure. Stand up and walk around, smiling, looking 100 per cent well again.

VOCABULARY & SPEAKING: body & health

> *Language reference, Student's Book page 105*

1

- Ask students to look at the illustration at the top of the page. Point out that different parts of the body are labelled A to J. Students then label the words from the box with the parts of the body in the picture.
- When they have finished, students can work in pairs to compare, and then list as many other body parts as they can.

A	eye	E	stomach	I	head
B	neck	F	chest	J	back
C	ear	G	throat		
D	mouth	H	nose		

Language notes: parts of the body

- As well as the parts of the body in exercise 1, students may suggest (or ask about) some of the following: *forehead; cheeks; chin; jaw; lips; tongue; arm; elbow; hand; palm; fingers; thumb; wrists; bottom; leg; thigh; knee; ankle; heels and toes.*

Language notes: aches & illnesses

- An *ache* is a pain that isn't very strong, but often lasts for a long time. The word often comes as part of some common compounds: *headache; stomach ache; earache; backache.*
  NB *Heartache* is an emotional rather than a physical pain!
- *Hurt* is not a reflexive verb (though it is in many other languages), ie we say *My head hurts* not ✗ *My head hurts me.*
- *Medicine* is uncountable. If you want to count it, you need to say the container or amount, eg *a bottle of medicine.*
- *Pills (tablets)* are a kind of medicine.
- Make sure students know how to spell and say *ache.* /eɪk/; *cough* /kɒf/; *stomach* /ˈstʌmək/.

2

- Students can work in pairs to describe the problems of the four people in the illustration, using sentences from the table.
- Students could start sentences with *I think ...* or *Maybe ...* if they are not sure what problems the people have.

Possible answers (from left to right):
Woman 1: She's got a headache / a pain in her neck / a hangover.
Man 1: He's got a stomach ache / His stomach hurts.
Man 2: He's got a cough / a cold / flu / a temperature.
Woman 2: She's got a pain in her back / Her back hurts.

3

- Students decide what medicine might help each of the people's problems.

Aspirin and paracetamol are both *pain killers* and can be helpful when a patient has a headache, a hangover, a cold or flu.
A prescription for antibiotics may be given when an illness is caused by *bacteria,* eg an ear infection.
NB Antibiotics are useless for colds and flu which are always caused by viruses, not bacteria, as are most coughs and sore throats.
In the case of back pain, an appointment with a specialist may be the best solution.

4

- Pairwork. Students discuss the questions about illness and going to the doctor.

LISTENING

In this listening, there are two separate dialogues between a doctor and patients. In the first, a woman describes her symptoms to the doctor and he diagnoses flu. In the second, a man describes his fear of flying and the doctor tells him he has stress.

1 🔘 2.30–2.31

- Students listen to two patients at the doctor's and decide why they are happy when they leave.

> The woman is happy because she isn't seriously ill.
> The man is happy because the doctor says he's not well enough to travel and he hates flying.

🔘 2.30–2.31

---

1 D = Doctor   S = Sarah
S: Hello.
D: Come in, come in, take a seat.
S: Thanks.
D: Now, how can I help you? What seems to be the matter?
S: Well, lots of things, actually.
D: Mmm?
S: I've got a headache all the time. And a cold.
D: And a cough.
S: Yes. And it hurts everywhere. I mean, I've got pains in my back, my chest, my neck, everywhere. I just feel awful.
D: OK, well, let's start by taking your temperature, OK? Hmm, let's see. 39 degrees – that's quite high.
S: Nothing serious, is it? Is it flu?
D: Yes, it's probably flu. But it's nothing to worry about. Now. Anything else? Any other symptoms?
S: Well, I suppose I'm feeling a bit depressed. But maybe that's normal. There are lots of problems at work at the moment.
D: Well, that's understandable. I hope everything works out. Anyway, you've got flu and you'll need to take four or five days off work. Rest as much as possible; stay in bed. Take some aspirin or paracetamol for the pain.
S: OK.
D: I'll give you a prescription for some strong paracetamol, and I'll give you a letter for work. Four or five days and you feel much better. OK?
S: Oh, right, thanks. I was worried that it was something much more serious. And a few days off work is always good – even when you're ill!
D: But make sure you rest, eh?

2 D = Doctor   R = Roger
D: Ah, Mr Hunter, good morning.
R: Morning.
D: Nice to see you again. What seems to be the matter?
R: I've, er, I've had a stomach ache for a few days. It really hurts. Very bad, you know, I don't even want to think about food.
D: So, you're not eating anything?
R: Not really, no. I mean, coffee, I'm drinking coffee, that's about the only thing I can take at the moment.
D: Just coffee?
R: Yes, I mean, the thing is I've got a meeting in New York later in the week, and I hate flying, and every time I think about getting in the plane, my stomach hurts, and sometimes I get a headache, sometimes I feel cold, sometimes I feel hot, or hot and cold, you know, and I'm not hungry, and I think of that plane, and I think, no, I can't, I mean, you know, what if the plane crashes or something, and then I get this really, really big, big headache, and my eyes hurt, here, my eyes, behind the eyes, you know, it's really painful.

D: Calm down, calm down. Now, I think that it's probably not a very good idea for you to go to New York. Not this week, anyway.
R: What?
D: Well, it seems to me that you are not well enough to travel. Your symptoms point to stress, extreme stress. I'll write a letter for your work, OK? But I think you should see a specialist. Someone who can help you with your fear of flying. But first of all, you need to eat.
R: You mean, I won't have to fly to New York?
D: Here, I'll write the letter, but you must promise that you will eat something, all right?
R: I'm feeling better already!

2 🔘 2.30–2.31

- Students listen to the recording again and complete the doctor's notes with words from the box.

1	cough	6	stomach ache
2	back	7	cold
3	flu	8	eyes
4	depressed	9	stress
5	paracetamol	10	specialist

3

- Students can discuss the questions about going to the doctor's in small groups.

FUNCTIONAL LANGUAGE: at the doctor's

> *Language reference, Student's Book page 105*

1

- For each phrase a–j, students must decide if it's something that a patient typically says or a doctor says.

aP bD cD dD eP fD gP hD iP jD

2 & 3 🔘 2.32

- Students use the phrases from exercise 1 to complete the dialogue.
- Students then listen to check.
- Pairwork. Students practise reading the dialogue with a partner.

1	what's the matter?
2	I feel awful.
3	Where does it hurt?
4	I'll have a look at you.
5	It's very painful.
6	it's nothing to worry about.
7	What's wrong with me?
8	Is there anything I can take for it?
9	I'll give you a prescription.
10	I think you should take a few days off work.

🔘 2.32

Doctor: Come in. Take a seat.
Patient: Thank you.
Doctor: Now, <u>what's the matter</u>?
Patient: <u>I feel awful.</u> It's my back.
Doctor: <u>Where does it hurt?</u>
Patient: Here and here.

> **Doctor:** OK. <u>I'll have a look at you.</u> Take off your shirt. Does this hurt?
> **Patient:** Yes, it does. <u>It's very painful.</u> Is it serious?
> **Doctor:** No, <u>it's nothing to worry about.</u>
> **Patient:** <u>What's wrong with me?</u> Do you know?
> **Doctor:** I think you've pulled a muscle.
> **Patient:** <u>Is there anything I can take for it?</u>
> **Doctor:** Yes, <u>I'll give you a prescription.</u>
> **Patient:** Thank you. And what about work? Is it OK to work?
> **Doctor:** No, not at the moment. <u>I think you should take a few days off work.</u> And come back and see me in ten days.
> **Patient:** OK. I'll make an appointment with the receptionist. Thank you. Bye.

Language notes: at the doctor's

Prescription
- When you go into a chemist's, there are two kinds of medicines you can get: *Prescription medicines* are only available if your doctor *prescribes* them for you. *Non-prescription medicines* can be bought *over-the-counter* without any permission or restriction.
- Students often confuse these three words: *prescription*; *receipt* and *recipe.*
  A *prescription* is a piece of paper given to you by a doctor that says which items of medicine you can get at a chemist's.
  A *receipt* is a piece of paper that says that you have paid someone for something (or have given them something).
  A *recipe* is instructions for cooking a meal.

Collocations
- You *swallow* tablets or pills, but you usually *take* medicine. You don't ✗ *eat* medicine.
- You *make* an appointment. You don't ✗ *arrange/get* an appointment.

Phrases
- In the phrase *I'll have a look at you*, the word *have* is a so-called *delexicalized verb,* ie it has no specific meaning of its own. In this phrase, it allows the speaker to use *look* as a noun rather than as a verb. The alternative sentence *I'll look at you* seems to have exactly the same meaning, although it's possible that *I'll have a look* suggests a shorter, less threatening examination.
- In the phrase *Where does it hurt*, we can't say exactly what the word *it* refers to. This is an example of the *dummy subject* necessary because English verb phrases always need a subject.

4
⊙ *Methodology Builder 8: Roleplay, page 27*
- Students follow the instructions to prepare a roleplay. Make sure that students have sufficient preparation time for the roleplay.
- Pairwork. Students do the roleplay twice so that both partners get to play both roles. Remind students that they can use the phrases in exercise 1.

PRONUNCIATION: sentence stress

1 💿 2.33
- Tell students to look at the joke. Check if they understand it, then point out that three words are underlined. Ask students to listen to the recording and decide how those words are stressed.

Alternative presentation
- With books closed, tell students that they are going to listen to an English joke. Before the first playing, ask them to listen and decide if it's funny or not. Play the recording and then check that they have understood the joke by asking a few check questions:
  1 *What did the doctor do for the patient?* (Answer: *He took an X-ray.*)
  2 *What was in the picture?* (Answer: *nothing*)
  3 *Why is that funny?* (Answer: *The doctor wants to say that there is nothing wrong and the patient is well, but it sounds as if the patient has nothing inside his head. In other words, he is very stupid!*)
- Tell the students that you will play the recording again and they should listen to pick out the words that sound most stressed. You may need to play the recording three or more times to allow students to agree on the answers.
- When students have agreed on particular words, you can tell them to open their books and see the printed text. Don't worry if students have different answers from each other or from the book. It is often difficult for students to learn to hear stressed words.

 2.33

> **Patient:** Doctor, doctor, what did the <u>X</u>-ray of my <u>head</u> show?
> **Doctor:** Absolutely <u>nothing</u>!

Language notes: sentence stress
- Students saw in lesson 6B on page 59 that individual words have their own stress. But there is also another kind of stress, this time associated with sentences. Many teachers and students call this *sentence stress* and this is therefore the name used in this coursebook, although this name isn't completely accurate.
- In fact, this kind of stress (strictly speaking called *prominence*) affects groups of words known as *tone units* rather than sentences, ie sections of speech with one main stress. The main stress is known as the *tonic syllable* and, in addition to this, there may also be one or more *secondary stresses*. Changes in prominence make substantial differences to the meaning of language.
- Here are some ideas for helping your students notice patterns of sentence stress:
  Mark sentence stresses when you write sentences up on the board.
  Tap, clap, hum the rhythm of sentences.
  When you use poetry texts and songs in class, focus on the sentence stress.
  Get students to work out sentence stress patterns themselves, by listening to recordings and marking texts.

2 & 3 💿 2.34–2.36
- Pairwork. Students practise reading the other three jokes, taking special care to stress the underlined syllables.
- Students listen to the recording to compare with their own readings.
- You may want to let students listen to the recording while they are preparing their own dialogues.
- You could use the recordings for shadow readings (see next page).

Extra task: shadow reading

- A good way to work on sentence stress is to try some shadow reading exercises. Select a short text (six to ten lines) that students also have a copy of, eg a piece from the Student's Book.
- Ask students to first listen to you reading it twice. (If you prefer not to read yourself, use a recording.)
- The third time, ask students to read aloud simultaneously with your reading/the recording, trying to keep up with the speed and following the rhythm. Let them mumble their way through (ie speaking quietly).
- Repeat the reading a number of times. Each time encourage students to speak louder.
- Students will need quite a number of goes before they can shadow read a text successfully.

 2.34–2.36

1
Patient: Doctor, doctor, I'm seeing <u>double</u>.
Doctor: Take a <u>seat</u>, please.
Patient: Which <u>one</u>?
2
Patient: Doctor, doctor, I've got a <u>memory</u> problem.
Doctor: How long have you <u>had</u> this problem?
Patient: What <u>problem</u>?
3
Patient: Doctor, doctor, I feel very <u>nervous</u>. This is the <u>first</u> operation I've ever had.
Doctor: Don't worry. It's <u>my</u> first time, too.

Cultural notes: Doctor, doctor jokes

- The phrase *Doctor, doctor* is a common opening line for jokes. Other similarly popular opening lines are: *A man walks into a bar …; An Englishman, an Irishman and a Scotsman …; Knock knock.*
- If the examples of *Doctor, doctor* jokes in the pronunciation section aren't enough for you, here are a few more you might want to drop into the lesson!
  1 *Doctor, doctor, everyone keeps ignoring me.*
    Next!
  2 *Doctor, doctor, will I be able to play the violin after my operation?*
    Yes, no problem.
    Great – because I couldn't do it before!
  3 *Doctor, doctor, I think I'm a bell.*
    Give me a ring tomorrow!
  4 *Doctor, doctor, I've just swallowed some film!*
    Oh dear. I hope nothing develops.
  5 *Doctor, doctor, I swallowed a 20-pound note last week.*
    Has there been any change since then?

IF YOU WANT SOMETHING EXTRA …

❯ Straightforward Teacher's Resource Disc *at the back of this book*

Answer key

10 REVIEW
❯ *Student's Book page 157*

1

1	since
2	since
3	for
4	since
5	for
6	for
7	since
8	for

2

1	finished
2	wanted
3	has been
4	began
5	has provided
6	has never been
7	won
8	has known
9	left
10	went
11	began
12	hasn't seen

3

1 A: Good morning, Mr Riley. I ~~didn't see~~ <u>haven't seen</u> you for at least two weeks. What's wrong with you?
2 A: How long ~~do you have~~ <u>have you had</u> the pain?
3 A: When exactly ~~have you stopped~~ <u>did you stop</u> smoking?
4 A: So you haven't had a cigarette ~~since~~ <u>for</u> two days?
5 B: Well, ~~I am~~ <u>I've been</u> under a lot of stress in the last few days.
6 A: No, but come back and see me if the pain hasn't ~~been~~ <u>gone</u> away in the next few days, OK?

4

1 a   2 b   3 a   4 a   5 a

5

1	suffer
2	operation
3	specialist
4	check-up
5	symptoms
6	treatment
7	weight
8	pressure

6

Students' own answers

10 WRITING
❯ *Workbook page 83*

Model answer

One night, a wild boar was looking for food on the edge of a forest. At the same time, a pet Pekinese dog was out in the garden of a small farmhouse. The dog heard noises in the trees and went to see what was happening. When the boar saw the Pekinese, it was terrified and started to run. The dog chased after it. The boar ran into the garden and then into the house, smashing a door.

The sound of the breaking glass woke up the elderly couple inside. The couple were horrified. They could see something by their bedroom door. The man turned on the light next to the bed. At that moment, the boar jumped into bed and the elderly couple ran out of the room. A short time later, the dog arrived and started barking at the boar.

After a while, the couple realized the boar was frightened of the dog. The man got out of bed and carried the dog outside. He found a chain and attached the dog to a fence. In the end, the boar left the garden and returned to the forest.

11A | Things

WHAT THE LESSON IS ABOUT

Theme	Personal possessions
Speaking	Pairwork discussion: describing a favourite possession
	Pairwork – Communication activity: describing & guessing objects
Listening	Monologues: two people talking about things they wanted when they were younger
Grammar	Infinitive of purpose
Functional language	Paraphrasing
Vocabulary	Personal possessions
Pronunciation	*Th-* sounds: /θ/ and /ð/

IF YOU WANT A LEAD-IN ...

Teach a key word: things

- Write these sentences on the board:
  Could I have one of those … , please?
  *When I go on holiday, I like to take all my favourite …
  with me.*
  What are the green … in the window?
  I remember a time when … were very different.
  Do you know where I left my … ?
- Set a thirty-second time limit and ask students to work in pairs and think of different words to complete the sentences. When they have finished, collect suggestions, eg *cakes; CDs; boxes; people; book,* and write them on the board.
- Tell students that they must now find just one word that fits every gap.
- There may be other possible answers, but *things* is the most likely word. Point out that *things* can be used instead of all the words the students first suggested. Explain that *things* means any objects that we don't want to name (or we don't know the name of), especially objects that belong to us personally.
- Ask students to make some true sentences about themselves using the word *things.*

VOCABULARY & SPEAKING: personal possessions

❯ *Language reference, Student's Book page 115*

1
- Students label the photos (A–K) with the names of the items in the middle. This should be a relatively simple task, so don't spend more than a little time on it.

A	a computer		G	a watch
B	a car		H	a phone
C	lipstick		I	sunglasses
D	a pen		J	a motorbike
E	a TV		K	an MP3 player
F	a credit card			

2
- Students could work in pairs to discuss the questions.

3
- Ask students to think of one of their favourite possessions and to think about the four questions. Tell them to choose something that is not in the pictures.
- Pairwork. Students make new pairs with different partners from the previous task. They then describe their choice of possession to each other.

Language notes: personal possessions
- The following items in the list are usually uncountable: *lipstick*; *sunglasses*. *Sunglasses* can be counted using *pairs,* eg *two pairs of sunglasses.*
- *Mobile phones* (UK) are usually called *cellphones* in the US.
- A *computer* can also be called a *PC* (*personal computer*). A PC in a fixed place in your home or office is known as a *desktop PC.* One that you can carry around with you is a *laptop.* The screen that you look at is called a *monitor.*
- A *credit card* allows you to borrow money. *Debit cards* allow you to spend money that you already have in your bank account. You can use many of these *bank cards* at an *ATM* (*cashpoint/cash machine/autobank*). ATM stands for *Automated Teller Machine,* but no one ever says that!
- The following are some common types of car:
  Five-door is a car which has four normal doors and a large opening back door (also called *Hatchback*).
  Estate is a long car with five doors and space to carry large objects in the back.
  Convertible is a car with a roof that you can open (eg when it is sunny).
  Sports car is an expensive, stylish, fast, small car, often with only two seats.
  SUV (Sports Utility Vehicle), also known as *4x4* (pronounced 'four-by-four') or *off-roader,* is a big, high car capable of carrying more than four people and able to drive off-road on rough and hilly land.
- Motorbike means 'motorcycle'. A *moped* is a small, slow motorbike (with limited speed and limited engine capacity).
- An *MP3 player* is a portable music player that contains a *hard disc drive.* It is able to store and play back large quantities of music in computer-readable form. MP3 is a popular way of storing musical data; there is some loss of quality but tracks take up relatively little storage space.
- Common kinds of pen are *ballpoint pen* (or *biro*) and *fountain pen* (one that uses refillable liquid ink).

LISTENING

In this listening, the first speaker describes how much she wanted to have a credit card when she was younger to impress her business clients. The second speaker describes how much she wanted to have her own car when she was younger to give her independence.

1

- Ask students to look at the four photos at the bottom of the page and ask: *Are these things fashionable? Would you feel proud to own one now?* Students discuss when the items were fashionable.

> The car is a Capri Mark 1600 (as described by Katy in the audioscript). These were in use from 1974.
>
> Early mobile phones were very big and heavy like this one, which probably dates back to the early 1980s. People rather rudely called them *bricks*!
>
> The American Express card was issued before built-in computer chips became standard.
>
> The computer is an early Apple IIc personal computer from the early 1980s. It has a mouse but note the green screen display and that the keyboard and processor are all in one piece.

2 🎧 **2.37–2.38**

- Tell students that they will hear two women talking about things they really wanted when they were younger. Students must choose which of the four items they talk about.

> Susan: American Express credit card
> Katy: Capri car

🎧 **2.37–2.38**

> | Susan | I was just starting in business, a small advertising business with my sister, and in those days it was hard for women to run a business. Most of our clients were men, and we took them out to restaurants and ball games, you know, we took them out to make them feel good, to impress them, too, of course, and we wanted them to take us seriously. Then, one evening, I was in a restaurant and the woman at the table next to mine, when the check came, she held up this little card to pay. American Express, I think it was. I really, really wanted a card like her. So, I spoke to my sister, and she agreed it was a good idea, and we filled in a form to apply for a card. The first time I used it, you know, to pay for a meal with a client, he was really impressed. He signed the contract right there in the restaurant! Best investment we ever made! |
> |---|---|
> | Katy | What did I really want when I was younger? Independence, really. I was living with my parents and it took me ages to get into town to go out for the evening. And I needed some way to get home because the last train was really early. So, anyway, I was saving up to buy a Mini, but when I saw my first Ford Capri, I took one look at it and knew that was what I wanted. It took me two years to get enough money, but, in the end, there I was, the owner of my very own sexy Capri Mark I 1600, metallic yellow and sexy sports wheels. It was the biggest change in my life. I've done hundreds of thousands of miles in it. And I've still got it, actually. |

3 🎧 **2.37–2.38**

- Tell students to listen to the recording again and complete the sentences with *S* or *K*.

> 1 S   2 S   3 K   4 K   5 S   6 K   7 K   8 S

Extension task

- Students discuss with a partner what they really wanted when they were younger and whether they got it. Allow students a little thinking time before they start talking.

Web research task: things

- ❯ *Methodology Builder 1: Using Web research tasks, page 2*
- Set a time limit, eg ten minutes. Tell students they have a budget of 1,000 US dollars. Their task is to find the most amazing thing on the web that they can buy for that money. It must be just a single thing. Students should then print out a picture of their item (if possible) and try to sell their item to the class by explaining what it is and why it's great. The class can only agree to buy half of the items, not all of them.

Web search key words

- *unusual shopping*

GRAMMAR: infinitive of purpose

Grammar box

- ❯ *Language reference, Student's Book page 114*
- ❯ *Methodology Builder 22: Using Grammar boxes, page 106*

1

- Students underline all infinitives in the sentences. They should then decide which ones fit the description in the grammar box and are infinitives of purpose.

> 1   to pay
> 2   to spend
> 3   to pay
> 4   to buy
> 5   to get
> 6   to live
> *Infinitives of purpose: 1, 3, 4, 5*

Language notes: infinitive of purpose

Infinitives in general: a quick reminder

- The present infinitive is the basic form of a verb. It has no endings to show change of person. It has two forms: infinitive with *to*, eg *to run*, and infinitive without *to* (base form), eg *run*.

Infinitive of purpose

- The meaning of the *to* infinitive in this structure is exactly the same as *in order to*, eg *She filled out a form in order to get a card.*
- The person who will do the infinitive action is the same as the person who does the action mentioned earlier in the sentence. For example, in the sentence *She wanted a credit card to pay for meals in restaurants*, the person who will pay for meals is the same person who wanted the credit card.

- If we stop a sentence before the *to* infinitive, we still have a good sentence, eg *She wanted a credit card* or *She filled out the form.* The infinitive of purpose adds more information to the sentence and explains why the action was done.
- This structure cannot be used in the negative: ✗ *She phoned the bank to not get a penalty charge.* To convey this meaning you must use *in order not to*, eg *She phoned the bank in order not to get a penalty charge.*
- Watch out for errors in which students use *for* + infinitive, eg ✗ *I want for to go there.*

2

- Students make sentences by joining the phrases in columns A and B with *to*.
- Tell students that all the sentences make a complete story, and although a number of answers are possible, there is only one set of answers that makes a coherent story.

1	b	I worked overtime to earn more money.
2	a	I saved £5,000 to buy a car.
3	g	I wanted a car to go away at the weekends.
4	f	I went to a garage to look at the new cars.
5	d	I asked a friend to come with me to help me choose.
6	c	We went for a drive in one car to see if I liked it.
7	e	Then we went back to the garage to pay for it.

3

- Use *car* as an example. Ask students to think about the different things they do with a car, eg *go to the shops.* Collect five or six more ideas. Then ask students to think of one or two more unusual uses for a car, eg *hiding from the rain; using the wing mirrors to check your make-up,* etc.
- Pairwork. Now ask students to find five or six different uses for each of the other things.

FUNCTIONAL LANGUAGE: paraphrasing

❯ *Language reference, Student's Book page 114*

1 🌐 2.39–2.40

- Start by introducing the idea of paraphrasing (see *Language notes* below). Students listen to the recording of two people talking and complete the sentences.

1	computer
	send emails with
2	shoe
	go to the beach

Language notes: paraphrasing

It's a kind of X / It's a sort of X
- These phrases mean:
  It is an X.
  OR
  It is like X (but it may not be exactly the same).
  For example, if I say *It's a kind of computer,* I mean it is a computer, OR it is like a computer (but maybe not exactly the same).
- In fluent speech, note the pronunciation of these items is often weakened:
  kind of = /ˈkaɪ·ndəv/ (or /ˈkaɪ·ndə/)
  sort of = /ˈsɔːtəv/ (or /ˈsɔːtə/)

Paraphrasing

- This is an important communication strategy, when (a) we can't find the best way to explain something, or (b) our listener hasn't understood what we said and we need to try again and explain it in a different way.
- We can paraphrase a word by:
  saying a synonym or a word with a very similar meaning, eg *mug* > > *it's a sort of cup*
  naming a bigger group that the item is a member of, eg *Alsatian* > > *it's a sort of dog*
  describing the use, appearance or some other feature of an item, eg *tyre* > > *it goes on a wheel on a car.*
- Often we may use vague language, eg *sort of, kind of,* to indicate that what we are saying isn't 100 per cent accurate.
- For example, if you can't find the word for a *yacht,* you could say any of the following:
  It's a boat; It's a sort of ship; It's a kind of boat; You use it on the water; It's a thing you sail in; It's a sort of sailing boat; You use it to go sailing; It's got sails.
- Normal everyday colloquial speech contains a lot of paraphrasing. Speakers often use meaningless filler phrases like *you know* to give themselves more time when they are trying to describe something, eg *It's a, you know, boat.* Such phrases are often considered uneducated or careless English.

💿 2.39–2.40

> 1
> Good afternoon, I'm looking for a – I'm sorry I don't know the right word. It's a kind of computer, a little one that you can put in your pocket. You know, it's a thing you send emails with, I think. In fact, I'm not really sure what you do with it. But you know what I mean. A little computer. It's a present for my grandson.
> 2
> Good morning. I'm looking for some, erm, what do you call them? You know, they're a sort of shoe. Well, not really a shoe, but, erm, well, yes they're a sort of shoe, really. You use them to go to the beach. In the summer. You see all the young people wearing them. Do you know what I mean?

2

❯ *Communication activities, Student's Book page 126*

- Pairwork. Students secretly think of one of the items and describe it to their partner without pointing to it or naming it. The partner must decide which object is described.
- Although this is a sort of guessing game, be careful that the game element doesn't obscure the practice. There is a danger that the listener will jump in immediately to guess an object. You may want to set a rule that the student describing must be allowed to finish their description before the partner is allowed to make a guess.

PRONUNCIATION: /θ/ & /ð/

❯ *Methodology Builder 28: Voice, page 145*

1 🌐 2.41

- Students listen to the recording with two different sounds /θ/ and /ð/.

💿 2.41

> /θ/ thanks, thing, thousand
> /ð/ than, this, those

Alternative presentation

- Write *th* on the board. Tell students that they will hear a number of words starting with *th*. Ask them to listen to the first recording and write down the words.
- When all six words have been heard, ask students to work in pairs and check if they have the same words. They should then discuss and agree together how to divide them into two groups to show different pronunciations of *th*.
- After checking, continue to the second recording and ask students to add all the new words they hear to the correct group.

> ### Methodology Builder 28
> ### Voice
>
> - *Voice is when we add a vibrating, buzzing sound from our vocal chords (found in the throat) to a phoneme.*
>   **Recognizing voice**
> - *Here is a useful way of distinguishing voiced and unvoiced sounds. Try it with your students:*
>   *Put your hand over your voicebox (around the middle of your throat, where your Adam's apple is). Say a number of voiced and unvoiced sounds. Notice how the area vibrates for the former, but not for the latter.*
>   **Comparing voiced and unvoiced /θ/ & /ð/**
> - *Your students can experiment with voice by first working with some familiar pairs of sounds, eg /f/ and /v/ and then extending their learning to /θ/ and /ð/.*
>   *1 Ask students to first say the unvoiced sound, eg /f/.*
>   *2 Ask them to lengthen the sound so that it lasts for a few seconds.*
>   *3 Ask students to think about how they are making the sound. Agree that the essential features are:*
>   *(1) a movement of air.*
>   *(2) some friction when the air is blocked by tongue and teeth.*
>   *4 Then ask students to say /v/, lengthen it, and consider how they make it. What is different between the making of the two phonemes? Agree that for /v/ the key features are:*
>   *(1) a movement of air (same as /f/).*
>   *(2) some friction when the air is blocked by tongue and teeth (same as /f/).*
>   *(3) voice (the vibration of vocal chords).*
>   *5 Repeat the exercise with the sounds /θ/ and /ð/. Hopefully they will agree that they are, like /f/ and /v/, very similar sounds, but with the significant difference of having or not having voice.*

Language notes: /θ/ & /ð/

Students are sometimes puzzled about what is different between /θ/ and /ð/. Luckily, it is a distinct and teachable difference!
- The sound /θ/ is made by placing the tongue against the sharp points of the upper teeth and then blowing air through the small gaps!
- The sound /ð/ is made in exactly the same way but with added *voice* (see *Methodology Builder* on this page).

2
- Students can work in pairs. They use words from the box and put them into the correct column according to the sound.

The phonemic transcriptions are included after their words.			
/θ/:		/ð/:	
theatre	/ˈθɪətə/	their	/ðeə/
theory	/ˈθɪəri/	there	/ðeə/
think	/θɪnk/	they	/ðeɪ/
thirteenth	/ˌθɜːˈtiːnθ/		
thought	/θɔːt/		
three	/θriː/		
Thursday	/ˈθɜːzdeɪ/		

3 🔊 **2.42**
- Students listen to the phrases on the recording. Pause after each sentence for the students to repeat.

🔊 **2.42**

> What do you think of their theory?
> Do they think the same thing as the others?
> Let's meet on Thursday the thirteenth at three o'clock.
> They thought the theatre was over there.

IF YOU WANT SOMETHING EXTRA …
- Straightforward Teacher's Resource Disc *at the back of this book*

11B | Fashion victim

WHAT THE LESSON IS ABOUT

Theme	Clothes and fashion
Speaking	Groupwork: discussing clothes & appearance
Reading	*Office Worker Flip Flops Out of a Job.* Newspaper article about a man being fired from a job for wearing inappropriate clothes
Grammar	Modals of obligation (present time)
Vocabulary	Clothes

IF YOU WANT A LEAD-IN ...

Teach a key word: victim/fashion victim

- Write the word *victim* on the board. Pretend to steal something from a student (eg a pen) and then ask *Who is the criminal?* (Answer: *you!*) and *Who was the victim?* (Answer: *the student*). Elicit or explain that a *victim* is someone who has been hurt or had problems because of a crime, eg someone who has been robbed or murdered is the victim.
- Now ask students what they think a *fashion victim* might be. Don't confirm their guesses. Instead tell a short anecdote about Kim:

  Kim reads all the fashion magazines and spends all her money on new clothes. However, when she's not looking, some of her colleagues laugh at her clothes behind her back.

- Ask students why they think her colleagues laugh at her clothes. Elicit that she doesn't look good in the clothes (ie they don't suit her) and that people think she is foolish to spend all her money on them.
- Explain to the class that Kim is a *fashion victim*. This is someone who always tries to wear the latest, most fashionable clothes even if they don't look good on them, or are too expensive for them to afford.
- Tell students that the lesson will be about someone who has a different problem with clothes!

Test before you teach: modals of obligation

> ❯ *Methodology guidelines: Test before you teach, page xxi*

- Tell students to write three new rules about clothes people can wear in their school. Elicit an example if useful, eg *You must wear red shoes on Friday, You can wear jeans in maths lessons, but you can't wear jeans in English lessons.*
- When students have finished, tell them to keep their ideas until later.
- When you get to *Grammar* exercise 2, ask students to look back at their rules. Give them a few minutes to change them and correct the grammar. Then ask students to meet up and compare their ideas.

SPEAKING

1
- Groupwork. Students discuss the four statements.

VOCABULARY: clothes

> ❯ *Language reference, Student's Book page 115*

1
- Students match names from the box to the pictures A–S.

A	jersey	H	top	O	shorts
B	dress	I	trousers	P	sweatshirt
C	boots	J	socks	Q	skirt
D	shirt	K	underwear	R	T-shirt
E	cardigan	L	tie	S	jacket
F	jeans	M	suit		
G	scarf	N	trainers		

2
- Ask students to look back at the words in the box and answer the two grammar questions. Remind students that there may be more than one answer for the questions.

underwear is always singular uncountable
jeans, trousers and *shorts* are always plural

Language notes: clothes

- *Jeans* are trousers made from denim, a thick, strong cotton material. Denim is usually blue, but can also be black and other colours.
- *Trousers* and *jeans* are always plural although they are describing a single piece of clothing! If we want to specify that it is a single item, we can say *a pair of trousers* or *a pair of jeans*.
- We can't say ✗ *a trouser,* ✗ *a trousers,* ✗ *one trouser,* ✗ *one trousers,* ✗ *a jean* or ✗ *a jeans*, etc.
  We can use the plural word to talk about more than one pair, eg *three trousers, seven jeans* or we can say *two pairs of trousers* or *six pairs of jeans.*
- *A boot* covers a larger part of your foot than a shoe and usually also covers part of your leg.
- *Boots* and *trainers* are plural in exercises 1 and 2, and are usually used in the plural (because we have two feet!), but they can be used in the singular, eg *I picked up my boot.*
- A *dress* (countable) is a long piece of women's clothing that includes top and skirt in a single piece. As a noun it never refers to male clothing.
  Students often confuse the nouns *dress* and *clothes.* A common mistake is to use the noun *dress* as if it means *clothes,* for example when a male student says ✗ *I'm going to change my dress.*
  Dress appears as part of the compound nouns:
  Fancy dress is special clothes (for men or women) at a celebration or party so that you look like someone else, eg a celebrity or someone who does a particular job.
  Evening dress (uncountable) is smart formal clothes for men or women.
- A *jersey* is the same as a sweater or a jumper or a pullover.
- A *cardigan* is a jersey that opens, with buttons down the front.
  A *cardigan* is a clothing item named after a famous person, Lord Cardigan, who was a leader at the battle of Balaclava in 1854. (Another clothing item named after a famous soldier is the *Wellington boot.*)
- A *top* is a general word for clothes that a woman wears on the top half of her body.
- *Underwear* is an uncountable general word that includes:
  Male: *Vest* and *underpants* (AE *shorts*).
  Female: *Bra* and *knickers* (AE *panties*). These items together are as known as *lingerie* (uncountable).

- The verbs that commonly go with the noun *tie* are *wear*, *tie* and *undo/untie* and *take off*. So it's possible to *tie a tie!* Or *untie a tie!*
- *Trainers (sneakers)* were originally a sports shoe, though are now worn as a fashion item as well.
- *A suit* is a set of matching clothes items, usually including a jacket, waistcoat and trousers (or skirt) = *a three-piece suit*. A male suit is almost always worn with a tie.
  Make sure your students don't confuse *a three-piece suit* (/suːt/) with *a three-piece suite* (/swiːt/). A *three-piece suite* is a set of furniture comprising two armchairs and a sofa (settee or couch).
- Some common collocations for skirt are: *a long skirt*; *a knee-length skirt*; *a short skirt*; *a mini skirt*; *a pencil skirt*; *a tight skirt*.
- *A sweatshirt* is similar to a jersey but is made of thicker material.
- *A T-shirt* is so called because of its shape like a capital T.

3
- Pairwork. Students recall what other students were wearing in the last lesson.

Extension task
- You could ask students to turn their backs on other students and describe what the people behind them are wearing now.

Extra practice: describing clothes
- Before the lesson, you need to prepare a set of pictures of people, one picture for each student. These could be torn out of magazines.
- Give students one picture each. Ask students to work in pairs, but tell them not to show their pictures to their partner. Each student should describe the clothes (not the people) in their picture as well as they can. When everyone in the class has finished, ask all the students to come up to the front of the class and throw their pictures down on the floor (or onto a large table), still making sure that their partner doesn't see which is their picture.
- Each student should now try to find the picture that they think their partner described. Don't let them pick them up (because if they have got it wrong they will be taking someone else's picture). Their partner can confirm if it was the right picture.

READING
This newspaper article is about a legal case in which Philip Dale has taken his old company to court over human rights and sexual discrimination. They had fired him from his job for wearing shorts to work on a hot day.

1
- Students look at the headline and photo and explain a possible reason for the two people being dressed as they are. Students then read the article to see if their guesses were correct.

> He wore the shorts and flip flops to work because it was a hot summer day.

Extra task
- Ask students who they think the man on the left is. (Answer: *He's the lawyer who is defending Mr Dale. He is dressed formally for work. He could possibly be Mr Dale's boss, but the gown (a long loose coat that hangs down*

from your shoulders and worn by the legal profession when they attend court) suggests that he is probably Mr Dale's lawyer.)

Language notes: court
- There are two ways that we can tell that Mr Dale has gone to court to try and challenge his dismissal: he has a lawyer and the phrase *The case continues* (last line) which suggests that the newspaper is reporting a court case that has not yet finished.
- Your students will probably not know the noun *case*. In this meaning, a case is something that will be decided in court.

2
- Students read the text again and mark the sentences *T* (true) or *F* (false). They correct the false sentences.

1	T
2	T
3	F (He refused to go home and change.)
4	F (He does not have to work with customers.)
5	T
6	T
7	T
8	F (He thinks it's simple – they can't have some rules for men and others for women.)

3
- Pairwork. Students discuss the questions.

GRAMMAR: modals of obligation (present time)

Grammar box
- ➲ *Language reference, Student's Book page 114*
- ➲ *Methodology Builder 22: Using Grammar boxes, page 106*

1
- Students complete the text with the correct verb forms. Tell them that they cannot make decisions about the answers only on the basis of grammar. They must also consider the meaning of the sentence in the context of the whole text.

1	have to
2	do not have to
3	can
4	Do children in your country have
5	have to
6	have to
7	can
8	must
9	have to
10	can

Language notes: modals of obligation
Must & have to
- In colloquial UK English, *have to* is the same as *have got to*. NB The word *got* is fixed and never changes form, eg *He's got to leave now, Have you got to finish that report?*
- Grammar books outline guidelines for choosing between when to use *must* and *have to*, but they are notoriously hard for students to apply successfully.

- At this level, you may want to avoid going into reasons for choosing between the two items. It's safe to present them as meaning the same when they are ways of talking about rules and things that are necessary, ie *external obligation* (obligation from things that are outside the speaker, like notices; rule books; orders; printed regulations etc).
- If you do want to offer more detailed guidelines, the most important point of contrast with *have to* is that *must* generally relates to *internal obligation* (something that the *speaker* feels is necessary).
- *Have to* is more common with obligations that come regularly and repeatedly, eg *I have to get to the station by 8.15.*
- Remember that *must* has other functional uses, eg logical deduction (*It must be the doctor*).

Don't have to
- *Don't have to* means that it is not necessary to do something, although it is possible and you can do it if you wish.
- Students often confuse this with *mustn't*, which is a prohibition, ie it says that you are not allowed to/not permitted to do something.

Can & can't
- *Can* (like *must*) has a number of different meanings. In this lesson students look at the meaning that something is *possible* or *allowed*.
- *Can't* is a possible negative, but *mustn't* is also possible.

Summary
- The following table summarizes these curious forms:

Positive	Negative
must (obligation)	*don't have to*
have to	*don't have to*
can (possibility)	*can't* (possibility)
can (permission)	*mustn't* (prohibition)
can (allowance)	*can't* (prohibition)

2
- Pairwork. Students use the topics in the box to discuss rules in their workplace, college, school, etc.
- Remember to check the *Test before you teach* lead-in task if you did it at the start.

3
- Students complete sentences so that they are true for them. They can use information they discussed in exercise 2, but you might want to allow them to go on asking their partner questions during the writing task.

> Many answers will be possible, but it's important to check that all missing words are *bare verb infinitives*.

Extra practice: modals of obligation
- Put students into small groups of four to five. Tell the groups that they have been asked to design a completely new game for a special event called *The Crazy Olympics*®. The new sport must have only 10–15 rules. Write the first two rules on the board:
  1 You must play with …
  2 You must try to …
- Elicit some possible endings for these. For example:
  1 … a ball / seven balls / an Indian elephant / mobile phones.
  2 … get all the balls in the lake / find your own phone in the forest / lead the elephant to the bath.
  Remind students that these are *Crazy* Olympics®!
- Now ask groups to agree at least ten rules like your examples. They must have at least three *must* sentences and at least three *don't have to* sentences.
- When they've finished, the class can decide which game is the craziest!

IF YOU WANT SOMETHING EXTRA …
❯ Straightforward Teacher's Resource Disc *at the back of this book*

11c | Camden Market

WHAT THE LESSON IS ABOUT

Theme	Shopping, street markets & business success
Speaking	Pairwork: giving a presentation on shopping in your town
Reading	*Home comforts*. Magazine article about a successful businesswoman
Grammar	Modals of obligation (past time)
Did you know?	Guide book about shopping in London

IF YOU WANT A LEAD-IN ...

Teach a key word: market

- Tell the class that yesterday morning you bought some onions and potatoes. Ask where they think you bought them. Some students will probably name some shops and possibly a market. If they don't mention a market, explain that you didn't buy them in a shop but inside a large building (or in the open air), where there were many different sellers. Ask what the difference is between a *shop* and a *market*. (See *Language notes* on this page.)

Test before you teach: had to & didn't have to

❯ *Methodology guidelines: Test before you teach, page xxi*

- Ask six students (all male or all female) to come to the front of the class. Tell the students to follow your instructions. Ask the rest of the class to concentrate and remember exactly what happens.

    Say to A: *You must walk to the door.*
    Say to B: *You must sit down in your seat.*
    Say to C: *You can walk to the door if you want to.*
    Say to D: *You can sit down in your seat if you want to.*
    Say to E: *You must walk to the door.* (But prevent the student by physically stopping him/her moving.)
    Say to F: *You must sit down in your seat.* (But prevent the student by sitting there yourself!)

- Tell students that they have to stay where they are while you write the following sentences on the board (changing the pronoun if necessary):

    1 She didn't have to walk to the door.
    2 She couldn't sit down in her seat.
    3 She had to walk to the door.
    4 She had to sit down in her seat.
    5 She couldn't walk to the door.
    6 She didn't have to sit down in her seat.

- Ask students to work in pairs, copy the six sentences and agree which sentence is about which student. Tell them that only one sentence is correct for each student. They should write the students' names next to the right sentences.
- When they have finished, tell them that you will check the answers later in the lesson. Also ask some check questions, eg *Was it necessary for her to walk to the door?* (Answer: *Yes, because the teacher said she must do it.*)
    (Answers: *1 C, 2 F, 3 A, 4 B, 5 E, 6 D*)

READING

This magazine article is about a woman who started selling candles at a market store, and who has now set up a chain of successful international home and furniture shops.

1

- Students look at the photos and say if there are any places like this near them, and if they have ever bought anything from these types of places.
    NB The photo on the left is of a shop selling fashionable household furniture. The photo on the right is the front stalls of Camden Market in London.

Cultural notes: Camden Market

- **Camden Town** is an area in the north of London, about ten minutes by underground from the centre of London.
- The market at **Camden Lock**, next to Regent's Canal, began in 1974 as a craft market, but has grown a lot over the years and now includes a market for all kinds of products, including fashion. There are hundreds of shops, bars and entertainment venues. Many Londoners and tourists visit it. Originally only open at the weekend, you can visit it all week long, though Saturday and Sunday is the time it really comes alive.

Tourist hints
- If you go to the market, use *Chalk Farm* underground station rather than *Camden Town* station.
- Try a walk along the canal – or take a boat trip to London Zoo.
- Watch out for the huge crowds at the weekend. Beware of pickpockets!

Portobello Road
- Another popular market area in London (also mentioned in the text) is **Portobello Road** in the Notting Hill area of West London. This market, open on Saturday only, specializes in antiques and people say it is the world's largest antiques market.

2

- Students read the article and decide how the photos connect with the text.
- Ask students if they can guess what the title of the article means.

This article is about Kyra Komac who owns 25 furniture shops. She began her business career by selling candles at Camden Market.

Language notes: shopping

- When you go shopping, you will usually buy things either from a *shop* or from a *market*.
    A *shop* is a building where you can buy things, usually run by a single owner or company.
    A *market* is an area where many different sellers offer a range of products. It might be an *indoor market* or in the open air, ie a *street market*.
    A *shopping centre* (US *mall/shopping mall*) is a large building that includes many shops, restaurants, entertainment facilities and possibly a market area.
- The word *shop* is frequently part of compounds, eg shoe shop, clothes shop, antique shop, chemist's shop, specialist shop, corner shop (a local shop such as you find on the corner of two streets).
- A *store* is a large shop. The word is often used in a compound, eg a furniture store, a department store, a DIY store. The word was considered mainly American English but has become more common in UK English in recent years.

- *A megastore* is a recently-invented word meaning a large shop, especially one that specializes in stocking a wide range of goods of a particular kind, eg music and video recordings.
- *A chain of shops* is a group of shops that have the same name, similar products and are owned by the same company.
- *A branch* is one shop that is part of a larger chain.
- *A stall/market stall* is a place in a market or shopping area where you can sell things. It may be just a table or it could be a small building with an open front window.

Language notes: home comforts

- *Home comforts* are the familiar personal things that you have in your home and which you miss if you go somewhere else, especially somewhere that you consider less pleasant or less comfortable. A person might say *I'm enjoying this conference but I miss my home comforts.*

3

- Students re-read the text and decide the order of events.

> Correct order: 7, 4, 6, 8, 1, 2, 5, 3

4

- Students can work in pairs and discuss the questions.

Extra discussion

If any of your students have worked in shops or markets, you could add a short pairwork or whole-class discussion on this topic, using some of these questions:
- *Was it a full-time or part-time job?*
- *What did the shop/market stall sell?*
- *Was it a big or small shop/market stall?*
- *What were the customers like? Friendly? Rude?*
- *Did you enjoy working there?*
- *Did you get a discount?*
- *Did you buy a lot there yourself?*

Cultural notes: small beginnings & big business successes

- The chain of Home Comforts stores mentioned in the text is fictional, although it is similar to a number of other personal success stories in business. Two of the best known success stories are the Body Shop and Virgin:
  Anita Roddick opened the first Body Shop in Brighton in 1976. The shop specialized in soaps, cosmetics and toiletries. It always had a strong ethical basis, including policies of fair treatment for shop staff and fair trade with poorer countries. Nowadays, the chain has over 500 shops in more than 50 countries.
  Richard Branson made his fortune by creating the Virgin company, which has an airline, a record label, a radio station, a cola (that sells more than Pepsi in Europe) and many other successes. But he started small by creating a student newspaper while he was at school, a discount record shop and then releasing a record on the new Virgin label – *Tubular Bells* by Mike Oldfield – that sold millions and established the basis of the Virgin fortune. Recent ideas of his have included starting commercial flights for tourists and launching a chain of high street banks.

GRAMMAR: modals of obligation (past time)

Grammar box

> *Language reference, Student's Book page 114*
> *Methodology Builder 22: Using Grammar boxes, page 106*

1

- Students can work in pairs and decide which four sentences (a–d) go in which space.
- You could point out to students that all the sentences are from the magazine article. Students may want to look back to find the original context of the sentences.

> 1 c   2 d   3 a   4 b

Alternative presentation

- The lead-in *Test before you teach* would also work well as a presentation for the grammar exercises here.

Language notes: past obligation & possibility

- The table summarizes the grammar points in this lesson.

Present (positive)	Past (positive)	Past (negative)
must (obligation)	had to	didn't have to
have to	had to	didn't have to
can (possibility)	could	couldn't

- The most important thing for students to remember is perhaps that the past of *must* (when it is used to talk about obligation) is *had to* not *must* (or any variation of *must*)!

2 & 3   2.43

- Students complete the text using the four phrases.
- Students then listen to the recording and check their answers.

1	had to	4	had to	7	could
2	didn't have to	5	couldn't	8	had to
3	couldn't	6	didn't have to		

> ### Methodology Builder 29
> ### Gap-fill exercises
>
> - *Gap-fill exercises such as Grammar exercise 2 in this lesson can sometimes seem a necessary but duller part of your teaching. Here are a number of ways to vary the work on them. These are not simply for fun and variety. By changing some variables, eg listening rather than reading, we may be adding a useful added ingredient of challenge to the task.*
>
> **Doing the gap-fill: speed-do the task**
> - *Books closed, explain the task's instructions clearly. Tell students that they have to do the whole task in exactly one minute. Start them by saying 'go' (or blowing a whistle!). After a minute, say 'stop' and make students immediately close their books. Ask students how they felt about doing it quickly. Was it possible? If the general opinion is that it was completely impossible, negotiate a new (still fast) time limit for a second attempt. To check, tell students to first look through the exercise more carefully, without a time limit, and see if they want to change any of their original answers. Only then, go through the answers together.*

Listening gap-fill

- *Do the task with books closed and you reading the text. Students will need to listen closely to you reading the text. Whenever there is a gap, make a* beep *noise instead (or a noise of your own choice!) and ask them to write down their choice for each blank. When you have finished, let them look at the text and see if they think their first answers were good, before you go through answers together.*

Teacher does the work!

- *Instead of getting students to do it, do the task yourself on the board. Ask students to watch you and check if you get all the answers right. Make two or three errors and see if people spot them. If someone challenges you and says an answer is wrong, play devil's advocate and vigorously deny it. Force students to persuade you that they are right and your answer is incorrect. Get students to teach you how to correct your sentence.*

Mark the teacher!

- *In the same way, you could do the task on paper before class and hand out copies in class for students to mark.*

Checking the gap-fill: partial answers

- *At first, only give partial answers. For example, in Grammar exercise 2, initially tell them only how many of each choice there are, eg There are three 'had to' answers. This will make students check their answers to see if theirs fit this information, and it may cause them to re-think some choices.*

Student teachers

- *Ask a student to come to the front and be the teacher. Hand the student the answers and let them go through the class's answers. Encourage them to ask people for reasons. NB If you do this, make sure you really do hand over to the new teacher. Don't hang around, signalling or mouthing things, taking over, etc. Instead disappear to the back of the class or somewhere out of sight and let them get on with their task autonomously. If you strongly disagree with something they did, you can always gently point it out at the end. Make sure you thank and congratulate your temporary teacher.*

🔊 2.43

My twin brother and I are the oldest in a family of seven. When I was a teenager, I <u>had to</u> look after my brothers and sisters until my parents came home from work. My brother was really lucky – because he was a boy, he <u>didn't have to</u> do anything. I <u>couldn't</u> see my friends or go out because I <u>had to</u> do my homework when my parents got home. I wanted to go to college, but I <u>couldn't</u> get a place because I did badly in my exams. I got a job where I <u>didn't have to</u> work in the evenings, so I <u>could</u> go to evening school. For ten years, I <u>had to</u> work and study really hard, but I finally got the qualification that I wanted and I became a teacher.

4
- Students write an ending for each sentence to say something true about things they *had to/didn't have to/could/couldn't do* when they were young.
- Pairwork. Students compare answers and discuss them.

DID YOU KNOW?

1
- Students read the text and decide how many kinds of shop are mentioned.

> antique shops; international chains; department stores; mega-stores; (specialist) bookshops; shops for computers, TVs and other electronic equipment; clothes shops; small specialist shops; designer clothes shops (in Bond Street)

2
- Pairwork. Students discuss the questions about London.

Extra speaking task: designing a Metro

- If your town has no underground railway system, ask students to work in threes and design a new Metro. (If your town already has a Metro, ask students to design two new lines.)
- Write these rules on the board:
  Maximum: two lines
  Maximum: nine stations
  Maximum: one change
- Students must decide the structure of the lines and exactly where they will place the stations. They will need to consider which places most people need to travel from and to. Remind students to think about shops; school; entertainments; housing areas etc. They should also consider any difficulties, such as hills and rivers, etc. If possible, provide photocopies of a simple map of your town for this activity. Students can mark their lines and stations onto the map.
- When they've finished, students can show their designs to each other. They should try to explain why they have chosen to place the lines and stations where they did. The class could vote for the best design.

SPEAKING

1
- Pairwork. Students choose a shopping area and prepare a presentation using the cues given.
- You may want to assign areas of the town to pairs so that everyone does not prepare the same presentation.

IF YOU WANT SOMETHING EXTRA …

> ❯ Straightforward Teacher's Resource Disc *at the back of this book*

11D | Looking good

WHAT THE LESSON IS ABOUT

Theme	Shopping for clothes
Speaking	Pairwork discussion: shopping
	Pairwork roleplay: in a clothes shop
Listening	Informal dialogue: dialogues in a clothes shop
Vocabulary	*Fit, go with* & *suit*
Functional language	In a clothes shop
Pronunciation	Word linking

IF YOU WANT A LEAD-IN ...

Discussion starters

> *Methodology Builder 15: Using Discussion starters, page 63*

- How often do you go clothes shopping? What sort of shops do you go to?
- How do you shop? Do you buy on impulse or do you take your time? Do you like to try things on?
- Which of the following is most important to you and why: the label, the price, the shopping experience, the quality?

Introducing the theme: clothes shopping

- Ask students to write down the last five clothes or shoes they bought. Ask them to think about why they bought them. Did they really need them or was it something that looked nice in the shop? Write these words on the board: *cheap; expensive; large; never; size; shop* and *colour*.
- In small groups, ask students to meet up and tell each other about the things they bought. Each student must try to use all the words when speaking.

SPEAKING

1
- Pairwork. Students discuss the questions about shopping for clothes.

VOCABULARY: *fit, go with* & *suit*

1
- Students match phrases in column A with their meanings in column B.

1 c	2 a	3 b

Language notes: fit, go with & suit

Meaning
- If clothes *fit* you, the *size* is correct for you.
- If clothes *suit* you, they *look good* on you.
- If some clothes *go with* something else, they look good when they are together with something else.
- If some clothes *go well* together, the things look good when they are worn together.

Possible problems
- The verb *suit* has no connection with the noun *suit* (formal clothes including jacket and trousers/skirt). A suit can suit you – but so can any other piece of clothing.
- The verb *fit* can be used without an object, eg *It fits!* But you don't usually say ✗ *It suits!*
- In a sentence such as *The shirt suits you,* or *The shirt fits you,* students need to note that the subject is *The shirt* and that it is a normal active sentence. However, the sentence cannot normally be turned around to make a passive ✗ *You are suited by the shirt* ✗ *You are fitted by the shirt.*

2
- Groupwork. Put students into small groups to discuss the three questions about the pictures.

3
- Students work in the same groups and discuss the next three questions.

Alternative task
- If you would like an alternative task, ask students to talk about clothes they have bought themselves and why some didn't fit/suit them. If you use this alternative task, students will probably need to know the regular past forms:

infinitive	past	past negative
It fits me	It fitted me	It didn't fit me
It suits me	It suited me	It didn't suit me

LISTENING

These are four separate, short, informal dialogues which take place in or around clothes shops. In each, two people talk about whether an item of clothing suits or fits them.

1
- Ask students to look at the four photos and elicit ideas. You could try to elicit what the people in the photos might be saying in order to recycle some of the vocabulary from the previous section.
- Write some of their ideas on the board. Students can use this as a checklist while they are listening to the recording in exercise 2.

2 ● 2.44–2.47
- Students listen and match the dialogues 1–4 to the photos A–D.

1	D
2	A
3	C
4	B

3 & 4 ● 2.44–2.47
- Ask students to make sentences.
- Play the recording again. Students listen to the dialogues again and check their answers.

1	That kind of thing really suits you.
2	Let's see if they have my size.
3	I don't think they go together.
4	You'll see what I mean.
5	One size bigger would fit you better.
6	The length looks about right.
7	I can always come back tomorrow.

🔘 **2.44–2.47**

1
A: Ooh, that looks nice! What do you think?
B: For you maybe, not for me.
A: Do you think so?
B: Yeah. That kind of thing really suits you.
A: All right, come on. Let's go in.
B: You know you can't afford shops like that!
A: You never know. Let's see if they have my size.
B: Come on, let's go and have a look.
2
A: Hey, look. This one would go well with my new trousers.
B: I don't think black goes with brown at all.
A: It's not black. It's grey. Anyway, who says that black doesn't go with brown?
B: I dunno, I just, I don't think they go together. Why don't you try it on? You'll see what I mean.
A: All right. I believe you.
B: Anyway, the shirt you're wearing suits you just fine.
3
A: How do I look?
B: You look great.
A: You really think so?
B: Yes. Really. Although it's a bit tight perhaps. Perhaps one size bigger would fit you better.
A: But I couldn't find the next size.
B: Well, just wear a thin top under it, and then it'll be OK.
A: That's a thought. It's a summer jacket anyway, isn't it? I'm not exactly going to wear a heavy sweater or anything, am I?
4
A: Do they fit at the back?
B: Yes, the length looks about right. But they don't really go with the boots you're wearing.
A: They feel comfortable. But perhaps I'll try on the next size.
B: No, they're fine. Take them. They look really good on you. Seriously.
A: You're just saying that because you want to get out of here.
B: No, I'm not. You look almost smart. Get them.
A: No, I'm going to think about it. I can always come back tomorrow.

PRONUNCIATION: word linking

1 & 2 🔘 2.48

- Ask students to look at the five sentences. Point out the curved lines are linking words and elicit what students think that means. Establish that these marks show that the words are linked when pronounced, ie they seem to connect to each other.
- Tell students to listen to the short extracts from the previous dialogue and listen to how this linking sounds.
- Students can then practise saying the sentences in pairs.

 2.48

What do you think?
Let's go and have a look.
Why don't you try it on?
That's a thought.
I'm going to think about it.

Language notes: word linking

- When we speak normally in English, words often link together. Sometimes two or three words together can sound like a single longer word. This feature is known as *juncture* or *linking*.
- The simplest aspect of linking is when a consonant from the end of a word seems to carry over and sounds as if it starts the next word. In *Pronunciation* exercise 1, this happens with:
    That's a /ðæt…sə/
    think about /θɪŋ…kəbaʊt/
    about it /əbaʊ…tɪt/
    try it /traɪ…jɪt/
    it on /ɪ…tɒn/
- With some words that have a letter *r* in their spelling the /r/ sound isn't usually pronounced in UK English, eg mother /ˈmʌðə/; four /fɔː/; bare /beə/; fire /ˈfaɪə/, etc. However, we often add a linking /r/ sound if the following word starts with a vowel. For example, notice the difference between the pronunciation of the following words when said on their own and the pronunciation of them together:

Word(s)	Pronunciation
four	/fɔː/
apples	/ˈæpəlz/
four apples	/fɔːˈræpəlz/
clear	/klɪə/
address	/əˈdres/
clear address	/klɪrəˈdrəs/

- In *Pronunciation* exercise 1 the linking /r/ is seen in:

Word(s)	Pronunciation
We're	/wɪə/
in	/ɪn/
We're in	/wɪrɪn/

- The linking /r/ is also possible after some words ending in vowels, though this doesn't feature in the lesson:

Word(s)	Pronunciation
banana	/bəˈnɑːnə/
ice cream	/ˈaɪskriːm/
banana ice cream	/bənɑːnəˈraɪskriːm/

- Another linking sound is /w/. This features in the exercise:

Word(s)	Pronunciation
go	/gəʊ/
in	/ɪn/
go in	/gəʊˈwɪn/

- Other linking features in this lesson include:
    A tendency to lose some sounds. This feature is known as *elision*.
    A tendency of some sounds to change so they sound like another. This feature is known as *assimilation*.
- The speaker has a lot of choice about how much assimilation and elision they want to use, so, for example, a sentence such as *What do you think?* can be said in a number of ways. The examples below are all possible pronunciations of the sentence, featuring varying degrees of linking, assimilation and elision:
    1 /wɒt duː juːˈθɪŋk/
    2 /wɒt duː jəˈθɪŋk/
    3 /wɒ dəjəˈθɪŋk/
    4 /wɒdjəˈθɪŋk/
    5 /wɒtʃəˈθɪŋk/
    6 /wɒdʒəˈθɪŋk/

- The pronunciation in these examples is progressively more reduced:

  No. 1 is an unnatural word-by-word pronunciation. Many students will start speaking in this way, but they need to know that it sounds strange to give every word its full pronunciation like this.

  Nos. 2, 3 and 4 are typical everyday pronunciations. These are suitable for students to try saying themselves.

  Nos. 5 and 6 are much more reduced, fluent examples. It's useful for students to know that this pronunciation is possible and to get practice in hearing examples of speakers using language in this way, but it's probably not sensible to try and get students speaking like this at Pre-intermediate level.

- Another phrase from the exercise that demonstrates elision and assimilation is *Shall we go …*:

  1 /ˈʃæl wiː ˈgəʊ/
  2 /ˈʃælwɪgəʊ/
  3 /ˈʃæwɪgəʊ/
  4 /ˈʃwɪgəʊ/

  No. 1 is a fairly unnatural word-by-word pronunciation.
  Nos. 2 and 3 are normal fluent pronunciations.
  No. 4 is a fast, very reduced pronunciation.

FUNCTIONAL LANGUAGE: in a clothes shop

1 & 2 🔊 2.49
- Students use the phrases in the box to complete the dialogue.
- Students then listen to check their answers.

1	A: Can I help you B: I'm just looking.	3	A: try this on 4 A: Have you got it B: I'm afraid not
2	A: Excuse me. B: I'm looking for A: What size	5	A: I'll take this B: How would you like

🔊 2.49

> **1**
> **A:** Good morning, sir. <u>Can I help you</u>?
> **B:** No, thanks. <u>I'm just looking</u>.
> **2**
> **A:** <u>Excuse me.</u>
> **B:** Yes, madam. How can I help you?
> **A:** <u>I'm looking for</u> a black jacket.
> **B:** Certainly. <u>What size</u> are you?
> **A:** Medium.
> **3**
> **A:** Can I <u>try this on</u>, please?
> **B:** Of course, the changing room is over there.
> **4**
> **A:** How does it fit?
> **B:** Fine, fine. <u>Have you got it</u> in green?
> **A:** <u>I'm afraid not</u>, sir.
> **5**
> **A:** <u>I'll take this</u>, please.
> **B:** Certainly, madam. <u>How would you like</u> to pay?
> **A:** Credit card.

3
❯ *Methodology Builder 8: Roleplay, page 27*

- Pairwork. Student A is a shop assistant at a clothes store. Student B is a customer. Students read their role cards and take a minute or two to prepare to speak. They then do the roleplay together.

Language notes: in a clothes shop
Offering help
- Nowadays in the UK, many shops are fully self-service so customers have limited exchanges with shop assistants. Even so, assistants will often come over to ask *Can I help you?* or *Do you need any assistance?*
- If you don't want help, the standard reply is *No, thanks. I'm just looking.* It would be rude to say just ✗ *No.*
- If you do want help, you can say *I'm looking for … .*

Trying things on
- If you *try something on*, you put the clothes on in the shop in order to see if they fit you and suit you. You will usually do this in a *changing room*.

Asking about different colours and sizes
- If you like the clothes but don't like the colour, you can ask if they have it in a different colour by asking *Do you have this in red?* or *Have you got this in red?*
- Similarly, you can ask about a different size: *Do you have this in a 12?* or *Have you got these in size 45?*

Deciding to buy
- When you decide you want to buy something, you tell the shop assistant *I'll take this.* You don't usually say ✗ *I'll buy this* or ✗ *I want this* (although these are both possible).

IF YOU WANT SOMETHING EXTRA …
❯ Straightforward Teacher's Resource Disc *at the back of this book*

Answer key

11 REVIEW

● *Student's Book page 158*

1

2 He bought a new car to impress his girlfriend.
3 She called the restaurant to book a table for this evening.
4 He spoke to his boss to ask for a pay rise.
5 She went to the changing room to try on the jeans.
6 She's started swimming to get fit.
7 He used a thesaurus to find a better word.
8 She always reads the newspaper to look at her horoscope.

2

1 b 2 a 3 b 4 a 5 b 6 b

3

1 c 2 e 3 d 4 b 5 a

4

1 You could smoke almost anywhere a few years ago.
2 Did you have to wait a long time?
3 You don't have to say 'Sorry' all the time.
4 I couldn't find anywhere to park my car.
5 We had to get a new car after the accident.
6 I have to work overtime this evening.
7 You can't wear hats in many churches.

5

1 Can you tell me where the ~~change~~ changing room is, please?
2 Do you like shopping for ~~clothe~~ clothes?
3 Excuse me, have you got this suit ~~on~~ in a darker colour?
4 I like this top. Can I try ~~on it~~ it on?
5 I really like your jeans. Where did you get ~~it~~ them?
6 I'm sorry, this doesn't ~~suit~~ fit. Can I try another size?
7 She's gone to the department store to buy some ~~underwears~~ underwear.
8 What size ~~trouser~~ trousers do you take?

11 WRITING

● *Workbook page 85*

Model answer

My favourite possession is a carpet. I bought it from a shop in Kabul when I was working in Afghanistan. I often used to go and have tea with the shopkeeper when I was there. The carpet wasn't very expensive but it is special because it reminds me of my old friend. I have had it for ten years now.

It's quite small and light. I love the warm colours: different kinds of reds and browns and some small white and blue lines. The pattern is very simple: rows of triangles. It makes me feel very calm when I look at it. A friend of mine says the pattern is actually Iranian, not Afghan. I don't know, but I know I like it!

I don't use the carpet on the floor. It hangs on the wall behind my computer. In all the places I have lived for the past ten years, I have had it in front of me. It's like an old friend!

12A | Around the world

WHAT THE LESSON IS ABOUT

Theme	Explorers & adventurers
Speaking	Groupwork: discussing famous explorers
	Pairwork discussion: planning a 'round the world' trip
Listening	A news report about the American adventurer Steve Fossett
Vocabulary	Phrasal verbs
Grammar	Prepositions of movement
Pronunciation	/ɜː/

IF YOU WANT A LEAD-IN ...

Teach a key word: explorer & adventurer

- Write the two words *explorer* and *adventurer* on the board and ask directly: *What does an explorer do?* If students can't answer, give a definition:
  An explorer may:
  go on journeys to places that are unknown to most people; go to places where few (or no) people live; discover new things on their travels; try unusual ways of travelling.
- Check understanding by asking if the following are explorers or not:
  Mike went on holiday to the south of Italy. (Answer: *no*)
  Susie walked to the South Pole. (Answer: *yes*)
  Dagmar skateboarded from the north of Scotland to the south of England. (Answer: *not really*)
- Ask directly: *What does an adventurer do?* If students can't answer, give a definition:
  An adventurer may go to unusual places and do exciting or dangerous things, eg hang-gliding in the valleys of the Caucasus mountains.
- Check understanding by asking if they know of any adventurers (maybe famous people in their country).

SPEAKING

1
- Groupwork. Students discuss the four questions.

Cultural notes: explorers & travellers

Christopher Columbus (1451–1506)
- Italian navigator who sailed west across the Atlantic Ocean to find a sea route to Asia, but discovered the Americas instead.
- When Columbus died in 1506, he still believed that he had discovered the east coast of Asia!

Roald Amundsen (1872–1928)
- A Norwegian explorer who was the first man to travel the north-west passage in his ship Gjoa in 1903–1906. He and four others in his team reached the South Pole a month before Englishman Robert Scott.

Marco Polo (1254–1324)
- Venetian traveller and writer, who spent 17 years travelling along the Silk Route through China and Asia, and wrote about his adventures when he returned to Italy. His book *The Travels of Marco Polo* became very influential in Renaissance Europe.
- Some historians think Polo never went to the East at all and all the tales are invented.

Jacques Cousteau (1910–1997)
- French oceanographer who invented the scuba-diving equipment.
- Cousteau believed in making scientific information available for ordinary people to understand. He was a pioneer of documentary films and a huge influence on TV filmmakers.

Neil Armstrong (born 1930)
- American astronaut who, in 1969, was the commander of Apollo 11, the first manned lunar landing mission. He was the first man to walk on the Moon.
- As well as the famous Moon mission Armstrong was also a pilot on the pioneering Gemini series of space flights, and took part in the first ever docking (joining together) of two spaceships in orbit around the Earth.

2
- Keep the same groups. Students discuss the question.

GRAMMAR: prepositions of movement

1
- Students match the prepositions in the box to the correct illustration A–H.

A	into	E	along
B	around	F	past
C	across	G	over
D	out of	H	through

Language notes: prepositions of movement

There are a few points about the pictures you may want to mention:
- Picture A shows an open box and the arrow is moving from outside to the inside. If the box had a solid closed top, the preposition would be *onto* not *into*.
- To move *across* something you move from one side of it to the other. The illustration in the coursebook illustrates a sentence like *He jumped across the river,* where the places are on different levels. The preposition is also possible where all items are on the same level, eg *She walked across the field.* This picture shows that idea:

- *Along* means that you move, following a road, a river or other line, eg *He walked along the path.* You can be *on* the line or *next to* it, eg *They sailed along the Channel coast.* So both of these pictures show *along.*

- Abstract pictures (as used in this lesson) are a very clear way of conveying the meaning of these prepositions. However, it's also very helpful to offer pictures linked to full sentence examples based on real objects and locations, preferably local ones that all students will be familiar with. The sentences could be something like:
  She walked across Kitale High Street.
  They walked along the Danube shore.
  Mike had to drive around the building site in the centre of Kutaisi. etc.

2

- Students read the sentences about explorers and decide which is the correct preposition to complete each one.

1	past	5	through
2	across	6	over
3	around	7	into
4	along	8	out of

3

- Ask students to imagine their journey from home to school in as much detail as possible. You could allow students thirty seconds of thinking time before they start describing their journey to their partner. They should use as many prepositions as they can.

LISTENING

In this listening, there is a news report about the death of the American adventurer Steve Fossett. It goes on to describe his achievements.

1 2.50

- Allow students a short time for them to read the questions before playing the recording.

1	because he has died
2	space travel

2.50

More than a year after Steve Fossett disappeared, while flying over the Sierra Nevada Mountains, police have confirmed that they have found the remains of his body. Fossett was 63 and one of the world's most extraordinary people. With 116 world records in five different sports, Steve Fossett was a hero and an inspiration to thousands.

Perhaps his greatest achievement was to become the first person to fly solo in a balloon around the world. During the journey of more than 33,000 kilometres, Fossett had a number of serious problems and he almost called the attempt off. At the start, he had to put off his departure for three hours because of a problem with wind, but finally managed to take off, flying past Sydney and New Zealand and over the Pacific Ocean. At one point, his burner stopped working; later, there was a fire in the balloon, but Fossett was not a man who gave up easily. This was, after all, his sixth attempt! The difficulties were sorted out and he carried on with his epic journey. He arrived back in Australia after just under fifteen days.

Fossett had both determination and endurance. As a young man, he enjoyed mountain climbing and cross-country skiing, but one of his great early achievements was, on his fourth attempt, to swim across the Channel between England and France. He twice took part in a 2,000-kilometre dog race in Alaska, he twice drove in the 24-hour motor-racing Classic at Le Mans in France, and he also drove in the Paris to Dakar Rally. As a sailor, he set world records for sailing around the world and across the Atlantic, along with records for speed sailing. In total, he set 32 world records in a boat. It seemed that Fossett was a man who could do anything. Sadly, he is with us no more.

2 2.50

- Students listen again to the recording and complete the sentences with the correct number.

1	63	4	6	7	32
2	116; 5	5	4th		
3	33,000	6	2,000		

3

- Students can work in small groups to discuss their opinions about Steve Fossett.

PRONUNCIATION: /ɜː/

1 2.51

- Students listen to the recording and repeat the phrases. Each phrase has two examples of the sound /ɜː/.

2.51

The phonemic transcription is included after each phrase.
first person /fɜːst ˈpɜːsən/
third world /θɜːd wɜːld/
journey to work /ˈdʒɜːnɪtə wɜːk/
word search /wɜːd sɜːtʃ/

2 & 3 2.52

- Students should now be clear what the /ɜː/ sound is. In this task, they must find the one word in each group of four that does not contain the sound /ɜː/.
- You could allow one to two minutes of individual thinking before students compare answers with a partner.
- Students then listen to the recording and check their answers.

1	heart	3	record
2	compare	4	interest

2.52

The phonemic transcription is included after each phrase.
1   burn /bɜːn/; circle /ˈsɜːkəl/; heart /hɑːt/; journey /ˈdʒɜːni/
2   birth /bɜːθ/; compare /kəmˈpeə/; early /ˈɜː(r)li/; nervous /ˈnɜːvəs/
3   earn /ɜːn/; girl /gɜːl/; heard /hɜːd/; record /ˈrekɔːd/
4   interest /ˈɪntrəst/; learn /lɜːn/; nurse /nɜːs/; service /ˈsɜːvɪs/

Language notes: /ɜː/

- The sound /ɜː/ is a long vowel sound, like /ɔː/ in lesson 10C on page 101. In other words, it is possible to continue saying the sound for two seconds, ten seconds, thirty seconds. Try saying really long vowels as an exercise with your students.
- Many stressed syllables spelt with -er-, -or- and -ir- have the /ɜː/ sound – though, interestingly, in UK English the /r/ sound is often not pronounced.
- The /ɜː/ sound is the distinctive sound of hesitation in English. When you don't know what to say, you can just say er (pronounced /ɜː/). This is a very useful thing to learn and being able to er successfully is an important step to sounding confident in English!

Vocabulary: phrasal verbs

1
- Draw attention to the italic phrase in sentence 1, and explain that it is possible to say the meaning of *left the ground* in a different way. Elicit which phrasal verb from the box is suitable. Agree on *took off*.
- Students read the six sentences and do questions 2–6.

1	took off	3	put off	5	carried on
2	called off	4	sorted out	6	gave up

2
- Students cross out the item that is not possible in each sentence.

1	weather	4	world
2	the Atlantic Ocean	5	good health
3	his wife	6	ship

Language notes: phrasal verbs

- **call off:** If you *call off* something, you *cancel* it. You can cancel a concert or a wedding but not the weather, because it is not possible for a human to do this! However, you can call off something *because* of the weather, eg *We called off the wedding because of the weather.*
- **carry on:** If you *carry on* something or *carry on* doing something, you *continue* to do it. You can continue seeing someone or continue with your studies, but you can't continue an ocean. To make a sentence about this you would need to add a verb, eg *Are you going to carry on studying the Atlantic Ocean?*
- **give up:** If you *give up* something, you stop doing something that you have been doing regularly until now. You can stop doing a job or smoking, but not your wife or husband. However, you can give up *doing something* with your wife, eg *He has decided to give up eating out with his wife.*
- **put off:** If you *put off* something, you delay it or postpone it for a later date. You can delay decisions and meetings, but you can't delay the world because it is not something that happens or has a set date and time.
- **sort out:** If you *sort out* something, you find a way to solve a difficult problem, or find a solution to a difficult or negative situation. You cannot sort out things if they are positive and going well. You cannot sort out good health because it is not a problem.
- **took off:** Things *take off* when they lift off the ground and go into the air. Ships do not normally do this (except in action films).

Methodology Builder 30
Pelmanism (memory game)

- *Pelmanism is a useful card game which helps students to recall grammatical or vocabulary items and their relationships to each other. Prepare a pack of about 16–40 cards containing pairs of cards that go together, eg vocabulary items and illustrations; phrasal verbs; past simple verbs and infinitives; questions and replies, etc. If you have a very small class, you can use these cards with the whole group; otherwise prepare enough packs so that small groups can work with them.*
- *Pelmanism is a basic memory game. The cards are laid out on a table so that the backs of all the cards are visible (but no one knows what's on the other side).*

- *Each player, one by one, turns over two cards attempting to reveal two that make a match. If they do this, they can keep the cards and have another turn. Otherwise, they turn the cards back (upside down again) in the same locations, and the next player has their turn. As the game goes on, students will have to try and remember which card was where. The winner is the player with the most cards at the end.*

Speaking

1
- Tell students to imagine that someone has bought them a plane ticket and they can fly round the world. They can choose five stop-overs (a brief stop for a day or two). Ask students to make a list of the five places where they would like to stop.

2
- Pairwork. Students compare their lists and agree a list of five places that they would both like to go to. Students then plan a route around the world, agreeing on what they would both like to do at each place they stop.
- It would be good if students could have a photocopy of a basic world map to work with. Alternatively, they could copy an outline map from the board.
- Allow some time at the end of the task for students to look ahead at the instruction to exercise 3, and prepare their presentation.

3
- Pairs report back to the rest of the class. When they've finished, students agree which journey is most interesting.
- If you have a large class, you could group pairs together for this stage.

IF YOU WANT SOMETHING EXTRA …
- Straightforward Teacher's Resource Disc *at the back of this book*

12в | Let's dance

WHAT THE LESSON IS ABOUT

Theme	Carnivals and festivals
Speaking	Pairwork discussion: talking about festivals
	Presentation: describing a festival
Reading	Email travel diary: an email describing Trinidad Carnival
Vocabulary	Festivals
Grammar	Relative clauses

IF YOU WANT A LEAD-IN ...

Teach a key word: festival

- Write on the board: *Rio.* (If your class is in Brazil, write *New Orleans* instead.) Ask students what they know about this place. They will probably suggest carnival or festival. If they don't, tell them that one of the most famous things in this place is when people go on the street and dance and celebrate. Ask if anyone knows the word for this. If they don't know, tell them that is a *carnival.* Ask students to list six important vocabulary items that they know about carnivals. Tell them that they can check the items as they study this lesson.

Test before you teach: relative clauses

❯ *Methodology guidelines: Test before you teach, page xxi*

- Write these sentences on the board:
    1 *She was a singer. She had very long legs.*
    2 *I went into a shop. The shop sold 22 kinds of bread.*
    3 *Tom was an actor. I met him at a party.*
- Ask students to rewrite each pair as a single sentence. You can look around at what they write. It's quite likely that they will use conjunctions such as *and* and will avoid relative pronouns. Tell students that you won't check these sentences now but will come back to them later in the lesson.
- When you have taught relative clauses, ask students to look again at their sentences and tell you what they wrote. Acknowledge all good answers (even ones without relative clauses). If they didn't use relative clauses, see if they can do so now.
(Answers: *She was a singer who/that had very long legs*; *I went into a shop which/that sold 22 kinds of bread*; *Tom was an actor who/that I met at a party.*)

Cultural notes: Let's Dance

- When someone says to you *Let's Dance*, it's an invitation to join them in a dance. Many dance instruction books have titles like *Let's Dance the Cha-Cha* or *Let's Dance the Tango.*
- The phrase features as part of the chunk *Let's dance the night away* (Let's dance all night until the morning comes). The phrase features in a number of songs, eg Justin Timberlake's song, *Take Me Now*, includes the lines *Wanna show you / That there's no better way / Let's dance the night away.*
- In 1983, David Bowie used the phrase as the title of an album and single, *Let's Dance*, which became one of his biggest hit records.

SPEAKING

1
- Pairwork. Students discuss the questions.
- Students may not know much about festivals in their own country. This would be a good Web research task.

Web research task

❯ *Methodology Builder 1: Using Web research tasks, page 2*

- Ask separate groups of students to each find out about a different festival in their own country.
    1 What are the festivals called?
    2 What is the reason for the festival?
    3 Where is it held?
    4 What happens?
    5 What special foods or drinks are there?
- When students have found information, they can report back to the class.

Web search key word
- *festival* name of country

Cultural notes: festivals

- **Rio de Janeiro** is probably the most famous carnival centre in the world, although carnival is also celebrated all over Brazil. It starts on the Saturday before Lent and finishes on Shrove Tuesday (the exact date varies every year as it is linked to Easter). The major event is the Samba Parade with amazing floats and costumes after which there are balls (glamorous dances) and club dancing all around town. If you're thinking of going, be warned that it is very expensive if you want to attend any of the special events, and hotels are booked months in advance. Don't even think of sleeping on the beach! And remember, if you want to join in the fun by throwing tomatoes, make sure you squash them first as tomatoes can be very hard!
- **Venice** holds the most elegant carnival in Europe, which has a long history back to the 14th century. It is particularly famous for the traditional costumes and masks that participants wear. In the past, these disguises meant that everyone was equal – no one could tell if people were nobility or poor. Since 1980, the modern carnival has grown in popularity and is now a major tourist attraction, usually held in February. Each year the carnival has a different theme.
- **Valencia** in northern Spain holds an extraordinary fire festival called **Las Fallas** (the fires) in March every year. There are around four hundred massive *ninots* (giant paper statues), often looking like famous politicians and celebrities, some over nine metres tall. At the end of the festival, all the street lights are turned off at midnight and all the statues are set on fire.
- **Notting Hill Carnival** in the west of London began in 1964, when many immigrants from Trinidad and the Caribbean decided to create a festival as a positive response to poor living conditions and racism. Steel bands played on the streets and started the tradition of celebrating and dancing on the streets. Since then, the event has grown to become one of the largest street festivals in Europe, with over two million people attending. The carnival is held on the last weekend in August.

• The name **Mardi Gras** comes from French and means *Fat Tuesday*. In the Christian calendar, this comes before the period of Lent (when people give up foods and luxuries for 40 days). In many countries the days before Lent became a period of feasts, wine and craziness. The New Orleans carnival began in 1827, when some students put on wild costumes and danced in the streets. The event grew quickly and is now a huge celebration with parades, music and fun.

Language notes: festivals & carnivals

• Students may ask what the difference is between *festivals* and *carnivals*. In fact, the word *festival* is a general word that can include carnivals and many other things.

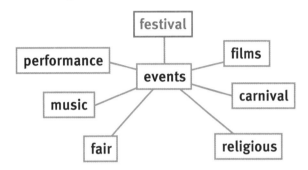

• A *festival* is a special event or series of events to celebrate something. This could include performances, a series of films, a public event such as a fair or market or a carnival.
• Popular festivals in the UK include pop festivals (lots of bands playing in the open air), eg Glastonbury, beer festivals and balloon festivals.
• A carnival always includes dancing or processions in the streets.

VOCABULARY & READING: festivals

▷ *Language reference, Student's Book page 125*

This email is a holiday diary describing Pam and Claire's trip to Trinidad to see a carnival.

1
• Students can work in pairs to decide which word from the box goes with each part of the picture A–H.

A	parade/procession	E	band
B	fireworks display	F	mask
C	speakers	G	costume
D	float	H	traditional food

2
• Explain to students that they are going to read an email travel diary written during a carnival in Trinidad. Ask them to read the diary and find which items from exercise 1 are not mentioned in the text.

fireworks display; mask

3
• Students write the phrases a–g in the correct gaps 1–7 in the email on page 118.

1 f   2 c   3 g   4 e   5 a   6 b   7 d

4
• Before students read the question, direct them to the text and ask them to look at line 5 and find the word *he*. Agree that it is a pronoun and ask them to draw a small circle around the word. Then ask students who the word *he* refers to. Agree that it refers to *James*. Ask students to draw an arrow back from the circle to *James*. The circle and arrow now show a clear illustration of how the pronoun refers to the noun. Now ask students to do the same for questions 2–5.
• Students then decide which word or words in the text the pronouns refer to.
• In order to answer the last question with names, students will need to spot the names *Pam and Claire* at the top of the email.

2	The soca competition (or soca music).
3	J'Ouvert.
4	The float (which was covered in speakers).
5	The writer (Pam) and friend Claire.

Language notes: festivals

Costume
• Your *costume* means the special clothes that you wear for a celebration, a party, a performance, etc.
• Be careful: students with some mother tongues confuse this word with the word *suit*. A *costume* does not mean a suit.
• *Costume* can be countable or uncountable.

Float
• As this is normally a verb, your students may be surprised to see this noun. A *float* is a large vehicle used in a parade. It is usually highly decorated and carries people and statues. A *float* often has a stage for singing and dancing at the back.

Parade
• A *parade* is when many people walk through the streets (or travel on specially decorated vehicles). There is usually music.
• A *military parade* is a large group of soldiers standing or marching together.

Procession
• This word is similar in meaning to *parade*, but it suggests a slow speed of movement.

Speakers
• The word *speakers* can refer either to people who speak at an event or as an abbreviation of *loudspeakers* (a box that lets you hear amplified sounds, eg from a CD player). In this task *speakers* mean *loudspeakers*.

Mask
• A *mask* is a special decorated object that you wear to hide your face usually either for a celebration, like a festival, or for criminal purposes such as bank robbery.
• *Mask* is also a useful verb, with a similar meaning to the noun. If you *mask something*, you hide it or cover it up, eg *She kept telling jokes to mask her sadness.*

GRAMMAR: relative clauses

Grammar box

❯ *Language reference, Student's Book page 124*
❯ *Methodology Builder 22: Using Grammar boxes, page 106*

1
- Whole class. Ask students to look at sentences 1–4 and quickly decide if they are good English or not. Agree that they are OK (because *that* can be used for people and things).
- Ask students to change *that* and put either *who* or *which* instead.
- To do this exercise students simply need to decide if the relative clause is about a person/people or about a thing.

1	who	3	which
2	which	4	who

2
- Ask students to read sentences 1–6 and cross out one unnecessary word in three of the sentences.

1	Pelau is a dish that ~~it~~ is …
3	… a soca competition which ~~it~~ started …
6	… a woman who ~~she~~ was …

3
- Ask students to join the pairs of sentences to make one sentence with a relative clause.

1	Venice has a carnival which/that is famous for its beautiful masks.
2	Belgium has an important festival which/that takes place in Binche.
3	The summer festival in Verona is for music lovers who/that like opera.
4	During the Rio carnival, the keys of the city are given to a man who/that is called King Momo.
5	At Las Fallas, the people of Valencia make statues of famous people which/that are burnt on the last night.
6	At Notting Hill in London, people wear costumes which/that cost thousands of pounds.

Weaker classes
- Remind students that they will only need to do two things: either use a suitable relative pronoun or lose the unnecessary ordinary pronoun.

Language notes: relative clauses
- Relative clauses help us to avoid repeating things unnecessarily. In the sentence *He was a tall man who always laughed at danger*, we are making one sentence instead of two. (*He was a tall man. He always laughed at danger.*)
- Relative clauses, like those in this lesson, tell us more information about something. In the sentence *He was a tall man who always laughed at danger*, the relative clause *who always laughed at danger* tells us more information about the tall man. So, in some ways, relative clauses are quite like adjectives.

- Relative clauses are usually started with a relative pronoun, eg *that, who* and *which*. Other relative pronouns not studied in this lesson are: *what; whom; whose; when; where; why*.
- Relative clauses can seem complicated and confusing to students and they are frequently a cause of errors:
  Students may assume words like *who, which*, etc are question words.
  They may think *that* is demonstrative, ie referring to a particular person or thing, eg *that house*.
  The sentences are quite complex to construct and students often simply avoid using them.
  Students often forget to omit the unnecessary pronoun (see example in the grammar box in the Student's Book).
  Students can use the wrong pronoun, eg using *who* when they are not talking about a person: ✗ *This is the shop who I talked about.*
  Students may say *what* instead of *that*, eg ✗ *I saw the information what was on the noticeboard.*

SPEAKING

1
- Ask students to think about a festival they have been to. They should make brief notes to answer each question.
- If you think your class may mainly have been to the same festival, ie one in your own town, you may want to ask them to focus on the last four questions, or use the alternative task below.

2
- Students can work in small groups to talk about their festivals.

Alternative task
- If all students have attended the same festival, you could substitute this task by asking them to describe an imaginary festival.
- Ask students to work in pairs and to invent a completely new festival anywhere in the world. Tell them to imagine that they went there recently. Ask students to write down the name of this new festival, and then answer the coursebook questions about this festival. Both students in the pair should take notes.
- Divide the pairs up and put them into separate, small groups. Ask students to talk about their festival to the others in their group. Remind them that they are not just giving a dull description of the facts, but they should talk about their own (imaginary) visit there. You could ask each student to start by saying *I went to the … festival.*

IF YOU WANT SOMETHING EXTRA …
❯ Straightforward Teacher's Resource Disc *at the back of this book*

12c | Global English

WHAT THE LESSON IS ABOUT

Theme	English around the world
Speaking	Discussion: talking about the English language in your country
Reading	*English as an International Language – no problem, OK?* Article: what type of English you should learn
Vocabulary	Countries & languages
Pronunciation	British & American accents

IF YOU WANT A LEAD-IN …

Discussion starters

> ❯ *Methodology Builder 15: Using Discussion starters, page 63*

- *Do you ever speak English outside the classroom? Where?*
- *Do you ever listen to English outside the class? Where?*
- *Why do you need to speak/listen to English?*
- *Do you find English difficult to use? Why?*
- *Are people helpful when you use your English?*

Teach two key words: accent & dialect

- Ask students what language they speak in Scotland. After any incorrect guesses, explain that, although there is a Scots language, most people speak Scottish English. This is a *dialect* of English – in other words it is very similar to English, but has some words and grammar that are different (eg the word *wee* means 'very small'). A dialect is a variety of a language that is spoken in a particular area or by a particular group of people.
- Ask if students think that Scottish English sounds the same as English in the south of England. Explain that it sounds very different from RP English (Standard English based on the pronunciation of the south east of England). An *accent* is the way people pronounce a language that shows where they come from.
- In the UK, there are many very different regional accents, eg a Liverpool accent, a Newcastle accent.
- English around the world has many dialects, eg Indian English, South African English, Singapore English (Singlish) and many different accents.

Alternative task

- If you are a confident user of an alternative dialect or accent yourself, you could introduce these words by actually asking your questions and teaching using the dialect/accent. In this way students will notice what you are doing and the point will be very memorable. If you can, demonstrate as many accents as you know.

Introducing the theme: Englishes

- Write the word *Englishes* in big letters across the board. Stand back and look (in a puzzled manner) at the word. Wait to see if students react at all. If they do, help the dialogue without giving any definite answers. If no one says anything very interesting, ask some questions:
  1. *What does that mean?*
  2. *Is that correct English?*
  3. *Is English a countable noun? Can you count English?*
  4. *How could you count Englishes?*
  5. *Is there more than one English?*

Don't explain what the word means at this stage, but tell students that they will find out during the lesson. (Answer: *The word 'Englishes' refers to the wide number of varieties of English now in use around the world. English is no longer a single language, but a whole family of dialects and varieties.*)

SPEAKING

1

- Ask students where they can see or hear English around their own town.
- If students are in a non-English speaking location, they may initially think there's very little English around, but on reflection they may think of a number of ideas.

Language notes: English around the world

- English has become a global language. It is a first language for many people (they grew up using it), but it is also the official second language in many countries (it is used alongside local or regional languages, maybe as the language of law, government or education). In addition, many English language dialogues around the world are not between two native speakers, but between two people who speak different languages and find that using English is a good way to communicate with each other. This is why English has become the international language of business. Similarly, if you are a tourist from Brazil visiting The Czech Republic, you will probably not know any Czech, so most things aimed at tourists are likely to be in English. In addition, English is the worldwide language of many other fields, eg science; computers; international college courses, etc.

Signs, notices, etc

- In any town that attracts tourists or business people around the world, you are likely to find many signs, notices and other printed material in English:
  - Shopping mall; shop; café; fast food; restaurant names; eg *Texas fried chicken, West End Shopping Centre.*
  - Product names and descriptions, eg *Ivory Moisturising Beauty Soap, Tomato ketchup.*
  - Words and phrases used in adverting posters, eg *I'm lovin' it, Coke is life.*
  - Fast food and café menus on the wall, eg *Mega-burger, French fries.*
  - Translated notices explaining directions, instructions and rules, eg *Public transport information, Entrance times and prices.*
  - Traffic and pedestrian signs and notices, eg *No parking, Stop,* etc.
  - Notices outside and inside buildings, eg *Entrance, No smoking, Closed,* etc.
  - Labels and explanations on goods for sale in shops, market stalls, etc, eg *Special offer.*
  - Leaflets, booklets, guide books, publicity magazines, etc.
  - Labels and information in museums, exhibitions, etc.

People speaking and using English

- Tourists, business people and visitors can often be overheard in trams, buses, cafés, etc speaking English.
- English may be heard in TV films, at the cinema, etc. In many countries films are *dubbed* (they use actors to speak in the local language instead of the original

language). For language learning, it is much more beneficial to hear the original sound of actors' voices. In order to understand, the viewer must read *subtitles* (translations written on the bottom of the screen).

- Many international TV channels (eg *CNN*) are in English.
- People often need to speak English on the phone to relatives, work contacts and friends in other countries.
- Many computer games played around the world are in English. People who play online games or use internet chat-rooms and forums communicate in English.
- Many other languages have borrowed words and phrases from English and mixed them in with their language.

VOCABULARY: countries & languages

> *Language reference, Student's Book page 125*

1

- Students read the list of cities and decide which countries they are in.
- Students can then check their answers with their partner and agree the order of countries (from 1 = nearest to 12 = furthest) in relation to the country the students are currently in.

2	Hungary	7	China (People's Republic of China)
3	Brazil		
4	Russia (Russian Federation)	8	Turkey
		9	Spain
5	Saudi Arabia	10	France
6	Japan	11	Italy
		12	Poland

Extra questions

- Ask students to decide which cities in the task are not capital cities of their country. Can students name the capitals of these places?
  (Answer: *Brasilia is the capital of Brazil, not Sao Paolo. Ankara is the capital of Turkey, not Istanbul.*)
- Ask students to determine the correct order of the towns from west to east, starting with Madrid.
  (Answer: *Madrid; Paris; Rome; Budapest; Warsaw; Athens; Istanbul; Moscow; Riyadh; Beijing; Tokyo; Sao Paolo.*)

2

- Students add the languages from exercise 1 to the table.
- When this is done, students should try to add one more language in each column.
- Some possible additions to each column are shown in brackets in the answers below.

ending in '-an': Hungarian; Russian; Italian (Korean; German)
ending in '-ish': Turkish; Spanish; Polish (English; Kurdish)
ending in '-ese': Portuguese; Japanese; Chinese (Vietnamese)
with other endings: Arabic; French (Hindi; Swahili; Hebrew)

Extra task: country names & stress

- Write the following table on the board:

1	2	3	4	5	6
☐ ◻	◻ ☐	☐ ◻ ◻	◻ ☐ ◻	◻ ◻ ☐	other

- Write *Russia* on the board and ask students to think about how the word is pronounced, particularly the *stress* pattern. Point out that the images at the top of

each column show different stress patterns. Elicit which column's stress pattern fits the word *Russia* (Answer: *column 1; 'Russia' is a two-syllable word with the stress on the first syllable*).

- Put students into pairs and ask them to go through all the other country names which have more than one syllable (and city names too if you wish), and place them in the correct columns. To check, don't just say *yes* or *no*, but ask students to pronounce the names, and then offer a correct model yourself for comparison. Ask students to check if their pronunciation matches yours.
- NB These are usual British English pronunciations of these places. Students may find these stress patterns odd if they are noticeably different from names they know well in their own pronunciation.
- *Hungary* and *Tokyo* could be said as two-syllable names.
- Students from many countries seem to find the ◻☐ two-syllable names particularly difficult. Students will often say Madrid, Brazil, etc, as ☐◻.

1	2	3	4	5	6
☐◻	◻☐	☐◻◻	◻☐◻	◻◻☐	other
Russia	Brazil	Hungary			Saudi Arabia
China	Japan	Italy			
Turkey					
Poland					
Paris	Madrid	Tokyo	São Paolo	Budapest	
Warsaw	Beijing			Istanbul	
Athens					
Moscow					
Riyadh					

3

- Ask the class: *Who can say 'hello' in another language?* You may also want to find out the literal meaning of the greeting and the appropriate response. For example, in the Georgian language, the greeting actually means 'I wish you victory' and the response means 'And to you victory'.
- Get the student to teach the word/phrase to the class by saying it clearly a few times, and allow other students the chance first to repeat it and then to say it to each other.
- Go on to elicit more *hellos* in different languages.

4 & 5 🔘 **2.53**

- Students can work in pairs to discuss which languages are most widely-spoken and complete the list.
- Students listen to the recording to check their answers.

3	English	6	Arabic
4	Spanish	7	Portuguese
5	Russian	8	French

🔘 **2.53**

The most widely-spoken language in the world is Mandarin Chinese with approximately 1 billion speakers. Next comes the Indian language family of Hindi, Bengali, Punjabi and so on. More than half a billion people speak one or more of these languages. After that, we have English which also has more than 500 million speakers (including speakers of English as a second or third language). The next language on our list is Spanish, with speakers in Spain, Central and South America. Next is Russian, followed by Arabic. At number seven on our list is Portuguese with about 200 million speakers and finally, at number eight, is French with about 130 million.

READING

This article discusses the different types of English used in the world now: UK and American English, regional dialects and accents, and English used by non-native speakers. It argues that there is no correct English to learn; it depends on the type of English that is right for your situation.

1

• Pairwork. Students discuss the three questions.

> 1 English has over 400 million speakers as a first language. It is a first language in: Antigua, Australia, the Bahamas, Barbados, Bermuda, Dominica, Gibraltar, Grenada, the Grenadines, Guyana, Jamaica, New Zealand, St. Lucia, St. Kitts & Nevis, St. Vincent, Trinidad and Tobago, the UK, the US.
>
> 2 Students may find it easiest to understand the language variety they have been educated in. This might be a local variety of English or an international standard variety such as 'British English' or 'American English'.
>
> 3 This is entirely a matter of opinion and personal choice. Neither is 'better'. If a learner is more likely to meet or work with people who speak one variety then this may be the most useful to learn. Generally speaking, there are few comprehension problems between English speakers using these different varieties.

2

• Students read the article and find out whether the writer thinks it is better to learn American or British English.

> The author says it doesn't matter – it depends on the reasons for learning English.

3

• Students read the article again and answer the six true or false sentences. They correct the false sentences.

> 1 F (The differences in the grammar are small.)
> 2 T
> 3 F (There are many different British accents.)
> 4 T
> 5 T
> 6 F (English as an International Language is a language that is different to both American and British English.)

4

• Students discuss the three questions. This could be done as pairwork or small group work, but it may also be successful as a whole-class or big-group discussion. You could try dividing your class into two groups and arrange them so that students can sit and chat easily with other people in their group. There may be a rich exchange of views. When they've finished, the two large groups can come back together to see if they reached similar conclusions.

Extra discussion

For students learning English in an English-speaking country:
• *Some regions have a recognizable local English sometimes known by a descriptive name such as Jamaican English or Indian English, or by a humorous name such as Hunglish or Spanglish. Is there a local variety of English in your area? What is it called?*

• *If you speak with the local accent and use local words, do people consider you a good English speaker?*
• *Why do people try to learn different accents?*

PRONUNCIATION: British & American accents

1 2.54

• Direct students to the words in the box. Tell them they will hear each word spoken twice, once in a British English accent and once in an American English accent. They must decide which speaker is British and which is American.
• If students cannot do this easily, tell them the answer after the first listening and then play the recording again, pausing and pointing out some distinctive features.

> The first speaker is British. The second is American.

2.54

> 1 answer ask banana castle dance example France glass
> 2 answer ask banana castle dance example France glass

Language notes: British & American accents

As well as some stress differences studied in this lesson, the standard American accent differs from the British accent in a number of ways. For example:
• The /r/ sound is often heard at the end of words (eg *father*) in American English (AE), where it would not be pronounced in British English (BE).
• Words pronounced with /ɑː/ in BE tend to be closer to /æ/ in AE, eg *can't*.
• When it comes in the middle of a word, the sound /t/ is pronounced more like a /d/ in AE, eg *better*.
• For more information on American and British phonetic charts please visit www.soundspronapp.com © *Adrian Underhill and Macmillan Education.*

2 2.55

• Tell students they will listen to some more words spoken first by an American and second by a British speaker. This time the students must decide how the stress is different between the American speaker and the British speaker, and mark the stress on the words.

US	UK
address	ad**dress**
ca**fé**	**ca**fé
cigarette	ciga**rette**
magazine	maga**zine**
weekend	week**end**

 2.55

> address, address
> café, café
> cigarette, cigarette
> magazine, magazine
> weekend, weekend

IF YOU WANT SOMETHING EXTRA ...

⊙ Straightforward Teacher's Resource Disc *at the back of this book*

12D | Global issues

WHAT THE LESSON IS ABOUT

Theme	Global issues
Speaking	Pairwork: discussing global issues
Listening	Informal dialogues: three dialogues at a party
Vocabulary	Global issues
Functional language	Agreeing & disagreeing
Did you know?	Oxfam

IF YOU WANT A LEAD-IN ...

Teach a key word: global issues

- With books closed, write *global issues* on the board. Ask students what *issues* means (important subjects people talk or argue about); and what *global* means (something that affects every country or every person in the world).
- Ask for some examples of global issues, eg poverty; lack of food; global warming; nuclear power, etc.

Discussion starters

❯ *Methodology Builder 15: Using Discussion starters, page 63*

- *Are you worried about the environment? What is the most serious environmental problem in the world now?*
- *Which scientific advances worry you most?*
- *Will there always be poor people in the world?*
- *Can the rich nations help the poor more than they do now? Will a global economy help to improve the living standards of everyone throughout the world?*
- *What other big problems are there that affect the world?*

SPEAKING & VOCABULARY: global issues

❯ *Language reference, Student's Book page 125*

1

- Students match the global issues at the top of the page to the headlines torn out from a newspaper.
- Students may not understand some of the global issues or headlines immediately. Tell them that you won't help them yet. You can discuss if they have learnt the meaning of unknown words after they have tried the reading task.

> health – F, H
> global warming – G, J
> internet – B, K
> education – A, L
> genetic engineering – C, M
> animal and nature conservation – D, I
> poverty – E, N

Language notes: vocabulary

- *Poor* is an adjective, eg *A poor person is someone with very little money. Poor* is also a noun. *The poor* are people who have little money and who own very few things.
- *Poverty* is a noun. It is usually used to describe the problem of a country or area having many poor people, eg *There is a lot of poverty in the south* is almost exactly the same as *There are a lot of poor people in the south.*
- The opposite of poverty is *wealth*.

2

- Pairwork. Students discuss the four questions.

Cultural notes: newspaper headlines

Online crime
- The increasing popularity of the internet has led to many new crimes, including *Identity theft* (where someone pretends to be you and gets money or products using your name), and *Diallers* (where your phone secretly dials an expensive overseas number, when you think you are just using the internet normally).

Rainforest reserve
- A *nature reserve* is a place which the government of a country says is protected. There are usually very strict laws about cutting down trees, hunting animals, etc.

Cloning sheep
- A clone is an exact copy of a living creature. The first animal to be cloned was Dolly the sheep in 1996.

Genetic engineering
- Also known as *GM* (genetic modification).
- Genes are the biological instructions that parents give to their children. Genetic modification means 'changing the genes of a living thing'. Nowadays, many plants and vegetables are being modified to make them stronger or make it harder for them to catch diseases. Many people believe that this is dangerous and protest against it.

Hostels for homeless men
- In large cities with many homeless people who sleep on the streets, charities or local government often set up hostels where people can sleep, wash, eat, etc, at no cost.

Save the Javan rhinoceros
- The Javan rhinoceros is one of the most threatened species of animal in the world. It is believed that there are only about 50–60 animals left alive. Animals like this are known as *endangered species.* Other endangered animals include the Giant Panda, the blue whale, the gorilla, the tiger and the chimpanzee.

LISTENING

In this listening, there are three short, separate, amusing dialogues which take place at a party. The speakers all talk about global issues.

1 🌐 2.56–2.58
- Ask students to listen to three dialogues and decide which of the global issues in the picture at the top of the page are being discussed.

> Dialogue 1: health / genetic engineering
> Dialogue 2: internet
> Dialogue 3: global warming

2.56–2.58

---

1 M = Man   W = Woman

M: Hiya.

W: Hi.

M: Can I get you a drink? Do you want some crisps?

W: A juice, please. But crisps, no. I try to avoid junk food.

M: Oh, I think they're quite tasty myself.

W: They taste of chemicals, and genetically-modified potatoes. I prefer to eat natural, organic food, if I can.

M: I see what you mean, but I still think they're quite tasty. Nothing wrong with a crisp or two, surely?

W: Well, I'm sorry, but that's not the way I see it. I think we should all eat organic.

M: Yes, yes, I agree with you, but not all the time, maybe. And some of that organic food is a real waste of money.

W: I'm afraid I disagree. It's not just about taste. It's about saving our planet. I'm worried about it, even if you're not. Now, sorry, will you excuse me?

M: So you don't want me to get the juice for you, then?

2 M = Man   W = Woman

M: Have you heard about this new internet virus that's going around?

W: Yeah, a friend of mine got it on her laptop, and she's lost everything.

M: That's terrible. God knows why people spend their time inventing viruses.

W: But I don't know what anyone can do about it. Maybe the United Nations could do something.

M: The United Nations? You must be joking! They never do anything about anything.

W: Well, I don't know. I'm sure the Americans could do something about it. I mean, if they wanted to.

M: Oh, definitely. But, well, I don't know … but the police could do something more about online crime. It can't be that difficult.

W: Yeah, you're probably right. Anyway, let's get a drink.

3 M = Man   W = Woman

M: 'Scuse me. Have we met before?

W: I don't think so. No.

M: Oh, well. Nice weather, innit? Nice and warm, eh?

W: Well, it's definitely very warm, but 'nice', no, I wouldn't say that.

M: You prefer it cold, then?

W: Definitely not. I just mean that there's nothing very nice about global warming.

M: Oh, you don't believe all that stuff about global warming? I don't care about that! You can't believe everything you read in the press.

W: Well, maybe, but it's not just the journalists. It's the politicians and it's the scientists, too.

M: Not all of them! And you can't believe everything the scientists say, either.

W: Perhaps not. But most scientists are very sure about global warming.

M: Well, you may be right. I don't really know a lot about it to be honest. My name's Ben, by the way.

---

2 2.56–2.58

- Students listen again and check their answers.
- Allow some reading time before students listen one more time to the recording. Students need to know what the sentences are before trying to do the task.
- Stronger students could try and predict (or remember) the answers before listening.

1	junk	5	online
2	organic	6	global warming
3	planet	7	press
4	internet		

Cultural notes: organic food & global warming

Organic food

- Organic food is grown or produced without using any chemicals, drugs or pest killers. There are very strict controls about using the word *organic* on foods.

Global warming

- Many scientists believe that the Earth's climate is changing and that it is getting hotter. This is mainly because of man's use of carbon dioxide, which is destroying important parts of the atmosphere. Other scientists say that this is just part of the natural changes in climate.

FUNCTIONAL LANGUAGE: agreeing & disagreeing

1 & 2 2.59

- Students put the phrases in the best places in the table.
- Students then listen to the phrases and repeat them.

1/2/3	c, d, f	6/7	b, e
4/5	a, g	8	h

Alternative presentation

- Write the four headings from the table on the board, and an opinion about something, eg *I think global warming is a serious problem.* Ask one student to say that sentence to you and respond with one of the phrases, eg *Well, maybe, but … .*
- Ask students to discuss and agree very quickly in pairs the exact words you said and which of the four headings it goes with. Collect feedback and write the phrase in the correct place. Continue with the others, using the same starter sentence, or elicit some different ones.

 2.59

Agree:	*Disagree:*
I agree with you.	I'm afraid I disagree.
Oh, absolutely … (definitely)	I'm not sure about that.
That's how I feel, too.	That's not the way I see it.
That's what I think, too.	*Strongly disagree:*
Partly agree:	You can't be serious.
I see your point, but …	You must be joking.
I see what you mean, but …	
Well, maybe, but …	

3
- Pairwork. Students complete the dialogue by using phrases from exercise 1 and continue it using their own ideas.
- NB The first gap needs to be filled in with a topic, eg *cloning*, *rainforests*, rather than an agreeing/disagreeing phrase. Weaker students may need you to help them notice that the second gap should be an *agreeing* phrase. This is because the 'But what?' question that comes afterwards is asking 'what we should all do about it'. The third gap probably needs to be a suggestion.

4
- Students can work in small groups. One student in the group reads out a sentence. The others make statements about whether they agree or disagree, using phrases from exercise 1.
- You could allow students some preparation time before the group work for students to read and think about the sentences and decide their own opinions.

DID YOU KNOW?

1
- Pairwork. Ask students to read the text about Oxfam and discuss the three questions.

Extra discussion
- Tell your class about some of the other popular UK charities listed in *Cultural notes* below. Ask students for their opinions on which ones they think are similar to an organization in their own country, and which would not be successful or popular in their own country and why.

Cultural notes: UK charities
Some other popular charities in the UK include:
- British Red Cross (voluntary health care, especially in emergencies)
- Cancer Research (searching for a cure for cancer)
- British Heart Foundation (researching heart disease)
- Mencap (for people with learning disabilities)
- Amnesty International (promoting human rights)
- NSPCC (The National Society for Prevention of Cruelty to Children)
- Shelter (helping homeless people)
- Royal National Lifeboat Institution (to provide a life-saving service for ships in trouble at sea)
- Salvation Army (a religious group helping homeless and poor people)
- RSPCA (the Royal Society for the Prevention of Cruelty to Animals)
- The National Trust (preserving ancient buildings and land in Britain)

Web research task
- ❯ *Methodology Builder 1: Using Web research tasks*, *page 2*
- Ask students to find a website for a charity that interests them, or from the list in *Cultural notes*. They should prepare to give a short report to the rest of the class about what the charity does and how people can help.

> ### ■ Methodology Builder 31
> ### ■ Revision activities
> - *When you finish using a coursebook, it is a good idea to plan some activities that allow students to look back and recall what they have done. Although the ideas below are suggested for this book, you could easily use them at the end of any course of study.*
>
> **Memory test**
> - *Tell students to close their books. Ask them to work in small groups and try to remember as many of the main grammar items from the book as possible, eg present perfect. They should write the list on a piece of paper. Set a time limit, eg six minutes.*
> - *Ask groups to pass their list on to another group. The new groups will check the list by looking through the book. Every item they correctly listed gets one point.*
>
> **Student-centred test**
> - *Give students fifteen minutes to look back through the book and write a test for other students. They should write the test clearly on a separate piece of paper for other students to read (or for photocopying).*
> - *You could set some specific requirements. Include:*
>   1 *Five grammar, vocabulary or function questions directly from the book. NB These must be questions that students will be able to do even when they can't see all of the original exercise.*
>   2 *Five sentences taken from anywhere in the book. The test writers must make a one-word gap in each sentence. The gap must be a grammar word, eg an auxiliary verb, a preposition, an article, etc.*
>   3 *Five definitions of words so that other students can guess the original word.*
>   4 *Five questions with information about people, places, etc from the book, eg Where was the futurological conference?*
> - *Quickly check that the questions are fair before other students try it. When ready, students do the test.*

IF YOU WANT SOMETHING EXTRA ...
❯ Straightforward Teacher's Resource Disc *at the back of this book*

Answer key

12 REVIEW
❯ *Student's Book page 159*

1

1	around
2	into
3	across
4	past
5	over
6	through
7	out of
8	along

2

1	off
2	on
3	up
4	off
5	out
6	off

3

1	who is
2	that has
3	that is
4	who have
5	which takes
6	who were
7	which have
8	that are

4

1 e 2 c 3 h 4 b 5 g 6 a 7 d 8 f

5

1	wage
2	global
3	viruses
4	organic
5	poverty
6	conservation
7	engineering
8	homeless

6

Students' own answers

12 WRITING

❯ *Workbook page 87*

Model answer

I don't believe that it is wrong for women to put their careers before their families. I do believe, though, that some jobs make it difficult to look after children. In many countries, it's expensive to give your children a good quality of life and education. Both parents often need to work to pay for their children's needs. Of course, we would all like to be able to have both a nice quality of life and lots of time for our children. But this is often not possible and we must make a difficult decision. In my opinion, the choice should depend on the parents' jobs. When both parents work long hours or often need to move house for their work, I think one of the parents needs to change their jobs.

I also disagree with the statement for another reason. A mother with a successful career may not be able to spend a lot of time with her young children. But when those children grow up, maybe they will be happy that their mother achieved her ambitions. A woman who finds it boring to stay at home might not be a good mother.

In my view, nobody can say what is right or wrong for mothers with careers. It depends on each family. Who really knows the right way to look after children?

Sounds App – Straightforward Second Edition

Available for Apple iOS devices (iPhone, iPad, iPod Touch) and Google Android-based devices, *Sounds: The Pronunciation App* allows you and your students to study, practise and play with pronunciation wherever you are.

The app contains:

Interactive Phonemic Chart

The chart shows all the sounds of English (switchable between British and American English), divided into vowels, dipthongs and consonants. Tap a symbol to hear the sound, hold to hear an example word.

Wordlists

Sounds comes with a vocabulary wordlist of around 650 high-frequency words. These feature phonemic spellings and audio recordings. By recording your own pronunciation you can work with problematic sounds. You can also purchase new wordlists directly inside the app. Premium App required for in-app wordlists purchases. **All levels of *Straightforward Second Edition* are available to purchase,** for just £0.69/$0.99 per level, and include **all** of the words and phrases from the Student's Books.

Practice and Quizzes

In the app you'll find three different practice modes, focusing on reading, writing and listening. In addition the quizzes introduce timed elements to add an element of fun into pronunciation practice. **All of the quiz and practice activities can be done using the Straightforward Second Edition wordlists** (once purchased and available in your app).

Teacher and learner support

We've included an extensive extra resource section in *Sounds* written by pronunciation expert Adrian Underhill (the author of *Sound Foundations* – the most thorough teacher's guide to phonology available).

For teachers we have three brand new downloadable lesson plans for teaching using *Sounds*, as well as Top Ten Tips for teaching pronunciation, a video of a complete introductory pronunciation workshop with Adrian and more! For students we have information on why pronunciation is important for all aspects of language learning, and Top Ten Tips for studying pronunciation.

For more information visit the website at www.soundspronapp.com